# Britishness since 1870

What does it mean to be British? It is now recognised that being British is not innate, static or permanent, but that national identities within Britain are constantly constructed and reconstructed. *Britishness since 1870* examines this definitition and redefinition of the British national identity since the 1870s. Paul Ward argues that Britishness is a resilient force, and looks at how it has adapted to changing circumstances since the 1870s.

Taking a thematic approach, *Britishness since 1870* examines the forces that have contributed to a sense of British national identity, and considers how Britishness has been mediated by other identities such as class, gender, region, ethnicity and the sense of belonging to England, Scotland, Wales and Ireland.

**Paul Ward** is senior lecturer in Modern British History at the University of Huddersfield. He is the author of *Red Flag and Union Jack: Englishness, Patriotism and the British Left, 1881–1924* (1988).

# Britishness since 1870

*Paul Ward*

LONDON AND NEW YORK

First published 2004
by Routledge
11 New Fetter Lane, London EC4P 4EE

Simultaneously published in the USA and Canada
by Routledge
29 West 35th Street, New York, NY 10001

*Routledge is an imprint of the Taylor & Francis Group*

Typeset in Baskerville by The Running Head Limited, Cambridge
Printed and bound in Great Britain by The Cromwell Press,
Trowbridge, Wiltshire

*British Library Cataloguing in Publication Data*
A catalogue record for this book is available from the British Library

*Library of Congress Cataloging in Publication Data*

Ward, Paul, 1964–
    Britishness since 1870 / Paul Ward
        p.   cm.
Includes bibliographical references and index.
1. National characteristics, British–History–20th century. 2. National
characteristics, British–History–19th century. 3. Group identity–Great
Britain–History–20th century. 4. Group identity–Great
Britain–History–19th century. 5. Great Britain–Civilization–20th
century. 6. Great Britain–Civilization–19th century. I. Title.
    DA566.4.W334 2004
    305.8'00941–dc22

                                                          2003020798

ISBN 0–415–22016–5 (hbk)
ISBN 0–415–22017–3 (pbk)

For Oscar and Georgia

# Contents

*Acknowledgements*                                                    ix
*List of abbreviations*                                               xi

**Introduction: Being British**                                       **1**

**1  Monarchy and Empire**                                            **14**

*Ceremony, celebration and the making of the nation as family  18*
*Overcoming divisions: nation, ethnicity and class  22*
*Politics, monarchy and imperialism  28*
*The monarchy and the end of Empire  31*

**2  Gender and national identity**                                   **37**

*Masculinity, Britishness and Empire in the late nineteenth century  38*
*Women and the nation 1870–1918  39*
*Women in Ireland, Scotland and Wales  42*
*The impact of the Great War  44*
*Gender and Britishness in the Second World War  47*
*Gender, 'race' and home in post-war Britain  50*

**3  Rural, urban and regional Britishness**                          **54**

*Finding the core of the nation  55*
*Regional identities  66*

**4  Spare time**                                                     **73**

*Sport and national identities  73*
*Sport, nation and Empire  74*
*Sport and nation in Scotland, Wales and Ireland  76*
*Regional and local identities in British sport  80*

*'Race', sport and identity  82*
*Discordant voices  84*
*Going on holiday  85*
*Resisting the Americanisation of culture  89*

**5  Politicians, parties and national identity**                                93

*Radical patriotism and the claims of the Conservatives  93*
*'Countervailing currents'  96*
*The First World War  98*
*Between the wars  100*
*British Fascism and Communism  101*
*Patriotism and politics in the people's war  105*
*The politics of European identity  108*

**6  A new way of being British: ethnicity and Britishness**                     113

*Continuities and varieties before 1945  116*
*The Second World War and the national community  123*
*Numbers and 'the other' in affluent Britain  125*
*Keeping Britain white: the politics of exclusion  127*
*Black and Asian identities in the UK  135*

**7  Outer Britain**                                                              141

*Holding together or pulling apart?  142*
*Wales  143*
*Scotland  149*
*Ireland and Northern Ireland  157*
*The end of Britain?  168*

**Conclusion**                                                                    170

*Notes*                                                                           174
*Bibliography*                                                                    211
*Index*                                                                           229

# Acknowledgements

I would like to thank the various colleagues at the universities at which I have taught and researched who have offered advice about how to proceed with this book. The historians at University of Westminster, Royal Holloway University of London and most recently the University of Huddersfield have provided the general career support and friendship that has made being a university lecturer so enjoyable. At Westminster, Martin Doherty and Tony Gorst taught me varied academic skills. Martin Francis, Alex Windscheffel, Liz Buettner and John Turner at Royal Holloway were supportive of this project from its beginnings, and Alex read much of the manuscript. Tony Stockwell was a Head of History in a million. At Huddersfield, Keith Laybourn and Sarah Bastow made many valuable suggestions on the whole book. Rainer Horn gave a newcomer's personal perspective on Britishness. John Ramsden shaped the book by commenting on both the proposal and the whole manuscript. I followed up leads offered by audiences and participants in research seminars and conferences at the universities of Central Lancashire, Monash, A Coruña, Manchester Metropolitan, Huddersfield and Calgary.

Students on courses at Royal Holloway and Huddersfield gave me many ideas for directions to take in research, and some of their contributions have gone directly into this book. I hope I have acknowledged them by name in the notes where necessary; it is certainly the case that in essays, projects, presentations and general class discussion, they have all pushed the ideas in this book forward. And it has been fun along the way.

I am grateful for financial support from the British Academy and the University of Huddersfield research grants scheme, as well as to the History Division and School of Music and Humanities at the University of Huddersfield. The maintenance of a comfortable research environment amidst a deep commitment to teaching makes Huddersfield very special.

Librarians and archivists at Royal Holloway, London Metropolitan Archives, the National Library of Scotland, the National Library of Wales, the National Library of Ireland, the Public Record Office of Northern Ireland, the Brotherton Library at the University of Leeds, Huddersfield Public Library, the Linen Hall Library, Belfast and the University of Huddersfield all contributed to the finished product through their professionalism and guidance. My appreciation also goes to Frances Brown for her efficient copy-editing and stylistic suggestions.

Jackie, Georgia and Oscar have helped out in so many ways with the writing of this book. Georgia in particular helped with some of the corrections and revisions, but the most important contribution made by all three has been to make my life very happy. Love to them all.

Huddersfield, September 2003

# Abbreviations

| | |
|---|---|
| BUF | British Union of Fascists |
| CPGB | Communist Party of Great Britain |
| CSU | Cymric Suffrage Union |
| EEC | European Economic Community |
| FA | Football Association |
| GAA | Gaelic Athletic Association |
| IRA | Irish Republican Army |
| JLB | Jewish Lads' Brigade |
| LCC | London County Council |
| NF | National Front |
| RAF | Royal Air Force |
| SNP | Scottish National Party |
| VAD | Voluntary Aid Detachment |
| WAAF | Women's Auxiliary Air Force |

# Introduction

## Being British

Since the 1970s there has been a sense of crisis about what it has meant to be British. But not only British. Far from being constants, as had been presumed to be, national identities have been recognised as constructed and reconstructed. This is not to say that national identities are 'false' or 'artificial', but this idea of the 'making of national identities' has opened them up to academic study, not least by historians, who are keen to locate continuities and changes in their historical context. National identities in many countries other than the United Kingdom have seemed to be more obviously contested. Disputes over borders in Europe have been frequent, and often bloody. Alsace-Lorraine was ceded by a militarily defeated France to Germany in 1871 and returned to France in 1919 after the Allies had defeated Germany. The collapse of the Austro-Hungarian Empire at the end of the First World War produced numerous new nations, and the reshuffling of Europe in 1945 again changed the nature of many nations. Poland, for example, was created, contracted, and expanded at the military and diplomatic whim of its neighbours, allies and enemies. Belgium has made great efforts to contain Flemings and Walloons within a single polity, as Spain has sought to enable autonomous government to its regions while maintaining national-political unity. In Yugoslavia and the Soviet Union, pluralism (of sorts) failed, with bloodshed as a consequence, in the 1990s. After 1945, decolonisation in Africa and Asia saw the foundation of new nations and national identities: sometimes formed against the backdrop of war, as in Rwanda, sometimes through more peaceful transformation, as in South Africa. The Americas too have experienced contests over what it means to be national. In Canada, French-Canadians have urged autonomy for Quebec, and after the terrorist attacks on the World Trade Centre in New York, US American identity has been redefined. The list of 'national' problems is as universal as the nation as a political and cultural form.[1] The apparent stability of the United Kingdom across much of the twentieth century has made its current 'crisis' appear profound. Being British is no longer seen as innate, static and permanent. Indeed, it is seen as under threat. In this book I examine the definition and redefinition of national identities within the United Kingdom since the 1870s. This period embraces the 'new' imperialism from the 1870s onwards, around which conservative political forces constructed claims to a monopoly on patriotism and versions of national identity, and also includes the decades since the Second World War when notions of Britishness have been challenged by the end of Empire, Commonwealth immigration, 'Americanisation', European integration and the re-emergence of Celtic nationalisms. The book, therefore, seeks to locate the current perception of crisis in its historical context.

What is meant by 'Britishness' is, of course, a complex issue. I argue that across the period since 1870 the majority of Britons, that is people living in the United Kingdom, have adopted cultural and political identities associated with the existence of this multi-national polity. Many commentators believe that states that contain more than one nation are fundamentally unstable and that the United Kingdom of Great Britain and Ireland began its inevitable process of dissolution as soon as it was created by the Act of Union of 1800, if not before with the union of England and Scotland in 1707. In this view, there was only a transient and unstable sense of a British national identity, and it has recently been argued by Christopher Harvie that there was only a brief moment of Britishness, between 1939 and 1970.[2] This has been accompanied by arguments from some that Britain, and therefore Britishness, is no more. Tom Nairn, who forecast the break-up of Britain as early as 1977, declared in 1999 that we were now in a period 'after Britain'.[3] But Harvie and Nairn are Scottish nationalists of sorts. They describe, but also seek to promote further, the crisis of Britishness. They are entitled to do so, but the historian's task is more about analysing the past rather than prophesying the future. Harvie and Nairn are not alone in deciding that the death of Britain is occurring or has occurred. Others have declared that England/Britain has been 'abolished' and that, therefore, an elegy for England is needed.[4] The sense of crisis is shared by British Conservatives, some of whom see the future in the emergence of a more insular English nationalism,[5] others in a strengthened British unionism.[6] But still others see a sense of crisis. Darcus Howe verbally and visually portrayed a crisis among white English people in his three-part television series *White Tribe*. 'These are people who are in a crisis', he said. 'Something is finished; there's nothing in its place. And anything can happen.'[7] This apparent consensus does suggest that there is a profound sense of crisis in Britishness, that its future is limited. On the other hand, there are others who see major advantages in continuing British- ness. The New Labour government of Tony Blair has sought to defend Britishness through developing political institutions in Scotland, Wales and Northern Ireland, but also, with limited powers, in London with referendums in some English regions in the future. Many Conservatives also see a future for Britishness. John Redwood declared categorically that 'The United Kingdom is my nation, rather than England or the Wokingham district. That is a fact of history.'[8] And while Howe saw a crisis in white English identity because too many people had a taste for American line dancing and French wine (and male black strippers), Yasmin Alibhai-Brown and others have argued for a new Britishness that positively embraces cultural diversity.[9]

So what then is Britishness? Some historians, sociologists and political scien- tists have seen Britishness as some form of economic or cultural imperialism imposed on Scotland, Wales and Ireland/Northern Ireland by English ruling elites. Hence Stephen Haseler argues: 'For what is often meant by "national identity" is really "state identity" (identification not with the four nations of the British Isles but with the over-arching nation-state of the United Kingdom.'[10] For Haseler, therefore, Britishness was an imposition of the English on the non-English, who maintained their diversity in this colonial situation.[11] A much more convincing explanation of Britishness has been provided by Linda Colley. She argues that Britishness was a separate identity alongside other identities. She sees Britishness being 'forged' between 1707 and 1837 in conflict with an external 'other'. War with Catholic France confirmed the centrality of Protestantism in Britishness for much of the nineteenth and twentieth centuries, though surviving much longer in Ulster than elsewhere. The crucial point for Colley was that it was possible to be Scottish and British, Welsh and British and so on, since 'Identities are not like hats. Human beings can and do put on several at a time.'[12] Further, Colley sees Britishness as a creation of the Scots in the eighteenth century as a device to defend their nation's position as junior partner within a wider state. This formulation means that Colley's interpretation is compatible with that of Keith Robbins, who has suggested that it was 'the blending of "the English", "the Scots" and "the Welsh"' that produced the 'British'.[13] Both of these interpretations enable 'the British', those people who live within the United Kingdom,[14] to be responsible for the development of their own identities. They allow for the inconsistencies, contradictions and flexibility of daily identity formation. Britishness is what people mean when they identify themselves individually and collectively as 'being British'. This identification relates to the political, economic, social, cultural and personal surroundings they find themselves in at the time they choose to think about their Britishness. This might appear as a highly empiricist approach, but to classify the national identities of nearly 60 million people in one theory does not do justice to the complexity of people's identities. Hence, Britishness has never been a stable force, easy to describe because it is fixed. In that sense, Britishness has always been in a process of formation. Homi Bhabha has so perfectly commented that a nation is always 'caught, uncertainly, in the act of composing itself'.[15]

Britishness has always been unstable. This has led some to argue that it was always in the process of 'unravelling' rather than of forming a collective identity. In this approach, the past is plundered to find examples of the expression of difference and diversity and then this is associated with the inevitability of the break-up of Britain. The revolution in Ireland between 1916 and 1923 is seen as the ideal type of behaviour for the non-English nations of the UK. Expressions of Welsh and Scottish distinctiveness are seen as being demands for separation. The infinite variety of discord and dissent is celebrated as a persistent challenge to the United Kingdom. This welcome recognition of diversity is associated in many ways with the post-modernist influence on historical study. Yet a new 'grand narrative' has been imposed, whereby the disuniting of the kingdom is seen as inevitable. But because it took so much longer for the Scottish and Welsh to discover their 'historic task', further explanation is required. In the past, some historians sought to explain why the British working class refused to act in the revolutionary manner expected of them.[16] Now many commentators ask a similar question of the Welsh and Scottish – what has delayed their 'historic task' of nation building? This book will not ignore the persistent challenges to the state in the United Kingdom since 1870, but it will argue that equal, if not more, attention needs to be given to agreement and consent in understanding the formation and resilience of Britishness over a century of rapid and radical change.

I started from the fundamental premise that ordinary working- and middle-class people played the major part in constructing their own identities. Their constructions are certainly shaped by external influences, many of which are imposed or coercive, particularly, but not only, in wartime. My approach here is in stark contrast with the supposition of an idealised form of behaviour suggested by Haseler when he argued that 'Real middle classes are radical and liberal. They also tend to be internationalist.'[17] Implicitly, this means that the British middle classes – in England, Scotland, Wales and Ireland – were unreal, because they were often conservative and were frequently nationalist. The book looks at the actions and reactions of 'real' people without making assumptions about the way in which they *should* act. This leads on to the next point, now generally accepted as a cliché yet not always taken into account in the assumptions of the break-up of Britain. Laurence Brockliss and David Eastwood described the British Isles between 1750 and 1850 as 'a Union of multiple identities'. 'Every Briton in 1800', they have argued, 'possessed a composite identity.'[18] So too did Britons in 1870 and in 2003. Arthur Aughey also stresses that people frequently have a duality of national identities. He quotes Wassily Kandinsky, the Russian artist, who said that the twentieth century would be the century of 'and' over 'either/or'.[19] In many nations, identities are frequently multiple and relatively unproblematic. The notion of being Irish-American is well accepted. Galicians frequently consider themselves Spanish; Germans sometimes consider themselves to be Bavarian. In the United Kingdom, as elsewhere, identities of place have frequently been multiple, combining allegiance to street, neighbourhood, locality, town, county, region, nation(s) and even a global empire.

The frequent intermingling of different people from within and without the United Kingdom has also enforced a necessity for multiple identities. A quarter of people living in Wales and 10 per cent of those living in Scotland in the 1990s were not born in those nations.[20] In any 'English' university seminar room, the numbers of students with Irish, Scottish, Welsh, Ukrainian, Polish, African, Asian and Caribbean names are testimony to the intermingled nature of the British Isles.

In addition, other identities have been held simultaneously with these identities of place. Individuals have considered themselves to be mothers or fathers, sisters or brothers, socialists, liberals or conservatives, working class, middle class or aristocratic, gay or straight, with none of these categories being mutually exclusive. The varieties are endless, and while some are incompatible – one person cannot at the same time be a teenager and a pensioner – not all are so. Britishness has more often than not been compatible with a huge variety of other identities, and that has been one reason for its continuing hold. This book argues that 'Britishness' has been a flexible identity, and that fact has enabled its persistence. And persisted it has. Of course, the dissent of millions of people needs to be taken into account across the last 130 years. In 1918, for example, half a million Irish people, nearly half of those who voted, did so for Sinn Féin, a party committed to withdrawal from the UK parliament at Westminster and the establishment of the Dáil Éireann in Dublin.[21] This act marked the birth of a nation. On the other hand though, the change in Ireland can be seen as cataclysmic, caused by the experience of the First World War, the Easter Rising of 1916, and the repression imposed by the British state. T. P. O'Connor, Irish nationalist MP for Liverpool, certainly believed that 'Before the executions [of the 1916 Rising leaders] 99 per cent of Nationalist Ireland was Redmondite, since the executions 99 per cent is Sinn Féin.'[22] In April 1916, the majority of nationalist Ireland supported a moderate form of devolutionary and parliamentary nationalism. This form of nationalism may not have embraced Britishness but it could certainly accommodate itself to remaining part of the United Kingdom. Two sides can also be seen in Scotland in the late twentieth century. In a 1997 opinion poll, one in four Scots decided that they were 'Scottish not British', but the same poll revealed that one in three of the Scottish considered themselves at least equally British and Scottish.[23] It is of immense significance that these 'British' people retain their Britishness in the face of the crises of national identity.

It is even possible to see ways in which Britishness has been strengthened in recent years. This can be seen in the construction of black and Asian 'British' identities, and the Labour government's desire to use devolution to nations and regions within the UK to strengthen Britishness. A further example emerges from the writing of history. A. J. P. Taylor has been widely quoted as an exponent of an Anglocentric version of history writing, but that he is so frequently condemned shows the way in which British historiography has moved towards being more truly 'British'.[24] Historians such as Hugh Kearney, Keith Robbins, Jeremy Black and Norman Davies have been seeking to popularise a new history that fully takes account of the interrelationships between the separate parts of the British Isles or 'Atlantic archipelago', as J. G. A. Pocock described it in his pioneering 'plea for a new subject'.[25] Some of these writers are pessimistic about the future of the UK, but implicit within their interpretations is a pluralist sense of Britishness, shared by the current government, and reflected in the invitation to Linda Colley to deliver a lecture at Downing Street on Britishness. There has also been a resurgence of Scottish and Welsh historiography, which equally represents a strengthening of a sense of distinctiveness within those nations, but which does not necessarily imply incompatibility.[26] English history has also partly taken on a regional focus with the emergence of academic journals devoted to *Northern History* (1966) and *Southern History* (1979), though again, such journals operate in the context of British history.

There has been a recent spate of books on 'British' history, but fewer books on Britishness in the modern period. There are some honourable exceptions. Linda Colley's *Britons: Forging the Nation* was groundbreaking, locating the emergence of Britishness between 1707 and 1837, as a combination of the deeds of elites and common people. In particular, she emphasises the role played by women in the forging of the nation. Keith Robbins has also contributed extensively to the historical literature about the formation of Britishness in the nineteenth and twentieth centuries, offering an alternative interpretation to Colley. Where Colley saw being British as an overarching identity compatible with other identities, Robbins stressed that Britishness has emerged from a 'blending' of other identities.[27] Generally, though, there has been a tendency to focus on Englishness.[28] Other books, about identities in Scotland, Wales and Ireland, reject the idea of Britishness as anything other than an imposition of the English, whose roots in the 'periphery' were shallow.[29] In many ways, historians are better served by books that consider the formation of Britishness in the medieval and early modern periods, which look for ideas that sought to unite the kingdom rather than tear it apart. This has been a major achievement in the face of what was until recently a conceptual orthodoxy in which nationalism and nations were seen as modern inventions.[30] Most interpretations of the nineteenth and twentieth centuries, though, look for decline in a sense of British national identity. The three-volume collection of essays that emerged from a History Workshop conference in 1984, edited by Raphael Samuel, had their origins in seeking to understand the widespread British patriotism associated with the Falklands War.[31] Many of the speakers and writers desired to prove how ephemeral such patriotism was, how it was manufactured or invented, and how it was contested and rejected by a variety of opponents of Margaret Thatcher and her patriotic predecessors. The subtitle of the volumes, 'the making and unmaking of British national identity', had the suggestion of a chronological narrative.

This is the approach taken by two recent books on Englishness-Britishness, by Richard Weight and Robert Colls.[32] Weight's *Patriots* is about the end of Britishness. He states clearly at the start that it is 'a book about why the people of Britain stopped thinking of themselves as British and began to see themselves instead as Scots, Welsh and English'.[33] This emerges from his argument that the United Kingdom and Britishness were functions of capitalism, imperialism and Protestantism, and that therefore British national identity was enforced upon the lower classes, colonies (including Wales, Scotland and Ireland) and non-Protestants, who resisted at each point, and, in the case of the Scots and the Irish, '[e]mboldened by the victories they won', moved onwards towards devolution and autonomy.[34] With the economy facing decline in the regions, the Empire coming to an end, and Protestantism being attacked by secularisation and the growth of new non-Christian religions, English insensitivities led to the inevitable crisis of Britishness at the end of the twentieth century. He doubts whether the United Kingdom will last another century.[35] Weight provides a detailed, clear and wide-ranging argument, but he assumes too easily that *British* national identity is imposed, whereas Scottish, Welsh, Irish and English national identities are more organic and therefore more real and permanent. He does not confront the possibility that Scottishness, for example, might also serve the purposes of historic forces, such as a globalised capitalism that needs national peculiarities to create niche markets, or that it too has been historically linked to Protestantism that faces decline. Alternatively, and more likely, it might be suggested that, for much of the twentieth century, Britishness was an identity accepted, put together and lived by the majority of the people within the United Kingdom. It was certainly not the only identity. It was, as Robbins has argued, a blend of other national and regional identities, and as Colley has argued, an identity that in other ways existed above these identities.[36]

Robert Colls' argument is that such multiple identities in the United Kingdom have been so unstable as to be doomed to inevitable destruction. Colls views Britishness as a much weaker force than Weight does. There existed a British state, he argues, but not in any real sense a British collective identity.[37] There was Unionism, but this was political rather than cultural, and it was wrought with tensions. 'How could one be authentically Scottish and loyally Unionist at the same time?', he asks, referring to Tom Nairn's argument that the dilemma entailed mental illness.[38] Colls eventually comes to the conclusion that *all* national identities are fundamentally unstable, as he states that 'it is difficult to think of a national identity – *any* national identity – that can be pluralist and normative at the same time'.[39] In the British case, he thinks the crisis will emerge in an unavoidable constitutional dispute between the Scottish and British parliaments, since 'no Scottish parliament, not even a Unionist one, is going to miss the opportunity of using the Edinburgh parliament against the London one'.[40] He also argues that the state and Englishness belonged to the dominant, male classes and that women in particular found themselves outside the state, as the evidence of miners' wives and Greenham Common feminist-pacifists in the 1980s indicates.[41] Certainly, as chapter 2 of this book argues, women's relationship to the nation has been ambiguous, but most women have felt comfortable within the nation, and have made great efforts to be part of the nation, rather than as Colls suggests locating themselves in the local and the universal but outside the nation.

Weight and Colls share the interpretation that Britishness and the British state have been in continual crisis from at least the 1940s, and that in the near future that crisis will not be able to resolve itself. The argument of this book is that the period from the 1870s to the present has been about the continuing definition of Britishness. Britishness has continued to be made across the whole of the period. While there are certainly deep tensions, Britishness is still in formation. In the period between 1870 and 1914 this was on the basis of a widespread adherence to the monarchy and the British Empire, but was also associated with the strength of the British global economy. Between 1914 and 1945 the context of the development of British national identity changed. The Empire remained a central part of Britishness. But the economy had weakened. This enabled the emergence of nationalist parties in Scotland and Wales, but most people in those countries continued to believe they were British, looking to the Conservatives deliberately to uphold the Union or to the Labour Party to provide all-British solutions to all-British problems of economic weakness. In addition in this period, two World Wars contributed powerfully to the sense that the British had common purpose. Out of the second of these wars emerged a new form of Britishness that entered into people's everyday lives through a national welfare state.

The dismantling of the British Empire between the 1940s and the 1990s removed a major prop to Britishness. The monarchy, weakened by the end of its imperial role, did however provide a sedative to relieve some of the pain of the loss of Empire. The legacy of Empire, mass non-white immigration, challenged the racialised version of Britishness that rested on a myth of ethnic homogeneity. The 1960s and 1970s saw political nationalism grow stronger in Wales and Scotland, and the re-emergence of the impact of Irish nationalism in Britain (it had never gone away in Northern Ireland). This was the moment when the end of Britain began to be widely predicted. But the prophecy of change is more exciting than the prophecy of continuity, even where the forces of continuity are far stronger. Thatcher's election victory in 1979, even if it was based on only just over 40 per cent of the votes cast, did suggest a desire for territorial integrity and political order. The 'project' of the Thatcher governments was to make Britain great again, in the face of a sense of decline. That four general elections were won by the Conservatives (one under John Major, no less a Unionist than Thatcher) should suggest the strength of Britishness in this period. But it was not only Conservatives who felt British. Despite massive social divisions in early 1980s Britain, a survey undertaken by Richard Rose suggested that 86 per cent of people in Britain were 'proud' to be British. The survey was conducted before the Falklands War. Rose went further though. His research suggested that while the proportions differed between those who were 'very proud' and 'quite proud' in England, Wales and Scotland, the totals of those who were proud in each nation were the same. He concluded that, 'Because national pride is so widespread in Britain, it is normal in the literal sense, that is, it is the norm to which nearly everyone conforms.'[42]

Thatcherism, however, was also in the process of removing yet another prop of Britishness. The welfare state had been constructed around Labour's version of Britishness forged in the Second World War and afterwards. Most people were proud of the welfare state as a 'British' institution, but Thatcher who claimed to be a British patriot proclaimed her intention to make people less dependent on the state. In this circumstance there was a substantial rise in support for devolution of power and, in some cases, for independence for Scotland and Wales. The break-up of Britain, it seemed, was back on the agenda. Certainly things had changed. Many young people, Scots, Welsh and English, saw national identity as less important than a huge variety of other identities. Their cultural influences were localised versions of a global culture – of black music, of Asian and Italian food, of drugs from Morocco and the Lebanon that were trafficked through European cities such as Amsterdam. At the same time, the landslide election of Labour in 1997 brought to Westminster a government with a more flexible attitude to national identity than any since the pluralist Liberal governments of the late nineteenth and early twentieth centuries. That British pluralism emerges at the same time as demands for change accounts for the ability of Britishness to adapt to changing circumstances. But this should be seen not as the product of some unionist or English conspiracy but rather as a reflection of the adaptive sense of Britishness of much of the United Kingdom population. This returns us to the basic premise of this book, that people have been actively engaged in the construction of British national identity, and that this too has made Britishness a resilient force.

Some will say, an 'English' historian would say that, wouldn't he. It is worth therefore coming clean in advance. I was born in the south-east of England, to parents born in England (one in east London, the other in Newcastle upon Tyne). Until I was thirty-five I lived and worked in the south-east, then I moved to Huddersfield. But such a description hides a range of conflicts in my own 'British' identity. Both my parents had Irish surnames, Moran on my mother's side and Ward on my father's. An academic colleague from Northern Ireland used to mock me that they were Irish 'knacker' names. I went to a Catholic primary school in a garrison town during the Provisional IRA's campaign against mainland Britain. Each morning my brothers and sisters and I had to walk past a Church of England school where our right to be resident in Britain was sometimes questioned. Our school was subject to numerous retaliatory bomb threats after each IRA attack. Perhaps it was these experiences that led to my first political activism around the fringes of the Socialist Workers' Party in the late 1970s. I attended a Troops Out of Ireland meeting in, probably, 1978. I joined the Anti-Nazi League about the same time. My early politics already addressed the multi-national and multi-ethnic nature of the United Kingdom (not that I knew it). I eventually joined the SWP, which for a long time rejected identities of place entirely in favour of a workerist and internationalist identity. I was a loyal member for many years, but felt a little dismayed in the 1990s when the party refused to discuss a programme of political reform based on republicanism in the four nations of the United Kingdom. Somehow, and I think through the inspirational teaching of John Ramsden, a Conservative historian with a much more open mind than I had, I ended up researching the relationship of the labour movement and national identity in Britain between the 1880s and 1920s. This suggested to me, first, that people do adopt multiple identities of class, socialism and nation, even when people like me did not want them to, but secondly that the break-up of Britain would be a progressive act, breaking with an imperialist and monarchist (British, not English) past. But the achievement of this progressive act is much more difficult than those like Nairn, my political allies in many ways, suggest. This book seeks to explain the strength of Britishness, because it constantly amazes me: I see identities other than those of class no longer as false consciousness, but as part of the complexity of being human. I remain, after ten years of academic research on national identity, ambiguous in my attitude to Britishness. I now take it for granted that the vast majority of people do adopt national identities (even though these are historical constructions they are no less real) and I would far rather see the emergence of an open and inclusive version of Britishness that not only welcomed diversity but was constituted of that diversity than I would the emergence of a racialised Englishness in response to the break-up of the United Kingdom. It is hard being Anglo-British right now. But then, it has never been straightforward. And it has frequently been harder being ruled by the Anglo-British.

This book has been self-consciously written as a history book. It does not (often) seek to make political judgements on the past. Given its wide scope, it relies on the work of other historians in many ways, but in parts it is based on archival research of printed and non-printed sources, on diaries, letters, newspapers, pamphlets and contemporary books. It uses quantitative sources where they have been available, but it tends to make greater use of qualitative sources because they cast greater light on the complexities of individual and collective identities. It has tried to retain a Britannic rather than Anglocentric approach in each chapter. It seeks to examine, across a range of themes, the forces that have contributed to a sense of Britishness, while also giving due weight to the ways in which Britishness has been mediated by other identities, such as those of class, gender, region, ethnicity and the sense of belonging to England, Scotland, Wales and Ireland. It also looks at some of the processes by which adherence to Britishness has been encouraged or discouraged by politics, leisure and other forms of culture. Each chapter seeks to examine the whole period from 1870 to the present, though the focus in each differs in order to enable some detailed discussion. There has, of course, been a process of selection. National identity intersects with a wide variety of other identities, and impacts upon people's lives in numerous ways. Religion might, for example, have been given a separate chapter, or analysis of national identity by age across the period might have been undertaken. These issues have not been ignored, but the chapters have been constructed around what I considered the most important themes, which could also incorporate and organise discussion of the abundance of areas in which Britishness had played a part.

In the first chapter, the relationship of the various national identities of the United Kingdom with the monarchy and Empire are examined. Between the 1870s and 1950s, the rule of the British and their kith and kin overseas was perhaps the most significant aspect of Britain's world image. The extent to which the British themselves internalised this image has been strongly debated, not least because the answer to this enigma has so much bearing upon the impact of the end of Empire on the British and Britishness. The monarchy pre- and post-dated the British Empire. Royalty in Britain gloated over its imperial role and retained a sense of imperial mission long after the Empire had transformed itself into a 'Commonwealth' that really did not look to Britain for leadership. The chapter considers the ways in which the royal family has been seen as central to British national identity in the imperial and post-imperial United Kingdom. It suggests that the British monarchy provided a way in which diversity and unity could be celebrated, not as something imposed from above, but through the participation of thousands, indeed millions, of people. The monarchy validated different social and national identities, while stressing unity within the kingdom.

Chapter 2 examines a different sort of identity, that of gender. Its purpose is to show that Britishness has been mediated by other identities that the British have adopted, in this case of being men and women. It argues that while Britishness has often privileged males with most significance, women have not been any less enthusiastic in asserting their Britishness. It also addresses the argument that Britishness has become 'feminised' since the end of the First World War and that the association of the British nation with the family acted as an important component in the war of ideas against Nazi Germany but also tended to exclude non-white people from Britishness after 1945. It concludes by arguing that the perception of a breakdown of traditional family life since the 1960s has contributed to a sense of the break-up of Britishness.

There is a change of direction in chapter 3, which in its first part focuses on the historiographical debate about the relationship between towns, the countryside and the idea of national identity. It argues that the association of Britishness with a rural idyll has been exaggerated, and that the urban has been incorporated substantially into ideas of national identity. This is confirmed by the continuing hold that myths about the Second World War have within 'British' memory, but also by the reinforcement to a sense of Britishness provided by regional identities within England, identities which tend to be based on urban experiences: scousers are Britons from urban Liverpool, Brummies are Britons from urban Birmingham, Geordies are Britons from urban Newcastle. Yorkshire is associated as much with Bradford and Huddersfield as it is with the Dales and the North York Moors.

Chapter 4 trawls through various aspects of popular culture in order to examine the ways in which Britishness has been part of the everyday experience of Britons in the last 130 years. It discusses the contradictory, yet simultaneous, processes by which sport in the United Kingdom has acted both to unite and divide collective identities. There is nothing more English than cricket, or more Welsh than rugby, for example. The chapter also considers the central role holidays have played in the construction of Britons' images of themselves. Finally the chapter explores culture as a site of conflict over the influence of the UK's most important ally since 1917, the United States of America. The USA may have aided British victory in 1918, 1945 and the Cold War, but for many it has been seen as at the cost of Americanisation of British culture.

Chapter 5 examines the political contests over national identity in Britain since the late nineteenth century. It argues that the ownership of patriotism has never been firmly in the hands of one party or another, and that, for the major parties at least, the extent to which they shared ideas about what it meant to be British confirmed the basic stability of British politics. At the same time, it meant that the electoral advantage of being associated with the dominant ideas of Britishness was transferable. In 1900, the Conservatives won a khaki election, but in 1906 they lost another, given that the election was fought on issues associated with the impact of the war in South Africa (Tariff Reform, 'Chinese slavery', 'national efficiency'). This happened again when the Conservatives won, as part of a National coalition in 1931 and 1935, but were devastated by Labour's victory in the khaki election of 1945. The last part of the chapter examines the political debates over European integration since the 1960s.

Chapters 6 and 7 are substantially longer than the others, because they address what are currently considered the most important aspects of Britishness since the 1960s. Chapter 6 discusses the relationship between 'ethnicity' and Britishness. It seeks to address the experience of both immigrants and their descendants and the 'host community' in coming to terms with the diverse nature of the population of the United Kingdom. As far as I know, nobody has been assaulted or murdered over the issue of European integration, yet the right of non-white and other immigrants and their descendants to be British has frequently been violently opposed in the United Kingdom. The chapter attempts to examine the wide variety of experiences of the encounter with Britishness raised by the global nature of the human population. The chapter does examine the simultaneous sense of separateness and integration within the UK. While it certainly does not seek to provide a whig view of progressive acceptance, it does take a fundamentally optimistic view of the ability of Britishness to become a diverse collective identity. It places the emphasis here on the post-colonial confidence of young black and Asian Britons since the 1980s rather than on any innate tolerance associated with being British.

The final chapter examines the experiences of Ireland, Scotland and Wales within the United Kingdom. Its fundamental argument is that people in these nations have been central to the construction of Britishness in the last 130 years. It does not underestimate the extent to which Britishness has been contested and opposed, particularly in Ireland and Northern Ireland. It does, however, argue that in Ireland until 1916 the majority of the population supported continued association with Britain at the same time as demanding limited political devolution. It suggests, therefore, that in different historical circumstances certainly, it is possible for Britishness to survive the challenge of devolution in the present. It suggests that unionism has been a much stronger force in the United Kingdom than the electoral support of the Conservative Party alone suggests, because, in fact, the Liberal and Labour Parties, not to mention more radical parties such as the Communist Party of Great Britain and the British National Party, have been unionist. Northern Ireland is different, because for possibly a majority of the nationalist population there, the fundamental damage to their tolerance towards Britain was inflicted between 1916 and 1921. Virtually nothing that the Unionist state did between 1921 and 1972 was intended to repair that damage, and the British state has participated in the continuing alienation of the Catholic northern Irish.

Ernest Renan, a French writer on national identity in the late nineteenth century, suggested that nations were 'not something eternal. They had their beginnings and they will end.' They existed, he said, by virtue of 'daily plebiscites' by their members.[43] This provides an essential warning that nations and national identity are not permanent and unchanging, that they are the products of constant recomposition, renegotiation, contest and debate. The inevitability of the transitory nature of nations does not, however, mean that the end has arrived for Britishness. This book argues that in Britain between the 1870s and the beginning of the twenty-first century the majority of people in the United Kingdom came through such discussions of their national identities with a belief that they shared more in common, as Britons, than they had differences. Certainly the nature of Britishness had changed, and in many ways had been weakened, but Britishness was alive and well.

# 1  Monarchy and Empire

From at least the late nineteenth to at least the late twentieth century monarchy was seen as central to British national identity. Between 1876, when Disraeli gave Queen Victoria the title of Empress of India, and 1953, the monarchy was fundamentally entwined with the idea and reality of the British Empire. They were seen together as forming two basic foundations upon which Britishness could be built. As Robert Roberts recalled of his schooldays in Salford before the First World War, loyalty to the nation and state was loyalty also to both monarch and Empire:

> We drew Union Jacks, hung classrooms with flags of the dominions and gazed with pride as they pointed out those massed areas of red on the world map. 'This, and this, and this', they said, 'belong to us!' When next King George [V] with his queen came on a state visit we were ready, together with 30,000 other children, to ask in song, and then . . . tell him precisely the 'meaning of Empire Day'.[1]

The coronation of Elizabeth II in 1953, after the loss of India from the Empire (though not from the Commonwealth), continued to link monarch to Empire. David Cannadine has pointed out that the coronation

> was still avowedly an *imperial* occasion, with the queen's dress containing embroidered emblems of the dominions, with Regiments of Commonwealth and colonial troops marching in procession, with the prime ministers of the Dominions and India present in the Abbey, and an assortment of heads of state from various exotic colonial protectorates.[2]

The monarchy was seen as a device to maintain the loyalty of the dominions and colonies. Arthur Balfour, prime minister from 1902 to 1905, pointed out that 'The King . . . is the greatest constitutional bond uniting together in a single Empire communities of free men separated by half the circumference of the globe.'[3] Divisions within the United Kingdom too, it was hoped, could be overcome through the unifying vehicles of monarch and Empire. On the outbreak of war in 1939, for example, George VI became patron of the Empire

Day Movement.[4] This chapter therefore discusses the monarchy and imperialism together, because they were intended in many ways to perform the same function of forging Britishness, and because they were seen as so fundamentally linked. As David Cannadine has argued, there was a convergence between hierarchy and the British Empire, with the monarchy at the top.[5] It is clear, though, that there are also separate issues involved between monarchy and Empire, not least the survival of the centrality of monarchy to nation after the ending of Empire. Sir John Stokes, Conservative MP between 1974 and 1992, could therefore still argue in 1984 that 'The monarch embodies the whole nation and gives us a sense of history, continuity and cohesion', without reference to the Empire in British history.[6]

Furthermore, the historiographies of monarchy and imperialism in relation to British national identity have been largely separate. The study of the domestic impact of imperialism was pioneered by John MacKenzie in his book *Propaganda and Empire*. He argued that British society was subject to an ideological imperialist barrage through 'vehicles of imperial propaganda' from which there was no escape for the population between the 1880s and the 1960s. The British people received the imperial message from school textbooks and teachers, juvenile literature, youth movements, the churches, music hall, theatre, propagandist societies, exhibitions, cinema, radio and political parties, mainly, but not exclusively, the Conservatives. The imperial message also appeared in commercial advertising and packaging. Imperialism itself became a commodity to be sold to the British public. MacKenzie quotes John Julius Norwich, who remembered that in the 1930s, 'Empire was all around us, celebrated on our biscuit tins, chronicled on our cigarette cards, part of the fabric of our lives. We were all imperialists then.'[7] John Benson has, though, noted that while 'consumption played some part in fostering British national consciousness, it also helped to reinforce other forms of identification – especially with the Dominions, with England, Wales and Scotland, and with particular regions and localities'.[8]

In this view, the big imperial celebrations, often part of royal occasions, were but part of a continuum with everyday expressions of imperialism. This connects with the recent conceptual work of Michael Billig, who describes 'banal nationalism' as 'the ideological habits which enable the established nations of the West to be reproduced . . . Daily, the nation is indicated or "flagged" in the lives of its citizenry.'[9] We might want to invoke the term banal imperialism rather than nationalism (while nonetheless not repudiating the links between the imperial and the national), but it should be clear that while empire and imperialism were extraordinary, exciting and out there, they were also centred in the metropolis, indeed in the cities, towns, villages, suburbs and homes of the imperial British 'race'. As Raphael Samuel has remarked, 'the imperial and the domestic' were linked.[10] They were often linked through the monarchy in architecture, coins, stamps and letterboxes as well as in 'an amalgam of names, places, buildings, images, statues, rituals and observances'.[11]

In the view of MacKenzie and the 'Manchester school', imperialism held sway over British culture and values from the onset of 'new' imperialism in the

1870s, surviving the First and Second World Wars and into the 1960s.[12] Michael Caine in *Zulu* in 1963 consoled the British that as their Empire fell the whole affair had been marked by dignity and bravery, involving not only soldiers of different classes, signified in the overcoming of the tensions between the aristocratic and middle-class officers, but also with the involvement of a Welsh regiment signifying the 'British' nature of the Empire. At a critical moment in the battle, the Welshness of these British soldiers is vocally revealed when the men break into the singing of 'Men of Harlech'.[13] Imperialism was therefore pervasive in British culture even after the end of Empire.

Two alternative interpretations can be set against the MacKenzie approach. Richard Price provides a necessary nuance to the debate by his implicit argument that the impact of imperialism in Britain was affected by other social identities. Writing in the early 1970s, Price stressed the importance of class. In his study of the impact of the Boer War on metropolitan Britain he argued that the working class were largely indifferent to the war in particular and the Empire in general, being more concerned with 'the immediate and material', that is the everyday struggle for life.[14] Hence when the relief of Mafeking from an extended siege by the Boers was enthusiastically celebrated by large parts of the British population in May 1900, Bernard Porter, sharing Price's approach, suggests that, 'For the working classes who participated . . . the whole occasion was probably little more than a celebration of the safety of their comrades in uniform.' Porter continues that between the wars, 'as ever a good proportion of the working classes proved impervious to Empire Days, Empire Songs, Empire Essay Competitions, "Empire Meals on Empire Day", and all other ingenious ploys of the imperialists'.[15]

These and like-minded historians suggest that the outpourings of public imperialist enthusiasm came from the middle class, who were denied the class loyalties of the aristocracy at one end of society and the organised working class at the other and looked instead to nation and Empire for a sense of collectivity.[16] The advantage of this approach is that it does see responses to imperialism as mediated by the social position of the individual, but it is rather a product of its time in its exclusive concentration on social class.

A third approach to understanding the impact of the Empire on the British comes from the imperial historian P. J. Marshall. He argues that the experience of imperialism did not divert the British but 'seems to have accentuated certain trends already recognizable in pre-imperial England [*sic*]' among which were a sense of uniqueness and superiority.[17] While there is much to be said for this argument, given the clear evidence of a sense of authority and dominance among the English, at least, before imperialism, including the assumption that they were God's Englishmen, it does rather underestimate the effects of imperialism on British society.

The monarchy has been absent from the discussion so far because it appears pretty much only as an appendage to imperialism despite its longer life – before and after – than the British Empire. MacKenzie, for example, sees monarchism as a component of an 'ideological cluster' comprising 'a renewed militarism, a devotion to royalty, an identification and worship of national heroes . . . and racial ideas associated with Social Darwinism' that constituted imperialist patriotism.[18] Monarchy does, however, have its own tradition of literature examining its relationship to national identity. First, there are the numerous celebratory materials accompanying royal events. These usually placed much emphasis upon the historical aspects of the ceremonial. The age of the institution was portrayed as an important part of the association of royalty to national identity. The King George's Jubilee Trust, for example, explained the purpose of its production of *Official Souvenir Programme of the Coronation of His Majesty King Edward VIII*:

> One of the principal objects of producing the Programme is to enable His Majesty's subjects throughout the world to follow the Coronation service word for word when, as is expected, this is broadcast from Westminster Abbey. The section devoted to explaining the Coronation Ceremonial will help them to realise the symbolic character of the service, and will bring them in close touch with the historic ceremony.[19]

Such programmes were widely circulated, if not so widely read, and therefore retain importance in terms of the historical reading of royal ceremony. A second approach shown by literature on the monarchy is biographical. Royal biographies have been variously hagiographic, official, scurrilous, for entertainment and scholarly.[20] A third recent approach has been the sceptical; works by Tom Nairn, Stephen Haseler and Edgar Wilson seek to explain the popularity of the monarchy, but also in turn seek to contribute to the end of the United *Kingdom*.[21] In a sense, the products of these three varied approaches are primary source materials for examining attitudes towards monarchy in the time that they were written.

The fourth approach has more deliberately set out to examine the interrelationships between the monarchy and British society. In 1937 the newly founded social anthropological organisation Mass-Observation used observers to record people's reactions to the coronation of George VI. In the same period, Kingsley Martin, editor of the *New Statesman*, wrote about 'the magic of monarchy'.[22] It is in this tradition that historians have more recently approached the monarchy in relation to national identity. David Cannadine has argued that the monarchy was unpopular until the 1870s, after which its loss of political power and the development of cheap media enabled the 'invention of tradition' which contributed to the increasing popularity of the monarchy. Cannadine implicitly argues that traditions such as the elaborate ceremonial of jubilees and coronations were largely the work of a few individuals who intentionally sought to bring the monarchy more to the centre of the nation; so, in the Edwardian period, Viscount Esher, Edward VII and Elgar all contributed to the development of royal pageantry.[23]

The purpose of such pageantry was to cope with the stresses of a modern, urban, industrial society through an emphasis on the legitimacy and continuity of the monarchy in Britain. William H. Kuhn has usefully criticised Cannadine's approach, pointing out the wider involvement than a narrow range of elite figures in the invention of tradition. He points out that more Liberals than Conservatives were involved in aiding the monarchy's rise to the centre of national identity.[24] Frank Prochaska sees the development of the monarch's popularity as a result of the interplay of the royal family and the public through joint activity in pursuit of charitable ends. In this relationship, benefits came to both sides. The monarch not only supported charities through direct donations (Queen Victoria distributed £12,535 to 330 charities in 1882), but also provided patronage which encouraged citizens to charitable endeavours. In 1887 £80,000 was contributed by 2 million women as a 'Women's Jubilee Offering' to the Queen. At the end of the twentieth century the Prince of Wales's Charities handed out £1,367,230 in a single year and the involvement in AIDS charities by Princess Diana brought much praise. Prochaska's conclusion about the 1920s and 1930s, when monarchies across Europe had toppled, is that, 'There was more to the [British] monarchy's survival strategy in the interwar years than salesmanship and insubstantial pageant. With its extensive network of patronages, the monarchy was well placed to assist the voluntary sector to deliver an array of much-needed social services.'[25]

This chapter continues by examining two ways in which the monarchy sought to establish its centrality to the nation: the function of royal ceremonial and celebration; and the development of the idea of a royal *family*. Both sections will show the profound links between monarchy and Empire, but also how the two could be so easily disengaged. Responses to the monarchy and Empire, as explained above, were affected by the variety of social identities of the British people, and the main part of this chapter suggests ways in which monarchy and Empire have been mobilised to overcome potential divisions to develop a sense of Britishness.

## Ceremony, celebration and the making of the nation as family

The celebration of the monarchy as the centripetal force of the nation must occur in the public domain. The monarch must be in touch with the people. The most noticeable way in which this occurs is in the construction of cere-monial and ritual and the celebration of these by the populace. There is there-fore a dialogue occurring between the monarchy and its subjects. The monarch performs in the public arena, and the people, by acting as a willing audience, by actively participating in the spectacle, ensure the continued centrality of the monarch to the nation but also seek to ascribe values to the nation. Hence the sociologists Edward Shils and Michael Young described the 1953 coronation of Elizabeth II as 'a great act of national communion'.[26]

Cannadine has described how 'Between the late 1870s and 1914 . . . there was a fundamental change in the public image of the monarchy, as its ritual, hitherto inept, private and of limited appeal, became splendid, public and popular.'[27] Developments in the media in the twentieth century enabled an increasing proportion of the population to be involved in such ritual, even if only as spectators from afar. The role of the British Broadcasting Corporation (BBC) has been crucial. The first Director-General, Lord Reith, 'rapidly recognised the power of the medium [radio] to convey a sense of participation in ceremonial which had never been possible before', and in the post-war period each significant royal event from the coronation onwards has been televised live.[28] Mass-Observation noted of the 1937 coronation: 'The most potent means of unifying behaviour was the broadcasting of the ceremony and processions, and of the King's speech. It meant that a very high proportion of the population spent the day listening in and thus partaking in the central events.' Asked what they found the 'most stirring incident' of the day, many respondents who listened to the radio mentioned hearing the cheering and shouting of the crowd in London, and two others recorded (in note form) 'People quiet in pub to hear King's speech' and 'Spontaneous rising of audience in cinema for relay of *God Save the King* after the King's speech.'[29] It seems, therefore, that most affecting was the sound of others showing their loyalty to the monarchy, which encouraged the sense of being part of the nation. Such scenes were then reproduced in the cinema. *South Riding* (1938), a feature film about improving the housing conditions of Yorkshire, ends with the opening of a new housing estate and school on the Coronation Day of 1937. Children, firemen and nurses and other people representing the community, sing 'Land of Hope and Glory' and there follows a patriotic speech from the chairman of the council.[30] As has already been mentioned, between the late nineteenth century and the mid-twentieth century, royal events were also imperial events and it is clear that participants could extend their sense of belonging to the Empire. Again Mass-Observation recorded reactions in 1937. A twenty-seven-year-old male schoolteacher, describing himself as 'inactive Left' in politics, told how he 'felt tearful at the sight of the mounted escorts from distant parts of the world, the Indians, the Australians. It affected me to think that England's influence reached so far.'[31]

Active participation in the organisation of royal events was widespread. These were not events organised at a national level alone. The collaboration of tens of thousands was needed for the successful outcome of major royal occasions. The London County Council (LCC), for example, in 1911 took 100,000 schoolchildren to the Festival of Empire at Crystal Palace at the invitation of the new king, George V. This entailed organising ninety-six trainloads of children under the supervision of 6,000 teachers and an organising committee of twenty-three.[32] In 1935, under Labour control, the LCC arranged for 70,000 children to watch the silver jubilee procession from stands in The Mall and Constitution Hill; in 1937 and 1953 the numbers were reduced to around 35,000 children. Each of these events involved council officials and teachers in immense extra and unpaid work in what amounted to nation building. There was also no shortage of offers of voluntary help from the general public. In 1911 a south London scoutmaster offered himself and one hundred Scouts to help with the day's organisation, and stressed their qualifications that, 'This troop has already formed a guard of honour four times for King George.' In

1953 a man from Ilford wrote to the LCC 'to offer my services as a seat steward or a similar job. I will not be requiring any pay for the duty as I am only too pleased to offer my services on this great day.'[33]

It was not only through the big royal and imperial events that people felt connected to the monarchy, the nation and the Empire. The charitable work of the monarchy has been crucial in securing public approval, but Prochaska also points out that royal involvement in the recognition of the charitable works of the public plays an important role in the transformation of civic into national pride. Royal acknowledgement involved validating citizenship so that in turn citizenship was associated with patriotism and loyalty. The impact of even indirect contact with royalty could be profound. During the First World War, Mrs E. M. Bilbrough described the impact of receiving a letter from Queen Alexandra in recognition of her husband having raised a substantial amount of money for blinded soldiers: 'it's not everyone who can claim the distinction of having received a letter of gratitude from a Queen! and written in handwriting, not even typed, which makes a great difference.'[34] In 1943, Mrs Lightfoot related another encounter:

> I was chosen to represent the East Riding at a [Women's Land Army] tea party at Buckingham Palace and was sent a new pair of breeches for the event. I travelled up to London with the girls from the West-North Ridings. This was so thrilling, I could hardly believe it was real, but shall never forget it. We were presented individually to the Queen and then had tea and Her Majesty and [the] Princesses came to talk to us.[35]

In wartime the monarch was involved in the validation of the patriotism of as many people as possible. George V made 450 military inspections and visited 300 hospitals between 1914 and 1918. He also bestowed 50,000 decorations. Harold Nicolson noted that 'the soldiers in training, the soldiers at the front, the sailors at Scapa Flow, Rosyth, Invergordon, Harwich and Dover, above all perhaps the workers in the munitions factories, were aware of his constant presence among them'.[36]

The monarchy therefore sought to make physical contact with the British people. In terms of royal ceremonial this was mainly in the public space, but through what Walter Bagehot called the 'interesting idea' of 'a family on the throne' it was possible to connect the monarchy and the people in the domestic space also.[37] Dorothy Thompson has pointed out that Queen Victoria was the first monarch, indeed the first public figure, to combine both public and private roles, through her marriage to Prince Albert.[38] Victoria had nine children, and if after the death of Albert in 1861 she was criticised for her prolonged mourning and absence from public life, it was impossible to deny her maternal role. With her reluctant return to public life at the encouragement of Gladstone and Disraeli and her growing popularity, her gender became increasingly important as she developed into the matriarch to the nation and Empire.[39] The family life of the royal family, Bagehot argued, brought the monarchy to the attention of women in general; it brought 'the pride of sovereignty to the level of petty life'.[40] In the family, women had enormous significance. The suggestion that a nation was a family therefore enhanced the importance of women despite their exclusion from national political processes until 1918. Furthermore, a domestic monarchy did not mean the complete passivity of women. As Frank Prochaska has argued, in the late nineteenth century 'Royal women commonly reflected and reinforced the prevailing idea that the female sex had a particular calling or social purpose.'[41] Women were able to take part in national life through philanthropy, which in turn sometimes meant validation of women's efforts by the monarchy in the award of patronage and honours.

The idea of a royal family could therefore be seen as a method of appealing to women. That is not to say that men too did not find the association of family life and monarchy attractive, but alternative appeals could also be made to men. Edward VII, married but an obvious adulterer, was admired by many for what was seen as his manliness and spirit.[42] While never seriously threatened after 1837, the monarchy was always most secure when a family resided at Buckingham Palace. With the accession of George V, clear roles were played within the family. George V was confirmed as father of the Empire in the Durbar in Delhi in 1911, and during the First World War Queen Mary established her Needlework Guild to encourage women to sew for their husbands, fathers, brothers and boyfriends serving in the armed forces. The royal parents also shared in the anxiety over their sons, who served in the navy and the army.

The monarchy was faced by a crisis when George V died in 1936. He was succeeded by his eldest son, David, who became King Edward VIII. Through 1936 the constitutional implications of Edward's relationship with the divorced and remarried American Wallis Simpson became apparent to the National government of Stanley Baldwin. Edward did not seem to have the stability and maturity that marriage was thought to bring to a man, especially since Edward was not fully given to observing political neutrality. In December 1936, Baldwin warned Edward that he could not continue to serve as prime minister if the king chose to marry Wallis Simpson. Baldwin was secure in the knowledge that the Labour Party would not form an alternative government and that the conservative middle class would provide little support for a 'King's Party'. The prime ministers of the white dominions, including de Valera in Ireland, had been consulted and supported Baldwin. On 10 December 1936, Edward abdicated.[43]

While the damage to the monarchy caused by the abdication should not be exaggerated, 'the representation of the royalty as a family group' became 'the key factor in a new "restoration" of the monarchy'.[44] Edward's brother, Albert took the name George VI to establish his links not only with his father but also with his father's familial lifestyle. Albert had married Elizabeth Bowes-Lyon in 1923 and they had two young daughters, Elizabeth and Margaret, who alongside their parents became subjects of newsreel and press representations of the royal family. As Golby and Purdue argue, under George VI there was a 'depiction of the monarch as father as well as King – as the head of a family which, although royal, shared the typical hopes, joys and concerns of respectable families throughout the nation'.[45] In the late 1930s, the ban on cinematic depiction of Queen Victoria was lifted, and the theme of the two enormously popular films made by Herbert Wilcox, *Victoria the Great* (1937) and *Sixty Glorious Years* (1938), was exactly the role of the monarch in a national family extending throughout the British Empire. Anna Neagle, who played the Queen in both films, said that she saw working-class women in the north of England weeping as they left the cinema.[46] During the Second World War, fought on the 'home front' to a much greater extent than the First, the royal family established itself once more as head of the national family.[47] With victory in the war, the marriage of Princess Elizabeth to Prince Philip provided a respite from the austerity of Labour Britain in the 1940s, and for the next four decades royal weddings provided a media staple. There were of course blips in the good fortune of the royal family in their personal relationships, but it was not until the 1990s, with the collapse of the marriages of three of Queen Elizabeth II's four children, that the sense of a moral, family example of the monarchy to the people was dispelled. Virginia Woolf in the late 1930s described the family life of Britain's monarchy as a 'domestic paradise', and if family life could be represented as so fulfilling then so could belonging to the national family.[48]

## Overcoming divisions: nation, ethnicity and class

Representation of the monarch as head of the national family helped to overcome internal social and geographical divisions. The United Kingdom consists of four nations united by the monarchy. There were concerns that the monarch was too closely associated with England and Englishness. John Davies points out that during her reign Queen Victoria spent seven years in Scotland, seven weeks in Ireland and a mere seven days in Wales.[49] Therefore, Queen Victoria, head of state of the United Kingdom of Great Britain and Ireland, spent fifty-six years of her sixty-four year reign in England. The 'Celtic periphery' has been seen as the weak link in support for the monarchy. It is clear that proximity to the monarchy bred loyalty because opportunities arose more often to celebrate royalty and, in turn, to have one's efforts validated. In 1953, for example, there were protests that only London's schoolchildren would be given the opportunity to watch Elizabeth II's coronation procession. MPs, councillors and newspapers from the north of England complained. The *Manchester Daily Despatch* reported that 'The North is indignant because the 30,000 schoolchildren who are to have a special view of the Coronation procession are all to be from the London area.' It quoted the Mayor of Blackburn saying that 'It is unfair', and the chair of Leeds City Education Committee remarking that 'Children all over the country will be disappointed.' The Labour MP for Birmingham Sparkbrook, Percy Shurmer, raised the issue in the House of Commons, and while the explanation that the exclusion of children from outside London was due to the logistical difficulties of accommodation was logical, it was not satisfactory. This conflict did not reflect a north–south division so much as the provinces versus London, as the headline in the *Eastbourne Gazette* testifies: 'Eastbourne Not Among 30,000.'[50] The solution was a royal progress through the provinces in 1954.

On the whole, however, since the nineteenth century the monarchy has acted as a force encouraging a sense of Britishness, and between at least 1870 and the 1960s the same could be said for imperialism. In large part this was because the celebration of monarchy and imperialism and the link implied to Britain was compatible with the display of a sense of Scottishness, Welshness and some forms of Irishness. Monarchy and Empire provided opportunities for establishing the compatibility between the distinctive national identities of the United Kingdom and a sense of British identity. This was a two-way process. It could be argued that the use of symbols of Scottishness, for example, emerged from the English interest in 'tourist Scotland' encouraged by Queen Victoria's liking for the Highlands and her decision to build a royal residence at Balmoral. Prince Albert himself designed the house using 'Scottish baronial style' externally and making much use of tartan internally.[51]

Likewise in Wales, royal events were replete with symbols of Welshness utilised in the invention of the 'tradition' of the investitures of the Prince of Wales in 1911 and 1969. John S. Ellis has pointed out that in 1911, 'although wrapped in a shroud of medievalism, the ceremony of investiture was a very modern invention' of a Liberal government seeking to utilise the monarchy to strengthen 'a sense of Britishness reconciling ethnic diversity within a multinational state'.[52] Within this modern invention, it was Welshness that was emphasised. Wales was portrayed as Welsh-speaking, the ceremony took place in the castle at Caernarfon, and dragons, leeks and daffodils were much in evidence to invest a Prince of Wales born in Surrey. Irishness too was adopted for celebration by and of the monarchy. Following his coronation in 1911, George V made a visit to Ireland during which Dublin was decorated with royal crowns alongside Irish shamrocks and harps.[53] Yet while monarchy utilised such symbols it is clear that in many cases Scots, Welsh and Irish accepted the utilisation of their national symbols and did so themselves in celebration of monarchy and Empire. In 1932, at the depth of the depression that saw 36.5 per cent of insured Welsh workers unemployed, Princess Elizabeth was presented with a three-quarters scale model of a little Welsh thatched cottage built with Welsh labour and materials. Presented in the name of 'the people of Wales', the gift aimed to signify both Welsh distinctiveness and Welsh loyalty. In 1944 suggestions came from Wales that Princess Elizabeth, now heir to the throne, should be made 'Princess of Wales'.[54]

In Scotland, imperialism was celebrated because it allowed a celebration of Scottish achievements, especially the military success of Highland regiments, the administrative success of the numerous Scottish colonial administrators and the religious success of the Missionary Movement.[55] Indeed Protestantism tied all parts of the UK to the Empire. Welsh Nonconformists, too, welcomed the evangelising process of British imperialism.[56] In Ireland, radical nationalists defined themselves by their opposition to monarchy in the adoption of the description

republican, and celebrated their opposition to imperialism so that in 1900
W. B. Yeats could warn that 'Whoever stands by the roadway cheering for
Queen Victoria cheers for that Empire, dishonours Ireland and condones a
crime . . . her crime in South Africa.'[57] The Unionist Irish on the other hand
celebrated imperialism and monarchy as signs of their own Britishness. The
(Protestant) bishop of Down and Connor and Dromore declared in 1917 that:

> We cannot realise the best that is in us as a people except through associa-
> tion with England. The British Empire is an Irish Empire as well as an
> English Empire . . . Ireland has need of England and England has need of
> Ireland in order to carry on that glorious work which Englishmen, Irish-
> men, Scotchmen, and Welshmen working together have so wonderfully
> accomplished.[58]

The British Empire was therefore seen as a joint venture: it was a British rather
than an English empire, and indeed in the colonies of white settlement the
proportions of Scottish, Welsh and Irish to English were much more evenly balanced and 'Celtic' cultural pursuits were able to become the more central.
While in Britain the Scottish formed only 10 per cent of the population in 1901,
in Australia they comprised 15 per cent, in Canada 21 per cent and in New
Zealand 23 per cent.[59] In imperial India a major social event of the year was
the celebration of St Andrew's Day, which enabled 'satisfaction with two patrio-
tisms, for Scotland and for empire'.[60] Clearly, the emigration of Irish Catholics
caused by poverty and distress was unlikely to lead to an emotional attachment
to the British imperial venture, and Irish dissent contributed to the conscription
crises in Australia and Canada during the First World War. Nonetheless, emigration from the British Isles gave many a sense of Britishness, which in no way
undermined their dual identities of Scottishness, Welshness or Englishness.

In the metropolis, sharing in the economic prosperity of Empire further
aided integration of the various parts of the United Kingdom, but this also
enabled a sense of national-cultural distinctiveness. MacKenzie has described
how the River Clyde visibly connected Glasgow to the Empire through its economic importance and maintained Glasgow's claim to be the second city of the
Empire. Yet the Clyde also remained a Scottish icon.[61]

The monarchy also validated national distinctiveness through royal visits and
tours to the Celtic periphery. Mention has already been made of the scarcity of
Victoria's visits to Wales, but she took the necessity of maintaining the strength
of Unionism and loyalism in Ireland more seriously, visiting Dublin in 1900 at
the age of eighty-one. In 1903 Edward VII was greeted enthusiastically despite
organised nationalist opposition to the visit. James Loughlin suggests that the
generous Land Act of 1903 extending mortgages available to Irish tenant
farmers to buy their land played some part in this, but also that Edward had
had the flags on Dublin Castle flown at half-mast when Pope Leo XIII had
died.[62] Some Unionists felt that the monarchy could have done more. Alick
Crawford suggested so in a private letter on the eve of the First World War:

'Whatever their faults may be through the crushing power of Popery, the Irish people, South and West, are warm-hearted, and had Royalty visited and mingled with them I doubt if ever a Home Rule Bill would have reached Parliament.'[63] In 1921 George V opened the Northern Ireland parliament, and while his speech was conciliatory, it was clear that the royal visit was designed to show Ulster loyalists that the monarchy was concerned for their welfare.[64] Such royal visits have been intended to prop up potential weaknesses. In 1944 a tour was undertaken through South Wales to make amends for the decision not to make Elizabeth Princess of Wales.[65] In 1999 in the wake of devolution, Elizabeth II opened the assemblies in Scotland and Wales. The monarchy was widely seen in Scotland as being English in the late twentieth century, and devolution and the family crises within the royal household were seen as potentially threatening to the popularity of the monarchy in Scotland. An opinion poll in 1991 suggested that if Scotland became independent only 43 per cent of Scots would wish to retain the Queen as head of state, while 48 per cent favoured an elected president. Faced with such concerns the Prince of Wales has sought to re-establish his links with Scotland. In May 2000 he told the General Assembly of the Church of Scotland that 'Scotland is certainly where a very large and special part of my affections lie – not only for the people of Scotland and the incomparable beauty of Scotland's scenery, but also for the glories of Scottish culture.'[66] Nonetheless there is enough residual loyalty to the monarchy in Scotland to ensure that the Scottish National Party does not wish, at present, to take the path of republicanism despite the majority of members holding such sentiments. The story of the popularity of the monarchy is not solely one of decline, since an opinion poll in September 1998 suggested that 61 per cent of Scots would vote to retain the British monarch as head of state in an independent Scotland.[67]

It is worth pointing out that the British monarchy is not alone in facing the complexities of multiple, and potentially fragmentary, identities of place. Britain is not peculiar in being a composite nation. King Juan Carlos, for example, has specifically set himself the task of maintaining a sense of Spanishness within the seventeen 'autonomous communities' that now make up Spain. His desire to be 'king of all the Spaniards' has been strengthened by his recognition 'within the unity of the kingdom of the state, of regional peculiarities as an expression of the diversity of peoples who make up the sacred reality of Spain'.[68]

The British monarchy has also sought to overcome other divisions within society in order to instil a sense of national unity. Not only has the United Kingdom been formed from four nations but it has also been subject to waves of immigration. Both the monarchy and imperialism have acted as integrative factors in drawing immigrants into British society, though of course imperialism also has a relationship with British racism. Jonathan Schneer has written about Sir Mancherjee Merwanjee Bhownaggree, the Conservative MP for Bethnal Green at the turn of the twentieth century, who fought the 1900 election on the slogan 'Into one Imperial whole! One with Briton [*sic*] heart and soul! One life, one flag, one fleet, one Throne!'[69] At the end of the twentieth century, the death of Princess Diana provided a method through which immigrants could feel integrated into the nation. As Dorothy Thompson explains:

> There seems no doubt that this public manifestation of grief gave some
> people who feel excluded from the major currents of public and political
> life an opportunity to join in a national manifestation which was earning
> the applause of the establishment and the media. Diana's status as mother
> of the future monarch gave her death a national significance.[70]

Diana's interest in Islam, however ephemeral, and her relationship with Dodi Al-Fayed had the effect of validating immigrants and their descendants, and one response was the visible mourning of Diana in British-Asian communities.[71] Likewise other groups, such as women and homosexual men, usually marginalised in terms of national identity were able to show their patriotism in the open displays of grief.[72] Affective behaviour replaced the stiff upper lip, and while some saw this as unwelcome, others saw in it the adaptability of Britishness. The *Daily Mirror* proclaimed that 'In our grief for Diana, there is none of that old British reserve. We are united as never before. And we want the world to know it. It is the new British spirit. The spirit of Diana, proclaimed loud and proudly throughout the land.'[73] Such comments suggested that the new national identity was more inclusive and that it had been cleansed of the taint of imperialism.

At the same time, however, Britain's imperial experience could, and did, build a sense of superiority close to the heart of Britishness. P. J. Marshall has wisely pointed out that racism is a feature of non-imperial as well as imperial societies and that the most virulent recent British racists tend to be too young to have direct experience of Empire.[74] Nonetheless, the British Empire was built upon ideas of Social Darwinism, which were transmitted to people in Britain. Numerous imperial exhibitions in Britain contained living tableaux representing an image of life in the colonies that was bound to encourage a sense of superiority. In 1899 the Greater Britain Exhibition in London included a 'Kaffir Kraal' with 174 Africans, a further exhibit was 'A Vivid Representation of Life in the Wilds of the Dark Continent.' In 1924–25 the Wembley Empire Exhibition included 175 Chinese people in its Hong Kong exhibit, and seventy Africans peopled the West African section as representatives of the various tribes.[75] Mary Wade recalled her feelings as a schoolgirl at the 'African village' at the North East Coast Exhibition in 1929:

> Despite all the poverty around us, perhaps this was our first injection of a
> superiority complex. With furniture in our homes and desks in our class-
> rooms, surely we were very fortunate! Home cooking did not vary much,
> but leek puddings and tettie hash was certainly more appealing than any-
> thing the Africans were eating.[76]

Perhaps the greatest potential division in British society since the 1870s has been that of class, and here too monarchy and Empire can be seen as integrative. It could be argued that the aristocracy and upper middle class were brought together by a shared public school education that was imbued with imperial patriotism.[77] But the monarchy also played a role in bringing the middle class to the centre of society. In the early nineteenth century the monarch had been head of Society, that is the exclusive aristocratic social circle centred on London, but the family of Victoria and Albert played at being middle class and certainly displayed middle-class values. As Thomas Richards argues, 'Victoria was a domesticated monarch whose public image resided not in the trappings of the upper class but in the middle-class ethos of frugality, self-denial, hard work, and civic responsibility.'[78] With the monarchy prepared to act in a manner acceptable to the middle class, in turn that class was prepared to utilise the monarchy as 'a theatre of loyalty, which gave its separate elements a sense of belonging, unity and purpose'.[79] This was often undertaken through charitable works, for charities with royal patronage, and in turn the middle classes, were rewarded in the New Year and Birthday honours lists or in personalised letters. George V, for example, wrote to Miss Storey in March 1919, donating £25 to her fund to provide Bovril for British soldiers serving overseas.[80]

It has already been shown how the royal family has made journeys into other countries of the United Kingdom. In a sense a further element of the monarchy's popularity is based on its willingness to travel into the other country of the working class. Since important centres of the industrial working class were to be found in Wales and Scotland it was often possible to combine such visits. Hence in June 1912 King George V and Queen Mary went to South Wales, where they laid the foundation stone of the National Museum of Wales and then ventured into what Queen Mary called 'the heart of Keir Hardie's constituency'.[81] Hardie had been elected Labour MP for Merthyr Tydfil in 1900 and was prone to making anti-monarchist statements which had resulted in his exclusion from royal events. This visit was an attempt to resist the rise of Labour but also to prevent the wave of industrial action then sweeping across the United Kingdom from undermining the monarchy. It was indeed at times of industrial unrest that the monarchy felt most at risk, so in the 1920s and 1930s it seemed beneficial to appoint the Duke of York (later George VI) as royal ambassador to the industrial working class. Between 1920 and 1935 he visited between 120 and 150 factories, earning himself the family nickname of 'the foreman'. The Duke of York also acted as president of the Industrial Welfare Society which organised annual camps for public school and working-class boys, and the Duke of York ensured that he attended at least one day each year.[82] The culmination of his involvement came when he became king after his brother's abdication. The *News Chronicle* on 6 April 1937 recorded that the King had 'surprised and delighted four workpeople' by inviting them to Westminster Abbey for the coronation service. These four were clearly intended to be representative in a number of ways: 'one is a Scotch woman weaver, another a South Wales steel works foreman. Then there is a girl employed at a Birmingham electricity works and young pit worker at Chesterfield.'[83]

Hence the monarchy also sought to integrate the working class at times of national celebration. During armistice week in 1918 George V made five drives through the poorest parts of London in an open carriage, and in 1935 made four similar drives.[84] Nicolson described the success of such contacts; he wrote of George V that 'He was just as much King in Whitechapel as King in White-hall . . . so they [the working class] bought flags for their children; and stood in their millions smiling affectionately as the King and Queen drove by.'[85]

During the Second World War, royal visits took on a new importance, especially those to bombed areas, which, as Queen Elizabeth noted, became far less tense after the bombing of Buckingham Palace.[86] As Angus Calder has observed, 'The monarchy, with its essential, mystified role . . . had been given new stature by the comportment of George VI and his smiling Queen as they toured the ruins', and the ruins were so often in working-class areas.[87] The monarchy made the working class part of the nation, as it had also sought to incorporate Scotland, Wales and immigrants into the United Kingdom.

## Politics, monarchy and imperialism

Imperialism and royalty frequently lessened class, gender, national and ethnic divisions. This mostly meant that these issues did not emerge in party politics. The rise in the popularity of the monarchy in the nineteenth century was enabled by the monarch's substantial withdrawal from party politics, but it remained clear that the monarchy would always support the social system over which it presided.[88] Radical parties of the left were at a disadvantage when the head of state represented a hereditary and hierarchical social structure.[89] Yet despite this the monarchy has rarely been an issue in British politics. There has certainly been opposition to the monarchy, though it has tended to take the form of criticism of the behaviour and financial affairs of the royal family rather than republicanism. It is indeed difficult to disentangle the desire to abolish the monarchy from the desire to strengthen it through reform. There has been a hysterical streak among supporters of the monarchy that sees any suggestions for change in the organisation of the affairs of the royal family as treasonable. Hence in 1957 when Lord Altrincham made some mildly offensive comments about the speaking style of the Queen in a small circulation journal, a member of the League of Empire Loyalists physically assaulted him in the street. Likewise, in 1955, Malcolm Muggeridge found himself temporarily banned from the BBC for calling the monarchy a soap opera and suggesting that some people saw the Queen as dowdy and banal.[90] At certain points, criticism of the monarchy has emerged from the fringes of politics in Britain, but it has never been a very strong growth.

In the 1870s the absence from public life of Queen Victoria, who remained in extended mourning for Albert, did allow criticism of monarchy to emerge briefly into the limelight. Between 1870 and 1874, it is often noted, eighty-four republican clubs were formed, and such prominent figures as Joseph Chamberlain and Sir Charles Dilke were prepared briefly to see potential political capital being possible from supporting such criticism.[91] But as Golby and Purdue point out, 'The roots of republicanism had never been more than fragile and it was very much a minority interest.'[92] Republicanism attracted more attention than it warranted at the time because of the sense of anxiety among Britain's elites brought on by the increasing urbanisation of the nation. The focus of historians on the small wave of anti-monarchism in the 1870s says much about the weakness of republicanism in the period since. Frank Prochaska has recently drawn attention to royal fears about republicanism in the years immediately after the First World War and the Russian Revolution, but the threat then was implied in the militancy of the labour movement rather than being explicit in its rhetoric.[93]

Certainly it would be wrong to dismiss the importance of challenges to the centrality of the monarchy to Britishness by republicans, radicals and socialists. Antony Taylor has catalogued the occurrence of anti-monarchism since the end of the eighteenth century, much of it articulated and reported through the radical *Reynolds's Newspaper* from the 1880s to the 1950s, but perhaps his conclusion about the outbreak in the 1870s can be applied to the whole period since then: 'the anti-monarchist campaign was a pariah. It existed almost entirely outside the political mainstream.'[94] But for all that, it was not always entirely without effect. In April 1917, H. G. Wells suggested that the Russian Revolution had provided a model for the removal of 'an alien and uninspiring court'. Stung by the criticism, in May the royal family adopted the new dynastic name of Windsor, with its deep English associations.[95]

It is clear that the Conservatives saw the monarch as an ally in the nineteenth century but also as a method of securing votes for their party at elections. As the party of the established order they encouraged the formation of such organisations as the Primrose League, which sought to uphold the constitution, defined by them as the monarchy, the Church of England and the British Empire. Disraeli sought to associate himself with the monarchy through the Royal Titles Act of 1876 that made Queen Victoria Empress of India. The potential here was to continue the politicisation of the monarchy from outside, yet many of the Conservatives' opponents on the left in the nineteenth and twentieth centuries have seen such politicisation as potentially damaging to their fortunes and they have therefore stressed the politically neutral nature of the monarchy. The monarchy was therefore removed from politics, and protected from criticism, not by its most apparent supporters but by its potential opponents. In the 1860s it was Gladstone who showed greatest concern about the threat to the monarchy posed by Victoria's absence from public life and he sought to stabilise British society by encouraging the Queen to play a greater role in public ceremonial.[96] Likewise in 1911 it was a Liberal government that sought to utilise the investiture of the Prince of Wales and a royal visit to Ireland to reinforce their pluralistic version of Britishness.[97] In the 1960s it was a Labour government that presided over the investiture of Prince Charles.

Between the wars the Labour Party leadership came to see criticism of the monarchy as fundamentally damaging to their electoral performance. But some in the party were republicans and in 1923, for the only time, the party conference debated its political position on the monarchy. George Lansbury, for the

executive, declared himself a republican, but he argued successfully that capitalism, not the monarchy, was the source of poverty and that the party should not
'fool about with a question of no vital importance'.[98] In such a way the Labour
leadership continued the depoliticisation of the monarchy. Constitutionally conservative, the British Labour Party was perfectly happy to cohabit with the
monarchy. Martin Pugh has stressed the strength of monarchism in the Labour
Party, seeing the party's adaptation to Conservatism as aiding its rise in the first
half of the twentieth century.[99] It was possible for much of Labour to welcome
celebration of the monarchy by pointing to the association of monarchy with
democracy. The *Daily Herald* in 1937, for example, editorialised that, 'The King
is neither a dictator nor a Party man. He is a constitutional King in a Parliamentary democracy. And yesterday was the celebration of that democracy by
all people, irrespective of Party.'[100] Herbert Morrison wrote of the coronation in
1953 that 'when the people cheer the Queen and sing her praises, they are also
cheering our free democracy'.[101]

The Blair Labour government declared itself to be constitutionally radical,
prepared to abolish the House of Lords and devolve power to Scotland and
Wales, and yet discussion of the monarchy remained 'Labour's last taboo'.[102]
Where it was discussed within the party it was with the intention of *modernising*
rather than abolishing the monarchy by removing its associations with the
'musty smell of Empire . . . the odour of Europeans-Only Clubs, of soldiers
drilling on the parade grounds of Lucknow and Cawnpore, of *Pax Britannica*,
which turns the stomachs of democrats in a multi-racial, European parliamentary democracy'.[103] New Labour sought politically to manage the divorce of
monarchy and Empire for the sake of the former.

Measuring the impact of imperialism on British politics is complicated. In
large part this is because all mainstream parties accepted the necessity of ruling
the Empire. Again, Disraeli and the Conservatives were most associated with
the 'new' imperialism in the late nineteenth century, and the party believed that
elections could be won on the back of a populist imperialism. Certainly this
seemed to be the case in the 1900 'khaki' election as Britain fought the Boers
for control of southern Africa. The Conservatives won 402 seats as against the
Liberals poor showing of 184.[104] And this Conservative achievement was
founded on the use of slogans such as 'Do you vote for Queen or Kruger?' and
'Briton [Conservative] v. Boer [Liberal]'.[105] The portrayal of their political
opponents as enemies of the Empire suited the Conservatives, but it did not
provide the full picture. Certainly there was opposition to this imperial *war* from
Liberals and socialists, but except in a very few cases that hostility did not
extend to imperialism.[106]

The British left was always able to distinguish between varieties of imperialism. They did not like jingoism and rowdyism at home and they did not like open
exploitation in the colonies. But most of the British left believed that if imperialism was to exist then it was better conducted by Britain than anyone else. Britain
in the world, it was believed, was a force for good. This had been the spirit
behind the massive support for petitions against the slave trade and slavery in the

early nineteenth century.[107] In the late nineteenth century a powerful group within the Liberal Party described themselves as Liberal Imperialists, and within the labour movement open imperialists could be found such as Robert Blatchford. The Fabian Society refused to declare itself against war in South Africa in 1899–1902, and went on to establish the Fabian Colonial Research Bureau in 1940 which argued that Africa should be developed economically and socially, but should remain within the British Empire for the foreseeable future.[108] In Britain, there was no anti-imperialist opposition, beyond a few marginal Marxists, and that suggests that elections could be fought between varieties of imperialism. In 1906, the Liberals took their revenge on the Conservatives' attempts to forge imperial unity around tariff reform. It was widely believed that duties on non-imperial goods would raise the price of foodstuffs. Here, it seemed, was an election in which material interest outweighed the idealism of Empire of the mainly working-class electorate. But in fact, what the Liberals presented to the electorate was an alternative free trade and benevolent imperialism.[109] In a sense all elections in Britain between the 1870s and the 1950s were imperial elections, but a consensus between most parties on the necessity for British imperialism meant that this did not often translate into open conflict.

## The monarchy and the end of Empire

The coronation in 1953 was an imperial occasion. As Gordon T. Stewart has pointed out, the news, on the morning of the coronation, that Mount Everest had at last been conquered by Edmund Hillary, an imperial Briton from New Zealand, set the seal on the claims that Britain was entering a new and imperial Elizabethan age. Yet Stewart points out that Tenzing Norgay, the Sherpa who reached the summit with Hillary, subverted this grand imperial narrative by his rejection of Britishness.[110] In 1956 Britain failed to achieve its imperial objectives at Suez, and the reality of the weakness of British power in relation to that of the United States of America became more readily apparent. In the wake of the Suez reverse, if not necessarily because of it, Britain decolonised in earnest. Between 1960 and 1964 numerous independent African nations were created from Britain's former empire. By the end of the decade, Britain had withdrawn from its self-imposed defence commitment 'East of Suez'. Britain's empire was at an end. The Queen consoled herself that she remained Head of the Commonwealth, and continued to take much interest in its development. Many of the British people consoled themselves that Britain's distinctiveness now resided in its monarchy. In 1966, one commentator noted of the monarchy that

> its existence means safety, stability and continued national prestige: it promises religious sanction and moral leadership; it is 'above party' focus for group identification; it means gaiety, excitement and the satisfaction of ceremonial pageantry; it is an important, and perhaps increasingly important, symbol of national prestige.[111]

In other ways too the monarchy replaced the Empire. The BBC in the 1950s and 1960s began to see imperialism as controversial and looked increasingly to the monarchy to supply national events for broadcast, unsullied by political contention.[112] More recently, as the Blair Labour government looked to rebrand Britain, some saw the monarch as able to play a role in removing the deadweight of imperialism from the British image. Mark Leonard suggested that Britain should capitalise on the entry into a new millennium by 'organising a tour by the monarch of all sites where there is still bitterness about Britain's past – from Ireland to Iran – to heal difficult memories and to signal that Britain has moved beyond its imperial heritage'.[113]

Historians and other commentators dispute the extent of the burden of this deadweight on British identity.[114] It has been noted that the process of decolonisation in the 1950s and 1960s did not result in bitter political debate, as it did in France. France's war to prevent Algerian independence was so vicious, involving torture and murder, that the belief in the universal liberating and civilising mission of French imperialism was severely damaged. The end of Empire in France, therefore, involved a re-examination of national identity.[115] In Britain the process of the end of Empire was part of a wider consensus that incorporated agreements over national identity. That both major political parties agreed the need to bring the Empire to an orderly end cannot be doubted, but this process was not straightforward. In the late 1940s and early 1950s, as parts of the Empire were discarded, others, like Africa, were being *increasingly* exploited.[116] The consensual decision to bring the Empire to an end was a rushed judgement, certainly based on an awareness of long-term weakness, but that was a recent awareness. Crucially John Darwin argues that the end of Empire was not accompanied by a belief in the end of Britain's global influence. This was, he argues, the preservation of global power through the modification of Britain's relationship to its former colonies.[117] If geographically the Empire ended, it continued to exist in the British imagination. Robbins argues an alternative view: the lack of debate over the end of Empire reflected its lack of importance even during its greatest geographical extent between the 1880s and the 1930s.[118] Weight takes a similar line: 'Most Britons cared little about the Empire and [therefore] did not mourn its passing.'[119] It seems that the impact of the end of Empire on British identity needs to be approached with the same method with which the impact of imperialism has been approached in this chapter. The impact was varied and uneven across the population and across time. The impact on the ruling elite, schooled in imperial values and a sense of Britain's mission to govern, is likely to have been quite profound. Sir Charles Johnston, governor of Aden, commented on the impact of the Suez crisis that 'it is something which has happened inside us'.[120] It was this group that dismantled the Empire, but they could seek consolation in the method by which they were able to proceed. For these people, as Darwin argues, 'Decolonization was the continuation of empire by other means.'[121] The Ministry of Defence civil servant Sir Michael Quinlan explained (in an interview with the historian Peter Hennessy) the continuing influence of Empire on British foreign policy:

We have a certain sense of ourselves, born of history which does mean that we view what we might do rather differently from some of our partners. If you compare ourselves and Italy, we are about the same size, about the same wealth, about the same population. We are not in a more obviously threatened strategic position yet we spend . . . twice what Italy does on defence. Now, that I think only in the end can be explained by having a different view of what kind of contributor we are in the world.[122]

The supposed opponents of this class shared many of the same assumptions. The progressive critiques of Britain's 'archaic' social structure in the 1960s, which was blamed for Britain's decline, often referred back to the glory days of Empire. Anthony Sampson saw Britain's problems as stemming from 'a loss of dynamic and purpose' as 'those acres of red on the map dwindl[ed]'.[123]

A further area of debate emerges in the discussion of the impact of the end of Empire on the emergence of nationalisms in Scotland and Wales. Tom Nairn has seen the end of Empire and the 'break-up of Britain' as parts of the same process.[124] Robbins, on the other hand, has argued that while the two developments coincided, this was coincidence indeed. He points to crises in the nation-state in non-imperial nations, such as Canada and Spain. In addition, he argues that the emergence of nationalisms in Scotland and Wales pre-dated the decline of Empire.[125] Certainly we should not see the process as formulaically or inevitably connected, but nationalists have undoubtedly commented on the association. In the 1930s some nationalists saw Scottish and Welsh self-government emerging out of the development of imperialism. John Torrence argued that, 'The Empire has become the Commonwealth. Scotland remains, a relic of the old, absorbing centralising spirit of the defunct Empire . . . Scottish Nationalism is an inevitable fruit of Imperial evolution.'[126] By the 1950s the attitude towards Empire had become much more negative. H. W. J. Edwards commented that 'The Empire is now in a ramshackle state . . . The black folk of the Gold Coast have already reached a stage of self-government which puts them ahead of Wales.'[127] Here Wales was seen as a colony rather than part of the metropolitan imperial power, and such a view was continued in the late 1960s by the small group who argued for a trans-Celtic revolution, as they invoked 'the final and irrevocable collapse of the old "British Empire"'.[128] Since the link was being established in the minds (or mentalities) of some nationalists then the interdependency of the end of Empire and the development of nationalism at the end of the twentieth century should not be rejected. David Marquand overstates that connection, arguing that 'Imperial Britain was Britain . . . Empire was not an optional extra for the British; it was their reason for being British as opposed to English, Scots or Welsh.'[129] Nonetheless, imperialism did provide a sense of common purpose to disparate Britons, and its passing has removed that particular sense of commonality.

It might also be suggested that the election of Margaret Thatcher as prime minister in 1979 was in part a response to the crisis of the 1970s of which the 'break-up of Britain' was a component and to which the end of Empire seemed to have contributed. The 1977 silver jubilee had temporarily masked the extent of division in the United Kingdom. Economic crisis, problems with nationalism, unemployment and strikes all contributed to a desire to celebrate the continuity of the monarchy. On the one hand, thousands of street parties were held, yet on the other the Sex Pistols' punk anthem 'God save the queen' reached number two. While more attended the street parties than bought the single (some may well have done both), disrespect for monarchy was evident. Such attacks brought a backlash, and Thatcherism could be seen as representing an English nationalism (or English-dominated unionism) that sought to re-establish both Britain's place in the world and England's place in the United Kingdom. Roger Scruton, a right-wing philosopher, certainly saw Englishness making 'less and less sense as the empire dwindled'.[130] Thatcher sought to give back that sense. Thatcher's ministers sought to strengthen the UK's leadership in the world. Chris Patten, Conservative minister and later the governor of Hong Kong who presided over the colony's transfer to China, celebrated the role of the British Council in taking British culture to the far-flung parts of Africa, as he recalled with pride seeing Ethiopians queuing to borrow books from the British Council's library in Addis Ababa in 1988. 'I asked one young man the subject of the book he was clutching under his arm. "It's about great British Explorers," he replied. "Like Shackleton and Scott".'[131] As David Cannadine has remarked, 'The British Empire may have vanished from the map, but it has not vanished from the mind.'[132] Patten was celebrating the continuing hold of British culture even where military and political control had gone. That Ethiopia had been an independent state rather than a British colony enabled him to make such comments without being seen as an old-style imperialist. Other aspects of what Salman Rushdie has described as the refurbishment of imperialism in the 1980s included the making of films and television programmes in imperial settings which maintained white Britons at the centre of the story, as in *The Jewel in the Crown* (14 parts, 1984), *The Far Pavilions* (6 parts, 1984) and *A Passage to India* (1984). Even *Gandhi* (1982) enabled many of the British to congratulate themselves on their own role in ending the Empire. This confirmed that Empire was benevolent, a gift to the natives, because in the end, the British genius for governance was taught to the imperial population. So in Rushdie's view, 'British thought, British society, has never been cleansed of the filth of imperialism.'[133] The continuing hold of imperialism emerged during the Falklands War of 1982. The Conservative Alan Clark saw the war as the 'very last chance for redemption' from imperial decline, and Margaret Thatcher spelled out the imperial theme in her speech celebrating the victory in the Falklands, which consoled Britain for its wider loss of Empire. That triumph, she argued, showed that Britain was still 'the nation that had built an Empire and ruled a quarter of the world'.[134] This was a message that much of the population welcomed.

In the last two decades of the twentieth century, the monarchy seemed less able to console the nation at the loss of the status implied in formal Empire. Partly this emerged from Thatcher's refusal to listen to the Commonwealth over combating apartheid in South Africa through sanctions, which reportedly angered Queen Elizabeth. But in addition a series of personal crises rocked the royal family, which brought its centrality to national identity into question. These crises revolved around the wealth of the monarchy and the reaction of the monarchy to the breakdown of the marriages of the Queen's children. Many Britons had experienced divorce, and it might have been presumed that the royal family might have been able to present itself as a modern family experiencing modern problems, but it became apparent that the royal family and court were seeking to tarnish the reputations of the women who dared to leave the royal family. Princess Diana, however, fought back, using the media to portray Prince Charles and the royal family as vindictive and closed. The reaction of the monarchy to Diana's death certainly brought criticism of their behaviour, though the depth of crisis should not be overstated. It was certainly the case that Diana contested the monarchy's version of national identity. Her ability to appeal to plural identities was much greater than theirs; for all Prince Charles' suggestion that he would be defender of faith rather than defender of *the* faith, his public persona remained rather too distant from the day-to-day lives of the population. The deaths of Princess Margaret and Elizabeth, the Queen Mother in 2002, combined with the celebration of the Golden Jubilee, however, have enabled the royal family to reassert the more traditional notions of Britishness which they have sought to represent. It was estimated that over a million people were in central London on the two jubilee bank holidays (one the usual Whit holiday, the second providing an additional holiday for the purposes of celebration). *The Guardian*, a newspaper that had been calling for a debate on the position of the monarchy, decided that 'this is one of the best mornings the monarchy has ever had' and that there existed 'an unusual rapport between monarch and subjects'.[135] The monarchy had learned the lessons of Diana's death to bring new parts of the population into royal celebration. One part of the procession down The Mall had been staged by the Notting Hill Carnival organisers, and the highlight of the jubilee celebrations for many people had been the pop concert at Buckingham Palace. This was then 'a much more inclusive set of events than in the past . . . in the past, it has been their show, not ours. This time we were all invited.'[136] At the end of her thirty-five-day tour through the regions and nations of the kingdom, the Queen thanked her subjects for their loyalty and showed that she considered that the jubilee events had been successful:

> I have been profoundly moved by the affection shown and by the warmth of the response to my Golden Jubilee. It has been for Prince Philip and me a summer of great joy and happiness, and a celebration of all that binds us together as a nation: the heritage of our past, the values of our present, and the shared challenges of the future that lies ahead. I thank you all for your loyalty and support.[137]

At the beginning of the twenty-first century, therefore, it seems that while the fact of Empire has passed, it retains some ability to make its mark on ideas of British national identity. From the 1870s to the 1950s the monarchy had become interlinked with this imperial Britishness, and had shared in the sense of superiority this had given to many/most (white) Britons. The sense of Empire and monarch as central to the national identity spread widely through the population, through the class system, to women as well as men, and to the far reaches of the United Kingdom. Of course, much of this was challenged at various points, but probably only in a sustained way in Ireland and only then by the republican element within nationalism. Elsewhere, a share in imperialism and monarchy was aspired to. When the Empire fell, this was absorbed into the sense of national identity as a sign of strength. The British had given to the world the gift of self-governance. The continuing existence of the royal family, particularly when headed by a Queen who looks set to match the longevity of the imperial matriarch Victoria, served to remind many Britons that Britain remained, timeless and continuous. As one journalist reported of the Golden Jubilee in 2002: 'as the royal family stood on the balcony of [Buckingham] Palace, there came a rousing version of Land of Hope and Glory, followed by God Save the Queen. Clearly, for a great many Britons the old ones are still the best.'[138]

Monarchy and imperialism may have underpinned the development of Britishness from the 1870s to 1950s, but in terms of national identity they were fairly easily disentangled. The Queen may have continued to hold the Commonwealth in high esteem as part of her function and identity, but from the 1960s onwards there was no inextricable link between Queen and Empire in British national identity. For many, nostalgia for the imperial past continued, and remained an important component in the forging of a sense of unique Britishness, but others believed that it was necessary to come to terms with the impact of the end of Empire. This impact was not uniform among all Britons. But neither was the impact formulaic. It should not be assumed that it was the English middle-class or aristocratic male who had been most imperialist or most monarchist. As the next chapter argues, Britishness was gendered, but that did not mean that women felt excluded from national identity.

# 2 Gender and national identity

Despite its function to unite the nation across its internal divisions, Britishness has not formed a monolithic identity. It is mediated by other identities, of place, of class, of religion. It is further mediated by identities of gender. To be British is not necessarily the same for women as it is for men, for girls as it is for boys. For much of the period since 1870, contemporaries used the phrase 'separate spheres' to describe the differences in the social construction of men's and women's place in British society. Men in this description were assigned to the public sphere of work, politics and ultimately war. The nation as the main organising arena for such public activities provided men with a stage on which to play out their masculine roles. Women's proper sphere was private: home, hearth and domestic responsibilities.[1] 'Separate spheres' has always been an inadequate characterisation of women's (and men's) roles in nineteenth- and twentieth-century British society, but most representations of Britishness have fallen into line with this public–private demarcation. Historians have become increasingly aware that gender roles, both masculine and feminine, are socially constructed and are therefore subject to change across time (and space).[2] This chapter therefore seeks to examine the intersections between gender and national identities in Britain since 1870. It does so by examining the gendered nature of the nation, but also of the roles assigned to men and women within it. To ensure that men are not neglected within such a discussion, it begins by discussing the construction of notions of masculinity associated with the nation, and particularly with the British Empire. However, it does also aim to question a popular opinion among feminists that women are somehow 'outside' the nation. Indeed, the campaign for the parliamentary vote by women was part of a wider campaign for citizenship, a claim to be allowed full involvement in the affairs of the nation, and a desire to be seen as patriots alongside men. To explore this, the focus of this discussion will be women's role in the First World War. The impact of that war on national identity and masculinity was profound, and it has been argued that in the interwar years the nation (and Empire) were feminised or domesticated. Hence the challenge posed to masculinity and its version of national identity since the emergence of a feminist movement was continued. The reactions to such a challenge in the interwar years will therefore be discussed. Women's participation in the Second World

War was greater than in the First, and the characterisation as a 'people's war' suggests greater integration of women into the nation. Women's relationship to the state, however, remained ambiguous and the role they were allowed to play was limited. Women's employment and independence raised questions about men's place within the nation, particularly when American (Hollywood) models of womanhood encouraged self-expression and freedom from unhappy relationships. In this context, British cinema representations were concerned to portray a woman imbued with Britishness constructed against the American 'other'. Women's relationship to the nation therefore remained conditional upon certain standards of behaviour, and this is representative of a wider ambiguity within legal definitions of nationality revealed by immigration and nationality laws. In the post-war period, the domestication of Britishness continued. In this period, however, constructions of Britishness as centred in the home were used to exclude immigrant and black women from the nation. But a notion of Britishness linked to standards of behaviour enabled some (white) women to be targeted as instigators of national degeneracy, as the welfare state enabled the rise of a so-called 'dependency culture' connected to single motherhood. Ironically, such attacks came to a head under Britain's first woman prime minister, Margaret Thatcher, who prided herself on her patriotism. The final section of this chapter discusses the beliefs about gender and nationhood revealed during the Falklands and Gulf wars. Through this discussion, this chapter argues that national identity in Britain has been gendered. The nation has often been associated with men and their actions. However, while women's relationship to the nation was often viewed as ambiguous, that did not prevent many women seeking to make a contribution to nation through active participation.

## Masculinity, Britishness and Empire in the late nineteenth century

Many nations have been personified as female, and Britain has been no exception. Britannia is an ambiguous figure, in that she is seen to carry weapons for her own defence, but the centrality of a female figure encourages men to her defence.[3] In order to love one's country one must assign to that country features worth defending; the least problematic way is to define the embodiment of the nation as its women and children whom men can defend. In the late nineteenth century, this provided a clear distinction within the nation between the public and private spheres. Man's ultimate function was constructed as the conquest, extension and defence of the 'Greater Britain' of the Empire. The 'new imperialism' of the late nineteenth century was accompanied by a reconstruction of the central tenets of masculinity, from moral earnestness and religiosity to athleticism and patriotism.[4] In such a way the nation and maleness became entwined.

Young boys and men were trained for service in the Empire. In public schools, games were used as training for citizenship; cricket, rugby and football were exclusively for boys and men.[5] Britain's national and imperial heroes were represented as muscular Christian adventurers.[6] State schools mimicked the curricula and focus on games of public schools, and the message of a manly patriotism was further encouraged in youth movements such as the Boy Scouts and Church Lads' Brigade. Baden-Powell warned his recruits that, 'Every boy ought to learn how to shoot and to obey orders, else he is no more good when war breaks out than an old woman.'[7] Whether such persuasion was successful or not, the representation of patriotism was that it was intrinsically male and likewise that a leading component of masculinity was patriotism. Males were privileged within the nation, but in return more was expected from them in terms of service to the nation.

Perhaps the clearest point at which the relationship of men to the nation was revealed was in the wearing of military uniform. As Joanna Bourke has pointed out, at the beginning of the twentieth century, 22 per cent of men between 17 and 40 years old had some experience of military service, and between 1916 and 1918 and 1939 and 1963, young men were called up to serve the nation.[8] In popular terminology, the nation turned its boys into men in the process of training them to be patriots. But even those males outside the military services were expected to co-operate in shaping the nation. The *Boy's Own Paper* told its readership in 1879 that 'In the workshop, on the farm, / At the desk, – where'er you be – / From your future efforts, boys, / Comes a nation's destiny.'[9]

## Women and the nation 1870–1918

In the late nineteenth century, therefore, a form of masculinity in which adventure, virility, courage and chivalry were paramount became linked to British national identity. It encouraged young men either to defend Britain at home or to aid in the extension of the Empire overseas.[10] The polar opposite of this active manliness was a concept of femininity that entailed docility, domesticity and subservience. For some historians, influenced by feminist thinking, the nation has been a male construct in which women have played little part. This follows from Virginia Woolf's statement in *Three Guineas*, written in 1938, that, 'as a woman, I have no country. As a woman I want no country. As a woman my country is the whole world.'[11] In the wake of the recovery of women's history in the 1960s and 1970s, feminist historians have focused upon women who did see themselves as 'outside' the nation, such as pacifist and internationalist women.[12] Such a reading of women's place within the nation was reinforced by the ambiguous legal relationship between women and nationality. Under naturalisation acts in the nineteenth century, British women marrying 'aliens' were dispossessed of their Britishness. Under Edwardian welfare legislation, British women married to 'aliens' were barred from receipt of old age pensions. It was not until 1948 that British women could retain their legal Britishness on marriage to foreign men, and only in 1983 did it become possible for women so married to pass on Britishness to their children.[13] The ambiguity of women's legal relationship to nationality does indeed suggest that the nation belonged chiefly to British men, and that women's role was defined by their subordinate relationship. Much social reform aimed at improving women's lives was bound by their usefulness in terms of producing the next generation of male Britons. Following Britain's poor showing in the Boer War, in part owing to the poor physical condition of potential military recruits, the 'endowment of motherhood' for imperial purposes was widely supported. During the First World War, women were encouraged to produce more future soldiers in 'National Baby Week'. Marie Stopes' campaigns to encourage the use of contraception within marriage in the 1920s and 1930s had eugenicist objectives, and William Beveridge's report on the social services in 1942 was suffused with pro-natalist sentiments. Women, while providing the wombs from which the nation would grow, were at the behest of the patriarchal nature of Britain.

Against this view must be set more recent work that seeks to explore the embeddedness of women, including feminists, within an imperial and therefore national culture at the beginning of the twentieth century.[14] This interpretation enables historians to draw women's contribution to constructions of British national identity back from the margins of history.

The contribution of working-class women is difficult to determine, but from among the middle class and aristocracy women were prepared to make a significant offering to the nation. It should immediately be noted that this was a voluntary addition to patriotic activism, but also that limits were imposed upon what women could do by the strength of separate spheres ideology.

From 1900 onward there was a significant sense of foreboding about Britain and the Empire's safety, especially in the face of Germany's apparent expansionism. Encouraged by government, British men were urged to come forward to prepare for the nation's defence through the regular armed forces, the Territorial Army and Officer Training Corps in the schools and universities. The ultimate demand was for men to fight, and if necessary die, for Britain. This was indeed the leading argument against women's suffrage. Women, it was argued, were not biologically equipped to fight, and hence were excluded from full citizenship by exclusion from the parliamentary vote. In addition, the militancy of the suffragettes led to fears about the moral health of the nation. Despite this, women's campaign for the vote was not designed to challenge the existence of the nation, but entailed a desire to belong and participate within the nation, as is suggested by the women's suffrage societies processions for George V's coronation in 1911.[15]

Women were enabled to have a place within preparations for war, though only in the role of support services. Alongside the Edwardian reorganisation of the male armed forces, women's nursing services were overhauled. More than 50,000 women offered themselves for the Voluntary Aid Detachments to nurse Britain's fighting men in the event of war. As Summers has pointed out, women's motives for joining were varied; participation symbolised 'citizenship, social legitimation and personal challenge'.[16] Outside official structures women also participated within right-wing pressure groups such as the Primrose League (attached to the Conservative Party), the National Service League and Navy Leagues. They also organised their own groups, including British Women's

Emigration Association, Victoria League and the British Women's Patriotic League formed in 1908.[17] Within this latter body, women limited their own involvement to the traditional private sphere of instilling patriotism in children, and in particular encouraging boys to enlist in the services, and in 'buying British'.[18] Many women saw themselves as 'daughters of Empire', with a role to play, however much limited by their gender. This was clearly explained by the Girls' Friendly Society in 1900:

> The task that you are called to do
> Is quite as hard as War's brave deeds,
> True British pluck will pull you through –
> See to the soldier's needs!
> Brave daughters of Empire, come,
> Give to your Queen, assist your Lord,
> From village, shire and city home,
> Give your wealth with open hand!
> From North and South, from East and West,
> Joint Daughter – hearts from distant shores!
> Your Empire asks of you your best –
> Pour out your richest love and stores![19]

Hence when war with Germany did break out in 1914, many women had already anticipated the event. J. M. Winter has examined the impact of the First World War upon British national identity, remarking that once war started, '"Englishness" [*sic*] was everything "Germanness" was not.'[20] Germany was said to have violated Belgian neutrality as a rapist would violate an innocent woman, and this provided a gendered means to reinforce already existing notions of Britishness as concerned with honour, decency and fair play, as well as the defence of small nations against the German bully. Such a version of Britishness was widely shared in British society.[21] When alleged German atrocities were publicised, poignancy was given to the gendered nature of patriotism. Germany's 'frightfulness' towards women and children in turn enhanced the patriotism of British women. The immediate reaction was a desire to be active in defence of Britain and Britishness, but this activity was restrained by the continued hold of separate spheres ideas. These ideas, like those of national identity, had been formulated in the decades leading to the war. British national and gender identities were not created in response to the German 'other', but were brought into focus. Caroline Playne, in her history of the war written in 1931, remarked that, 'The great era of knitting set in; men should fight but women could knit.'[22] Despite the inadequacy implied in this statement, women's knitting was intended to show solidarity with the nation of which they felt part. Women's restricted role in society forced much patriotic activism to be confined within the home. For example, Viola Bawtree wrote of herself and her sisters that, 'We three girls eat margarine now instead of butter. Sylvia says we do it because we can't afford butter, but I like to imagine we're doing it because every patriotic person does so, and because we're loyal Britons – it goes down easier that way.'[23]

The experience of war, far from radicalising women, enhanced the devotion of many to their country. Shortages could be borne by validating them as patriotic duty, air raids provided a way of being involved in the war, and hostility to Germans within Britain – women in Liverpool rioted against Germans after the sinking of the *Lusitania*[24] – encouraged some women to see themselves as playing their part in defeating the enemy.

Once allowed, women joined the women's auxiliary services in large numbers. More than 100,000 women served in volunteer corps such as the Women's Volunteer Reserve, the Women's Legion and the Women Volunteer Motor Drivers. Around 50,000 other women joined the Voluntary Aid Detachments (VAD) of nurses. Further, 90,000 joined the official women's services – the Women's Army Auxiliary Corps, the Women's Royal Naval Service and the Women's Royal Air Force.[25] Greater numbers of women entered war industries, and while economic need certainly played a part, patriotism was by no means negligible.[26]

Undoubtedly some women, and men, did oppose the war, and the numbers grew as the length of the war increased. In 1916 and 1917, the Women's Peace Crusade was organised by the deliberately named Women's International League, but its membership of around 2,000 reveals it as a minority organisation.[27] For most women, the uncertainty regarding Britain's ability to win increased their determination to work for that end, and early 1918, when the German Spring Offensive seemed to be sweeping all before it, revitalised a nation that had indeed grown war-weary. The end of the war in November was greeted with immense relief, but was seen as a validation of British institutions and character. Crowds, in which women were well represented, gathered in large numbers at the Houses of Parliament, Downing Street and Buckingham Palace. For one woman, the end of the war proved Britain's rightness. The Kaiser, she wrote in the last entry of her war diary, was 'Dethroned; crushed; conquered; humiliated; disgraced.' She celebrated Britain's triumph and her own role in it: 'The War is over! and *We* have won the war, & glory, honour and victory is *ours*.'[28]

The First World War enhanced the integration of women into the nation, even if through lack of the vote they had not been consulted about the direction of Britain's foreign policy. As an anonymous feminist writer in the Liberal periodical, *The Nation*, had written in 1914, 'Women belong to the nation as much as men, and they fall as readily into the national attitude.'[29] The First World War certainly provides much evidence for such a claim.

## Women in Ireland, Scotland and Wales

A gendered sense of British national identity was further mediated by the multi-national nature of the United Kingdom. In Ireland, some women rejected Britishness as Irish nationalists. Women's organisations took up Gaelic themes, in particular labelling their organisations with Gaelic names, such as Inghinidhe na hEireann (Daughters of Erin, formed 1908) and Cumann na mBan (League of Women, formed 1914). But Irish nationalism was dominated by masculine perceptions of what it meant to be Irish. While Ireland was symbolised as feminine, as Cathleen ni Houlihan, this entailed men arming to defend 'her' in traditional ways. The language of nationalism was the language of manhood and manliness, and women were encouraged only to 'assist'.[30] To many nationalists, the connection with Britain was as violating as the German invasion of Belgium, and the reassertion of Irish masculinity could only take place through separation from the United Kingdom. As with British patriotism, women's role was circumscribed, though Roman Catholic assumptions about gender roles underlay Irish nationalism. The outcome of the Irish revolution, in which women such as Maud Gonne, Constance Markievicz and hundreds of others had played an active part, led to mixed results. Certainly the Proclamation of the Irish Republic in 1916 asserted equal rights for Irishmen and Irishwomen, but there was a call for a return of Irish women to domesticity in the wake of the war of independence. The poet Katherine Tynan, in a volume celebrating the establishment of the Irish Free State, wrote that 'The need of our nation . . . is *not* the Amazon. It is for the conservative woman, careful for all the sanctities, all the securities, all the safeguards of the House of Life.'[31] Of course, this mirrored the position of women in British patriotism. Hence nearly a quarter of a million Ulster women signed a version of the Solemn League of Covenant, which did not pledge them to resist the imposition of Home Rule by all means which might be found necessary as it did for men, but gave them a supporting role.

Sometimes women asserted their claims to political representation through language of difference from Englishness. Before 1918 among Welsh women the demand for votes was pressed using Welsh language and ideas. The Cymric Suffrage Union was formed in 1911 at the instigation of Edith Mansell Moullin, who emphasised the Celtic love of liberty. Members of the CSU wore Welsh costume and had an enthusiasm for 'pethau Cymru' (things Welsh).[32] While Welshness was emphasised, in fact the CSU was an organisation formed in London, emphasising the British context of the suffrage campaign. In addition, the CSU endorsed the investiture of the Prince of Wales in 1911 through a telegram declaring themselves to be 'loyal, though unenfranchised'.[33] Other Welsh feminists pointed to the ancient or 'true' Britishness of the Welsh. Gwyneth Vaughan argued that

> I may be wrong, but I fancy the Saxon has not the courtesy of the Celt to women. At any rate it is a matter of history that British women enjoyed more liberty than the Saxon and the Norman. All our great men believe in the equality of the sexes, and we would very soon have equal political rights if it depended upon Wales.[34]

Here difference and unity are implied in the assertion of a British history for Wales. This desire for unity also appeared in, for example, the existence of a

Queen Victoria Institute for Nursing in Cardiff and in Welsh women's contribution to the war effort in 1914–18 (and again in 1939–45). In Scotland, feminists asserted Scottish distinctiveness through symbolic use of the thistle, particularly apposite given that purple, green and white were the colours of the suffragettes.[35] Scottish and Welsh feminists were integrated into United Kingdom-wide organisations and sought votes for Westminster parliamentary elections.

Women who can be considered conservative also contributed to a sense of Britishness in Scotland and Wales. While not as strong as elsewhere the Primrose League had branches in Wales, which sought to defend the union, the monarchy, the (Anglican) Church and the Empire. That the flag day had its origins in 1914 in Glasgow also provides evidence of integration into Britishness. The founder of the movement, Mrs Arthur Morrison, explained her motives:

> It occurred to me that if a street collection was held it would raise a large sum of money in the least possible time with a minimum of expense and from the magnificent manner in which the whole Empire had responded to the call of the Motherland I decided that no more suitable emblem could be sold than the Union Jack.[36]

The Glasgow flag sellers wore red, white and blue scarves and collected £3,800, which weighed five tons, in order to provide comforts for soldiers during the First World War.

## The impact of the Great War

That (some) women were able to vote in the general election of 1918 suggested to contemporaries, if not to historians, that women's active participation in the defence of the nation in war had been rewarded.[37] Whatever the reasons, that women could now vote marked a greater entry of women into the affairs of the nation. Alison Light has seen the impact of the war on English national identity as profound. She has argued that:

> in these years between 1920 and 1940, a revolt against, an embarrassment about, and distaste for the romantic languages of national pride produced a realignment of sexual identities which was part of a redefinition of Englishness . . . the 1920s and '30s saw a move away from formerly heroic and officially masculine public rhetorics of national destiny and from a dynamic and missionary view of the Victorian and Edwardian middle classes in 'Great Britain' to an Englishness at once less imperial and more inward-looking, more domestic and more private – and, in terms of pre-war standards, more 'feminine'.[38]

There is much to be said in favour of such an argument, and it does reinforce the crucial point about national identity that it is a historical construction that is fluid and contested. Light, and many of the other historians considered here, do not consider the elision between Englishness and Britishness. Most of their arguments can be assigned to Britishness generally, rather than Englishness separately. To avoid slippage in the usage of terms, I have employed the terminology of Englishness-Britishness, which implies applicability to both national identities, except in quotation where the original usage has been maintained.

Light marshals her own evidence from literary sources: the works of Ivy Compton-Burnett, Agatha Christie, Jan Struther (author of the Mrs Miniver column in *The Times*) and others. Hence she argues that, 'The readers of Agatha Christie's detective fiction in the [interwar] period . . . were invited to identify with a more inward-looking notion of the English as a nice, decent, essentially private people.'[39] Miss Marple, the elderly Englishwoman amateur investigator, perfectly at ease in her garden in rural England represented this ideal perfectly.

Some historians, such as MacKenzie and Constantine, argue that there was an expansion in the amount of imperial propaganda in the interwar years owing to the utilisation of new forms of media. Radio and cinema were both used to encourage a sense of national identity. Whether in Exeter or Edinburgh, Belfast or Bala, the British public could listen to and watch the same radio programmes and cinema releases. This potential problem for Light's argument does in fact strengthen the domestication of Englishness thesis. These new media placed greater emphasis on women and the family unit. Where women had been excluded from much mass leisure prior to 1914, radio and cinema allowed access to all but the poorest, and both were central to the family.[40]

While great stress was still placed on Empire themes, the tone of the message had changed in line with the domestic nature of the new media. The establishment of the Empire Marketing Board by the Conservative government in 1926 provides an example. Preserved by the Labour government of 1929–31, more than £3 million was spent between 1926 and 1933. The EMB domesticated imperialism through pamphlets, lectures, posters and films. A typical instance was its publication of a recipe for the King's Empire Christmas pudding, which sought to link monarch and Empire firmly to the family and home. The EMB emphasised the reciprocal beneficial relationship of the Empire, using slogans like 'Keep Trade in the Family' and 'Remember the Empire, Filled with Your Cousins.'[41] Likewise, the BBC gave much coverage to imperial and royal events, and again the weight was on these as occasions for families to come together with the nation. The highlight of the year was the monarch's Christmas broadcast, first staged by George V in 1932, which because of its success immediately became traditional.[42]

As well as providing coverage for Empire Day, the BBC also saw Armistice Day as essential to its output. In the commemoration of the nation's war dead, women played a major part. The *Methodist Recorder* remarked in 1922 that 'Remembrance Day is only a national spirit because it is first and foremost a family spirit . . . The mother and sister at home will not forget – they above all others.'[43]

It seems possible therefore, that women, or feminine images at least, were playing a greater part in representations of the nation, which was more often depicted as a family in which women were more equal partners. The focus of the message was on the home, and the audience was more often seen as the real family.

There are, however, many problems with such an approach. Not least, J. M. Winter has suggested an alternative interpretation. He argues that in the 1920s the commemoration of the war dead was egalitarian, enabling all classes to come together to mourn the nation's dead. By the 1930s, however, there had been a return of elite masculinity into Englishness-Britishness. He provides R. C. Sherriff's successful play and film, *Journey's End*, as an instance of the rehabilitation of the manly virtues of the officer class, restoring the links between bravery and heroism as central to Englishness.[44] The peril posed to masculinity by women's visible patriotism during the war, it has been argued, led to male hostility towards women, rather than to their acceptance.[45] Part of such hostility was an attempt to re-establish a sense of English-British masculinity against such threats to manliness. Graham Dawson and Andrew Rutherford have seen the deliberate promotion of T. E. Lawrence to hero status in this light.[46] The mechanisation of warfare on the Western Front had removed control from the individual, and the disabling of thousands of soldiers had, sometime literally, removed the masculinity from many men.[47] John Buchan at the Ministry of Information (the government's propaganda bureau) had therefore instructed Lowell Thomas 'to search the Middle East for war stories more uplifting than any to be found in the Flanders quagmire'.[48] Thomas went on to create the myth of Lawrence of Arabia, not merely as a hero, but as a manly, English-British hero.

We can further see such a construction in middlebrow literature and cinema. Sapper's *Bulldog Drummond* (1920) and Alexander Korda's 1939 cinema version of A. E. W. Mason's *The Four Feathers* made manliness central to service to the nation and Empire. Therefore, feminisation did not have it all its own way. It was contested. Faced with the entry of women into the public, national, male sphere, there was a concerted reinforcement of masculinity within national idioms.

Neither should we see women's role as entirely leading in the direction of feminisation. Many female patriots in the First World War had attempted to breach the male sphere, accepting the need for the supposedly masculine traits of aggression and militarism. Thousands of women entered the women's auxiliary forces. Flora Sandes joined the Serbian army and fought alongside male soldiers.[49] Others celebrated the killing by proxy of Britain's enemies. One woman wrote to her fiancé congratulating him on his activities on the Western Front: 'Your enterprise on the 28th must have been very successful. I'm particularly glad about the [German] prisoners & I hope you killed lots more.'[50] While femininity has often been constructed as being associated with life giving rather than taking, some women have challenged such notions by their actions and language. As Caroline Playne commented on women during the First World War, the 'souls of women were as much possessed by military passion as the souls of men'.[51]

The interwar years were, therefore, a time of contention between gendered versions of Britishness. In many ways, British national identity had been domesticated and the quiet, suburban and rural version of national identity championed by, say, the Women's Institute was in the ascendant.[52] This was enhanced by the rise of deliberately masculine European Fascism which threatened Britain's desire for peace. Against the new Nazi 'other', it was, as Light says, the domestic, civilian and 'feminine' version of Britain that was emphasised. But coincident with this was a desire to revive more traditionally masculine virtues of national identity.

## Gender and Britishness in the Second World War

Women's participation in the war effort was greater between 1939 and 1945 than it had been in the First World War. It has been suggested that if all women workers are taken into account, full-time, part-time and voluntary, that 'a whopping 80 per cent of married women were working to aid the war effort',[53] and much of the historical literature has been concerned with the impact of this involvement upon women's status.[54] Few works discuss the impact of war on women's sense of national identity, though there is a growing literature on representations of women in a national idiom, especially in cinema.[55] Noakes suggests that experience of the war was gendered, despite the 'people's war' rhetoric of propaganda. She argues that men's involvement in the armed forces was supported by a gendered interpretation of the war mainly through army education. Likewise, she argues that women were encouraged to see the war as women. She concludes that

> Women's magazines and army education publications did provide their readership with models of femininity and masculinity for women and men in wartime. They described very gendered ideals of active citizenship. The ideal female citizen kept the home running, and continued to pay attention to make-up and clothing while contributing to the war effort through war work or careful home management. She made a vital contribution to the war effort while maintaining her femininity. The ideal male citizen joined the armed forces, where he learnt to forget divisions of class, status and politics, subsuming them beneath the common bond of masculinity.[56]

Noakes' argument does draw out the ambiguous nature of women's relationship to the nation, even in wartime. Much of the propaganda designed to counteract careless talk that could cost lives presented women as the main danger. Posters such as those which declared 'Keep Mum. She's not so dumb' fused the image of woman as sexually predatory with spying. But the danger came not only from directly handing information to the enemy, but also from the 'easy girl' who spread venereal disease to the nation's disadvantage. As Gledhill and Swanson conclude in their discussion of such female images, in these representations, 'women are a danger to the nation: at worst they constitute an internal enemy'.[57] The mixing of white British women with black American men aroused the biggest fears. As Sonya Rose has commented, 'The women and girls who could not or would not put aside their "foolish world" to rescue the nation were being constructed as anti-citizens – in contrast to those who were self-sacrificing.'[58] It should be noteworthy here that women as much as men were condemnatory of such 'moral laxity' which threatened the health of the nation.[59]

Even where women did not play a dangerous role, they were seen as a problem for the nation to solve. Women, and especially those of the working class, were seen as dissociated from the war effort and therefore from the nation. Mass-Observation reports argued that women's support for the war needed propagating because

> the tendency of working women to leave all the difficult things such as politics, ARP, opinions about world affairs, to their husbands, has come up many times in our surveys. The average housewife's horizon does not include these extra, unexpected problems; no one explains them to her in a way which shows her that they are as much her concerns as a man's.[60]

Women were seen as passive and easily influenced. Propaganda was needed to encourage their participation. The importance of women to the war effort was recognised, hence 'the everyday lives of women became a central focus in the management of a nation at war'.[61] Propaganda emphasised that women's work within the home equated to a contribution to fighting the war. But patriotism could also provide a release for some women. Summerfield has pointed out that within some families with a patriarchal and authoritarian father, the enhanced importance of the nation in wartime led to conflict. For such fathers, 'The extension of patriotism to include releasing daughters for war service contradicted his values concerning the patriarchal control of women at home in wartime.' For other fathers (and husbands) the needs of the state took priority over patriarchal authority, and daughters (and wives) were emancipated, in both senses of the term.[62]

The threat to British womanhood did not only come from the enemy. Britain's propaganda ally, Hollywood, supplied models for women outside the pale of Britishness. Hollywood women were glamorous and given to follow their hearts rather than their 'duty'. Women went to the cinema more than men and were therefore more likely to become Americanised than men.[63] The British cinema industry, geared up to total war, sought to distinguish British women from these models. British women could, in the British cinematic model, have powerful emotions, but in the end these could be brought under control, for the sake of family and nation. Women's emotional restraint was called for, as Celia Johnson showed in *Brief Encounter* (1945). The film sensitively carries us through the meeting and (non-sexual) relationship of Laura Jesson and Dr Alec Harvey (played by Trevor Howard). Together they decide not to go through with an affair, to think of their families, and to conform to British behaviour of stoicism and emotional restraint.[64] Harvey's behaviour conforms to the delineation made by Sonya Rose of a 'temperate masculinity'. Male Britons in wartime were to be courageous and physical, but they were contrasted to the hyper-masculinity of Nazi Germany, where soldiering was the essence of manliness. The British soldier was part of the family, concerned for mothers, women and children.[65] Harvey, too, thinks of others before his own gratification. In *Brief Encounter*, both men and women, because they are British, have stiff upper lips, however much they might quiver.

Within Britain, there were fears that the war was damaging the health of Scotland. Male Scottish MPs were outraged that young Scottish women were being sent to English factories (at the rate of 400 a month by early 1942). As Summerfield argues, 'They claimed that the Scots girls were not properly supervised, billeted or paid, but the nub of their criticism was a nationalistic possessiveness about "their" young women.'[66]

There were, therefore, fears about women's relationship with the nation and that relationship did remain ambiguous. However, the contemporary perception of women's potential dissociation from the nation must be contrasted to the evident patriotism of the majority of women during the war. Noakes remarks that

> Many [M-O] panelists used the language of 'the people' when writing about the war, describing themselves as one of the 'people', and writing about the nation as 'we'. One women wrote in 1940 that 'as a people we have had some very bad moments . . . and endured them', while another woman, writing in 1942, described a set of national characteristics, commenting that 'we are always slow to start, but when we do, we gather strength and confidence, and we shall continue our efforts until we have won the victory'.[67]

Even where the status of women was clearly unequal with that of men, women responded in patriotic terms. Women in the WAAF played only a supporting role to the RAF, yet as one WAAF wrote, '"The War" means something deeply personal to the WAAF. It's "our" war. We're fighting it, RAF successes are personal ones. And tragedies . . . '[68] Examples like these could be multiplied. Despite the forebodings about women, they felt that they belonged to the nation and were giving service in equal measure with the men.

That is not to say that all divisions were overcome. Class feeling was apparent in the support for compulsion of women amongst the working class, who in many ways saw it as necessary to compel lazy, cosseted middle-class women into war work.[69] Neither was ethnic division surmounted. In the first month of war, Miss Pringle, a Liverpool teacher involved in the distribution of gas masks, reported that one of her friends having queued for one and a half hours had heard people who 'commented on the Jews in the crowd. She hoped the masks were disinfected.'[70] Regional divisions also surfaced. Doris White wrote that

> We were now an eighty per cent girls' workroom, and how we rowed with each other. Country girls versus Londoners . . . So we sat in our respective places for our tea-breaks and tolerated each other. A trip over someone's handbag, or the accidental knocking of someone's coat off its hook would result in, 'Bloody Londoner, go back where yer came from'. I kept quiet while my pals returned the fire with 'Bloody country swedes' or 'Bloody onion treaders'.[71]

Divisions were not therefore entirely overcome, but this should not prevent the recognition that in wartime women and men thought more in terms of their attachment to the nation. For much of the time, most women shared with men a sense of the German, Japanese and Italian enemies that contrasted with a representation of Britishness that embraced parliamentarism, gradualism, liberty and the countryside.

## Gender, 'race' and home in post-war Britain

During the post-war period attempts were made to restructure British national identity. There was a move back to peacetime normality to overcome the upsets about gender in wartime, seeking to settle gender tensions thrown up by women's wartime mobility. There was at the same time a reassertion of manliness as heroic. This occurred despite the continuity of the location of home as the centre of the nation. This in turn contributed to a racialisation of British national identity in the face of black immigration from the Commonwealth and former colonies.

The 1950s saw an attempt to re-establish domesticity as women's primary occupation.[72] In response to the tensions thrown up by women's mobility in wartime, there was a concerted effort to concentrate women's endeavours within the home. This attempt was made all the more difficult because increasingly women were entering the workforce. Between 1947 and 1949 nearly a million extra women found paid employment.[73] Women's magazines led a drive towards domesticity that while it was compatible with paid employment stressed the primacy of the home and family in women's lives. By the mid-1950s, magazines such as *Woman* and *Woman's Own* were read by 58 per cent of women.[74]

This reformulation of women's roles, accommodating work and domesticity, was accompanied by efforts to reconstruct men's relationship to the nation. Again this can be seen most clearly in British cinema. During the war, the 'fit young man' in the armed forces had been privileged over the non-combatant male, but the nature of the war had made it essential to pay due regard to women's war efforts.[75] After the war, much less consideration was paid to the role of women. Films like *The Cruel Sea* (1953), *The Colditz Story* (1954) and *The Dam Busters* (1955) reinstated individual, often middle-class, men as national heroes. This was also a reaction against the egalitarian portrayal of the Second World War during its occurrence.[76] Indeed, in Britain's wars since 1945, as Noakes has remarked about the Falklands War, 'gender divisions were seen in very sharp relief; men went away to battle while women waited at home'.[77] Even in the first Gulf War, when women were for the first time occupied within the field formations of the British armed forces, they were seen as problematic.

The reassertion of masculinity after the war was accompanied by a strengthening of codes of behaviour for the male. Sir Ernest Barker in 1947 assigned 'the idea of the gentleman' as one of the constants of the English character. He marked out its central features as 'stoicism with . . . chivalry' and 'manliness'.[78] In politics, this resulted in tensions between what Martin Francis has described as the need for 'authenticity' to attract the electorate and a belief that 'Uncontrolled emotion . . . transgressed a conception of British (or at least English) national identity which was rooted in self-restraint.'[79] Geoffrey Gorer in his 'empirical' study *Exploring English Character*, published in 1955, saw gentleness, tolerance and abiding by the law as central to Englishness.[80] Throughout the 1950s, English-British gentleman, such as Edmund Hillary, Roger Bannister, David Nixon, Rex Harrison and Ian Carmichael, supplied role models around which national character could be maintained.[81]

It may at first seem contradictory to associate the reconstruction of masculinity with the location of the nation within the home. Yet these were complementary projects. Masculinity and femininity were 'restored' in harmony within the home, in turn aiding national unity. This unity was often built in opposition to the presence of black migrants from Britain's former Empire.[82] In this construction of Britishness, all other divisions were submerged. Wendy Webster has argued that in the post-war period, 'Differences between white and black were constructed through an opposition between an Englishness, characterised by the privacy of domestic and familial life, and "immigrants", who were characterised in terms of an incapacity for domestic and familial life, or domestic barbarism.'[83] In a series of quasi-anthropological studies of immigrant 'communities', commentators conflated diversity into homogeneity of immigrants on the one hand and white Britons on the other. Elspeth Huxley argued that

> Caribbean domestic habits and customs collide with our own. Most West Indians . . . like loud music, noise in general, conviviality, visiting each other, keeping late hours at weekends, dancing and jiving . . . Most English prefer to keep themselves to themselves and guard their privacy. Ours is a land of the wall, the high fence, the privet hedge – all descendants of the moated grange.[84]

In this reading of cultural differences in Britain, Huxley found the source of British domesticity in the medieval period, implicitly closing Britishness off forever to immigrants. Whereas in the 1930s, walls had been built, literally, between council housing estates and owner-occupied middle-class suburban housing, as at Cutteslowe in Oxford, now figurative walls were being erected between classless white Britons and the black other. But further to this, Huxley's stereotype could perhaps be more aptly assigned to those young people emerging as teenagers in 1960s Britain. Yet the consequence of applying such a description to generational differences was that the decline of Britain would emerge from the perceived permissiveness of the 1960s.[85] If the nation consti-tuted the white heterosexual family unit then outsiders within the nation would extend far – to homosexuals, to single mothers, to black people, and even further to youth. In the context of the Cold War, gay men were seen as a threat to national security, with homosexuality being associated with susceptibility to blackmail and espionage.[86] It was nothing new to see homosexuality as a degen-erative national force. During the First World War, the *English Review* had warned of 'the moral and spiritual invasion of Britain by German urnings [homosexuals] for the purpose of undermining the patriotism, the stamina, the intellect, and the moral[e] of British Navy and Army men, and our prominent public leaders'.[87] By the late 1960s, accompanied by the processes of the end of Empire, the notion of masculinity associated with public leadership was under threat. As Marcus Collins has noted, the notion of the gentleman suffered repeated attacks, from the 'Angry Young Men', the critique of the influence of public school on British society and economy, and the failure of 'gentlemen' such as the Conservative cabinet minister John Profumo, who in 1963 lied to the House of Commons about his affair which appeared to have implications for national security. These attacks culminated in Monty Python, which came to be seen as archetypal British comedy, denigrating the 'Upper-Class Twit of the Year'.[88] Many of these attacks were associated with the 'permissiveness' of the 1960s, which came to be seen by the New Right as contributing to the British crisis in the late twentieth century. Roger Scruton mourned the effects of the impact of the post-war changes in *England: An Elegy* (2000):

> Having been famous for their stoicism, their decorum, their honesty, their gentleness and their sexual Puritanism, the English now subsist in a society in which those qualities are no longer honoured – a society of people who regard long-term loyalties with cynicism, and whose response to misfortune is to look round for someone to sue. England is no longer a gentle country, and the old courtesies and decencies are disappearing. Sport, once a rehearsal for imperial virtues, has become a battleground for hooligans. Sex, freed from taboos, has become the ruling obsession.[89]

England's 'crisis' was gendered, as he saw men and women no longer conform-ing to traditional 'English' notions of behaviour, which could in turn be linked to the end of Empire. As Stuart Ward has argued:

> Ideas about the British 'character', for example, became difficult to sustain as the external prop of the imperial world was progressively weakened. Notions of duty, service loyalty, deference, stoic endurance, self-restraint and gentlemanly conduct were insidiously undermined by the steady erosion of the imperial edifice.[90]

In many ways, Margaret Thatcher sought to reverse the freedoms of the 1960s as part of her project to put the great back into Great Britain.[91] Of course this was not undertaken without dissent and opposition. Sometimes, this opposition rejected the nation as the essential identity, as with the women's peace camps against nuclear weapons, which foregrounded an internationalist women's identity.[92] But more often, from the 1960s onwards, black, gay and feminist Britons have contested the notion that they are 'enemies within' the nation and have asserted their right to be seen as equal citizens.

Britishness has been gendered throughout the period from 1870 to the present. For much of the earlier part of the period, the ideology of separate spheres firmly delineated the roles that could be played by men and women within the nation. This did not, however, mean that women sought to renounce the nation. Many accepted the limited role they could play as Britons, and after the vote had been secured much emphasis remained on the different rather than equal role of women within the nation. The wars highlighted the subordinate role of women within the nation, but also enabled a renegotiation of roles. In the post-war period national identity was again reconstructed. For some, the impact of 'permissiveness' on Britain was a national disaster, weakening the nation while it faced a range of other challenges – the end of the Empire, nationalist demands in Ireland, Scotland and Wales, European integration and Americanisation. Paradoxically, it was Margaret Thatcher, a woman, who saw herself as the supreme patriot who could reverse such challenges.

# 3 Rural, urban and regional Britishness

By the beginning of the twentieth century, four out of five Britons lived in towns. Yet Stanley Baldwin, Conservative prime minister three times between the wars, described the 'sounds of England' as 'the tinkle of the hammer on the anvil in the country smithy, the corncrake on a dewy morning, the sound of the scythe against the whetstone, and the sight of the plough team coming over the brow of a hill'.[1] George Orwell, however, questioned whether it was possible to attribute the idea of nation to such a diverse country as England, not least because of its regional differences:

> Then the vastness of England swallows you up, and you lose for a while your feeling that the whole nation has a single identifiable character. Are there really such things as nations? Are we not forty-six million individuals, all different? And the diversity of it, the chaos! The clatter of clogs in the Lancashire mill towns, the to-and-fro of the lorries on the Great North Road, the queues outside the Labour Exchanges, the rattle of pin-tables in Soho clubs, the old maids biking to Holy Communion through the mists of the autumn morning – all these are not only fragments, but *characteristic* fragments, of the English scene.[2]

Of course, Orwell resolved that the nation did indeed have a single identifiable identity, made up of all these characteristics. This chapter begins by examining the importance of images of rural England within national identity. It argues that such a focus on the countryside as the source of the real essence of Englishness is problematic in a variety of ways. The focus on England is perhaps the most significant problem in a United Kingdom where most rural spaces actually lie in Scotland, Wales and Ireland. It is noteworthy that both Baldwin and Orwell use the word 'England', and while on this occasion Baldwin clearly restricted his comments to that part of the United Kingdom, both tended to think that the nation they were considering was Britain. There was also a major element of pro-urban thought within British national identity that has been neglected by contemporaries and historians alike. This section will involve a discussion of the attitudes of the garden city movement and other town planners to urbanity, and will also give consideration to the nature of civic pride, an extremely important sentiment which locates pride in nation as well as locality. The chapter will then turn its attention to the other aspect of Orwell's comments, that of the immense variety of regional identities and characteristics, looking at the ways in which various identities of place interlock. These regional identities, stronger in some parts of the nation than others, have not necessarily disrupted a wider British identity. Regional identities have often been associated with the working class, and as such have played a part in incorporating them into the nation.

## Finding the core of the nation

It has seemed to many commentators that the dominant sentiment in English-British culture is anti-urban and that the true source of the strength of English-British national identity is to be found in the countryside. The impact of city and town life on the physical and spiritual health of the British people has been roundly criticised throughout the twentieth century. C. F. G. Masterman, a Liberal, warned in 1901 that the new century's major problem was the emergence of the 'New Town Type' who would prove unable to manage the British Empire.[3] This association of urban life with national ill health has become supplemented by a view that the nature of modern cities has inflicted fundamental damage on the national way of life. Patrick Dunleavy has suggested that post-1945 mass housing 'has in many areas destroyed "a landscape of small houses" and the community life which went along with it', creating 'large flatted estates of uniform housing'.[4] Since the uncontrolled urban growth of the nineteenth century, towns and cities have been associated with crime, poverty, anonymity, unsanitary conditions and immigration, all issues blamed for corrupting a wholesome sense of national identity. The other side of this negative view of towns and cities has been a celebration of the countryside. The urban planner Patrick Abercrombie could write without embarrassment that 'the greatest historical monument that we possess, the most essential thing which *is* England, is the Countryside, the Market Town, the Village, the Hedgerow Trees, the Lanes, the Copses, the Streams and the Farmsteads'.[5] Such sentiments can be found again and again in English and British culture. Images of the real England emerge in Thomas Hardy's Wessex, in the Cotswolds of the Arts and Crafts Movement, in the tradition of English pastoral poetry, in children's literature, such as Kenneth Grahame's *Wind in the Willows* (1908) and the Beatrix Potter stories (1901–18). Versions of rural England formed a mainstay of imagery for propaganda in the First and Second World Wars. London Underground Railways during the First World War published a poster as a 'reminder of home' for 'their passengers . . . now engaged on important business in France and other parts of the world'. The illustration was of a village green with thatched cottages, and the verse was on a similar bucolic theme, beginning 'Mine be a cot beside the hill/ A bee-hive's hum shall soothe my ear;/ A willowy brook that turns a mill/ With many a fall shall linger near.'[6] The obvious disparity between the homes of most of London Underground's passengers and these images requires no comment. In the Second World War, a major series of posters by Frank Newbould entitled 'Your Britain: Fight for it now', issued by the Army Bureau of Current Affairs, was predominantly of rural imagery.[7] Such images have been seen by many to form the dominant discourse of Englishness. In particular, the historian Martin J. Wiener has been influential in establishing the idea that an attachment to 'nonindustrial, noninnovative and nonmaterial' values of the English countryside was so central to the 'English way of life' that British economic (and by implication political and diplomatic) decline can be explained by the substitution of the industrial spirit for the stability and order of the countryside.[8]

Undoubtedly there is a huge swathe of English (and British) culture devoted to celebrating the countryside as the true depository of national character and identity. However, that does not mean that Wiener's thesis should be accepted in its entirety, with all its implications. The Wienerite orthodoxy has in particular come under sustained criticism from Peter Mandler, who argues that the British political and economic elite did not embrace this version of anti-urban and anti-modern 'Englishness', which was in fact the product of an unrepresentative and uninfluential minority.[9] Numerous other criticisms can also be levelled at this version of Englishness, not least that, as David Lowenthal suggests, 'heritage countryside is less British than English'.[10] Much of the material based on the rural idyll focuses particularly on the south-east and the Cotswolds. Other parts of Britain and even England have often been excluded from this version of national identity. However, it is fair to say that it has been possible for non-English Britons to celebrate similar versions of national identity by reference to both the English and the non-English countryside. Ramsay MacDonald made England British when he commemorated the area around his weekend home in Buckinghamshire by designing a tour for visitors 'which should display the pages of national history' through visits to the churchyard where Gray wrote his 'Elegy', to Milton's cottage and to the churchyard where John Hampden had been buried by Puritan soldiers.[11] But he also celebrated his Scottishness by describing the area around Callander as 'the hills [where] Rob [Roy] still wanders'.[12] Rural upland Britain was further elegised as British. It was possible for the nation to be celebrated not only in hedgerow and cottage, but also in moor and mountain. In 1941 the Ministry of Information made a propaganda film entitled *The Heart of Britain*, devoted to northern England. Accompanied by the Hallé Orchestra and the Huddersfield Choral Society, upland landscapes were characterised as British. The opening sequence begins 'The winds of war blow across the hills and moorlands of Yorkshire and Derbyshire. They stir the grasses in the sheep valleys of Cumberland and ruffle the clear surface of Ullswater.'[13] While the film was the product of Humphrey Jennings, artistic filmmaker and propagandist, there is evidence in Mass-Observation reports that people did consider the countryside in a British rather than an English context. Both male and female respondents cited the 'country scenes' first when asked 'What does Britain mean to you?' While one referred to 'Devonshire chessboard fields [and] the Sussex Downs', another extended the list:

The leafy lanes of Warwickshire and Worcestershire, the peacefulness of the Cotswold country, the hills and mountains of the Lake District and North Wales, the romance of the Cornish coast, the splendour of the Scottish Highlands, and the almost loveliness of the Western coast of Ireland.[14]

The post-war Labour government continued this focus on the north and upland Britain as central to the national character when it established the National Land Fund of £50 million. Hugh Dalton, Chancellor of the Exchequer, explained its purpose:

> This money will be used to buy some of the best of our still unspoiled open country, and stretches of coast, to be preserved for ever, not for the enjoyment of a few private land-owners, but as a playground and national possession for all our people. I want the young people in particular to have free access to all the most beautiful parts of Britain.[15]

He saw the open countryside of upland Britain as more important than the southern products of enclosure that had created hedgerows and lanes, but in addition his statement suggests that while people of many political stances and social positions looked to the countryside, they often disagreed upon what its important aspects were.

Some historians have suggested that the urban working class did not share the enthusiasm of the middle and upper classes for the countryside,[16] while others have suggested that working-class political movements contested the meaning of the countryside, sometimes literally in the physical battles for access to the open land. In the 1930s up to 500,000 people regularly 'rambled'. In April 1932 the most famous 'mass trespass' took place at Kinder Scout when between 150 and 200 ramblers fought physically with police and gamekeepers to secure access to the Peaks.[17] These walkers did not seek to uphold the values of the hierarchical Englishness championed by Baldwin but sought instead to overthrow them.

A third line of criticism is that valuing the countryside and the national identity associated with it does not necessarily imply an anti-modernist stance. David Matless, a historical geographer, has for example found 'a powerful historical connection between Englishness and the modern' in the planning movements of the 1930s and 1940s. It is clear also that the popularity of the countryside between the wars was made possible by the harnessing of modern technology to leisure, particularly in the use of the motor car by the middle class, to create what Matless calls 'a motoring pastoral genre' in travel books such as H. V. Morton's *In Search of England* first published in 1927.[18] Morton has frequently been held up to be the typical travel writer celebrating the countryside, especially in this book, which sold one million copies. It certainly represented the desire for tranquillity in the wake of the First World War, as *In Search of England* opens with Morton's sentence: 'I believed that I was dying in Palestine.'[19] His desires turned towards England, and it was a rural England:

> [T]here rose up in my mind the picture of a village street at dusk with a
> smell of wood smoke lying in the still air . . . I remembered how the church
> bells ring at home, and how, at that time of year, the sun leaves a dull red
> bar low down in the west, and against it the elms grow blacker every
> minute.[20]

Morton recognised the disparity between his urban background and this visual-
isation of rural England, but remarked that 'This village that symbolizes
England sleeps in the subconscious of many a townsman'.[21] But to take *In Search
of England* as the whole of Morton's thought is a misrepresentation. Morton ven-
erated the countryside, but as part of Britain. As Michael Bartholomew has
argued, 'Morton did not avoid industrial towns and . . . when he wrote about
them he often ran against the grain of the Merrie England mode by presenting
them as places which, despite the disgrace of their slums, were exhilarating.'[22]
Morton combined the rural with the urban, the traditional with the modern.
This mix can also be seen in Hugh Dalton, champion of opening access to
upland Britain, who built himself a house in rural Berkshire that utilised the
high-modern architecture of flat roof and metal windows.[23] In many ways, the
rural and the modern could be integrated as successfully as the urban and the
modern.

All these criticisms have focused on the apparent British obsession with the
countryside but have argued that the meanings attached to the countryside by
different groups were varied and contested. It is, however, possible to make a
more fundamental criticism that much celebration of the British way of life has
emphasised the contribution of towns and cities. Sometimes it was noted that
far from reflecting disaster, urbanisation was a reflection of British strengths.
Charles Booth, leading investigator of London life in the late nineteenth
century, told a conference in 1901 that 'It is to be noted that increase of population in urban centres, and the need for space for industrial and civic purposes
are results of, and factors in, general prosperity.'[24] London in particular, but
other cities too, have been championed across the century as central to the
national way of life, particularly, but not exclusively, by individuals on the left of
politics, such as Sidney Webb and Herbert Morrison.[25] Leaders and officials of
the London County Council and Greater London Council were keen to see the
metropolis made central to Britishness.[26] In the post-1997 context of devolution,
Ken Livingstone saw his role as mayor of London as encouraging the development of London as a multi-ethnic and multi-racial community of 'Londoners'.
Livingstone emphasised the world city status of London and, in addition,
embraced a modernising influence on the city's architecture.[27]

One event when it was possible to celebrate urban Britain as heroic, stoic
and therefore typically British was during the Second World War at the height
of the Blitz. The 'people's war' was a war of the towns, with a heroism emerging out of the threat posed to urban spaces by massive aerial bombing. If
Britain could take it, then it was the towns and cities that stood at the centre of
this version of Britishness. There was also an element of civic competition in

reacting calmly to the Blitz. London experienced nightly bombing between September 1940 and May 1941, and became the exemplar to which all other towns and cities aspired, of a community-based heroism, of part-time firemen, air raid wardens and rescue squads, urban and collective, across class and gender, shown in numerous contemporary propaganda films such as *London Can Take It* (Ministry of Information, 1940) and *Fires Were Started* (Humphrey Jennings, 1942). This was Priestley's urban Britain responding heroically to war.[28]

*The Heart of Britain*, made by the Ministry of Information, portrayed the popular culture of urban people in the north. 'Just look at these Lancashire lasses cowering before the Luftwaffe', it commented ironically as it showed women factory workers playing boisterous games in air raid shelters. Particular parts of the British Isles could also stress their contribution to the war effort by playing up their modern, industrial and urban nature. Harry Midgley, first non-Unionist to join the Northern Ireland government in 1943, exulted in the six counties' contribution to the war effort:

> Thus it is that to-day all industry and commerce in this area is being increasingly harnessed to the national cause and the successful prosecution of the war. Northern Ireland linen, engineering and shipbuilding played an important part in the Great War of 1914–18 . . . We are determined that these great industries, along with our newer but equally great Aircraft industry, shall once again play an important part in smashing tyranny and liberating the peoples of the earth.[29]

Once we begin to locate the connection of urban and national life in British culture we need to begin to consider the balance between celebrations of urban and rural Britishness. One method by which the Wienerites have sought to suggest that this balance is in favour of the rural and traditional, rather than the urban and the modern, is by suggesting that social reformers have sought to solve Britain's problems by making the nation less urban. However, while the countryside must be seen as important, many reformers accepted urban Britain into their notions of Britishness, and sought to improve and adapt urban life within a national idiom. One arena for debate lies within the discussion of improvements in housing the nation across the twentieth century. The population of the British Isles, excluding southern and western Ireland, was already substantially urban by the beginning of the twentieth century. Urban housing was, therefore, a crucial social question. Many historians have seen the discussion of these problems as a rejection of the urban, as calls for reform became associated with the medieval past, of a chiefly rural and socially harmonious society enabling the emergence of an organic and united nation. Stanley Bader, in his study of the garden city movement, argues that its forerunners in the Arts and Crafts movement 'attracted a variety of types who sought to transcend an ugly present by both looking backward to a past "golden age" and then forward to new forms of "organic" community'.[30] The late nineteenth-century model 'villages' of Bournville and Port Sunlight, and the garden cities and suburbs of

Letchworth, Welwyn Garden City, Hampstead and elsewhere, have been seen as a revulsion against the urban realities of industrial Britain, as backward looking and reactionary. It is certainly the case that Raymond Unwin, the most influential garden city architect, looked back to the pre-industrial village for inspiration:

> There are houses and buildings of all sizes: the hut in which the old road mender lives by himself, the inn with its ancient sign, the prosperous yeoman's homestead, the blacksmith's house and forge, the squire's hall, the vicarage, and the doctor's house, are all seemingly jumbled together . . . Yet there is no sense of confusion; on the contrary the scene gives us that peaceful feeling which comes from the perception of orderly arrangement . . . The village was the expression of a small corporate life in which all the different units were personally in touch with each other, conscious of and frankly accepting their relationships, and on the whole content with them.[31]

But if Unwin rejected the modern city, many other housing reformers did not, seeking to deal with urban *problems* rather than dispersing urban *life*. Indeed many reformers embraced urbanism; thus Canon Barnett, a conservative figure, could write a pamphlet explaining how Edwardian Bristol could be reformed into 'The Ideal City', which 'will be large, with a quarter or half a million citizens. There will be room for a great variety of pursuits.' The effect of this ideal city life would be to create 'patriots, poets and adventurers', and as a seaport it would be linked to 'Englishmen . . . carving an Empire'.[32] Around the same time, Robert Bremner believed that 'the terrible problem of the slums is, year by year, growing more acute', but that London and Glasgow were 'great cities of the Empire' and that city life was 'wholesome'.[33] These and other reformers linked civic pride to social reform and also to their sense of the importance of the nation. Mark Girouard has pointed out the importance of civic pride in the construction of the English town, as citizens of town and nation built town halls, market halls, exchanges, courthouses, police stations, water towers, pumping stations, bridges, aqueducts, museums, art galleries, libraries, schools, gardens, parks and cemeteries.[34] Further, local government often had a symbiotic relationship with the monarchy as a national institution, and the opportunity of royal celebration was taken to enhance the reputation of the local council, both members and officials. The Borough of Chelmsford in 1911 issued a programme for its procession and festivities to celebrate the coronation. On pages 2 and 3 there were photographs of King George and Queen Mary, but on pages 4 and 5 the mayor and mayoress were given equal space to the King and Queen. On every other page throughout the programme, which is fifty-five pages long, prominent local people were pictured. The programme stressed the loyalty of Chelmsford and the benevolent way in which the councillors had governed the town. '[T]heir ability and devotion', it declared, 'are mirrored in the good management and "up-to-dateness" of the town.' This would be confirmed by the raising of the Union flag on the radio mast of Marconi, which had its factory and laboratories in Chelmsford. The signal for the raising of the flag would be given by the mayor through wireless telegraphy during the playing and singing of *God Save the King*.[35] The London County Council also stressed in its address to the new king that its civic works were an expression of its patriotism. On 9 June 1910 the councillors delivered their address in person to the King at St James's Palace, claiming the right to do so as 'the representative authority of the inhabitants of the capital of the Empire'. The address continued:

> We gratefully recall that Your Majesty and Her Majesty Queen Mary, as Prince and Princess of Wales, honoured the Council by inaugurating its electrified tramways system, visiting its suburban working class cottages at Tooting, and opening Rotherhithe tunnel, and by being present on other notable occasions associated with its municipal work.[36]

The LCC therefore drew together the routine aspects of its work with the ceremonial role of royalty, uniting the urban and the patriotic.

Given the nature of population growth and urbanisation in the nineteenth and early twentieth centuries, it was rational for socially conscious people of all political persuasions to consider the problems of urban life. Such calls for reform were linked to the fate of the nation, especially since the international context was one of rivalry with other powers and the ideological context suggested the 'survival of the fittest'. In 1899, Lord Walsingham, a Norfolk landowner, certainly saw the problem as urban:

> Look at the pure bred Cockney – I mean the little fellow whom you see running in and out of offices in the city, and whose forefathers have for the last two generations dwelt within a two-mile radius of Charing Cross . . . Take the people away from their natural breeding grounds, thereby sapping their health and strength in cities such as nature never intended to be the permanent homes of men, and the decay of this country becomes only a matter of time. In this matter, as in many others, ancient Rome has a lesson to teach.[37]

There was a widespread belief that the health of the urban population needed investigation and resolution. The 'condition of England [and Scotland, Wales and Ireland]' question was almost entirely devoted to the problems of towns, and rural poverty was neglected. Numerous social enquiries of towns and cities were carried out. Charles Booth's reports on London and Seebohm Rowntree's report on York were only the most famous. Such reports were, as Mark Freeman argues, 'concerned not only with the poor, but with the community as a whole'.[38] The community in question was that of the nation. In 1904 a government committee, formed to provide explanation for Britain's poor showing in the Boer War, reported on 'physical deterioration', which resulted in campaigns for 'national efficiency'.[39] While Walsingham and others saw the solution in a revitalised countryside, other reformers recognised the problem but looked for other solutions. 'No great city in England is without a housing question', Chesterfield Fabian Society argued (presumably including Chesterfield within that designation): 'overcrowding is rampant everywhere and brings with it its train of evils – infant mortality and adult demoralization: dirt, infection and crime'. But the Society did not call for the destruction of urban Chesterfield; rather it wanted town planning.[40]

The solutions to the problems of urban life were therefore often seen as urban solutions. The garden city movement deliberately chose to include 'city' within its name, and gardens too are more a product of towns than they are of countryside. Indeed, by 1907 the movement had become the Garden City and Town Planning Association, fully embracing urban life. Ebenezer Howard, pioneer of the movement, condemned 'crowded, ill-ventilated, unplanned, unwieldy, unhealthy cities' as 'ulcers on the face of our beautiful island', but saw his 'peaceful path to real reform' enabling 'each inhabitant' to 'enjoy all the advantages of . . . a great and most beautiful city'.[41] The marrying of town and country was for the benefit of both, and was designed to create healthy citizens, that is national inhabitants of cities.

This was highlighted in the demand for 'homes fit for heroes' after the First World War, when the link between housing and the nation was confirmed in the desire to ensure that returning soldiers should be well housed. Colonel David Davies MP linked Welshness to a wider British patriotism, when he told the Welsh Housing and Development Association, of which he was president, that 'our brave soldiers deserved the best that could be prepared for them at their homecoming . . . one of the most desirable features in the welcome we can give them is to show them that Wales has tackled in real earnest the proper housing of her people and especially her disabled heroes'.[42] The emphasis was often on the building of 'homes' rather than houses. In 1889, Earl Compton had stated that 'One of our most popular English songs is "Home, Sweet Home." The most lovable word in our language is "home", and English home life is held up as a pattern to other countries.'[43] Some historians have seen this post-war phase of house-building, encouraged by the Tudor Walters Report, as backward looking. John Burnett has argued that the

> proposals [of the Report] were remarkably far-sighted and progressive, yet the external design of the houses themselves – 'cottages' as they were described throughout [the report] – was firmly rooted in a vernacular, rural idiom which pictured groups of buildings of traditional appearance dotted about a landscape of winding lanes, trees and gardens.[44]

Much of this was due to the influence of Unwin on the committee, and the similarities between Burnett's interpretation and Unwin's views quoted above are obvious. It was certainly the case that the architects sought to use vernacular styles and local building materials where possible, but the desire to link houses with their localities was not about rejecting the modern or urban. These houses utilised new methods of construction and the lives within them were seen as engaging with modernity even if the political outcome was designed to be conservative.[45]

After the horrors of industrial, mechanised warfare, the attractions of a construction of the countryside as tranquil and unchanging were great, and it is not surprising that the past provided models for the organisation and design of housing. In the wake of the war, guild socialism was temporarily able to flourish as it applied 'medieval' organisation to building houses for local authorities.[46] However, there were also modernist influences between the wars, particularly from Europe, so the London County Council under Labour after 1934 was described as building 'giant blocks of flats, worthy of Socialist Vienna'.[47] In Leeds, the city council built nearly a thousand new flats in the Quarry Hill scheme, consciously modern and close to the heart of the city. A further pressure on this Labour council came from the National government. The Exchequer said that support for slum clearance would only be provided where 'The rehousing is effected on or near the central site by means of blocks of flats and should not be given in cases where the rehousing is effected by means of ordinary small houses erected on undeveloped land on the outskirts of the area of the local authority.'[48] Treasury parsimony, it seemed, won out over the rural Englishness of Baldwinism. Even where the inspirations were less modern, such as in the mock-Tudor of much house-building for private ownership (the act of purchase perhaps suggests something about the tastes of those who lived in the houses, more so than those who rented accommodation), it has been argued that suburbanisation was about the decentralisation of cities to create a conurbation that stretched southwards from Liverpool, and this was made possible by the continuing development of modern transport systems such as the London Underground, which created 'Metroland'. This truly was a modern, urban force rather than a desire to get 'back to the land'.[49] In the early 1970s, John Betjeman celebrated 'Metro-Land' in a television film of that name, in which he nostalgically examined the city clerk turning countryman again, but enabled only by being 'linked to the Metropolis by train'.[50]

The experience of the Second World War heightened the link between 'home' and nation. The 'Dig for Victory' campaign highlighted the importance of the garden as a source of food for urban Britain. *Ideal Home and Garden* turned its attention to encouraging an increase in the productive capacity of the garden rather than its aesthetic beauty.[51] The 'home front' became a reality and hundreds of thousands of houses were destroyed or badly damaged. Housing was a crucial issue in the 1945 general election, adding to Labour's landslide victory, since they had most fully embraced the ideas of the involvement of the state in the provision of housing. One thrust of Labour's housing and planning policy was the creation of 'new towns'. Andrew Saint argues that despite

> embody[ing] the most self-confident, collective strain in British post-war life – a strain which for a time seemed to be leading the nation toward an austere but just classless version of social democracy . . . their philosophy was rooted in a profound continuity in British culture, that of anti-urbanism

– the belief in the superior morality of the countryside and its patterns of life.[52]

However, if there is some ambiguity in the 'garden city' epithet, then there should be none in the designation 'New Town', which was categorically modern and urban, and still linked to the desire to construct a new Britain. What Labour would bring to housing was expressed in their manifesto: 'We stand for order, for positive constructive progress as against the chaos of economic do-as-they please anarchy.'[53] The experience of *laissez-faire* in the nineteenth and early twentieth centuries was blamed for the evils of urban life in Britain, rather than urbanisation itself. By the 1970s many of the products of this experiment in mass housing, in New Towns and high-rise flats, were denigrated as damaging to the traditional fabric of British society, the result of dogmatic and ideological planners whose inspiration came from abroad rather than from domestic origins. It might not be wise to refute such a view entirely by reference to a single quote from Richard Fitter in 1945, but nonetheless he is worth quoting:

> Much nonsense [he wrote] has been written about every Englishman being a countryman at heart . . . The illusion that all cockneys are pining for the delights of rural life has largely been exploded by the experience of evacuation in 1939, when no group came back to their homes more quickly than the London mothers, bored to death by a combination of nothing to do and the quiet of the country.[54]

Saint has made much of the opposition to the building of the first designated New Town of Stevenage in 1946. When the Minister of Town Planning, Lewis Silkin, visited the town his car was vandalised and the station name was changed to 'Silkingrad'.[55] Yet when Mass-Observation visited the area in which the town was to be built they found that 57 per cent of the thirty-one men and twenty women they asked were favourable to the new town idea. They concluded that 'Answers revealed a fairly widespread opinion that Stevenage "must move with the times"', and that in addition there were material reasons for wanting urbanisation. A watchmaker, aged thirty, told the Observers: 'I feel everything will be extended to a great extent, and the place can do with it. I've only a small place in a side turning. It's the only place I can get. Same with where I live. We can do with the building extension, and the place livening up.'[56] Certainly some opposed the scheme, providing evidence for a pro-rural and anti-urban outlook. A sixty-year-old car park attendant was hostile:

> I don't like to see the beauty spots being violated. My great grandfather was here, and his father before him. We belong here, and I shouldn't like to see the beauty taken away. If they are going to put factories up our countryside is going to be polluted, especially the air, and people come here specifically for that. I suffer from lung trouble, and the air at present is

grand for that. Have you seen the beauty of the place? That avenue of chestnuts up by the school and the parish church? You should see it.[57]

Here then was opposition linked to a sense of belonging and fear of despoliation of the beauty of 'our countryside', linked later to an opposition to development in one's locality, commonly referred to as 'nimby' or 'Not in my back yard'. Yet Mass-Observation found that only 19 per cent positively disagreed with the New Town plans. Likewise architectural historians have pointed out that post-war tower blocks were built as products of 'municipal pride' by elected councils. As David Gibson, a socialist councillor in Glasgow, explained in 1962:

> In the next three years the skyline of Glasgow will become a more attractive one to me because of the likely vision of multi-storey houses rising by the thousand . . . The prospect will be thrilling, I am certain, to the many thousands who are still yearning for a home.[58]

It was not only radicals who embraced the redevelopment of post-war Britain. Conservatives too welcomed the urban development which stemmed from freedom from state controls. One Conservative argued that, 'we believe that the social and economic forces which have shaped Britain into a cluster of big cities are the very forces which have established her place in the world'.[59] Such a statement shows a remarkable optimism about the urban future in the wake of the Suez crisis, and certainly confirms Mandler's conclusion that:

> If today we yearn to live in an 'old country', this may reflect not a horror of modernity deeply rooted in British culture, but a particular revulsion from the peculiar – and peculiarly cheap and brutal – vision of modernity inflicted upon Britain . . . by the governments of the 1950s and 1960s.[60]

The relationship between the rural and the urban was fundamental to national identities other than Britishness. The *Western Mail* reported that Welsh housing reformers 'desire to have more and better dwellings; they desire also that the homes of the people of Wales should express very clearly the artistic qualities which now largely lie dormant in the Celtic temperament'.[61] In Wales, nationalism was often associated with ruralism, and Plaid Cymru used rural Wales to counter Britishness, defining the people of Wales as the *gwerin*.[62] In the 1950s and 1960s Plaid Cymru mobilised much support in defence of the Welsh countryside at Tryweryn and Clywedog against the building of reservoirs to supply water to English cities. England was portrayed as an urban imperial power imposing itself on rural and colonial Wales.[63] However, Plaid Cymru were unable to convert emotional into electoral support on this issue, and the party's focus on rural Wales when four-fifths of the population live in towns and cities is a convincing explanation for the limited success of Welsh nationalism.

Other versions of Welshness embraced urbanism, though not necessarily wholeheartedly. Edgar Chappell, Edwardian socialist and housing reformer, argued that there had been an awakening of 'the national spirit' and 'a new demand . . . for the recognition of Wales as a separate political entity'. The devolution of administrative and government functions to Wales, in education and health, would be followed, he hoped, by greater Welsh control of Welsh affairs resulting incrementally in the need for a Welsh parliament. His chief concern however was with the location of the buildings that would house these new national functions. He wanted to avoid the squabbles that had occurred over the location of the National Museum, the National Library and other buildings in the previous decade. His solution therefore was to suggest the building of 'a new city in which might be embodied concretely the most desirable elements of Welsh National life'. Chappell argued that the best of Wales was to be found in the countryside, 'where men and women live in greater harmony with nature and are able to appreciate the things which inspired patriotism in their dead forefathers', but nonetheless Wales needed 'a Garden City capital' as a 'fitting symbol of a united and progressive nation'.[64] Cardiff had been bestowed with city status in 1903 and in 1955 became the capital city of Wales. With devolution, Cardiff has been self-consciously creating itself as 'the youngest capital city in Europe'.[65] Each of these developments can be seen as contributing to a sense of Welshness, but within the context of Cardiff as a British city.

In a British context therefore it is fair to say that the urban as well as the rural has been celebrated as contributing to national identity. The tranquillity offered by the countryside has figured in the versions of political moderation associated with the British national character, but so too has the dynamism of urban life. National identity has therefore been constructed from a combination of both rural and urban Britain. To push the argument forward into a discussion of regional identities, it is possible to mention the importance of urban life for Anglo-British literature. Charles Dickens, Aileen Armstrong on Yorkshire, A. J. Cronin, J. B. Priestley and Catherine Cookson all wrote popular novels that described and endorsed urban life, adding substantially to the tradition of English literature. Catherine Cookson, 'a child of the Tyne', celebrated northeast England in novels such as *The Fifteen Streets* (1952) about the neighbourhood in which she grew up, *Maggie Rowan* (1954) about coal miners and their families, and *Rooney* (1957) about a Tyneside dustman. Cookson's popularity meant that she became one of the twenty wealthiest women in Britain, and in 1993 she was made a Dame of the British Empire. When the publisher Heinemann published a series on landscape and literature including *Hardy's Wessex*, they recognised the links between urban landscape and literature by including *Dickens' London* and *Catherine Cookson Country*.[66]

## Regional identities

Urbanisation and industrialisation have been seen as strengthening the processes of nationalisation and globalisation of politics, economics and culture. Regionalism and regional identities are seen as victims of these processes, lessening in strength and importance. As José Harris has argued, in the mid-nineteenth century British society remained variegated and local, and the 'preservation of local autonomy and custom was seen as a quintessential feature of British national character and culture'.[67] The industrialisation of Britain from 1750 to 1850 had in fact strengthened local and regional identities, as the north in particular constructed a distinct image of itself composed of progress, industry, manufacturing, civic pride and municipal enterprise, which were contrasted to the values of the southern aristocracy and financial middle class – whereas the south talked, as the saying went, the north did. In addition, local identities were enhanced by the nature of government legislation in the nineteenth century, as local authorities were encouraged and later required to deal with the problems of urban society. As these problems became more complex, the central state took over a greater role, restricting local initiative and action, and in turn provoking a sense of regionalism that responded to government initiatives.

Of course, the definition of region cannot be taken for granted. Regions and regional identities are unstable and fluid. Manchester in the nineteenth century was firmly within Lancashire, yet had taken on a separate city identity by the twentieth. As Edward Royle has summed up: 'Region historically . . . is not a fixed concept, but a feeling, a sentimental attachment to territory shared by like-minded people, beyond the local administrative unit.'[68] The region, like the nation, he continues, is therefore an imagined community. But within the United Kingdom, national identities are more territorially fixed, and regional identities are more vague and less rigid. Regions are geographically unstable and the sense of regional identity is uneven in different areas. In particular the boundary between north and south is often mistakenly assigned to be 'north of Watford' rather than 'north of Watford Gap', a service station on the M1 motorway in Northamptonshire, rather than the town in Hertfordshire, only 10 miles north of London.[69] J. B. Priestley on the other hand considered that it was not until he reached the approach roads to Barnsley that he was in 'the true North country'. It was 'stocky figures and broad faces, humorous or pugnacious' and 'the stone walls' that signified 'the North'.[70] Regional boundaries, it seems, are in the eye of the beholder.

This stems from the fact that a clear definition of the term region is elusive, yet it usually is taken to form some sort of relationship with the core or centre of the nation. Regions are frequently defined and regional identities are often seen as being constructed in contrast to the centre. Hence Stuart Rawnsley has argued of the nineteenth century that, 'it was increasingly apparent that the North was being constructed as "other" to the emerging sense of Englishness constructed around the capital and the south of England'.[71] This fits well with José Harris' argument that in the early twentieth century there was a 'nationalisation of culture' as economic, political, social and cultural affairs came to be increasingly dominated from the south and from London in particular. The outcome was not necessarily a decline in regional identities, as the provinces responded to the domination of London by stressing their distinctive contribution to the nation and Empire. Sometimes this could privilege a particular region over all others and London, as illustrated by the arrogant confidence of a Lancashire cotton manufacturer before 1914:

> My lad, never again let anybody in Lancashire hear you talk all this child-ish stuff about foreign competition. It's right enough for Londoners and such like but it puts a born Lancashire man to shame as an ignoramus. It's just twaddle. In the first place, we've got the only climate in the world where cotton pieces in any quantity can ever be produced. In the second place, no foreign Johnnies can ever be bred that can spin or weave like Lancashire lasses and lads. In the third place, there are more spindles in Oldham than in all the rest of the world put together. And last of all, if they had the climate and the men and the spindles – which they never can have – foreigners could never find the brains Lancashire cotton men have for the job. We've been making all the world's cotton cloth that matters for more years than I can tell and we always shall.[72]

At other times, and more often, regional and other local identities were seen as part of a wider national identity. It seems that, in many cases, local and regional identities provided the building blocks for national identity, that the local area or the region could be visualised as the nation to which adherence was given. Hence in Lancashire, Patrick Joyce has seen a continuum between identities of street, neighbourhood, town, county, region, nation and Empire.[73]

Some of the disputes between regions and the capital can be seen as a desire for fair shares and recognition, supportive of the nation rather than hostile to it. Hence, as discussed in an earlier chapter, in 1953 questions were asked in the House of Commons about why it was that only London school children were to be included among the 33,000 who would see the coronation from the London County Council's stands. A campaign was run in the provincial press to see the inclusion of children from outside the capital in the celebrations.[74] In response to this the Queen undertook a royal progress through the provinces in 1954. In this way, regions came to be validated in return by the figurehead of national identity. Other members of the royal family could also perform this role. Princess Mary, the only daughter of George V and Queen Mary, married Vis-count Lascelles in 1922 and made her home in Yorkshire. Between her marriage and her death in 1965 she proved, as the *Halifax Courier* put it, 'a sort of regional viceroyalty', which combined 'the best features of regional self-esteem with a real strengthening of the national community'.[75]

It might be argued that a further consequence of the link between regional and national identities is located in the similarity between the characteristics assigned to regional groups. It is often the case that 'national' virtues are given a regional flavour, but remain varieties of the same basic components. This can be seen clearly in the attributes assigned to different regional groups during the Second World War, and particularly during the Blitz. J. B. Priestley had already begun the construction of a democratic Englishness from regional ingredients in his *English Journey* of 1934,[76] but during the war it became increasingly important for the nation to mobilise people's participation, and one method of achieving this was to incorporate the regions more firmly as part of the nation. Part of this process entailed the broadcasting of wireless programmes from the provinces. One such series was Wilfred Pickles' *We Speak for Ourselves*. In this he travelled the country presenting programmes from factories and other workplaces. These programmes celebrated regional and national identities alongside class with a combination of song and comedy involving the audiences.

*Wilfred*: Well done lads, well done. There's nowt caps a bit of a sing. It's good to hear folks sing these days now that Goering's doing his level best to shut us traps. All I can say is it takes a *lot* to keep Lancashire quiet, – aye, a lot more than we've had so far. The gradely folk aren't licked yet, – no, nor Merseyside neither . . . What about Oldham? Are you licked yet?

*Everyone*: NOOOOOO!!!

*Wilfred*: Nay I thought not! But it's funny y'know. You ought to be. The Germans think you are. Did you hear what [Haw Haw deleted from script] they said about you on t'wireless last week? They said there wasn't a smile to be seen in Lancashire; and that they weren't bothered about Oldham yet because there was nobody lived there but bald-headed bow-legged minders and consumptive women! (Roars of laughter from everybody.)[77]

This conjunction of a self-deprecating but defiant sense of humour, collective singing and regional accent was assigned to other regional groups. Most obviously this emerges in the portrayal of the stoic and cheerful cockney 'taking it' in London, and Mass-Observation commented on the emotional resilience of Liverpudlians, which had enabled them to maintain morale during and after the bombing of the city.[78] A further example is suggested in J. B. Priestley's novel and radio serial on the eve of the Second World War, *Let the People Sing*. Situated in the fictional but decidedly non-metropolitan Dunbury, the common people take on the values of American capitalism on the one hand, and those of the aristocratic and blimpish ruling class on the other, to defend the democratic right of the people to popular entertainment.[79] Wilfred Pickles took up a broadcasting project in wartime and post-war Britain to bring the variety and similarity of regional identities to the 'people'. In his autobiography, he explained how during the war

> I found I was learning a lot about ordinary people as I travelled from one end of these islands to the other. All over the country there was a quiet resolve to see things through and an astonishing confidence in victory . . . Among the dockers on bustling Merseyside where American supplies were rolling in by the boatload I found an intense determination . . . among the Scots at Oban . . . there was a characteristic challenge to anything that might come, and among the miners at Durham deep loyalty to the men in the Forces.[80]

These qualities are class specific. It is the working class that is seen as regional, as having accents and a locally based popular culture. Received Pronunciation, the approved non-accent, belonged to the British upper and upper middle classes, while regional accents were heard from those further down the social scale. In the 1970s a study in West Yorkshire found that the upper middle class dropped 12 per cent of aitches, while the lower working class dropped 93 per cent.[81]

Class divisions meant national fears. Gareth Stedman Jones has seen the manufacture of the cockney identity in the late nineteenth century as a response to the fear of the mob in an age of urbanisation. At a time when the East End was being compared to 'darkest Africa' as an unknown and threatening location, the cockney served to remove the sense of threat of the urban mass. He argues that the cockney came from a particular type of East Ender – the poor, rather than the very poor, situated between the casual and the skilled labourer. Such a stratum involved itself in just those forms of associational culture with which social commentators were likely to come into contact – the university and church settlements and clubs. They were also a conservative stratum, accepting social hierarchy and their place within it. The construction of the cockney was therefore part of 'the attempt to discover and embody a form of national spirit in the city dweller, to break down the anonymous and shabby crowds into a catalogue of particular types, and to incorporate them into a national community'.[82] Such a process can also be seen in the 1930s as George Formby and Gracie Fields provided a cinematic human face for the mass of unemployed in the regions of the United Kingdom. The impact of unemployment itself was regionally concentrated in those areas of heavy industry associated with export trade, damaged so severely by the First World War and the world depression. Formby and Fields both played out consensual responses to the depression, but which combined both the particularism of Lancashire and the universalism of the national. George Formby's catchphrase 'Turned out nice again' symbolised the optimistic fatalism of the northern working class, but also of a country ruled by the capable hands of a National government. Our Gracie in *Sing as We Go* (1934) showed how unemployment could be overcome by cheerfulness, song and class harmony. What was essential here was a sense of shared (national) interests that earned Gracie the role of the Lancashire Britannia, draped in the Union Jack.[83]

All these regional identities were conservative in the sense that they accepted the status quo, accommodated themselves to the Union Jack, and sometimes explicitly linked themselves to the monarchy, as in the case of the pearly kings and queens. There were, though, radical versions of regional identities. In the nineteenth century, the Manchester School of free trade political economists challenged the protectionist policies of the southern aristocracy. Later in the century, early British socialism celebrated its northernness through Robert Blatchford and the *Clarion* newspaper; and in the late twentieth century many people in the north pointed out that it was southern England that insisted on electing Conservative governments. In the 1990s, the British cinema industry reflected a popular resurgence of regional identity in films such as *Brassed Off* (1996) and *The Full Monty* (1997). In these films, masculine, working-class and community-rooted identities were seen as under threat by deindustrialisation.[84] Most recently the campaign for the north-east England regional assembly emerged from a sense of the neglect of the region in the Thatcher years. Its assertion of identity has been made visible in the erection near the A1 of the Angel of the North (1998). Sometimes, regional identity in the north-east has been anti-English, when 'Geordies' have supported Scotland against English sports teams, or have considered themselves 'Geordie' rather than English.[85] This was a complex identity, however, for in the 1970s many in the north-east borderlands were hostile to Scottish devolution because it was seen as likely to divert political power and finance northwards to Edinburgh, at their expense. In 2003, the Blair government decided that referendums would be held in some northern regions of England. But this was not evidence of a desire to break up England, for as Blair explained, his belief was that:

> Devolution has strengthened Britain because it has allowed the different parts of the UK to give expression to their diversity while celebrating the virtues that bind us together as a nation. We believe that devolution can offer the same benefits to the English regions.[86]

The construction of regional identities from outside the region has been a powerful force. James Vernon has examined the 'the English imagination of Cornwall as a primitive "Celtic" land of myth and romance'.[87] Originally, this construction sought to utilise Cornwall as 'the other' against which a more progressive and forward-looking Englishness was highlighted. However, given the sense of alienation of national identity associated with urbanisation, the Celtic and rural Cornwall (and Wales) were idealised as providing the essence of Englishness (and Britishness).[88] The region can further become a marketing tool for consumer capitalism. The famous Hovis television advertisement of a boy pushing his bicycle up a hill was designed to evoke images of the north as wholesome and bakery-made, as were the Allison advertisements of their loaves as bread 'wi' nowt taken out'.[89] In a globalising world, the 'authenticity' of marketed regional identities serves to sell. Whereas MacDonald's seeks to serve a globalised and uniform product around the world, Harry Ramsden's aims to provide Yorkshire fish and chips in any marketing context. This has further been transferred into a 'heritage' context; for example, Beamish, The North of England Open Air Museum seeks to portray the northern working class as a 'tough and resilient people' and as the 'embodiment of an undiluted and unchanging regional spirit'.[90]

Regional identities are also problematic in terms of migrants. Diane Frost has considered the position of West African Kru seafarers in Liverpool between the wars, and has concluded that 'the notion of "scouseness" was, and still is, something that black Liverpudlians are excluded from since to be "scouse" is to be white and working class. One only has to examine the crowds at Anfield.'[91]

On the other hand, the leading Labour figure J. R. Clynes suggested the way in which regional identities could accommodate ethnic diversity, given that he considered himself 'half Irish and wholly Lancastrian'.[92] At the Newcastle upon Tyne Asian Mela in 2000, anti-racist activists handed out stickers which read 'Geordies are black and white', providing another inclusive version of regional identity. This included black people in the regional identity but also implicitly acted to confirm regional identity as exclusive with its reference to Newcastle United, 'the toon army'.

Regional identities are therefore like national identities. They are problematic and varied. They entail the divisions that seem to fragment identities of place, but their fluidity has enabled them to survive the processes of modernisation and the development of communication. Ultimately, they complement the nation, allowing Britishness to emerge from an apparent diversity of regional identities in which often the same (national) values are validated.

# 4 Spare time

This chapter discusses the construction of national and other identities of place in the informal atmosphere of people's leisure time. It might be suggested that people have been more free to choose their identities when they have not been constrained by work, paid or unpaid, or membership of formal and involuntary associations, such as school, the armed forces, or even families. How people chose to identify themselves during their spare time might be expected to provide a good indicator of categories of collective distinctiveness. The range of spare time activities that could have been discussed is enormous. Cinema, fashion, eating habits or music might all have provided the focus for discussion.[1] This chapter will examine three main themes: sport, holidays and fears about the Americanisation of youth culture. Spectator sports have had a central place in popular culture since the late nineteenth century. They have reinforced over-arching national identities, but have also encouraged division through support for the individual nations of the United Kingdom. A different focus will be upon the British on holiday – both at home and abroad. Holidays and day trips have often been used to explore the 'real' rural Britain, but seaside resorts have also been areas where many of the rules of 'national character' no longer apply. A discussion of the British abroad in the late twentieth century will examine representations of the 'English' and their attempts to live up to them in their direct encounters with the foreign 'other'. Finally the chapter will discuss ongoing anxieties over the future of British culture in the face of the influence of American cultural forms among young Britons.

## Sport and national identities

The rise of spectator sports in the British Isles coincided with the transformation of national identities discussed in this book.[2] In the nineteenth century, as much of Britain's population experienced industrialisation and urbanisation, imperialism and modern war, they also watched Britain's footballers and cricketers, rugby players and, in Ireland, hurling and Gaelic footballers. But these were not just coincidences. Some observers have seen sport as separate from and different from external events. In 1915 the interests of those working in a railway factory were described as follows: 'Politics, religion, the fate of empires and governments, the interest of life and death itself must all yield to the supreme fascination and excitement of football.'[3] Yet watching (and playing) sports involved identifying with a range of identities associated with place, whether of the street, town, county, region or nation.[4] Sport became a central part of the identification of many people, not separate from their lives but an integral feature. The association of sport with national identity was particularly enhanced in the nineteenth and early twentieth centuries by the emergence of Social Darwinist ideas that suggested that virility and dynamism were necessary to national survival and that these characteristics were racially predetermined. But the multi-national nature of the United Kingdom meant that the representation of the 'nation' in sport would be complicated.

## Sport, nation and Empire

As spectator sports became popular at the end of the nineteenth century a concerted effort was made to associate some of them with the nation. In part, in a man's world, sport showed the same combination of team spirit, physical strength and territoriality necessary for the nation in a highly competitive world.[5] Major sporting events became national events, implicitly associating the British with the virtues of sportsmanship and fair play. Hence, events involving the participation of limited numbers of men came to symbolise something about the national way of life. The Oxford–Cambridge boat race, the Grand National and the Derby, the FA Cup Final, Test matches and Wimbledon became events in the national calendar, alongside those such as the trooping of the colour, Armistice Day and the monarch's Christmas message. The media encouraged a reciprocal relationship with sports, playing off the national nature of some to encourage the view that the media too were a quintessential part of the nation. For newsreel companies, this was partly a technical question. With cumbersome technical equipment, such staged events provided foreseeable news, but the new media were seeking also to establish themselves as national institutions. This can particularly be seen in the role of the British Broadcasting Corporation. Given a monopoly of national radio broadcasting in the 1920s, the BBC sought to establish itself as a consciously national institution, through radio in the 1920s and 1930s and through television after the Second World War.[6] Sport was also linked to the nation through the patronage of the royal family. In 1914 King George V attended the FA Cup Final, providing national respectability to a consciously working-class game. In 1923 a national setting was provided for British sport with the construction of Wembley stadium as part of the British Empire Exhibition. While the first FA Cup was played there in 1923, the official opening took place on St George's Day 1924.[7]

Sport also played a role in asserting Britishness throughout the Empire and, later, the Commonwealth. First, a sporting ability was seen as important to those taking up military, administrative and civilian roles within British dominions and colonies. The interview board of the Sudan Political Service, for example, 'attached considerable importance to the athletic records of candi-

dates. Such activity was regarded as an indication not only of physical fitness
. . . but of personality, initiative and capacity for judgement and control of sub-
ordinates.'[8] British public schools asserted the connection between sport,
national character and imperial governance and were echoed by a range of
popular culture aimed at boys lower down the social spectrum, who if not des-
tined themselves to run the Empire were to be imbued with the virtues of
team-playing, discipline and confidence. The most blatant link was made in
Henry Newbolt's 'Vitaï Lampada' in the late 1890s:

> There's a breathless hush in the Close tonight –
> Ten to make and the match to win –
> A bumping pitch and a blinding light,
> An hour to play and the last man in.
> And it's not for the sake of a ribboned coat,
> Or the selfish hope of a season's fame,
> But his Captain's hand on his shoulder smote –
> 'Play up! play up! and play the game!
>
> The sand of the desert is sodden red –
> Red with the wreck of a square that broke –
> The Gatling's jammed and the Colonel's dead,
> And the regiment blind with dust and smoke.
> And the river of death has brimmed his banks,
> And England's far and Honour a name,
> But the voice of a schoolboy rallies the ranks:
> 'Play up! play up! and play the game!'[9]

As well as teaching national values that would be of imperial use, sports served
the wider purpose of binding together British communities within the Empire.
As Holt argues:

> British sports served overwhelmingly to express and enhance the solidarity
> of colonial society. Providing amusement for those far from home isolated
> amidst an alien and sometimes hostile population, sport was not so much a
> luxury as a necessity, a means of maintaining morale and a sense of shared
> roots, of Britishness, of lawns and tea and things familiar.[10]

The nature of sport in the Empire was, however, paradoxical. While events
such as the British Empire Games, founded in 1930, were designed to pull the
Empire together, the 'bodyline' cricket tour of 1932, in which English bowlers
aimed at Australian batsmen's bodies, added to a sense of Australian nationalism. Matches against the mother country became a method of assertion of
national claims in the dominions and colonies.[11]

International matches, in cricket, rugby and football, all took on greater
meaning for Britain as British power declined. Martin Polley has argued that

Britain's leading role in the formulation of codes and rules for many sports has led to a deep-rooted British assumption of superiority, which has of course been shaken by successive defeats, particularly in football and cricket, with the effect of an increasing xenophobia associated with support for the English national teams.[12] In the wake of the Second World War when British friendship towards the Soviet Union was at its height, Moscow Dynamo football club toured Britain. George Orwell remarked on the animosity resulting from the tour that

> At the international level sport is frankly mimic warfare. But the significant thing is not the behaviour of the players, but the attitude of the spectators, of the nations who work themselves into furies over these absurd contests, and seriously believe – at any rate for short periods – that running, jumping and kicking a ball are tests of national virtue.[13]

In post-war England the significance of the 1966 World Cup victory over Germany has entered deeply into popular culture, with the Euro '96 tournament being marked by the nostalgic lament that 'football's coming home' after 'thirty years of hurt' in the pop song 'Three Lions' by the Lightning Seeds.[14] A halfway point between these two dates was marked by the release of the football and war film *Escape to Victory* (dir. John Houston, 1981) in which Michael Caine and Sylvester Stallone signified the successful Anglo-American alliance against Nazi Germany. Each England–Germany match has been accompanied by British tabloid newspapers resurrecting jingoist sentiments from the First and Second World Wars. After one England–Germany match in 2001, Marks and Spencer began to sell a tee shirt announcing the score: Germany 1 England 5. No other details were presumed necessary. The order of scores signified that, like both World Wars, this was an 'away win'.

Football is seen as a site for the reassertion of *English* nationalism in the face of the break-up of Britain as spectators paint the cross of St George on their faces.[15] Football had previously been, and continued to be, a method by which Scotland could successfully demonstrate its distinctiveness, but now England too played the separatist card. However, the 2002 World Cup, coinciding with the golden jubilee of Elizabeth II, saw Union flags and the St George cross being displayed in about even numbers. Sport has been a way of asserting English distinctiveness in the wake of the loss of Empire, devolution and economic crisis. Sometimes this has emerged from among spectators but government too has played a role. In 1975 the Labour government of Harold Wilson, a professed Huddersfield Town supporter, established the Sports Council, since it was argued that 'Success in international competition has an important part to play in national morale.'[16]

## Sport and nation in Scotland, Wales and Ireland

The relationship between sport and nation has been complicated in Britain by the multi-national nature of the United Kingdom. Much of the vocabulary (if not the virtues themselves) of the values associated with sport is associated more with Englishness than with Britishness. 'Fair play' and 'play up and play the game' are essentially southern English phrases. Likewise cricket is seen as quintessentially English, associated as its dominant version is with a southern version of the rural idyll of the village green set amidst thatched cottages and the Anglican church, or with public schools. A separate county version could accommodate county cricket frequently allowing the north to dominate, but cricket was ruled from the south. In football, Wembley stadium, built to celebrate the imperial connection in the 1920s, became symbolic of English football, and at worst of Anglo-Scottish rivalry.[17] Sport has played a role in identities in Scotland, Wales and particularly Ireland, defining their differences from England, though at different levels. Holt has argued that in the case of Ireland between the 1880s and 1920s this took the form of rejection of British sports, while in Scotland and Wales there was an assertion of difference *within* the framework of British sports.[18]

In Scotland and Wales, participants and spectators both took to sports also played in England but made those sports their own. In Wales, while football was popular along the south coast and in the north, it was rugby union that became part of the self-definition of the Welsh, and also a signifier of Welshness from without. Brian Roberts argues that 'rugby, communal singing and (rather less now) the chapels' provide the 'mundane' reply to the question, 'Do you consider yourself Welsh?'[19] Often, the 'mundane' gets closer to the unconscious sense of identity than more considered responses. In the late nineteenth century, rugby took hold in the mining valleys of South Wales, and absorbed both manual and white-collar workers to provide a confirmation of the sense of a democratic and classless culture so dear to Welsh identity.[20] In the 1890s rugby was given a Welsh pedigree in the Tudor game of *cnappan* to rival the alternative version of the sport's origin at an English public school. With a Welsh past, rugby was used as a method of providing Welshness for the migrants who swarmed to Welsh heavy industry.[21] While the Welsh language gave way to English as the language of assimilation and democracy in South Wales, rugby provided a distinctive form of culture to which to adhere. In 1905 Wales' national team defeated the unbeaten New Zealand All-Blacks in Cardiff. The victory was celebrated as a triumph of Welshness. The *South Wales Daily News* determined that

> The men that represented Wales embody the best manhood of the race . . . We all know the racial qualities that made Wales supreme on Saturday . . . The great quality of defence and attack in the Welsh race is to be traced to the training of the early period when powerful enemies drove them to their mountain fortresses. There was developed then those traits of character that find fruition today. 'Gallant little Wales' has produced sons of strong determination, invincible stamina, resolute, mentally keen, physically sound.[22]

While most of the team were Welsh-speakers, the captain and centre-three-quarter were both English-born, from Gloucester and Leicester respectively.[23] Wales celebrated out-performing England at rugby, affirming distinctiveness and skill, but the sport operated with a British and imperial context. Wales was seen to have saved the mother country's honour against the All-Blacks. This was seen as confirming the Britishness of Wales rather than contesting it. Andrews and Howell argue that 'The path to an Imperial Wales was reached through the promotion of a Welsh cultural nationalism', of which rugby formed a major component.[24] In 1881 the Welsh Rugby Union rejected the leek in favour of the Prince of Wales' royal feathers as the national symbol for the team, ensuring that Welsh rugby fell within royal confines.[25] Of course, the context of assertion changed. In the late nineteenth century urban, industrial Wales benefited from the imperial markets and a wider prosperity, allowing Welshness to flourish comfortably alongside the assertion of Britishness centred on monarchy and Empire. The dramatic decline of Welsh industry after the First and Second World Wars could raise the significance of matches against England. In 1977, Phil Bennett, Welsh captain, roused his team:

> These English you're just going out to meet have taken our coal, our water, our steel: they buy our houses and live in them a fortnight a year . . . Down the centuries these English have exploited and pillaged us – and we're playing them this afternoon boys.[26]

Morgan has argued that rugby diverted attention from political nationalism: 'Beating the English through skill with an oval leather ball appeared to be satisfaction enough', and the result of the 1979 referendum, when only 11.8 per cent of the electorate voted for devolution, suggests the profound difference between Welshness and Welsh nationalism.[27] Rugby in Wales has acted to strengthen a sense of distinctiveness, yet this has not resulted in nationalism.

For the tourist, Scotland's distinctiveness came in the Highland games. The monarchy began a long association with 'traditional' Scottish sports at the Braemar Royal Highland Gathering in 1866, and Anglo-Scottish aristocrats in fact and fiction enjoyed the sports of stalking and salmon fishing to relieve the tedium of elite life.[28] However, the major sporting identity in Scotland emerged, as in Wales, in towns and cities rather than in the countryside. Urban Scotland took up football with a passion. In 1886, as Gladstone introduced the first Home Rule Bill for Ireland, the Scottish Football Association began the process of withdrawal from the British FA Cup, establishing a separate Scottish league. While the same game would be played both sides of the border, Scottish football developed in a national rather than a British context.[29] Scotland took the annual match against England, the 'auld enemy', particularly seriously. Every other year, from 1923, it was played at Wembley, symbolic location of English football. By the 1930s tens of thousands of Scottish supporters, the vast majority working class, descended on London with their own symbols of national identity, tartan, bagpipes and banners of Wallace and Bruce.[30] In 1977 a pitch invasion by the

Scottish led to the destruction of the goalposts and the digging up of turf to take home. In 1989 the contest was ended. In this confrontation, Scottish football and culture could be shown as being distinct from and superior to those of England. If Scotland was junior partner in the Union, and in the interwar years the severe depression in heavy industry was revealing just how junior, then it was not inferior in terms of pride. Of course, the pleasure aspects of a weekend away might override those of national identity, but the alcohol-induced pleasure became part of the legend of Scottishness. In 1992, Jim Sillars suggested that the SNP's poor showing in the general election was caused by the 'problem . . . that Scotland has too many ninety minute patriots whose nationalist outpourings are expressed only at major sporting events'.[31] Chris Harvie, paraphrasing Marx, has aptly argued that 'sport made the Scots "of a nation" but not "for a nation"'.[32] In sport many Scots have expressed their Scottishness, while not necessarily seeing that as part of a political project towards independence.

Ireland was different. Where Wales and Scotland asserted difference within 'British' sports, nationalists in Ireland rejected any association with 'garrison' games. In 1884 the Gaelic Athletic Association was founded, self-consciously to reverse the Anglicisation of Irish culture. The GAA could muster mass support for the Irish games of hurling and Gaelic football – Croke Park in Dublin could hold 80,000 spectators – and in turn these could be mobilised in support of radical nationalism. John Redmond, leader of the Irish parliamentary party, was at home in the imperial parliament at Westminster (being a member of a landowning family he was accustomed to having more than one home), but the rejection of British sports by the GAA and its exclusion of those who served in the British armed forces was an explicit challenge to the idea of an inclusive cultural Britishness. The GAA was part of Irish-Ireland, and 'the outstanding example of the appropriation of sport by nationalism in the history of the British Isles and Empire'.[33] Five of those executed after the Easter Rising of 1916 had strong links with the GAA.[34] After partition, the GAA continued to claim authority over sports in the six counties of Northern Ireland, retaining its links to republicanism. It continues to see itself as a nationalist organisation:

> The Gaelic Athletic Association is more than a sporting organisation. Although it is dedicated to promoting the games of hurling, football, handball, rounders, and camogie, the Association also supports activities which enrich the culture of the nation and further Gaelic ideals, including the Irish language and Irish music and dance. The GAA endeavours to strengthen pride in the communities it serves.[35]

Clearly this led to problems in the six counties. Sport, like other aspects of civil society, was exclusive and disruptive in the north. The organisation of sport not only reflected existing divisions but reinforced them. As Cronin has argued, 'To understand the deaths in Northern Ireland as a battle between two identities on opposing sides of a sectarian divide is to understand sport.'[36] Identification with the GAA, Derry City Football Club and the Ireland national team marks people off as nationalist, probably Catholic and possibly republican, whereas support for Linfield FC and the Northern Ireland football team is a signifier of Unionism, Britishness and probably loyalism. Catholic and Protestant Irish migrants carried these rivalries to cities in Scotland and England. Sport, particularly football, in cities such as Glasgow, Manchester and Liverpool saw religious–ethnic divisions overlap with territorial competition.

## Regional and local identities in British sport

National identities are of course not the only identities in sport. Indeed in rugby, football and cricket they are probably not even the most important. In the nineteenth century, rugby, football and league cricket clubs became associated with urban areas as they emerged as mass spectator sports. These local teams provided the building blocks for county and national teams and there was no conflict in supporting Huddersfield Town Football Club and England, or Partick Thistle and Scotland in football, Wigan and the British Lions in rugby, and Essex and England in cricket. But the experience of this dual support was mediated by attachment to the locality and sometimes the region. This section looks at three examples of identities of place in sport. It examines a regional conflict between north and south, the experience of Yorkshire in cricket, and rivalries between local teams, and suggests that while there have been tensions these have often been accommodated in the compatibility between local, regional and national identities.

One conflict that emerged early in spectator sports was that between north and south, which could sometimes be an expression of the rest versus London. This conflict was apparent in football, rugby and cricket. In football for example, in 1882 the Blackburn Rovers FA Cup Final team was described by one local newspaper as 'the team who went to London to represent the town, the county and the provinces, against "Metropolitan" protection and "Metropolitan" monopoly'.[37] The FA Cup Final also provided an occasion for northern fans to visit the capital, where they sometimes realised their 'otherness' from the centre of the nation. Whereas supporters of Scotland visualised themselves as an invading army, northern supporters seemed more often to have imagined themselves as sightseers. In 1910 a Barnsley fan was quoted by *The Times* as saying: 'They don't know English i'London an' stare at us like we was pole-cats . . . and there's not a happy face in the streets. Why can't they be neighbourly?'[38] Such hostility continued into the interwar years, with Arsenal becoming the target for much northern hostility. In cricket, the conflict was with a southern, middle-class version of the game dominated by the Marylebone Cricket Club (MCC), the sport's governing body. It was often felt that selectors for the England team favoured southern over northern players, a discrimination based also on class differences between amateur ('gentleman') and professional. In rugby the Northern Union broke away from the Rugby Union in 1895 as the differences between amateurism versus professionalism, south and north, and middle and working classes became irreconcilable. The Rugby

League, as the Northern Union became in 1922, contributed firmly to images of the north and especially of northern masculine hardness, and remained a regional rather than national game, and therefore representative of one sort of mediation of national identity through sport.[39]

The second example of the mediation of national by local identities in sport comes from Yorkshire County Cricket Club. For much of the twentieth century (until 1992) the Yorkshire CCC sought to root itself in locality by a rule that meant that only those (males) born in Yorkshire could play for the team.[40] As the largest county in England and a with population of 4 million in 1911, Yorkshire considered itself a highly significant county, with a distinctive character that emerged in its cricket. From his research of a variety of Yorkshire publications, Dave Russell has compiled this catalogue of Yorkshireness, that could be applied to general Yorkshire and sporting identities:

> Yorkshire people were supposedly rough-mannered, brusque and blunt, if ultimately homely and hospitable, and with a strong sense of community obligation; naturally egalitarian to a considerable degree; canny and thrifty but generous in a crisis; hard-working, practical, temperate and phlegmatic; blessed with a dry wit; suspicious of strangers; competitive, with a hatred of losing, although never actually unsporting; and perhaps above all else, fiercely independent.[41]

But while this was a strongly held county (almost regional) identity, it was compatible with a cricketing national identity. Yorkshire was proud of its contribution to the England team, and this confirmed that Yorkshire people considered themselves the best kind of Englishmen (and women). In the context of cricket and elsewhere, Yorkshireness and Englishness-Britishness showed the compatibility of different identities of place.

The third example of the impact of identities of place in sport comes from the relationships between different teams located within a confined urban space. Mass spectator sports in an urban context generated strong town identities. According to Jack Williams, 'Supporting a town club was an expression of a town identity, an association with others from the town that asserted a collective geographical allegiance.'[42] Problems arose when there was more than one team associated with a town or city and where allegiances to those different teams represented dissimilar identities. This emerged in the association of some teams with Catholicism and others with Protestantism. Hence in Manchester, United was associated with the Catholicism of Irish migrants while the native, Protestant, population supported City. This rivalry emerged in its most bitter and enduring form in the second city of the Empire, Glasgow, as allegiances were split between Glasgow Celtic and Glasgow Rangers. Some historians have downplayed the significance of 'sectarianism' in Scottish football, hence Moorhouse has argued that 'in modern Scotland *talk* about ethnic antagonism is rather more prevalent than evidence of meaningful ethnic division'.[43] Others have categorised sectarianism as a variety of racism. Dimeo and Finn argue that sectarianism contradicts one central claim of Scottishness about the absence of racism in Scottish society.[44] At the centre of this clash is the adherence of Rangers to a Scottishness based on militant Protestantism with emotional links to Ulster Unionism. In 1992, while Sillars was lamenting ninety-minute patriots, Rangers chairman and managers showed that patriotism in Scotland was not confined to Scottishness when they publicly declared their support for the Union.[45] Among Rangers supporters, there have been links to both Linfield in Northern Ireland and Chelsea in England, suggesting further the 'British' and unionist nature of that support. In such circumstances the existence of a sizeable community of Catholics of Irish origin led to an ongoing tension within the city and its football.[46] Celtic was founded in 1887–8 as an Irish club within Scottish football.[47] Its support provides a good example of the construction of an opposi-tional national identity within the territorial boundaries of another nation. To support Celtic does not necessarily mean opposition to Scottishness, although in 1990 a survey showed that Catholics generally had lesser affinity with Scottish symbols than other Scots, but it does seem to reflect a sense of discomfort with the traditional version of Scottishness. It is to this latter version that Rangers has adhered, and indeed it has played a substantial part in its construction, pro-viding a public space in which Scottishness has displayed its hostility to Irish migrants and Catholicism.

## 'Race', sport and identity

In 1989 Norman Tebbit, an ex-Conservative cabinet minister, suggested that support for the England cricket team provided a wider test of the loyalty of immigrants to the British nation. His suggestion was 'that those who continue to cheer for India and Pakistan are wanting in Britishness'.[48] This was partially a point about class. Cricket played by Indian princes was likely to have proved acceptable to Tebbit. Certainly Ford Madox Ford suggested the integrative power of sport for people of the 'right' class. He described public school cricket and its power:

> We felt intensely English. There was our sunshine, our 'whites', our golden wickets, our green turf. And we *felt*, too, that Stuart, the pure-blooded Dahomeyan, with the dark tan shining upon his massive and muscular chest, was as English as our pink-and-white or sun-browned cheeks could make us . . . We could not put it more articulately into words than, 'He's been to *our* school.'[49]

As Polley has argued, 'sport has proved to be a significant location for the playing out of discourses over racial stereotypes, prejudices, politics and inte-gration'.[50] Since sport plays a major role in the way that many people identify themselves in day-to-day life, it has also provided an arena in which people think about the relationship of immigrants and their descendants to Britishness.

It is certainly the case that many aspects of sport have led to a greater sense of inclusion of migrants in a sense of Britishness. The participation of athletes in sports has foregrounded the multi-racial character of British society, and some sports historians have reinforced the need to open up the hidden history of migrants' involvement in a variety of sports. For example, Dimeo and Finn discuss the series of black and Asian players in Scottish football, from John Walker, probably of African origins, who played for Leith Athletic in 1898, through Abdul Salim, the first Asian player in Scotland, who played for Celtic in 1936, to Rashid Sarwar, an Asian-Scot signed for Kilmarnock in 1985.[51] By the late twentieth century, about 20 per cent of players in the English Premiership and Leagues were black, though Asian-British players were far fewer. In football, Viv Anderson, born in 1956 in Nottingham to Jamaican parents, was the first black player to play in the England football team, and in 1993 Paul Ince became the first black captain. The self-identities of athletes have also forced consideration of the national identity of immigrants by the wider population. The majority feeling about Zola Budd, a South African runner granted a British passport to enable her to compete internationally, was that she saw Britishness as a flag of convenience. The adoption of a pride in his British nationality by Linford Christie has, on the other hand, largely been greeted with praise by the media. Christie self-consciously wraps himself in the Union Jack, and has said that 'by representing my country, I'm trying to show there is really no need for the problems we have . . . black sportsmen are uniting the country'.[52] In 1998 Paul Ince and Ian Wright led the singing of 'God Save the Queen' at an international match in Morocco, and were widely praised by the British media for doing so.[53] This allegiance, fulfilling Tebbit's test, has encouraged the inclusion of black and Asian people within the nation, but that acceptance has often been limited and incomplete.

There remains much stereotyping of black and Asian people within a variety of sports, where agility and speed are seen as black characteristics and stamina and intellect are seen as white attributes.[54] In such circumstances, black players are seen as different kinds of Briton from white players. The stereotype extends to the belief that 'Asians can't play football', as one coach asserted.[55] Since football is seen as the national game, the logic of this statement is that those of Asian origin cannot be truly British. A further excluding aspect of sport is the widespread existence of racism, particularly among spectators of football and cricket. Cyrille Regis, who played for West Bromwich Albion in the 1980s, recalled that, 'When I was called up for England for the first time there was a letter, an anonymous letter saying "If you go to Wembley and put on an England shirt you'll get one of these through your knees". There was a bullet in the envelope.'[56] There have been and continue to be many racist actions associated with sport at all levels that seriously question the willingness of many participants and spectators to include black and Asian people within such a national fixation.

## Discordant voices

The association of sport with Britishness has of course been contested in many ways. Rudyard Kipling, champion of imperialism and proponent of military and spiritual preparedness for war to defend the Empire, referred to the 'flannelled fools at the wicket [and] the muddied oafs at the goals' in his verse 'The Islanders' (1902), meaning those who had diverted their attention from the Empire to the sport's field.[57] During the First World War there were some criticisms of sports continuance while the 'bigger game' was taking place in France and Belgium, even though the compatibility of sport and war was demonstrated by officers and men kicking footballs ahead of them as they went 'over the top'. It has already been mentioned that sport as 'national character' has overwhelmingly celebrated a masculine version of the nation from which many women (and men) have felt excluded. However, this section will focus on the role of sport as ambassador for the British (and perhaps more significantly the English) abroad. According to the *Guardian* in 2000, 'Britons are seen by young people in other countries as arrogant, xenophobic and frequently drunk.' The British Council, who carried out the survey upon which the *Guardian*'s comments were based, said that 'a big factor in Britain's reputation for drunkenness was the scenes of violence by football supporters abroad'.[58] In the last three decades of the twentieth century the association of sport with a sense of national character that was disposed towards tolerance, good order and fair play collapsed. In 1923 the first FA Cup Final was held at the new Wembley stadium. Fifty thousand too many spectators turned up, resulting in fans overrunning the pitch. The newsreel coverage of the event, however, showed a single mounted policeman on a white horse maintaining order among a crowd constructed by the media as typically English – well mannered, well behaved and respectful of his symbolic authority.[59] Football became associated with cheerful working-class crowds, vociferous in their support of their own teams but respectful of other teams' skills. During the General Strike in 1926, much was made of the football match between strikers and police in Plymouth, which was seen as evidence of fair play in the midst of a difficult constitutional situation. Since the 1960s, however, English football crowds have been seen as a stain on the nation's good name, because of football violence at both home and international matches. Jeremy Paxman, in his liberal elegy to a lost Englishness, points out that this sort of violence is not peculiarly English but that those involved in the violence see it as part of their Englishness: 'they see fighting and drunkenness as part of their birthright. It is the way they proclaim their identity.' Paxman suggests that football hooliganism is part of a tradition of an English association with disorder.[60] Such a 'tradition' can be traced through Hogarth's representations of violence in the eighteenth century to those of Charles Dickens in the nineteenth. *Barnaby Rudge* (1841) fictionalised the Gordon riots of 1780, representing London as a 'psychological space'.[61] Tony Mason on the other hand has persuasively argued that while there was violence associated with football even before the First World War, the nature of the violence changed in the 1970s and 1980s. Williams suggests that the change in the nature of football violence in the post-war period was linked to the decline of local community identities, which acted to police football supporters.[62] It is also the case that Scotland's supporters, the 'Tartan Army', now construct their identity as 'other' to England's hooliganism, involving alcohol consumption but combined with good-humoured and cosmopolitan boisterousness rather than the out and out xenophobic violence of the England supporters abroad.[63] Again, a warning is provided by Mason, who points to the parallel between modern hooliganism, associated with organised groups of young working-class males espousing local and national identities, and the violence of football in sectarian Glasgow in the 1920s.[64]

Sport has therefore been a significant area in the discussion and forging of national identities in the British Isles since the 1870s. Sport has not often acted to reinforce Britishness. In many sports, the component nations of the UK play in separate leagues or as separate national teams. In addition, sports have been a method by which Wales, Scotland and especially Ireland have asserted their difference from England. In the case of Wales and Scotland, this has been accommodatory, but Irish sport reflected and reinforced the nature of Irish national identity as distinct from Britishness. The relationship between sport, 'race' and national identity in the British Isles has also been ambiguous. Participation in sport has certainly enabled some black people to become icons of Britishness, but it is clear that their acceptance by many white people has been contingent and limited.

## Going on holiday

'What should they know of England, who only England know?', asked Kipling, privileging imperial Britons with greater knowledge of national identity than those whose lives had been spent entirely in the imperial metropolis.[65] But Kipling had a point. Identities are often formed in relation to the 'other', described by Rose as 'defining where you belong through a contrast with other places, or who you are through a contrast with other people'.[66] This section examines holidays, which have provided an opportunity for large numbers of the British people to contrast other places and peoples with those with which they were familiar. The numbers able to take holidays have expanded across the twentieth century, particularly as the result of easier mobility, the implementation of the right to paid holidays, established as the norm in the 1930s, and post-war affluence. As well as holidays within Britain, 25 million foreign journeys were made in 1986, with one-quarter being to Spain.[67] Rob Shields has associated the seaside resort in particular and the holiday in general with liminality, 'moments of discontinuity in the social fabric, in social space, and in history'.[68] This section argues that holidays, especially those at the seaside and abroad, have often been seen as spaces where many of the rules of 'national character' no longer apply. Some holidaymakers may have been seeking authenticity, sometimes the authentic nation, and an escape from modernity by holidaying in the countryside, but for many others, holidays have been about an escape from restraint, including that presumed to come from Englishness, for the middle and upper classes associated with the stiff upper lip and for the working class associated with 'respectability'. John Walton has explained how in Blackpool pleasures were policed with a light touch, but that limits to the loss of restraint were still imposed.

> This did not mean complete permissiveness: far from it. The aim was to provide a town centre in which all the visitors could mingle without people, property or sensibilities being outraged or threatened, and in which the broad working-class preference for sensation, variety, noise and bustle . . . could be accommodated without running riot and damaging other interests.[69]

Holidays, even within the British Isles, were sites of encounters with the exotic. On holiday 'the minutiae of daily life' are compared between home and holiday, [70] and choices are made between the 'British' and the 'foreign', between for example fish and chips and paella. The exotic was often embraced as spectacle. In 1930s Blackpool, for example, Mass-Observation recorded that, 'Powerful, often dominant in Blackpool culture is the Negroid, the Indian, the oriental and the Buddhist. These counteract the regular emphases of the rest of the year, spent in inland towns where the air is not so fresh.'[71] The Isle of Man marketed itself as foreign. 'Go abroad in the British Isles' was its slogan. And Cunningham's camp opened in 1904 celebrated its address as 'Switzerland', Douglas, Isle of Man.[72] The physical fabric of the seaside resort was built to stress exoticism and eclecticism. Mass-Observation described a holiday camp in Blackpool:

> Very Mediterranean-looking is the Squire's Gate Camp with rows and rows of tiled chalets, centred on the largest building with a bell turret, 'The Moorish Pavilion', a cross between a Spanish hacienda and a Swiss chalet. The 1,400 chalets among the sand-dunes, the manager calls 'Californian chalets'.[73]

As with the seaside, another form of architecture of leisure displayed similar exoticism to seaside building. In the 1930s cinema architects designed Italianate gardens, Moorish villages and Mediterranean vistas to provide the backdrop for escapist films.[74]

Often though, such buildings, on holiday and in the High Street, were brought into the arena of the known by their imperial connections. Brighton Pavilion built between 1815 and 1823 provides the best example, but in the late nineteenth and early twentieth centuries the imperial context of Britain was carried over into the building of resorts witnessing growing numbers of visitors as a result of a greater availability of disposable income. In this period, industrial workers, particularly in the textile industries, were beginning their 'traditional' relationship with the seaside holiday. They were met not only by the sea but by the extraordinary architecture of the Empire, and spectacular buildings given patriotic names such as the Victoria Pier, Empress Ballroom and Royalty Theatre.[75] The development of the relaxation of restraint eventually became familiar and its combination with nautical and imperial themes which were seen as central to British history made the seaside 'typically English'.

Sometimes conflicts between patriotism and holidays could emerge directly; in 1914 Blackpool Corporation decided to proceed with the Illuminations despite the war, and while patriotic motifs were illuminated, many visitors were outraged at the victory of commercial over national considerations.[76] There were casualties in seaside resorts in wartime. During the First World War, the German navy shelled towns along the east coast of England, and 'Remember Scarborough' became a recruiting slogan linking the seaside holiday with the national cause. Other casualties were cultural, as a popular wartime song showed:

> Has anybody seen a *Ger*man band
> *Ger*man band
> *Ger*man band
> I've looked everywhere both near and far,
> Near and far,
> *Ja*, Ja, Ja,
> But I miss my Fritz
> What plays twiddly-bits
> On the big trombone.[77]

Holidays often entailed an air of challenge to authority that fitted well into many readings of national character.[78] But the challenge posed was accommodated within what it meant to be English, and was absorbed as essentially harmless. Orwell noted in his discussion of comic illustrated postcards that, 'At normal times they are not only not patriotic, but go in for a mild guying of patriotism, with jokes about "God save the King", the Union Jack, etc.' Shields concisely summarises their usual subject matter: 'Red-faced bobbies, army colonels and majors, or other stiff-collared guardians of public morality and propriety are thoroughly catalogued in this genre, along with drunkards, embarrassed lovers, bathers, and prostitutes.'[79] But these have become aspects of the 'traditional' and 'national' seaside holiday. Walvin's history of the seaside holiday begins, 'The English summertime rush to the sea is so customary, so fixed a part of the nation's annual routines.' Pearson too discusses 'the essentially English phenomenon of the seaside holiday'.[80] Carol Reed's feature film *Bank Holiday* (1938), set in a seaside resort, was applauded by film critics as 'simple, human, humorous, in a truly British way'. The *New Statesman* welcomed it as 'notable for the authenticity of its scenes of jostling holidaymakers at the station and on the beach . . . To have conveyed to the commercial screen some part at least of the everyday life of the English masses is a rare achievement.'[81]

Orwell observed that low and vulgar comedy, the staple of seaside entertainment, was 'intensely national' and that 'startling obscenities . . . are only possible because they are expressed in *doubles entendres* which imply a common background in the audience'.[82] The seaside holiday, the release from restraint, was held within an adapted version of national identity, of the English on holiday. These measures of behaviour could be associated with the British more widely, so Blackpool was popular with Glasgow and South Wales holidaymakers, or holiday centres could be regional in identity. In 1891 *The Daily Telegraph* described how,

> as Margate is to the average Cockney, so is Morecambe to the stalwart and health-loving Yorkshireman. For it is allowed on all sides that Morecambe is true Yorkshire to the backbone . . . Yorkshiremen, Yorkshire lads, and Yorkshire lasses have selected to colonise and to popularise this breezy, rainy, wind-swept, and health-giving watering-place.[83]

In the post-war period, foreign holidays have become available to large numbers of the British people, and have enabled direct encounters with the 'other' in an alien setting. Culler has suggested that this has developed the tourist as a student of national identity and character:

> [T]he tourist is interested in everything as a sign of itself . . . All over the world the unsung armies of semioticians, the tourists, are fanning out in search of the signs of Frenchness, typical Italian behaviour, exemplary oriental scenes, typical American thruways, traditional English pubs.[84]

But such investigation takes place in the context of already formed images of the foreign other that may be challenged or may be confirmed by the actual meeting. As well as numerous media images, the marketing of holidays abroad has played on simplistic images of otherness to Britain and Britishness.[85] In 1930 Robert Graves described his life in Majorca, a Mediterranean island that would become familiar to millions of British holidaymakers after the 1950s. His description suggests the ways in which holidays (Graves' voluntary exile was a kind of extended holiday) are chosen and anticipated and enjoyed:

> [W]e live here in perhaps the best place anywhere – these are the Classical Hesperides where it never freezes and never gets too hot and where it costs nothing to live if one is content to go native, and where the population is the most hospitable, quiet, sensible and well-being that you can imagine. We are near the sea and Palma a big town, is within easy reach for any European necessities . . . We tried France and Germany first but of course though we knew the best parts it was no use; (the Germans are too serious and the French too false) it was just to confirm our previous choice of this island.[86]

In such constructions of foreigners, Britons are also constructing themselves. It is sometimes the case that Britons abroad have behaved in the ways that have come to be expected of them as (usually) English. In Spain, young British holidaymakers are known as *gamberros Ingleses*, English hooligans, and in turn the holidaymaker often loses all restraint. The stiff upper lip is entirely eliminated as respectable versions of national character themselves take a holiday. There has been, however, a trend of travel-writing (and broadcasting) in which the Englishness of the gentleman-traveller has lived on. In the late 1980s, Michael Palin, Monty Python satirist of the upper-class twit of the year, journeyed round the world in eighty days for BBC television. The series' accompanying book's blurb noted with nostalgia that 'he discovered . . . that the days are passed when a signed photo of Queen Victoria was enough to admit an Englishman anywhere'.[87] As Hsu-Ming Teo has argued, 'The experience of travel and tourism in post-colonial nations was thus refracted through the prism of British imperialism.'[88] Holidays have therefore played a part in the reinforcement of national identity in Britain in the twentieth century.

## Resisting the Americanisation of culture

At the beginning of the twentieth century, the British government decided on the policy of the appeasement of the United States of America.[89] This policy has rarely been challenged. Sir Anthony Eden sought a more independent role for Britain during the Suez crisis, but was displaced by the pro-American Macmillan. Edward Heath looked towards Europe but was replaced by the Atlanticist Thatcher. This policy of appeasement was based on the realisation of American strength and relative British weakness. In both the First and Second World Wars the American contribution proved essential in securing victory. Despite Leon Trotsky's prophecies of imperialist war between Britain and America in the 1920s,[90] many in Britain have seen the two nations as natural allies, given that the dominant forces within each are white, Anglo-Saxon and English speaking. Raymond Seitz, US ambassador to the United Kingdom in the 1990s, expressed the depth of this everyday 'special relationship' by pointing out that 'In 1996 there were more than one-and-a half billion minutes of telephone conversation between the United States and the United Kingdom, or, put another way, roughly three millennia of talk in one year.'[91] This desire for permanent peace has however been accompanied by deep anxieties over the impact of American cultural dominance. In part, this has been a racialised concern, fearing the impact of swing, jazz and, more lately, gangsta-rap on young British consumers, but there has also been a concern that American cultural products of the dominant consumer capitalism might have negative moral effects which in turn could lead to the destruction of indigenous British culture.

During the 1930s the American accent became a common sound in Britain. In 1933 63 per cent of fourteen to twenty-one-year-olds attended the cinema weekly, and already Hollywood dominated British screens. In the Rhondda Valley, the Welsh writer H. W. J. Edwards bemoaned that 'the delightful local accent is broken up by such words and phrases as "Attaboy!", "oh Yeah!" and "Sez you"'.[92] In 1927 a quota Act had been passed obliging cinemas to show a proportion of British-made films. But American films were popular among younger audiences, and young males in Britain could be heard sporting American accents. While the British government were happy to continue to rely on the British Board of Film Censors to maintain the 'moral' content of film,[93] many others thought that not enough was being done. Cinema was seen as a dangerous medium because it allowed the masses access to entertainment. Sidney Dark, editor of the *Church Times* in 1933, warned, in gendered language, that 'In this complex age it was race suicide to allow foreigners to impregnate falsehood into the lifeblood of this nation.'[94] Since foreign language films were the preserve of film clubs and middle-class audiences, it was Hollywood that was seen as the contaminator of British culture. Major Rawdon Hoare, cousin of a Conservative cabinet minister, commented on being served by a petrol station attendant who affected an American accent:

> He is only one among millions whose entire lives are being influenced by the American cinema. What good can all this do to England? Will it create patriotism? Will it create a desire to keep our great Empire together? I doubt it. But quite definitely it *is* creating a race of youths belonging to all classes whose experience of life is based largely on the harrowing and frequently sordid plots of American films.[95]

It should be noted here that two contradictory processes were occurring. On the one hand, some cultural commentators were condemning the American influence, while large numbers of (often young) Britons were embracing Americanisation. As J. B. Priestley noted in 1934, factory girls were 'looking like actresses'.[96] Roy Hattersley, taking a more politicised view than most might be expected to do, recalled that he and others felt 'a cultural – if not ideological – affinity with the United States. We were the children of the war, Hollywood movies and current affairs lessons about Roosevelt's New Deal. We felt at home in America.'[97]

The entry of the United States into the Second World War encouraged both these responses. Nearly 3 million Americans disembarked in the UK between 1942 and 1945.[98] In particular, many were concerned that young British women were consorting with American troops, even black soldiers (though marriage to black Americans was outlawed). But on the whole, attitudes towards America and Americans were positive. Mass-Observation repeatedly asked the question, 'How do you feel about the Americans?' The yearly percentage of people responding that they were 'favourable' was 45 in 1941 but 58 per cent in 1945. Once the war ended, opinions changed. In 1946 only just above 20 per cent were recorded as favourable to Americans. In 1945 American 'boastfulness', 'immaturity', 'materialism and commercial preoccupation' and 'morals' were cited as reasons for dislike. One man told Mass-Observation that the USA was not prepared to supply Europe with food yet was 'prepared to flood the world with their atrocious films, full of slop, bad manners, inaccurate history and the general marvellousness of the American people'. A working-class woman aged thirty-eight was prepared to be more generous, though she acknowledged the position of Americans in relation to her own nationality: 'I think they are a rather fine people and very good friends. But on the whole, I think the American character is not as fine as the British.'[99] Frequently it was the young who welcomed Americanisation, often because to them materialism was unproblematic. As a Cambridge teenager said, 'To go to their bases was absolutely fantastic because there was no shortage of anything. Each base was a little America with plenty of food and drink and fantastic great iced cakes.'[100] Immediately after the war, the Labour government raised concerns over the influence of American cinema. Harold Wilson as President of the Board of Trade again sought to limit the numbers of films from Hollywood.[101] Wilson believed that they corrupted morals, but also that cinema needed to become more representative of Britain as a whole:

> Speaking as an ordinary cinema-goer, I should like to see more films which genuinely show our way of life. I am tired of the sadistic gangster . . . films [made by] diseased minds which occupy so much of our screen time. I should also like the screen writers to go up to the North of England, Scotland and Wales and the rest of the country and to all the parts of London which are not so frequently portrayed in our films.[102]

Responses to Americanisation were, then, not always straightforwardly conservative. Wilson's attempt to protect regional culture against the onset of Americanisation also challenged elite versions of Englishness. While the attempt at restriction of American films failed in the late 1940s, the Ealing films did provide representations of non-metropolitan Britain, including *Whisky Galore* (1948) and *The Maggie* (1954). By the end of the decade, the 'Angry Young Men' had diverted the focus of literature to the north.

The youthful embrace of Americanisation remained a cause of concern for older Britons. In the 1950s the impact of another American cultural product began to provoke alarm. The 'horror comic', imported first as ballast in American ships, aggravated anger for their graphic depictions of violence, which were seen as having a morally deleterious impact on children.[103] This may have been simply a moral issue, yet the discourse was framed in terms of a wider threat. A letter-writer to the *Picture Post* in 1952 explained that 'it is not only American comics that should be banned, but also many of the other false practices that have been imported into this country. The sooner we return to a sane British way of life (built on traditional lines) the better for this great nation.'[104] Likewise, an article in *For Home and Country*, the journal of the Women's Institute, condemned the comics' representation of 'cruel and sadistic acts' and concluded by warning of the wider danger: 'No self-respecting family would permit them in their house, and we can have little respect for ourselves or for our nation if we continue to allow degenerate literature to get in to the hands of our children.'[105] In 1956 the Conservative government responded to such concerns, passing the Children and Young Persons (Harmful Publications) Act.

While America could be seen as culturally contaminating, in political terms its leadership of the 'free world' and democracy in the Cold War enhanced its reputation. While Orwell spoke for parts of the political left in his denunciation of Britain as 'Airstrip One' in *1984*, many others admired the modernity of the States, particularly as represented by John F. Kennedy in the 1960s. It has been these multiple responses to Americanisation that have characterised reactions. Whether it has been American television or the ubiquity of MacDonalds, some have seen a threat to national distinctiveness while many, and probably most, have embraced this transatlantic influence.

National identity is often associated with formal settings, but this chapter has shown that it has played a significant part in people's spare time. National identity is part of people's lives. It has occurred in the everyday and chosen activities of people. These routines have reinforced national identity through lived experience. In sport and leisure, sometimes it is Britishness that has been reinforced. At other times cultural pursuits have been disruptive of a coherent British national identity and have presented challenges, through the rejection of British games for example, or through the adoption of foreign cultural forms. But nonetheless, people have been brought face to face with identities of place in their daily lives.

# 5 Politicians, parties and national identity

Patriotism and ideas of national identity have long been the playthings of politicians. Until recently, the claim of conservatives, and in Britain this mainly means the Conservative Party, to patriotism has been seen as much more secure than that of the left. Recently, however, Tony Blair, through the linking of 'New Labour' to 'New Britain' may be in the process of fundamentally challenging the link between the right and national identity. It has been suggested that the Blair–Brown government has brought an end to the 'decline debate' that has raged in Britain since the end of the Second World War, causing a sense of instability in discourse of national identity.[1] Yet this challenge itself is not new. Across the century, however, Labour has adapted itself to conservatism, including patriotism.[2] This chapter examines the relationship between politics and national identity, arguing that while parties of the right have sought to secure hegemony over ideas of Britishness, the left in British politics has consistently contested this hold. At a number of points in the twentieth century, the political left convincingly repudiated the hold of the right on characterisations of national identity and in those circumstances has performed well in elections. This in turn has made some parts of the left more determined to utilise patriotic ideas. In Britain's context as a multi-national state, the parties of the left have also sought to challenge the monolithic unionism of the Conservatives by offering a more pluralistic framework for national identities in the United Kingdom. In this sense, it can be argued that party politics has, in the main, acted as a unifying force in Britishness.

## Radical patriotism and the claims of the Conservatives

During the wars against revolutionary and Napoleonic France in the late eighteenth and early nineteenth centuries nearly all social and political groups sought to claim patriotism for their own. In the eighteenth century the British aristocracy had modelled their lifestyles on French modes and fashions which had enabled their opponents to make patriotism and radicalism almost synonymous in meaning. Faced with a struggle for survival against revolutionary and Napoleonic France, and domestic opposition from radicals at home, the aristocratic elite decided there was a need to re-establish their authority by showing their attachment to the ways of life of the British nation. French fashions – wigs, powder, lace and silk – were given up in favour of more functional clothing, including uniforms.[3] As Peter Mandler has pointed out, the houses of the aristocracy were at this time beginning their long and deliberate transition from symbols of authority to symbols of national identity.[4] George III, with his German background, also wanted to establish his Britishness in the face of radical criticism of royalty. Such concern shows the extent to which radicals had possession of ideas of the nation. Patriotism was associated with a vocabulary of liberty and rights that made those in power uncomfortable. The idea of the 'freeborn Englishman' and of historic rights pre-dating the Norman Conquest gave radicals a powerful hold on interpretations of the nation's history with a tremendous resonance in a society undergoing fundamental transformation in the face of industrialisation and its accompanying urbanisation.[5]

The legislative changes wrought on society by the governing class overseeing this social and economic change were met with widespread opposition. Radicals only partially used a new language of class to define and mobilise resistance to measures like the new Poor Law of 1834 and the new police forces of the 1830s, and to the imposition of work-discipline in the new mills, but instead mainly continued to exploit the language of nation and liberty. Workhouses and uniformed police were condemned as novel and un-English methods of repressing the labouring poor.[6] Chartism too saw the use of this radical patriotism, and shows how the language of the freeborn Englishman was translated into the multi-national context of the United Kingdom after the Union with Ireland of 1801 and the migration of many Irish to the expanding industrial cities of Britain. Chartist demonstrations included banners employing such symbolism as 'a figure of Justice, holding in her hand a balance, supported by the British Lion, the emblems of Wisdom, Unity, Peace and Strength, surmounted by a British Standard', and the 'Red Rose of England, Harp of Erin [and] Thistle of Scotland'.[7] This accommodation of multi-nationalism also enabled radicals to uphold a sense of internationalism, based as it was on a view of the plurality of nations. Radicals concerned themselves with nationalisms that were struggling for liberty against tyranny, as were Polish and Italian nationalists.[8] In the British context, English, Scottish, Welsh and Irish radicals could unite against the tyranny of a state riddled with 'Old Corruption'. The grip of the aristocracy on ruling institutions encouraged an identification of radicals with the ideas of the nation and the people against the sectional interests of a clique. As Hugh Cunningham has argued, while the language of radical patriotism outlived Chartism, the use of a new discourse of class in response to the emergence of critiques of industrial capitalism provided a competitor within the radical armoury which was not always compatible with the language of nation.[9] Class became an important form of description and identity among radicals, but it was not all encompassing. The language of nation within radicalism continued, sometimes being employed alongside the language of class, as each described and criticised a situation of exclusion from power and the material comforts of life among the majority of the population. In the 1870s the agitation around the Tichborne claimant saw the language of patriotism forming the forefront of radicals' critique. In 1865, Tomas Castro, a returning emigrant from Australia, claimed to be Sir Roger Tichborne, the missing heir to the estates of a Hampshire landed family. When Dowager Lady Tichborne died in 1868 she left the estates to Castro, whom she recognised as her son. The rest of the family, however, legally disputed his claim and won. Castro was tried for perjury and gaoled for fourteen years. Radicals rushed to Castro's defence, since here was a case of aristocratic corruption and exclusion that disturbed the 'English' notion of 'fair play'. Drawing on the language of historic popular liberties, the Magna Charta Association was formed and an agitational newspaper published with the symbolic name of the *Englishman*. Its circulation reached 70,000 in the mid-1870s, suggesting the popular nature of the cause, mobilised around the language of nation, which proved flexible enough to cope with the complexity of the radical analysis of the affair.[10]

Radical patriotism had, therefore, survived into the second half of the nineteenth century. The governing parties in Britain, however, increasingly saw patriotism as a means of damping down potential conflicts within urban, industrial society. The attributes assigned to Englishness-Britishness by radicals could also serve the purpose of justifying the expansion of the Empire. Both Liberals and Conservatives saw advantages in associating their parties with the nation and patriotism. In the 1860s, Gladstone sought to draw Queen Victoria out of private mourning and into national duty.[11] It was, however, the Conservative Party which saw in patriotism a solution to anxieties about the effects of post-1867 mass politics. Disraeli in particular saw patriotism and imperialism as forces that could draw mass support towards a popular and populist conservatism. Patrick Joyce has described this as the politics of 'beer and Britannia', in which both elements referred to national identity.[12] The Conservatives sought to defend the public house as a site of working-class culture against the attacks of temperance reformers associated with the Liberal and labour politics, but they defended in this a context of a national culture of beer, beef and plum pudding. Hence, in 1872, Disraeli described the working class as 'English to the core'.[13] Some Conservatives built on this Englishness through hostility towards immigrants, Irish and Jewish, which in parts of Lancashire and London further strengthened popular Conservatism. This politics of the street found its ultimate expression in 'jingoism', which emerged during the Eastern Crisis of 1877–8. In this the Conservatives linked popular dislike of Russian tyranny and power to the idea of the Liberal and peace parties as enemies within the nation, and mobs organised by Conservatives disrupted peace meetings.[14] Jingoism was to re-emerge during the Boer War and the First World War and on each occasion was directed at opponents of the Conservatives.

Having suffered the ignominy of accusations of being a sectional party for half a century after 1832, the Conservatives embraced the association of their party with the nation. Under Disraeli and Lord Salisbury a concerted effort was made to reshape patriotism to suit the imperatives of an expansionist imperialist nation and those of a party suffering anxiety over its future in a period with increasing numbers of voters. Disraeli made clear the link when he declared in 1872 that 'the people of England, and especially the working classes of England, are proud of belonging to an imperial country'.[15] When the Liberal Party under Gladstone converted to support for Irish Home Rule in the mid-1880s, Salisbury sought to make the words Union, nation and Empire synonymous with Conservatism. This set of ideas was backed up through Conservative organisations that celebrated these aspects of the national identity. The Primrose League, founded in 1883, and with over a million members by the First World War, drew both working- and middle-class Conservatism into an aristocratic party and community.[16] As Rohan McWilliam has argued, 'The culture of Conservatism transcended class in favour of the nation.'[17] The dominance of Unionism after 1886 seemed to confirm that this strategy was an electoral success. The Liberal Party split over Home Rule. The Liberal Unionists allied to and eventually united with the Conservatives. During the Anglo-Boer War of 1899–1902 the Liberals were divided in their attitudes to war. The Liberal Imperialists, including Lord Rosebery, embraced what had now come to be seen as a traditional patriotism of imperialism, while the so-called Liberal Pro-Boers opposed the war. In such a situation the Conservatives were able to win convincing electoral victories in 1895 and 1900.

The success of patriotism and the appeal to Britishness expressed in Unionism are not, however, as straightforward as they seem. Cunningham has argued that 'the patriotic card worked less obviously to the Conservatives' advantage than has often been implied. Patriotism was as likely to divide the party as to unite it.'[18] A range of problems was associated with the political use of national identity. In a multi-national state, the Conservatives became associated with Englishness rather than Britishness, which led to a loss of political support in Ireland in the mid-nineteenth century and in Wales in the late nineteenth century. In 1895, the Conservatives had their best electoral performance in Wales between 1880 and 1924, yet they won only nine out of thirty-four seats.[19] Secondly, the policies associated with patriotism and imperialism were not always popular; indeed the campaign for 'fair trade' or 'tariff reform' associated with an attempt to construct an imperial economic bloc caused, in 1906, one of the most dramatic Conservative defeats of the twentieth century. In this election, the patriotic card failed, compounded by the apparent incompetence of the government during the war in South Africa.

## 'Countervailing currents'[20]

Such problems with patriotism and Britishness experienced by the Conservatives were made all the worse because the Liberal, Labour and socialist parties simply refused to accept the Tory claim to a monopoly on patriotism. The left-wing artist Walter Crane had no hesitation in visually representing Gladstone as St George championing Irish Home Rule, and fighting a dragon of rack rents, evictions, police brutality, coercion and tyranny.[21] Whereas the Conservatives saw Home Rule as a direct attack on the Union and Britishness, the Liberals saw it as a method by which the Irish could be reconciled within the United Kingdom, to the annoyance of some Irish nationalists.[22] For the Liberals, the United Kingdom had room for the multiplicity of national identities of England, Scotland, Wales and Ireland. The *Daily News* in 1910 argued that 'The nationalities within the British Isles are the natural units for devolution and their nationalization does not take from but strengthens a common Imperial patriotism.'[23] The Liberal Party's sympathy towards the demands of small nationalities within the British Isles can be seen as an important integrative factor in British politics.[24] Nor did the Liberals accept that only the Conservatives put the needs of the nation at the forefront of their politics. The Liberals sincerely refuted the claim that tariff reform was a patriotic policy, arguing instead that free trade was responsible for the prosperity of the United Kingdom and in that sense was a policy more closely attuned to the needs of the nation. Lloyd George called it representative of a more true patriotism than imperial bluster. He pointed to 'this little island in the sea . . . standing against Continents armed at all points with the most systematically devised tariffs, standing alone armed only with the weapon of freedom, and yet beating them all on land and sea'.[25] In 1900 the Conservatives fought and won a 'khaki' election. The abstract ideas of patriotism and imperialism appealed to all classes within the electorate to secure for the Conservatives and their Liberal Unionist allies 402 seats to the Liberal, Labour and Irish nationalist total of 265.[26] Yet in 1906, in an election fought on a range of issues associated with national identity and patriotism (tariff reform and imperialism, 'Chinese slavery' in South Africa, national efficiency), it was the Liberal version that triumphed, with the Liberals alone winning 399 seats, and Labour and the Irish accounting for a further 112 to the Unionists' 156. In British politics at the turn of the century, perhaps the zenith of popular imperialism, the Conservatives' grip on the politics of patriotism was far from complete.

In addition, the labour and socialist movement contested the right of middle-class parties to the claim on patriotism. Like Lloyd George, many socialists also often made use of the distinction between Conservative patriotism and a 'true' patriotism. C. H. Norman, a member of the Independent Labour Party, explained in the midst of the First World War that there were two sides to patriotism. 'Patriotism', he explained, 'is a passion impelling a person to serve his country (1) either in defending it from invasion; (2) or, in upholding the rights and liberties of the people.'[27] Most of those within the British labour movement accepted this latter definition and defined themselves accordingly as patriots. Hence, Henry Mayers Hyndman, founder of the Marxist Social Democratic Federation in 1883, described socialism as *England for All*; Edward Carpenter urged the coming of socialism in his song 'England, Arise!' and Robert Blatchford called his best-selling socialist book *Merrie England*.[28] If the Primrose League offered Conservatives a patriotic political culture, then the labour movement countered by its appropriation of May Day as a labour festival drawing on the English past. Held annually after 1890, the symbolism of May Day in Britain included internationalism but it also drew on an association with the English past, through the Maypole.

Like Liberalism, labour and socialist politics also acted as an integrative factor in British politics. The driving forces behind labour politics were James Ramsay MacDonald and Keir Hardie, both Scots who saw labour politics as acting best within an all-British context. MacDonald happily embraced a celebration of English history but retained a sense of Scottishness. Hardie made more of his Scottish past and of Scottish culture, commemorating Robbie Burns regularly in his speeches and writings. He appealed to the Welsh electors in Merthyr Tydfil to support him because of their shared Celticness; he hoped that a time would come when he would see 'the red dragon . . . emblazoned on the red flag of socialism'.[29] Yet for Hardie and MacDonald, winning the support of distinctive constituencies was the method by which to get elected to Westminster, the British parliament. Hardie had been MP for West Ham South between 1892 and 1895, and MacDonald's political career ranged from a candidature in Southampton in the 1890s, Leicester in 1906, Woolwich in 1921, Aberavon in 1922, and finally Seaham in the 1929 election. Hardie and MacDonald were deliberately British politicians, even if in addition they retained a sense of their Scottish identities.

All 'British', as opposed to nationalist, parties acted as centripetal forces within the British Isles. Party leaders emerged from all four nations of the British Isles, though no Irish Catholic rose to the leadership of a party until the emergence of Sinn Féin.[30] For most the history of the Houses of Parliament was to be celebrated as a British achievement even if much of that history had occurred outside the chronological life of the United Kingdom.[31] When the Houses of Parliament had been rebuilt after a fire in 1834 their royal character was designed to overcome religious and national divisions.[32] Many nascent politicians learned their crafts in local 'parliaments', for example that of the Neath Parliamentary Debating Society in the 1880s.[33] Ross McKibbin has argued that the role of such local parliaments 'in legitimating parliament can hardly be overrated'.[34] In addition they legitimated the politics of Britain and Britishness.

## The First World War

It was very much this parliamentary and constitutional version of Britishness around which the political parties rallied on the outbreak of war in 1914. German aggression against Belgium and France in August 1914 was presented as a product of the lack of representative parliamentary government. This was not a question of democracy, for in 1914 Germany had universal manhood suffrage while the complicated British electoral system excluded around 40 per cent of the adult males, as well as all females. However, in Germany the Chancellor was not accountable to the Reichstag whereas the British prime minister was accountable to the House of Commons.[35]

The nature of the war, requiring massive state intervention in the economy and society, conflicted with the central tenets of Liberalism, and therefore also the Liberal version of national identity associated with free trade and individual liberty. This conflict tore the Liberal Party apart, so that by 1918 Lloyd George, who became prime minister in December 1916, fought the general election campaign as 'the man who won the war' in coalition with the Conservative Party, in which pre-war imperialists, like Lord Milner, had found increasingly prominent positions.

The Conservative Party's patriotic appeal, based on protection and imperialism, had proved electorally unpopular in Edwardian Britain, yet the war vindicated the party in a number of important claims. Many within the party had warned of a 'German menace' for a decade before the war. In association with patriotic pressure groups with mass (though almost overwhelmingly Conservative) memberships, they had called for a massive programme of naval rearmament ('We want eight and we won't wait', they demanded) as well as some form of compulsory military service. In wartime such demands were met, and those who had made such demands in peacetime could claim foresight. With the dynamic demands for more effective prosecution of the war led by the Unionist Business Committee and Unionist War Committee, it was apparent that it was the Conservatives who could best play the patriotic card in the khaki election that followed the end of the war.[36] That is not to say that patriotism pushed all before it in politics, but for many years after the war it became normal for parliamentary candidates to stress their war service or that of close relatives. Even among Labour candidates in 1922 there were a brigadier-general, three colonels, one lieutenant-colonel, three majors, five captains and one commander.[37] Clement Attlee, leader of the party after 1935, continued to make use of his rank as major, validating his army service even in the 'pacifist' 1930s.

The labour movement had been divided in its attitudes to the war, but not because of a rejection of patriotism within the movement. Much opposition to the war confirmed the sense of national identity based on parliament and liberty. Before Germany invaded Belgium, the majority of the labour movement was preparing to oppose British intervention in a European conflict on the side of tsarist Russia, 'as being offensive to the political traditions of the country'.[38] The minority who continued to oppose the war after Germany's attack on Belgium still did not reject patriotism. Like most other opponents of the war, Ramsay MacDonald, who resigned from the chairmanship of the Labour Party when the majority decided to support the government in the war effort, consistently hoped for a British victory. 'Victory . . . must be ours. England is not played out. Her mission is not accomplished', he declared when *refusing* to take part in recruiting meetings in his Leicester constituency.[39] The opponents of the war accepted the representations of Germany as the antithesis of what Britain stood for. Germany represented aggression, militarism and the forces of tyranny, whereas Britain represented liberty, honour and the defence of small nations against bullies. Whereas during the South African War of 1899–1902 radicals accepted the epithet of 'pro-Boer', in the First World War they consistently rejected being labelled as 'pro-German'.

The political outcome of the war was a triumph for the Conservative version of patriotism and national identity.[40] In the general election of 1918 even the mildest criticism of the war effort was met by defeat at the polls. 'Pacifists' like MacDonald and Philip Snowden were defeated; but so too were H. H. Asquith and Arthur Henderson, who had remained committed to the war effort even after disagreements with their former colleagues in government.

## Between the wars

Between 1918 and 1939 there were seven general elections. The Conservatives won five of these, and also won more votes than the governing Labour Party in the other two. For fourteen years, Stanley Baldwin, a leader who deliberately set out to epitomise the English national character, led the party. Some historians have seen Conservative victory being consequent upon Baldwin's appeal to Englishness. Robert Blake has described Baldwin thus: 'Pipe-smoking, phlegmatic, honest, kind, commonsensical, fond of pigs, the classics and the country, he represented to Englishmen an idealised and enlarged version of themselves.'[41] In this view, Baldwin drew the nation together behind tranquillity and harmony in the wake of the destructive, industrial slaughter of the Great War, offering social peace behind the image of Englishness as parliamentary, moderate and rural.[42]

Of course, Baldwin's appeal to Englishness can be seen as exclusive rather than inclusive. Baldwin's sort of Englishness rejected socialism and socialists as foreign. If not as ruthless in his condemnation as some in his party, and if he often sought to act as defender of the moderate Labour leadership against their Communist critics, nonetheless Baldwin did seek to suggest that British politics had room only for particular parties that took national character and traditions into account. In addition, many within the Conservative Party sought to associate themselves with the national interest, portraying Labour and the trade unions as sectional, aggressive, militant and selfish. Hence the General Strike of 1926 was cast as the self-seeking actions of unpatriotic and anti-English trade unionists, determined to challenge the constitution and in turn to bring the nation to its knees.[43]

Sian Nicholas has argued that Baldwin's persona 'appeared to celebrate the best features of "Englishness" without obviously casting aspersions on "Welshness", "Scottishness" or "Irishness"'.[44] His Englishness had the potential to weaken the party's position in Wales and Scotland. He therefore adopted an appeal to Unionism that enabled Welshness and Scottishness to provide a distinctive contribution to Conservatism. He was prepared to play on the Scottishness of his mother's family, and in 1930, upon receiving the freedom of Inverness, he declared that he was 'half a Celt myself'.[45] Nevertheless, there was a tension between the Englishness of Conservatism and the Britishness implied by its unionism. This allowed Labour the opportunity to claim by default to be the party of Britishness. In Wales and Scotland, Labour began to replace the Liberals as the force combining radicalism and nationalism. This was despite the insensitivity of Labour's head office, which in 1918 refused to allow Welsh Labour autonomy within the party because the administrative structures of the United Kingdom were based on the integration of England and Wales.[46] Labour played an integrative role in the United Kingdom because it both was prepared to adopt ideas of national identity in Scotland and Wales, yet at the same time saw political solutions taking place within an all-Britain context, focused on the parliament at Westminster, which it saw as central to British history. In 1922 MacDonald explained that the ornate and elaborate ceremonial of the Westminster parliament was an 'inheritance from a rich history of conflict to establish liberty'.[47] In this context, parts of the Labour leadership were confident in their challenge to Baldwin's claim to represent the nation. In 1923, when Baldwin raised the standard of tariff reform as a method of reducing unemployment by protecting the home market from foreign competition, MacDonald replied:

> 'Protect our home market!' What an insignificant phrase that is alongside the Labour Party's policy: Develop our own country! . . . *We are going to develop our own country, we are going to work it for all it is worth, to bring human labour into touch with God's natural endowments, and we are going to make the land blossom like a rose and contain houses and firesides where there is happiness and contentment and glorious aspirations.*[48]

Labour and the Conservatives therefore contested the content of national identity in the 1920s and disputed each other's claims to be the party of patriotism. But there was an element of consensus within this dispute that the defining feature of British politics was its parliamentary nature. The consensus therefore extended to the rejection of radical or extremist parties as un-British.

## British Fascism and Communism

The two decades after the First World War saw Europe in turmoil. In Russia (and more briefly in Hungary and Bavaria) a Communist government had been set up; in Italy in 1922 Fascism crushed (a weak) parliamentary democracy; the Nazis came to power in Germany in 1933, and across Europe various conservative authoritarian forces either took power or challenged for it. Britain too witnessed some upheaval. Between 1919 and 1921 strikes stood at record levels; indeed in 1926 the nine-day General Strike brought the nation to a halt. Twice in the interwar years, Labour governments were formed, the second collapsing amid a financial and political crisis in August 1931. Yet despite such apparent chaos, the British parliamentary system survived, the two major parties retained their commitments to a constitutional monarchy, and threats to public order, while highly visible, were mostly marginal. Communism and Fascism in Britain on the whole failed to secure significant support. They remained marginal political forces, though achieving some localised success. The Communist Party of Great Britain, formed in 1921, found some support in so-called 'Little Moscows' of mining areas in Scotland, South Wales and County Durham. But Communist membership rose only from 3,000 in 1931 to 18,000 in 1939. The British Union of Fascists had 50,000 members in July 1934, but collapsed to 5,000 by October 1935 (after anti-Fascist demonstrators were expelled from the Olympia rally with extreme brutality in full view of a number of Tory MPs and newsreel cameras). The BUF saw some revival to around 22,500 in September 1939. Despite gaining some support in the East End, no BUF councillor or MP was elected in the 1930s. Hence Communism and Fascism in Britain 'failed'.[49]

The most popular explanation in the 1930s for such failure was that extremist politics were un-English, and that the British national character contained within it an innate moderation and common sense, indeed a gentleness that kept politics within the paths of compromise and parliament. Most historians now quite rightly reject the notion that British national character can be used as an explanation for the failure of extremism. As Andrew Thorpe declares:

> To argue that extremism failed between the wars because the British were and remain 'jolly good eggs' (implied in Baldwin's statement that Mosley was 'a cad and a wrong'un') seems rather dated and hollow. Generalisations about 'the national character' are probably best left out of consideration when discussing the reasons for the failure of political extremism.[50]

Historians have, therefore, rejected national character as an explanatory factor in the failure of extremism and have replaced it with economic and political reasons. First, while popular perceptions of the 1930s continue to view the decade as one of slump, depression, dole queues and poverty, a revisionist view of the decade sees it as 'the dawn of affluence'.[51] Falling prices enabled the majority of the population to improve their standards of living, despite high levels of unemployment, which never fell below a million between 1921 and 1939 and peaked at more than 3 million in 1932. What this meant was that a significant number were never economically impoverished to the extent that they sought radical political solutions to economic problems. The British experience of unemployment was such that it discouraged political activism. Because of its regional concentration it prevented contrasts being made between poverty and affluence, it was largely felt to be a temporary phenomenon, and it was greeted with fatalism. Not least, the existence of unemployment benefit prevented most disorder.

Second, political explanations are offered for extremism's failure. The Conservative and Labour parties simply provided very little space for more radical parties. Hence, throughout the 1920s and 1930s, Labour and the trade unions rejected all links with the Communist Party and its front organisations. The institutional hold on the organised working class remained strong enough to prevent their turning in significant numbers to Communism. Likewise the Labour and trade union opposition to Fascism was unflinching; attachment to the BUF was likely to lead to ostracism by former colleagues. The Conservative Party was in government (on their own or in coalition) for much of the 1920s and 1930s. For most on the right, therefore, staying within the party remained essential even if they opposed the moderate Baldwin leadership. In office the Conservatives ensured that they legislated for their core supporters – the middle class, who were offered deflation, low taxation, low interests rates, restricted public expenditure and a more or less balanced budget. The party's success in presenting these as 'national' as opposed to sectional measures was apparent in their electoral success within the National governments of the 1930s.[52]

Some historians have stressed the failure of the ideology, organisations and leadership of the Communist and Fascist groups, but clearly these can be no more than explanations that account for the limitation of the size of individual organisations rather than providing for their almost complete failure. Economic and political explanations are adequate to describe the marginalisation of extremism between the wars, but they do not provide complete answers. The idea of national identity must be reinserted within the argument, to place a cultural explanation alongside political and economic factors. The historically specific construction of Britishness in the 1920s and 1930s included a significant element that represented extremist politics as un-British, as foreign, as alien to British political tradition and custom but also to the 'national character'. An innate national character is not an explanation for the failure of extremism, but the wide acceptance of ideas about what constituted the national character may have acted as an obstacle to the growth of extremist parties. Crises in the economy and in politics were not dramatic enough to challenge these widely held ideas about a moderate, non-violent, constitutional Britishness, constructed rather than innate certainly, but powerful nonetheless. If many of the British believed themselves to be 'jolly good eggs', because they were British, then the rejection of Fascism (and Communism) was likely to have been reinforced by such a belief.

Such constructions of Britishness and the exclusion of Communism and Fascism as un-British are easy enough to find, coming from a wide range of sources. Most obvious were the attempts by the Conservative Party to link Labour to Communism, thereby arguing that both were foreign and unfit to govern in Britain. The 'Zinoviev Letter' used in the election of 1924 was the climax of such redbaiting. Revealed by Conservative Central Office, it purported to show how Communists would take advantage of a Labour election victory. The Labour Party certainly believed such accusations were damaging, and saw the solution as total dissociation from Communism. At conference after conference the Communist Party was alleged to be under orders from a foreign power, against the best traditions of the British, and alien to British thought. Frank Hodges, secretary of the miners' union, declared in 1923 that 'Russia had nothing to teach the political democracy of the Western world. British institutions had grown up in accordance very largely with Britain's own peculiar history.'[53] Labour figures played a significant part in constraining British politics with the parliamentary arena.

Baldwin in particular favoured a language of Englishness that stressed the moderation of British politics. In the 1920s he had been seeking to incorporate

Labour within the parliamentary tradition; in the 1930s he aimed his language at the BUF and CP, not to incorporate, but to exclude. The association of British Fascism with the German and Italian variants further damaged the Britishness of Mosley and his supporters. Foreign financing of the BUF and CP were perceived as especially harmful to those parties, because gold from Berlin, Rome and Moscow was seen as being spent in the German, Italian and Russian national interests. Connections to foreign governments also enabled attacks on the 'foreign' political methods employed by the CPGB and BUF. The violence of the Russian Revolution was seen as inimical to British parliamentarism, particularly because of the execution of the Russian monarchy. The BUF were more often attacked for bringing 'foreign' methods directly to British soil, especially in the wake of the 1934 Olympia rally. Three Conservative MPs present at the rally wrote in a letter to *The Times*:

> We were involuntary witnesses of wholly unnecessary violence inflicted by uniformed Blackshirts on interrupters. Men and women were knocked down and were still assaulted and kicked on the floor. It will be a matter of surprise to us if there were no fatal injuries. These methods of securing freedom of speech may have been effective, but they are happily unusual in England.[54]

What are, as usual, more difficult to measure are the effects of such attacks. In this instance, parties that sought to challenge the parliamentary tradition failed, but alternative explanations may sufficiently account for such failure. However, the constraint of ideas and language about what constituted national identity between the wars played a significant part in the restriction of the growth of radical parties. This is suggested by the reactions of the radical parties to accusations of being un-British. The BUF strongly denied that they were foreign in influence or ideas. 'Our members', Mosley said, 'were the very flower of the English people.'[55] The BUF celebrated the successes of Tudor England, but also of early nineteenth-century patriotic radicals like William Cobbett, Thomas Carlyle and Robert Owen. They also stressed the 'foreignness' of some of their opponents. 'Ragotski, Schaffer, Max Levitas, Fenebloom, Hyam Aarons, Sapasnick', Mosley read out to a Fascist audience. 'Old English names: Thirty-two of them out of sixty-four convicted since last June for attacks on Fascists. Thirty-two names of that character. Spontaneous rising of the British people against fascism!'[56] When faced with accusations that Fascist violence against Jewish and other opponents was un-British, Mosley declared that 'the only methods we shall employ will be English methods. We shall rely on the good old English fist.'[57]

After 1936 and the turn towards the strategy of Popular Fronts of all opponents to Fascism, even the Communist Party stressed its place within British history. In seeking to build alliances with non-communist parties and individuals, it utilised a radical democratic version of history that emphasised the Englishness-Britishness of radical politics. In 1936 the party organised a 'March of English History' in Hyde Park, and described the English as 'a people proud of their instinct for fair play, for the rule of law and justice'.[58]

This defensive response of the radical parties suggests that they saw such accusations as damaging to their potential support, and the pervasiveness of such accusations of un-Britishness suggest that opponents too saw it as an effective method of restraint. There is a fine line to be followed here. The failure of radical parties of left and right did not stem from an innate Britishness that favoured moderation, but the failure of such parties suggests the strength of constructions of Britishness and their wide acceptance among different sections of British society. The radical right between the wars contested the dominant ideas of 'national character' but were unable to compete with the accepted notions, except in limited areas such as east London, where they built on a tradition of anti-immigrant super-patriotism. The radical left on the other hand rejected the notion of national identity in favour of an international working-class identity associated with the Soviet Union. Their turn to national history to strengthen the Popular Front in the late 1930s did not enable them to break out of their isolation on the left, until the unwilling entry of the Soviet Union into the Second World War in 1941.

## Patriotism and politics in the people's war

During the First World War the Conservative Party enhanced its grip on the ownership of ideas of national identity and patriotism. This had contributed to the electoral success of Conservatism, especially under the semblance of the National government in the 1930s. The Second World War saw a reversal of the fortunes of the parties, despite the leadership of the Conservatives by that epitome of the bulldog spirit, Winston Churchill.[59] Churchill exhibited a heroic and imperial patriotism grounded in British history as a struggle for freedom, and he wrapped this in a full-bodied rhetoric which he had perfected over the four decades of his political career. His public speaking did draw attention to the contribution of the 'common people' but the focus seemed to be on social elites. The people were indebted to 'the few'. This was not the only message. Churchill did celebrate the people's role, but it was their role in his project. He referred to 'the spirit of the British nation . . . the tough fibre of the Londoners, whose forebears played a leading part in the establishment of Parliamentary institutions and who have been bred to value freedom far above their lives'.[60] Churchill's people were products of national history rather than the nation itself. Michael Foot, in 1958, suggested that Churchill 'is wrong about the English people . . . However, since the people only make the rarest of intrusions into his *History of the English-Speaking Peoples*, the point hardly arises.' Certainly, Churchill has emerged from the Second World War to be considered the twentieth-century's greatest Englishman.[61] But he did not have it all his own way during the war. There was a bitter contest over national identity between 1939 and 1945, played out at a cultural level but with political consequences. Churchill was a Conservative, yet while he was prime minister he saw himself as leader of the nation rather than leader of the party. During the 1930s he had been alienated from the party over its liberal policy towards India, the abdication and the policy of appeasement. Churchill's accession to power in 1940 was as the result of the fall of Neville Chamberlain, who had patriotically maintained the peace in the 1930s, as chancellor of the exchequer and as prime minister, but whose patriotism had been fundamentally questioned by the proximity of Britain to defeat in 1940. Baldwin had carefully built up the association of the Conservative Party with patriotism and ideas of Englishness in the 1920s and 1930s; he had portrayed the National government as above party, as had MacDonald, National prime minister between 1931 and 1935. As the result of a major financial crisis, MacDonald had abandoned his Labour cabinet, who could not agree how to resolve the crisis, and formed a new government with the Conservatives and Liberals. In 1931 MacDonald and Baldwin had, it seemed, put country before party. Yet the events of 1940, the fall of Norway and France and the retreat of the British Expeditionary Force to Dunkirk annulled the patriotism of 1931. The National and Conservative leaders were branded the 'guilty men'. 'MacDonald and Baldwin', three journalists including Michael Foot declared in a best-selling book, 'took over a great empire, supreme in arms and secure in liberty. They conducted it to the edge of national annihilation.'[62] Churchill's leadership was not, therefore, an endorsement of Conservative patriotism but a register of its weakness in 1940. He was a Conservative outsider precisely because of his patriotism.

Churchill was leader of a renewed coalition government, this time with full Labour support, rather than the rump that had backed MacDonald, Baldwin and Chamberlain. In the late 1930s some prominent figures within the Labour Party, such as Hugh Dalton and Ernest Bevin, had vocally criticised the foreign policy of the National government and had called for rearmament to combat Fascism.[63] Such people saw themselves as patriots, but they combined two forms of patriotism: the outward-looking patriotism that sought to defend the nation was drawn together with an inward-looking patriotism that concerned itself with the condition of the people.[64] In 1940, Labour, now within the government, pursued both of these patriotic agendas in tandem. Bevin for example linked socialism to the war effort:

> I have to ask you virtually to place yourself at the disposal of the State. We are Socialists and this is the test of our Socialism. I do not want you to worry too much about every individual that may be in the Government. We could not stop to have an election; we could not stop to decide the issue. But this I am convinced of: If our Movement and our class rise with all their energy now and save the people of this country from disaster, the country will turn with confidence forever to the people who saved them.[65]

This was the core of the idea of the 'people's war'. In radical patriotic vocabulary in the nineteenth century, the people and the nation were synonyms and the well-being of both was entwined. The obstacle to national well-being had been the vested interests of 'old corruption'. Now during the Second World War it was the 'old gang' of the Conservatives who stood in the way of victory in war and the war on poverty and ill-health. While many of the propagandists saw the 'people's war' in consensual terms, as the nation pulling together, another reading of the term was that it entailed a coercive realignment of ideas of national identity. In *The Lion and the Unicorn: Socialism and the English Genius*, George Orwell suggested that the common people (the nation) had always to some extent lived against the established order, and that a revolution was necessary to ensure both that the war could be won and that socialism could be established.[66] J. B. Priestley, who was second only to Churchill in broadcasting popularity, tied patriotism firmly into the material needs of the people: 'Britain is the home of the British people . . . before anything else it is their home.'[67] He too called for radical social change. In many ways, Priestley and Churchill could be seen as complementary, one valorising the homely (the little pleasure steamers evacuating soldiers from Dunkirk), the other offering 'blood, toil, tears, and sweat', the traditional needs of patriotism.[68] Yet that there was an important political contest being fought out was clear from Churchill's desire to have Priestley prevented from broadcasting on the BBC. Labour may have served alongside Churchill in the coalition for five years, but in 1945 he returned to form and branded Labour's socialism as foreign and un-British. In the 1920s he had called Labour unfit to govern. In 1945, as the concentration camps and extermination camps were being brought within the public gaze, he said that Labour would need some form of Gestapo to implement its programme. Labour counter-attacked. Throughout the war it had stressed a democratic and working-class version of national identity, and in 1945 Attlee was well able to rebut Churchill's accusations. Socialism was British and suited to British conditions, he argued. The outcome was a landslide for the Labour Party. It won 393 seats in the House of Commons to the Conservatives' 213.

Of course, there were limits to Labour's success. It had been achieved on 48 per cent of the vote, while four in ten of those who voted had supported the Conservatives. It is also possible to note the apathy and cynicism of many people in wartime Britain.[69] Nonetheless this was a victory for Labour in a political and cultural battle. As Hartley Shawcross taunted the Tories in the Commons, 'We are the masters at the moment and for a very long time to come.'[70] Labour's patriotism did not end with the war, and between 1945 and 1951 they established new forms of Britishness in the welfare state. The new health service and *nationalised* (rather than socialised) industries were deliberately labelled 'national' or 'British'. The welfare state was seen as a welfare nation. This form of Britishness, in which the state played a role in the everyday lives of its citizens, was to remain central to a sense of political nationhood until the 1980s. There was however an element of conservatism in Labour's legislation, or lack of it.[71] Having accepted the parliamentary nature of British socialism, Labour did not seek to reform the constitution, beyond reducing the House of Lords' delaying powers to one year. Herbert Morrison, Labour minister, told

Clement Davies, the Liberal leader, that 'We should not set up something new and different from the past.'[72] Morrison's book *Government and Parliament* (1954) confirmed his respect for the constitution as it stood.[73] In 1951 the Labour government sought to confirm its Britishness through the organisation of the Festival of Britain. The Festival celebrated the past, but also aimed to modernise national identity, to give Labour a forward-looking face. The Festival was a success; there were 2,000 events throughout the country and 18 million people visited the various sites.[74] In fact Labour lost the general election of 1951 despite winning more votes that the Conservatives. Churchill was restored to Downing Street and outward-looking patriotism, signified in the imperial context of the coronation in 1953, was once more dominant.

## The politics of European identity

Since the 1950s, British politics has revolved around how to respond to economic and diplomatic decline. There have been constant attempts by both Conservative and Labour governments to maintain British global influence in the world. In many ways this has been related to a sense that Britain has something special to offer to the world, linked to a belief in British difference and even superiority.[75] As Jean Monnet, architect of European integration, said of the British position in the 1950s: 'Britain had not been conquered or invaded: she felt no need to exorcize history. Her imperial role was not yet at an end.'[76] Throughout the 1950s, 1960s, 1970s and 1980s, governments attempted to maintain the British position in relation to the superpowers. In the early 1950s this involved an attempt to restructure the Empire into the Commonwealth. Lord Salisbury, Conservative leader in the House of Lords, was convinced in 1952 that, 'We were not a continental nation. But an island power with a colonial empire.'[77] The dismantling of the Empire in the late 1950s and early 1960s was not an abandonment of Britain's world role but an effort to retain it. Certainly, British policy-makers considered the attempt successful and continued to think in imperial and global terms.[78] This effort also involved the decision to develop nuclear weapons. In 1946 Ernest Bevin, Labour foreign secretary, had convinced the Cabinet that Britain must build an atom bomb. A civil servant recalled that Bevin had concluded, 'We've got to have a bloody Union Jack flying on top of it.'[79] In 1954 Churchill confirmed this belief in Cabinet, saying 'that we could not expect to maintain our influence as a world power unless we possess the most up-to-date weapons'.[80] There was, it seems, some measure of consensus between the parties on maintaining Britain's prominent position in the world. Where the disputes came was over the relationship that Britain should have with continental western Europe, which was moving towards economic and political integration after the Second World War.[81] The divisions between and within parties have been complex and labyrinthine. In 1961, Harold Macmillan, Conservative prime minister, decided to make enquiries about the response a British application for membership of the European Economic Community would receive. The Labour Party opposed the decision, with

Hugh Gaitskell suggesting that it would be a betrayal of a thousand years of British history.[82] In 1967, the Labour government of Harold Wilson made Britain's second attempt to join. In 1973 it was again the turn of the Conservatives to try, this time successfully. In the same year, James Callaghan, a senior figure in the Labour Party, called on his party to 'defend the language of Chaucer and Shakespeare'.[83] In 1975 the Labour government held a referendum on membership of the EEC. Just over two-thirds (17.3 million people) voted to stay in, while only a third wanted Britain to withdraw. Interestingly, the highest 'pro-European' vote was in England, where 68.7 per cent voted 'yes'. In Scotland, the pro-European vote was 58.4 per cent.[84] In some ways this reflected geography rather than nationality, because south-east England, closest to the continent, had a greater pro-EEC vote than other parts of the country. In the 1980s Thatcher emerged as the leading anti-European in her party and that contributed to her downfall, yet her successor, John Major, declared that, 'I will never, come hell or high water, let our distinctive identity be lost in a Federal Europe.'[85] Such anti-European comments did reflect at least part of public opinion. In 1992, a survey suggested that while 60 per cent of Germans and 52 per cent of French people felt European often or sometimes, only 28 per cent of Britons did so.[86] Furthermore, John Major had been widely ridiculed for his speech on St George's Day 1993 which proclaimed his love of his country, 'the country of long shadows on county grounds, warm beer, dog lovers and pools fillers, and as George Orwell said, old maids bicycling to communion through morning mist . . . Britain will survive [European integration], unamendable in all its essentials.'[87] Major's focus was masculine, English and suburban and showed the difficulties Conservatives had with 'Europe'.

By the 1990s the Labour Party was more pro-European than the Conservatives. In many ways, this was related to Labour's ability to consider national identity as a changing force rather than something static and fixed. Harold Wilson had offered a 'New Britain' in the 1960s, harnessing 'the white heat of technology' to a national economic plan. His New Britain was born in the north, and wanted to clear out the stagnation of southern upper- and middle-class Britishness. When this went wrong, the Conservative response was to close down on the idea of change in national identity. Bitter industrial relations, riots, rising unemployment, a balance of payments deficit, immigration and demands for devolution in the 1970s suggested to many Conservatives that Britain was dying as a great nation. As Robert Hewison has argued, 'By the time of the Queen's Silver Jubilee in 1977, the sense of national decline and dissension was endemic.'[88] The perception of crisis was so great in the mid-1970s that the Conservatives were prepared to appoint a woman to lead their party, and the electoral success of Thatcher in 1979 can in part be related to the desire to do something about this crisis, to restore a sense of national pride. But it was a traditional concept of Britishness that was invoked by Thatcher's Conservatives.[89] It was exclusive rather than inclusive, branding trade unionists, people on benefits and some black people as 'the enemy within'.[90] This was a Britishness based firmly on Englishness and unionism. It did not allow for renegotiation of the

political discourse of national identity. Thatcher could for example state categorically that 'we are a nation whose ideals are founded on the Bible'.[91] This
provided no space for religious diversity to contribute to national identity. In
such circumstances it was difficult for many Conservative Britons to see a way
for national identity to be reconciled to European integration. Thatcherites welcomed the single European market, but not the apparent loss of sovereignty and
distinct national identity that greater steps might imply. In addition, there was
sometimes explicit hostility to Germany in the highest reaches of the party. In
1990, Nicholas Ridley publicly expressed anti-German sentiments in the *Spectator* magazine, and a meeting of eminent historians was held at Chequers to
discuss the German question.[92] This concern about Germany was shared by
increasing numbers of the British after Germany's unification. Opinion polls
showed a marked sense of distrust of the newly powerful nation. In 1986, 26 per
cent believed Germany was Britain's best friend in Europe, more than any other
country, and well ahead of France. In 1992, after unification, only 12 per cent
continued to view Germany in such a light, well below France. British memories
went back to the Second World War. In 1977, only 23 per cent believed that
there was a strong possibility of the rise of Nazism within Germany. By 1992,
53 per cent held this view.[93] The Conservatives had recognised the diversity
of identities in the United Kingdom but they had insisted that they must be
subordinate to Britishness and the sovereignty of parliament. For many Conservatives, therefore, integration in Europe meant the subordination of Britishness
to Europeanness and the loss of sovereignty. It also seemed to some of them to
offer a successful electoral strategy.

The Labour Party on the other hand had frequently been on the defensive
about its claim to Britishness. There was therefore a much greater awareness of
the fluidity of identities and about the possibilities of multiple allegiances. Before
and after the First World War, British socialists had contributed to international
socialist organisations. Such participation had been based on a belief in the plurality of national identities. It had been possible to be socialist, British and
internationalist.[94] When Tony Blair reconstructed the party as 'New Labour' he
again invoked 'New Britain', as Wilson had done before him. He argued that 'It
was always short-sighted of the Labour Party to allow the Conservatives to wrap
themselves in the national flag and to monopolize and distort the idea of patriotism.' He offered, instead, a 'patriotism of the left'.[95] This patriotism sought to
redefine the nation, making it far less narrow than the Thatcherite conception.
Anthony Giddens, 'philosopher' of the Third Way, argued that 'National identity can be a benign influence only if it is tolerant of ambivalence, or multiple
affiliation.'[96] After Labour's electoral victory in 1997, minister after minister
came out to speak about the new Britishness. Gordon Brown, for example,
described how his 'vision of Britain comes from celebrating diversity, in other
words a multiethnic and multinational Britain . . . I understand Britishness as
being outward looking, open, internationalist with a commitment to democracy
and tolerance.'[97] With the party's renewed emphasis on packaging, such discussions were described as 'Rebranding Britain' and, worse still, 'Cool Britannia'.[98]

In addition, however, there were attempts to give 'New Britain' greater intellectual support, with Mark Leonard of the Demos 'think-tank' producing *Britain: Renewing Our Identity* in 1997 and *Reclaiming Britishness* in 2002.[99] A *Guardian* leader effectively summed up the attitude of the government in relation to national identity:

> [T]he government reckons Britain has far from outlived its usefulness. For it provides an umbrella which, by its nature, covers the range of people living on these islands. Invented as a cobble-together of distinct nations, Britishness contains the very idea of difference within it. So, just as you can be Scottish and British or Welsh and British, you can now be Pakistani and British or Jewish and British without any contradiction.[100]

The Labour government has, therefore, been prepared to see national identity as a flexible and inclusive concept, more able to accommodate diversity. It has enabled the Blair government to renegotiate the terms of the Union. Yet not all aspects of Blair's thinking relate to newness. There are some remarkably old-fashioned tones to several of Blair's statements. His summation of Britishness might suggest dynamism and innovation, but in addition it does rest on a particular view of the British past. He told the Labour Party conference in 1996 to:

> Consider a thousand years of British history and what it tells us. The first parliament in the world. The industrial revolution ahead of its time. An empire, the largest the world has ever known. The invention of virtually every scientific device in the modem world. Two world wars in which our country was bled dry, in which two generations perished, but which in its defeat of the most evil force ever let loose by man showed the most sustained example of bravery in human history. Our characteristics? Common sense. Standing up for the underdog. Fiercely independent.[101]

Blair's speech provides an example of the way in which British national identity in the second half of the twentieth century could still rely on the familiar themes of a traditional Britishness, on the 'uniqueness' of Britain in its economic and scientific development, in its role in the world wars, and slipped in here, with no condemnation, indeed with implicit approval, is Britain's imperial past. Blair managed to combine patriotism with willingness to integrate the United Kingdom more closely with the European Union. This was an easier task for Labour, a party that had always had internationalist pretensions, than for the Conservatives.

National identity has been a site of political struggle in Britain throughout the late nineteenth and twentieth centuries. Since the 1870s the political right has sought to claim patriotism as its own, and for most of the period until the 1990s it succeeded. There were intervals when the left was able to make good its own claim, as the Liberals did between 1906 and 1914, and as Labour did in the Second World War, briefly after 1964, and again after 1997. But there have been limits to this contest. The mainstream political parties have all adhered to a notion of British history that sees parliamentary government as central, and that has desired the continuation of the United Kingdom. The main difference has been in relation to the extent to which the Union and with it British national identity can be adapted to meet the needs of other identities within the nation.

# 6  A new way of being British
## Ethnicity and Britishness

For many people the greatest challenge to Britishness since the late 1940s has been black immigration. Enoch Powell was well supported in the late 1960s as he made a series of speeches expressing the racism of many white people in Britain.[1] Powell saw black immigration as destructive of the very existence of Britain:

> We must be mad [he said], literally mad, as a nation to be permitting the annual inflow of some 50,000 dependants, who are for the most part the material of the future growth of the immigrant-descended population. It is like watching a nation busily engaged in heaping up its own funeral pyre.[2]

It is noteworthy here that Powell saw the 'problem' as one not only of immigration but also of 'second generation immigrants', the sons and daughters of those who had actually travelled to Britain.[3] Now there are increasing numbers of 'third-generation immigrants'. All of these have faced the battle over national identity in their day-to-day lives, with questioning not only of their Britishness but also of their right to residence in the United Kingdom. At one extreme, in the five years between 1976 and 1981, thirty-one black people were murdered for reason only of their skin colour.[4] In 1986, one in four black residents of the London borough of Newham reported that they had experienced racist harassment *in the previous twelve months*. In 1993 official statistics recorded more than 130,000 racial attacks each year.[5] A major issue that has faced black and Asian people living in Britain is whether they can combine identities to be black and British, Asian and British or British and Muslim. This is a two-sided question. First, have immigrants and their descendants sought to identify themselves as British, in the sense of an allegiance rather than just through the act of residence? Here the term 'British' is used to include the potential for a sense of Englishness, Welshness, Scottishness and Northern Irishness, although of course none of these latter identities is a detached category. In a study of black identities in the late 1960s, two social investigators interviewed a 'black Welshman'. Born in Port Talbot, his father was from Ghana and his mother's parents had been Portuguese and Welsh. He was an actor who did not want to play the parts of immigrants offered to him, since, he said, 'I can't do a West Indian accent. I'm a black Englishman.'[6] The second part of the question is whether 'white Britons' have accepted the adoption of black, Asian and other hyphenated British identities, and importantly, whether conditions are attached to this acceptance. In response to both parts of the question, of course, individuals have adopted a range of positions, which themselves can change according to context. Some migrants and their descendants retain an exclusive sense of their original national (or other) identities, not least because some migrants are 'pushed' from their former homes rather than 'pulled' towards the United Kingdom, and the attitude to their residence is that it is temporary. Other migrants and their descendants have seen it as natural to identify themselves as British, in whatever combination of identities. Examples are provided by an early study of post-war migration to Britain. Jerzy Zubrzycki identified three main responses to the migration experiences of the Polish in the years immediately after the Second World War: assimilation, accommodation and conflict. Jan Kowalski, a member of the Polish intelligentsia who had found his way to Britain during the war and had served in the Polish army, was disillusioned by the defeat of Poland and its subordination to the Soviet Union and hence explained how 'I have . . . adapted myself wholly to British ways of life . . . After all – I eat their bread. Once I earn my living in this country – why should I stick to my pre-war national loyalties.'[7] Franciszek B. explained that he admired the English, but remained Polish, accommodating himself to Britain rather than assimilating into its ways. In part, this was because of the response he met from English friends, 'who have known me for a long time [but] very often instruct me in a very paternal manner about the a, b, c, of what is called "The British Way of Living"'.[8] The third form was conflict, expressed in the attempted suicide of 'Maria', who had migrated from a displaced persons' camp and been employed within an English family who not only were unkind to her but whose irreligious behaviour she found unacceptable.[9] 'White Britons', too, have adopted different attitudes towards non-white and immigrant people in Britain. Some have committed terrible crimes, of violence through attacks and abuse, and of indignity, through discrimination in housing, employment and leisure. Others have been indifferent. Still others have formed friendships and loving relationships. Mavis Stewart, who came to London from Jamaica in 1954 to be a nurse, recorded the variety of responses:

> We had learnt to think of England as the mother country so I thought I was leaving one home and going to another . . . Some patients would say: 'Take your black hands off me' or ignore you outside the hospital, but that wasn't the whole story. There were some nasty people and some who were nice. You could go into a newsagent's or grocer's shop or get on a bus and they wouldn't take your money because you were a nurse and they appreciated you.[10]

Social scientists have been concerned to try to measure the frequency of these various responses. One such example was the 'Colour and Citizenship' survey in the 1960s conducted by E. J. B. Rose and Nicholas Deakin. Through a complex questionnaire they concluded that

> [I]n the five boroughs, which have relatively high proportions of coloured children in their schools, over one-third of all white adults expressed views with no trace, or practically no trace, of hostility to coloured people; and almost another two-fifths seemed to be strongly disposed in the direction of tolerance. At the other extreme there emerged 10% of the white population whose antipathy to coloured people was almost unconditional.[11]

The issues of allegiance and acceptance impact upon each other. Immigrants and their descendants have recognised the hostility to them, and for some this has resulted in a rejection of Britishness. In turn, many 'white Britons' have looked for some sort of test of loyalty to impose on those they perceive as alien. In the First World War, Jewish men were under severe pressure to join the army to 'prove' that they were Britons first and Jews second. As well as Tebbit suggesting a cricket test, questioning whether Britons of West Indian, Indian or Pakistani heritage supported England or not in international cricket matches, David Blunkett, the New Labour Home Secretary in 'New Britain', which has sought to embrace cultural diversity, has suggested the implementation of 'light touch' naturalisation tests which suggest conformity to a normative Britishness. These ideas were supported by the 'Life in the United Kingdom' advisory panel, chaired by Professor Sir Bernard Crick, a champion of a definition of Britishness based on citizenship, which suggested that those applying to be British should show progress in learning English (or another native language) as well as an awareness of British history.[12]

   This chapter explores the tremendous range of relationships between ethnicity and Britishness in the United Kingdom since 1870. Its title comes from Hanif Kureishi, author of *The Buddha of Suburbia* (1990). His decision that 'a new way of being British' was needed applied not to black and Asian people: 'It is the British, the white British, who have to learn that being British isn't what it was. Now it is a complex thing, involving new elements.'[13] This chapter examines the experiences of the diverse population of the United Kingdom in relation to national identity over the last century. It is necessary before further discussion to point out that some of the terminology used can obscure the nature of ethnicity in Britain. Being black and white are not 'discrete categories'.[14] Ethnic groups are not self-enclosed, exclusive and unchanging. A working definition of ethnicity is that it entails a belief in some sort of cultural distinctiveness, or 'an identification based on shared cultural traits'.[15] This means that ethnicities are not fixed, as in the late nineteenth century it was presumed that 'races' were. Neither have there been clear-cut 'communities' in Britain since 1870, of the Irish and the British, of the Jew and the Gentile, of black and white, of the English and the others. Often, these have been 'imagined' communities, their existence emerging from a collective sense of identification. But the categories to which people have assigned themselves have not been separated rigidly along 'ethnic' lines. A white youth in

Southall described himself to researchers as belonging to 'English black' culture, expressing a sense of hybridity, an extremely useful concept for understanding multi-cultural Britain since 1870 (and before).[16]

Discussions of the relationship between national identity and immigration have tended to concentrate on post-Second World War experience of black and Asian immigration and descendancy. This chapter, however, will aim to place this experience both in the historical context of the continuity of immigration and by looking at the variety of 'waves' of incoming people. The main theme will be the discourse on British national identity that has continued since the late nineteenth century. It examines the continuities and varieties of the multi-ethnic nature of the United Kingdom and the debates in which this has resulted. After a brief narrative of migration and ethnic diversity before 1945 it will turn its attention to the responses of the 'host' population, not least because the assumption that 'You know who you are, *only* by knowing who you are not' is untenable.[17] This sentence could more usefully be turned around to read 'You know who you are not, by knowing who you are.' This explains better the way in which stereotypes have been constructed which, in many cases, have sought to exclude 'the others' from Britishness. It will be argued that when mass black and Asian immigration began in the 1940s, 1950s and 1960s, many Britons were already prepared to use racial categories to define Britishness. It will also discuss the role of the state in guarding the borders of the nation and national identity, and the tensions between immigration laws based on skin colour and 'race relations' legislation designed to enforce equality. Finally, the chapter will discuss the range of identities adopted by immigrants and their descendants. There is sometimes the tendency to see discourses of national identity being conducted only by the 'host' population, thereby excluding immigrants and their descendants from any historical agency. This discussion of identities will suggest that, far from being passive, it has been black and Asian people who have forced 'white Britons' to consider 'new ways of being British'.

## Continuities and varieties before 1945

It has become almost commonplace to stress in historiography that the United Kingdom is a nation of immigrants and their descendants. Hence, the historian Zig Layton-Henry has explained that

> Throughout its history Britain, especially England, has been a destination for immigrants and refugees. Early invaders, like the Angles, Jutes, Saxons, Danes, Norwegians and Normans, were attracted by hopes of booty and fertile land. Later immigrants, like the Flemings, Germans, Walloons and Dutch, were often invited . . . or were fleeing religious or political persecution.[18]

Likewise, Peter Fryer, in his excellent book *Staying Power*, begins by citing the evidence for African soldiers being stationed on Hadrian's Wall, thereby establishing that black people were in Britain before the English.[19] Rozina Visram has established that there is a 400-year history of Asians in Britain.[20] This is rigorous history being used to challenge what Tony Kushner has described as 'a pathological chronology . . . starting with the arrival of the *Empire Windrush* in 1948'.[21] Immigration has been an ongoing process in the British Isles, accompanied by waves of emigration. The island nature of 'Britain' has meant that it has stood at the intersection of sea routes, which has meant that its population has been as fluid as the sea that surrounds 'this sceptr'd isle'. Between 1815 and 1930, 11.4 million people emigrated from the British Isles, with about one-third of these eventually returning. This has been accompanied by a tremendous variety of migrations to the United Kingdom. The 1901 census revealed that more than a million people living in Britain had been born elsewhere (with just over half of these having been born in Ireland).[22]

In the late nineteenth century, the two major groups of immigrants were the Irish and east European Jews.[23] Given that the census recorded place of birth, it is fairly easy to establish the number of those born in Ireland who lived in England, Wales and Scotland. In 1871, the 566,540 Irish-born people constituted 2.5 per cent of the population of England and Wales. In 1931, there were 381,089 Irish-born people living in England and Wales.[24] In Scotland, the numbers were lower, but the proportions were higher. In 1891, there were 194,807 Irish-born people in Scotland, forming 4.8 per cent of the population. In 1931, there were 124,296 or 2.6 per cent.[25] By 1900, though, the 'culturally Irish' rather than the 'born Irish' were forming an increasing majority of the Irish Catholic population in England and Wales, and the children of Irish immigrants are not recorded as such in the census.[26] It has been said of the Irish in Britain that they occupied 'a curious middle place' in society, neither fully Irish nor British.[27] The proximity of Ireland meant that many of these migrants were temporary, working seasonally in Britain, migrating and remigrating, retaining links with rural Ireland but forming links with urban England, Scotland and Wales. In the nineteenth and twentieth centuries, social commentators such as Friedrich Engels and J. B. Priestley condemned the Irish as creators of slums, dwelling in 'Little Irelands' or 'Fenian Barracks'.[28] This sense of segregation in urban ghettos suggests a feeling of Irish community and identity, separate, distinct and opposed to those of the English, Welsh and Scottish in the same cities. In 1880, O'Connor Power, an Irish nationalist, remarked that the hostility of the British and the pride of the Irish combined to prevent 'the slightest tendency to amalgamation with those around them'.[29] In Liverpool, T. P. O'Connor was elected as Irish nationalist MP at every general election between 1885 and 1929, signifying a sense of political difference, at least among the Liverpool Catholic Irish. On his retirement, he was replaced in 1929 by David Logan, a former Irish nationalist councillor who represented the seat for Labour until the 1960s. But O'Connor also served as chief censor for the British Board of Film Censors. His conservative Irish Catholicism could be turned to the service of British morality. British cities saw the establishment of Irish cultural and political organisations; there were 1,500 members of the Gaelic League in London in

1902, for example.[30] Certainly, some Irish immigrants and their descendants maintained a sense of different and oppositional identity to the English. Anne Higgins recalled:

> We were under a kind of siege being Irish Catholics in Manchester in the thirties and forties . . . I suppose it was our accents but mainly our religion that set us apart from the rest . . . We had the Holy Days of Obligation and St Patrick's Day. They had Empire Day and Guy Fawkes Day and you would go and look through the railing of the local C of E school when they were having fun and games which you were a bit jealous of but at the same time despised. My mother would never let us, even if we could have afforded the uniform, join the Girl Guides or Boy Scouts because that was English and protestant as far as she was concerned . . . Because people were anti-Catholic and anti-Irish, you tended to go out of your way to assert the fact that you were proud of being Irish and Catholic whenever the opportunity arose . . . My religion, political beliefs and national identity were all inter-related when I was a child.[31]

Higgins was identifying the formation of a host community as well as her alienation from it, and in turn the assertion of her own Irishness. This does not provide the whole picture however. Recent research has suggested that the Irish in Britain were 'not wholly isolated from the host community, since even at a very local level where Irish immigrants dominated particular streets and courts and squares, they were seldom shut off or very distant from the native population'.[32] Another historian has noted how 'successive generations simply merged into the anonymous background of English and Scottish urban life'.[33] Of course, many descendants of Irish immigrants continued to consider themselves Irish, but it was a different kind of Irishness, often relating only to important occasions such as St Patrick's Day and Whit marches, to christenings, confirmations, marriages and funerals. But even in its contact with the Catholic Church, the tendency was recognition of the amalgamation of the Irish and British, since the Catholic hierarchy in England felt insecure in a country whose identity had been formulated from Protestantism and anti-Catholicism. The response of the Catholic Church was to stress its own Englishness and patriotism.[34]

The experience of the Irish before 1945, therefore, has shown the array of conflict and negotiation about the place of the migrants in British society and national identity. So too did the experience of Jewish migrants. Persecution of Jews in eastern Europe raised the Jewish population of Britain from around 60,000 before the 1880s to 300,000 by the First World War.[35] The experience of Jews in this period confirms that ethnic groups have not simply formed 'communities'.[36] Many of the migrants from eastern Europe saw themselves as refugees looking for temporary asylum, not as immigrants seeking to establish new lives. Some involved themselves in revolutionary politics, aimed at overthrowing the tsarist state in Russia, after which they would return. In addition, the majority could speak little or no English, dressed visibly differently from other people in Britain, and sought to ease the trauma of their migration through living in areas already inhabited by previous Jewish migrants. Some of the features of such migratory experience are captured by Lew Grade (Louis Winogradsky), the television producer, who migrated from Russia to Britain as a child in 1912:

> I have no memory of our upheaval at all. But on the few occasions I have heard my mother talk about the journey . . . to London, she spoke about the hazards involved and how unpleasant it had all been . . . We were met at the docks by my father . . . our first lodgings were in Brick Lane, in the East End. We were just one of the many Jewish immigrant families living in that area, and my initial impressions of the area were not good . . . For the first time in our lives we were really poor, and, on top of this, I could barely make myself understood because all I could speak was Russian.[37]

It is noteworthy here that the solution to this linguistic isolation adopted by the Winogradsky family in the first instance was to learn Yiddish rather than English. The immigrants were frequently poor and very 'foreign', and this caused concern to the more cohesive Anglo-Jewish community, which had adopted an important sense of Britishness in conjunction with their Jewish identity. They did often, however, feel extremely precarious about their acceptance within British society and attempted to Anglicise the new arrivals in order to temper hostility to immigration. One method by which this was attempted was through the Jewish Lads' Brigade, a youth movement on the model of the (Anglican) Church Lads' Brigade and (Nonconformist) Boys' Brigade.[38] The JLB believed there was a particular form of Britishness, associated with modest behaviour and military discipline. Hence, Dyan Hyamson urged the boys of Manchester JLB 'at all times to be quiet in dress, manner and tone, and concluded by pointing out that one could at the same time be a good Jew and a good Englishman'.[39] Jews had in any case been displaying dual identities. When London celebrated the relief of Mafeking from the Boer siege in May 1900, Jews in East London were reported by the *Jewish Chronicle* as taking a full part:

> The greatest display of flags was however in [Brick] 'Lane.' Every stall, every barrow had its flag. One could get 'Mafeking fish,' 'Mafeking oranges' and 'Mafeking lemons,' cakes l'kovod Mafeking and what not. Everything was being sold in honour of Mafeking and, every minute or so, one could hear patriotic airs sung and played; the Yiddish bands . . . being greatly in demand, and reaping a 'coppery' harvest for their selection of patriotic music. All were happy. The sentence 'Mafeking is relieved,' was like an abracadabra, opening the way to joy, levelling rich and poor, ending the terrible anxiety. 'Mafeking relieved. Mazzeltov, Mazzeltov.'[40]

Here, then, were the horizontal divisions of class and the vertical divisions of ethnicity being overcome through patriotic celebration. The success of the JLB, measured in its own terms, was that 535 of its 5,000 members died fighting for king and country during the First World War.[41] The assimilation of Jews, however, led to their decreasing visibility, which in turn led some opponents of immigration to harden their attitudes to the essential 'racial' differences of the Jews from the British.[42]

While the Irish and the Jews formed the largest groups of immigrants, there were many other sizable groups in the United Kingdom before the Second World War. There were Italians, French, Spaniards, Greeks, Indians, Africans and West Indians, who had migrated to Britain for a tremendous variety of reasons. London and Cardiff were the most cosmopolitan cities, but many other urban areas of the United Kingdom had fair-sized foreign minorities. Sometimes, immigrants did form 'communities', such as Jews in the Leyland area of Leeds or the Chinese in Limehouse. In other places, immigrants and their families were sprinkled more thinly. In 1941, a Mass-Observation report described Tiger Bay in Cardiff as 'a cosmopolitan community representative of nearly every nation on earth'. From the numbers registered for employment, Mass-Observation sought to categorise these people. Of those they considered 'foreign white', there were seventy-six Maltese, twenty-eight Portuguese, fourteen Irish and thirteen other 'varieties'. They described also a coloured population, of one hundred Arabs, eighty-four Africans, fifty-six West Indians, twenty-six Jamaicans, twenty-four Indians, eight black people from Great Britain, seven South Americans and six Japanese. Being in Tiger Bay, Mass-Observation reported, was 'like being in some foreign and far away town'.[43] The British Board of Film Censors agreed, for when in 1933 Wyndham Films sought to make a feature film about the area the censors insisted that it should not be set in South Wales. The story was relocated to a South American port and was passed by the censors.[44] Surely, though, this equation of variety was only possible in a port town of a global maritime nation. Laura Tabili, in her study of the political demands of these black seafarers and the response of employers, trade unions and the state to them, has pointed out the logic for discussions of post-war relations. She argues that 'Attributing [post-war black people's] problems to unfamiliarity ignores their centuries of life and work in Britain.'[45] There has, therefore, been a wide diversity of people living in the United Kingdom since 1870 and before. These diverse groups of people experienced diverse responses from the people already living in Britain. They were not all treated the same, but the majority did all experience the variety of responses, spreading from welcome through lack of concern to overt hostility. In each of these cases there were implications for how the 'host' population viewed the national identity of the migrants and their descendants.

Stereotypes were constructed for each different group. These could be malign or benign, but they were stereotypes nonetheless. David Feldman has outlined the stereotypes for Jews and Irish in late nineteenth-century London: 'the Jewish immigrant was described as temperate, moderate and self-controlled. The caricature of the Irish immigrant "Paddy" was the reverse of the Jew.'[46] Often, however, all immigrants and foreigners were branded together. Immigrants were seen as criminal, as competitors for work and as a danger to British women.[47] They were also seen as unwilling to integrate into British society. In 1909, Judge Rentoul lectured in London on 'The British Empire: Its Greatness, Glory and Freedom'. He described a week sitting at the Old Bailey and told his audience that 'Three-fourths of the cases tried were those of aliens of the very worst type in their own country. He had in mind before him the Russian burglar, the Polish thief, the Italian stabber and the German swindler.'[48] Tom King, MP for Lowestoft, addressing a mass meeting at Great Yarmouth in 1914, described how 'The Chinaman ate rice with a knitting needle, while a Britisher wanted meat and a knife and fork, he clothed himself with a loin cloth while the Britisher wanted a suit of clothes; and he lived in a nest, while a Britisher wanted a house.' It was this that enabled Chinese seafarers, he implied, to undercut the wages of the Britisher.[49] In this latter example, it is clear that hostile images of immigrants were used in contrast to the perceived characteristics of the British. Immigrants were also seen as threatening to British women, biological carriers of the British stock. Before 1914, Jews were seen as responsible for the 'white slave trade' in young girls, and the *Liverpool Courier* condemned relationships between Chinese men and British women:

> It is with shock that one sees such names as Mary Chung or Norman Sing . . . It is the ambition of a Chinaman to mate with an English girl, and his Oriental wit and passion is directed to this end . . . The propagation of half-bred Chinese and English in Liverpool is not a matter to be treated lightly . . . As a rule the son of Chinese and English parents is very low down in the scale of morality. Such a degraded type should not be allowed to grow up in our midst to be a source of contamination and further degradation for generations ahead.[50]

In 1933, the British Board of Film Censors banned Frank Capra's *The Bitter Tea of General Yen* across the British Empire because it dealt with the love of a Chinese warlord for a white woman.[51] This criticism extended beyond condemnation of the relationship in the short term to assigning it with destructive force for the nation in the future.

In 1946, Mass-Observation conducted 180 interviews on anti-Semitism. Of those interviewed, 45 per cent declared themselves to be 'definitely' or 'slightly' anti-Semitic. Following perceptions of economic competition and power over the country, the third reason given for hostility was Jewish 'clannishness'.[52] Hostility towards immigrants on the basis of their deliberate separation from British society has been frequent.

In each of these cases, immigrants were constructed as being responsible for the hostility that they received. This hostility ranged from minor, though no less degrading, day-to-day antagonism to more occasional outbursts of mass violence. These acts, big and small, categorised immigrants and their descendants as non-British. In a collection of essays that examines racial violence against the

Irish, Germans, black people, Italians and Jews, Panikos Panayi has correctly argued that 'No newcomers who have entered Britain in the last two centuries have escaped hostility on a significant scale.'[53] Throughout the nineteenth century there were anti-Irish riots, made all the more newsworthy because many Irish people refused to accept such attacks without fighting back. There were anti-Jewish riots in Leeds in 1901 and South Wales in 1911. Also in 1911, every Chinese laundry in Cardiff had its windows broken on a single night.[54] During the First World War, there were riots against Germans (and other foreign people) living in Britain, as well as against Russian Jews who refused to fight a war allied to tsarist Russia, which was of course responsible for their original emigration. Anti-black rioting occurred in 1919, as long-term enmity combined with increased competition for employment in the aftermath of war led to violence involving thousands of white people in Cardiff, Liverpool, Tyneside, Glasgow and elsewhere. In these riots, one-third of those arrested had Irish surnames, confirming that divisions were not between two homogenous groups of the British and the others.[55] In the 1930s, British Fascists continued the 'tradition' of day-to-day harassment of Jews. The Second World War, so often seen as different from the First, as a fight against Fascism and for freedom, was not without its anti-foreign violence within Britain. The war did little to increase tolerance, even though German intolerance was seen as one of the things against which Britain was fighting. One woman, the wife of the head of a company specialising in international relations, told Mass-Observation that 'I can't stand the sight of foreigners. I loathe the look of them and the sound of their voices.'[56] In June 1940, when Italy entered the war at Britain's lowest point, there were anti-Italian riots in Soho and elsewhere. A 'middle-aged working-class woman', watching the window breaking, displayed the connections between antipathy towards different foreign people:

'After they've cleared out the Italians, they'll clear out the Jews' she said[.] 'You'll see – and a good job too. I ask you why these foreigners be here, why should they be employed, and so many English out of work. It isn't right, is it? . . . make no mistake about *that*, we're going to win this war, after that it's going to be England for the English.'[57]

Of course, such hostility did not apply equally to all foreigners. Mass-Observation reported two other comments of note in its reports on national identity and attitudes to foreign peoples, whether allies or enemies. In April 1943, it was reported that 73 per cent were favourable to the Dutch, because:

The Dutch are more often thought to be like the English people than any other group of foreigners. Their dependability, sturdiness and toughness are highly praised; they are thought to be truly democratic in outlook, and a large number of people praise the administration of the Dutch Crown colonies.[58]

Here a foreign people was constructed not as 'other' to the British, but as similar to them because of their democracy and imperialism. Sometimes similarities were emphasised over differences, as with the belief that North Americans were somehow not foreign.

## The Second World War and the national community

The Second World War is often seen as having made 'scientific racism' untenable, though it certainly did not cure people of overtly racial statements that suggested the desire to treat all people of particular nationalities with extreme measures. In May 1945, as the Nazi murder camps were being publicised to the British people, Mass-Observation once more measured people's responses. A skilled male worker aged fifty gave his response to the 'German atrocities':

> Pretty disgusted with it, that's how I feel. What's more I'm very glad such facts have been brought to light. The Germans have a sadistic trait in them, and delight in the sufferings of other races. If you'll pardon my saying so, and I'm loathe to say what I'm going to say to a lady, but my feelings on this are very strong indeed – The only way to punish them is to castrate every prisoner of war before he's released. Destroy the German race once and for all. Every healthy German citizen, man and woman, is a potential breeder of a future army in the making.[59]

The Second World War found Britain divided by a decade of depression and unemployment, gave it purpose and created a national community. Of course, much of this is myth, but it has been a powerful myth nonetheless.[60] It is a myth that foregrounds homogeneity, community, pulling together and standing alone against the might of Nazi-dominated Europe. The divisions of class, region and gender were overcome, it is suggested, and the nation not only survived six years of war, longer than any other belligerent, but emerged triumphant.[61] Films such as *Millions Like Us* (1943) and *The Gentle Sex* (1943) represented the contribution of women from all parts of the United Kingdom and from all classes to the nation. The stoicism of the people in the blitzed cities and the bravery of a conscript army transformed the position of the working class. As Chris Waters has argued, 'formerly "a race apart," workers were rapidly transformed into "the British common people," taking up their new, and now apparently rightful, place in the national community'.[62] Alistair Bonnett has extended this interpretation to the transformation of the working class from marginal to 'whiteness' to central to constructions of ethnic homogeneity.[63] He points out that social commentators in the late nineteenth century had investigated the working class and discussed them as 'darkest England' in parallel to consideration of 'darkest Africa'. Whiteness had been associated with the ruling of the Empire, but this had been the role of upper- and middle-class men, whose claim to whiteness was impeccable. The working class had been constructed as dark-skinned, hence the shock of Lord Milner when he witnessed

English soldiers washing during the First World War: 'I never knew the working class had such white skins.'[64] There are of course problems with this interpretation, not least that the Labour Party, which saw itself as British and working class, had asserted the centrality of the working class to the nation since its foundation.[65] The Second World War might be seen as the confirmation of Labour's assertion. In 1945, for the first time, the majority of the working class voted Labour, and this can be seen as an act of patriotic class consciousness. The outcome was the creation of the welfare state that itself became a symbol of Britishness. This was 'welfare wrapped in the Union Jack'.[66] In subsequent years, immigrants would be portrayed by many as parasites on the welfare nation.[67] The Second World War constructed the 'people' as socially and ethnically homogenous, not just in the 1940s but also across the decades since. David Cesarani has accurately described the significance of the myth of the war:

> The resonances of war in British national identity continue to divide the population along racial lines. Thousands of West Indians and Indians served in the British armed forces in 1939–45, but this fact hardly registers in public memory of the war . . . The war is taken to evoke the British at their best, the qualities of Churchill's 'island race' . . . It helps construct a sense of nation and nationality that excludes the bulk of post-1945 immigrants.[68]

As Cesarani points out here, there is some demythologising to be undertaken. When Britain 'stood alone' it was an empire rather than a nation standing alone. Eight thousand West Indians joined the British armed forces between 1939 and 1945. Two-thirds of the 500 men entering Britain on the *Empire Windrush* in 1948 had served in Britain during the war. The British government produced a pamphlet called *West Indies towards Victory*, illustrated to show the skin colour of those fighting for the Empire. In 1943, the Ministry of Information made a film called *West Indies Calling*, in which Caribbean people, including the well-known Trinidadian cricketer Learie Constantine, detailed the West Indian contribution to the war effort.[69] Many male West Indian children born during and after the war were named 'Winston' in displays of patriotism.[70] Many Indians served in the merchant navy and in war factories in Britain, so that the Indian population of Birmingham and Coventry was around 900 in 1943. That the police referred to these Indians as 'a problem' reveals that the reception of dark-skinned imperial subjects was not always welcoming, even in wartime.[71]

The Second World War, therefore, encouraged migration at the same time as it created a new sense of a socially cohesive British identity. When black and Asian migration began in greater numbers in the 1940s, 1950s and 1960s, many of the British had already constructed a sense of their identity against which the 'other' would be compared.

## Numbers and 'the other' in affluent Britain

There has always been an attempt to inject an element of reasonableness into arguments for the exclusion of immigrants from British society and Britishness. Sir Wintringham Stable, a retired judge, told Welshpool Conservative Club in September 1970 that:

> I have not the slightest colour prejudice but I think England and Wales and Scotland are the homelands of their nationals. Of course we can absorb a certain number of strangers but it is absolutely impossible to absorb the vast number of immigrants we have let in. And the reason is that they do not want to be absorbed. What do people calling themselves multi-racialists really envisage in 100 years' time? A sort of hybrid race?[72]

The judge explained his desire to exclude in two ways. First, that there were too many immigrants to be 'absorbed' into Britishness, and second, that the immigrants did not want to be British anyway. In both cases, the problems rested with the immigrants. The 1971 census revealed that 6.6 per cent of the population resident in Britain had been born elsewhere.[73] Of course, not all these people were black or immigrants. The Irish remained the largest, but least visible, immigrant group in Britain, but there were increasing numbers of scare stories about the invasion and swamping of Britain by black and Asian people from Britain's former Empire. Powell, in 1968, used numbers as one of the main thrusts of his argument:

> In 15 or 20 years, on present trends, there will be in this country three and a half million Commonwealth immigrants and their descendants . . . [By] the year 2000 . . . it must be in the region of five to seven million, approximately one-tenth of the whole population . . . Whole areas, towns and parts of towns will be occupied by sections of immigrants and immigrant-descended population.[74]

Here again the threat posed by numbers of immigrants and their descendants was presented as a menace to the demography of the United Kingdom, with the implication that something culturally British was being injured, probably fatally. This implied an appeal to reason, particularly when combined with suggestions that Britain was a small island and had become overcrowded. The response of people of common sense was, therefore, that Britishness was a finite collective identity and could not accommodate all of these immigrants. The problem was, therefore, the immigrants. The solution was presented as the restriction of numbers. Tom Driberg, Labour Party chairman in the early 1960s, however, refuted the logic of this argument. He told the TUC that

> People talk about a colour problem arising in Britain. How can there be a colour problem here? Even after all the immigration of the past few years,

there are only 190,000 coloured people in our population of over 50 million – that is, only four out of every 1,000. The real problem is not black skins, but white prejudice.[75]

The discussion in the early part of this chapter has shown that a normative ideal of Britishness had been composed across the late nineteenth and early twentieth centuries. It did not rely on the arrival of black and Asian immigrants in the years after 1945 to become delineated definitively. Britishness was not constructed in opposition to 'the other', with the British only knowing who they were by knowing that they were not black. In many ways, indeed mainly, 'the other' has been constructed because the British had already decided what constituted their identity. As Bikhu Parekh has explained:

> It is wrong to suggest that my identity consists in my difference from others. I differ from them because I am already constituted in a certain way, not the other way round. My differences from them are derivative from and not constitutive of my identity.[76]

Of course, it might be argued that, given that the British Isles have had such a long history of immigration, the process of constitution began with the first waves of immigration and the issue is whether the chicken of national identity came before the egg of otherness. Sheila Patterson, in her study of West Indians in Brixton in the 1960s, argued that in an 'insular, conservative homogenous society – mild xenophobia or antipathy to outsiders would appear to be a cultural norm. It is extended in varying degrees to all outsiders, to Poles and coloured people, and to people from the next village or street.'[77] Setting aside the obvious point that the process of mass urbanisation in Britain since the eighteenth century seriously undermines Patterson's suggestion about insularity, she suggests that antipathy is the product of the newcomers' difference. The process of immigration was, therefore, long term and the 'British' had responded to each wave. The change in nature of the post-war migration, she argued, was that 'The coloured migrant, and particularly the Negro, appears to be the supreme and ultimate stranger.'[78] Difference, and particularly that of skin colour, was therefore seen as a problem in itself because it challenged the presumption of homogeneity and rigidity associated with Britishness.

Racism, hostility to black and Asian people and the belief that British national identity would be fundamentally damaged by their arrival in Britain pre-dated mass immigration. In 1948, a Royal Commission examining a perception of population shortage and labour scarcity asserted that immigration 'could only be welcomed without reserve if the immigrants were of good human stock and were not prevented by their religion or race from intermarrying with the host population and becoming merged in it'.[79] This goes a long way to explaining why the much larger migration of Poles and Irish in the early post-war period was not greeted by the same extent of enmity as black and Asian migration, though this is in no way to deny the hostility that both Polish and

Irish people experienced. It becomes clear that the issue is not one of numbers, especially given that from the late 1940s to the early 1970s the British economy, whatever its problems, was able to provide virtually full employment and increasing spending on social services. Given the age structure of the immigrant population, their demands on the welfare state were disproportionately small. In localised areas, there was continuing poverty, overcrowding and lack of opportunity, but racism and racial violence were not confined solely to those areas. The problem, as Driberg argued, was one of white prejudice, and the belief that black people should be excluded from Britishness.

## Keeping Britain white: the politics of exclusion

In Britain, the politics of racism have often been a function of defending a particular form of exclusive and racialised Britishness. This politics is often seen as the product of marginal, extremist or maverick politicians, who have adhered to the slogan 'There ain't no black in the Union Jack.'[80] Hence before the First World War, the British Brothers' League, with 40,000 members mainly concentrated in the East End of London, and a few Conservative MPs can be seen as having responsibility for the passing of the Aliens Act of 1905, which sought to prevent the entry of Jewish immigrants, though of course they had to secure the acquiescence of a majority of MPs.[81] Between the wars, the British Union of Fascists and other anti-Semitic groups are seen as chiefly responsible for hostility to immigrants. In the post-war period, there have been many derivatives of neo-Fascist and racist organisations, such as Mosley's Union Movement, the League of Empire Loyalists and the National Front, founded in 1967.[82] The NF wanted 'to preserve our British native stock in the United Kingdom . . . by terminating non-white immigration, with humane and orderly repatriation of non-white immigrants (and their dependants)'.[83] Then there were the maverick MPs, usually, but not always, Conservative. In the late 1950s, Cyril Osborne broke the apparent consensus of silence on the issue of immigration, demanding restrictions.[84] In 1964, Peter Griffiths, Conservative candidate, fought and won the election in Smethwick on the slogan 'If you want a nigger neighbour vote Labour.'[85] From the late 1960s to his death in 1998, the most notorious of all 'mavericks', Enoch Powell, railed against immigrants and their descendants. His chief concern was a racialised conception of cultural Britishness. It was impossible, he argued, for black people to become English. As he put it in 1968 (but not in the 'rivers of blood speech): 'the West Indian does not by being born in England become an Englishman. In law, he becomes a United Kingdom citizen by birth, in fact he is a West Indian or an Asian still.'[86] In 1989, faced with the potential for the migration of many Hong Kong Chinese when the colony reverted to China at the end of Britain's 'lease', Peter Townsend, the Conservative MP for Bridlington, declared that 'England must be recaptured for the English.'[87] There are many other examples of these outbursts, but despite their frequency the impression given is that they are the unfortunate outcomes of living in a society that prides itself on free speech. Hence the condemnation of racism is used to strengthen a version of Britishness that emphasises tolerance and decency, sidestepping the issue of racism in the speeches.[88]

The racist politics of the far right and the mavericks have had an impact on more mainstream discourses on national identity. Cause and effect can be recognised in the election of Griffiths in Smethwick, when the swing nationally was towards Labour, and the Wilson government's tightening of immigration restrictions in 1965. Again, while the Conservative leader moved swiftly to sack Powell from the shadow cabinet, the Conservatives under Heath stressed their anti-immigration stance in the 1970 general election. Powell had anyway pointed out that voluntary repatriation was official party policy. In 1977, the National Front secured 120,000 votes in the elections to the Greater London Council. Early the following year, the new leader of the Conservatives, Margaret Thatcher, moved to outflank them by declaring on primetime television that the white British were 'really rather afraid that this country might be swamped by people with a different culture'.[89] This comment seemed to have immediate political benefits as the party won a by-election seat from Labour in Ilford, and some historians (and others) have seen this as a successful strategy that accounts for the decline of the National Front in the late 1970s and early 1980s. Thatcher herself certainly saw it as a successful electoral strategy.[90] As Kushner and Lunn explain:

> To see the impact of fascist ideas solely in terms of membership of fascist organisations or votes received is surely naïve; indeed, current debates about the decline of the National Front do not seek to deny the pervasiveness of racism in British culture, nor the institutional bias within political and social structures. Moreover, this is part of the explanation for the National Front's decline.[91]

Thatcher was not seen as racist herself, but as recognising the xenophobia of many of her core supporters (as well as many Labour voters who could be won over on this issue).[92] In the 1980s there was a strong element within Conservatism of seeking to maintain an exclusive sense of British national identity, around standing up for Britain against European integration, by celebrating victory in the Falklands as part of an imperial and Churchillian tradition, and through tightening immigration controls on racial lines. In part, the Conservatives had been pressurised towards a more strident declaration on immigration and nationality, but there was also continuity of thought between the exclusive versions of Britishness of the 'mavericks' and the mainstream party. Norman Tebbit's defence of his version of national identity is too frequent and sincere to be cynicism. In 1989, the potential for mass immigration from Hong Kong on its reversion to Chinese rule provided him with the opportunity to outline his conception of a fixed and cultural Britishness:

> These islands of ours are already overcrowded . . . [G]reat waves of immigration by people who do not share our culture, our language, our ways of social conduct, in many cases who owe no allegiance to our culture . . . is a

destabilising factor in society . . . Most people in Britain do not want to live in a multicultural, multiracial society . . . It has been foisted on them . . . the fear is that they will be swamped by people of different culture, history and religion.[93]

Before returning to a discussion of the impact of immigration restriction on discourses of national identity, it is necessary to discuss the elements of politics that have had an integrative role, drawing people with different identities together. In the late nineteenth century, Irish people living in Britain were urged by Irish nationalists to vote along ethnic lines, using their votes to put pressure on the 'British' parties to implement Home Rule. In 1891, 40,000 people belonged to the Irish National League on mainland Britain, which suggests that many of the Irish thought nationally in politics. Members were not allowed to join English political parties, and politically the intention was to remain separate in order to enhance the position of Ireland. However, Steven Fielding has pointed out that:

> [T]he Irish in England did not reserve all their political energies for the battle for Home Rule. They were essentially Janus-faced and looked not only to matters in Ireland, but also to those in their country of residence, England. Thus, by the mid-1880s the Irish had become Liberals because of that party's support for Home Rule.[94]

By the 1920s, with the establishment of the Irish Free State, the Irish in Britain could now look one way politically. Most Catholic Irish in Britain transferred their political allegiance to Labour. As late as 1965, voting evidence suggested that the Catholic middle class were supporting the Labour Party disproportionately more than their non-Catholic class peers.[95]

Likewise, while some Jewish immigrants continued to see politics as centred on revolutionary politics in eastern Europe, many Jews engaged in the major British political parties. They frequently met anti-Semitic hostility, as during the Marconi scandal, when Liberal cabinet ministers were revealed to have bought shares in the sister company of Marconi, which had just been awarded a large government contract. While the major target was Lloyd George, Rufus Isaacs and Herbert Samuel were picked out by the radical right for particular abuse because of their Jewishness.[96] It is noteworthy, however, that Liberalism was acting to integrate Jews into British politics, as it had done the Irish. By 1945, there were twenty-eight Jewish MPs, and by 1974 there were forty-six. As Geoffrey Alderman has remarked, 'most Jewish MPs consider themselves as politicians who happen to be Jewish rather than Jewish politicians'.[97]

Immigrants and their descendants have been integrated further into British politics and identity through anti-racist and anti-Fascist campaigns. Tabili has shown how black seafarers and other workers challenged their unequal treatment by employers, trade unions and the state: 'Exploiting inconsistencies in the imperialist position, they appropriated the rhetoric of fair play [and] of entitlement derived from service in the world wars.'[98] By adopting British patriotism, black Britons demanded their due reward. In 1919, a black workers' resolution declared that, 'Some of us have been wounded, and lost limbs and eyes fighting for the Empire to which we have the honour to belong . . . We ask for British justice, to be treated as true and loyal sons of Great Britain.'[99] Forty-five years later, the first Race Relations Act (1965) sought to prevent discrimination on grounds of 'race, colour, ethnic or national origin'.[100] Subsequent Acts, in 1968, 1976 and 2002, extended the principle that all those resident in Britain should be treated equally. There was a sense here of the extension of British justice, by Labour governments. In addition, the election of black and Asian MPs and councillors for the mainstream political parties suggests integration, though in 1997 only nine MPs were elected, showing limited progress.

Conservatives too have played a part in the integration of immigrants and their descendants into British politics. Parekh has pointed out that while Thatcher shared much with Powell, she differed in that through representing a constituency in north London with a sizeable Jewish population she saw the possibilities of assimilation for others: 'Although not entirely happy with blacks and Asians and the concomitant cultural pluralism, she took the view that they can and should be assimilated into the British "stock" and way of life.'[101] This assimilationist project could be seen in the Conservative election poster designed to appeal to 'ethnic minorities' in the 1983 general election. Underneath a photograph of a black man wearing a business suit, it declared 'Labour says he's black. Tories say he's British.'[102] The implication was that this was an upwardly mobile, self-improving man who had absorbed Thatcherite values. The poster, therefore, assimilated black people into Conservatism, but in the process the implication was that Britishness should be emphasised over blackness; the two identities were not seen as simultaneous or equal.

Despite integrationist politics, both the legal and cultural status of black and other immigrant people in relation to Britishness have been qualified by the actions of the British state. There have been tensions between the actions of Labour governments in passing 'race relations' Acts, which have sought to enforce equality of treatment of all people resident in Britain, and immigration legislation which has been implicitly aimed at keeping the proportions of black and Asian people to an 'acceptable' level. Kathleen Paul has explained how 'policy-makers – politicians of both major political parties and senior civil servants – presumed in the wake of the Second World War that British national identity was a singular fixed entity, which it was their duty to protect and preserve'.[103] Immigration legislation, in 1962, 1965, 1968, 1971 and 1981, was all therefore coded with the implicit attempt to prevent the expansion of the non-white British population. R. A. Butler, Conservative home secretary in the early 1960s, responsible for framing the first legislation that would exclude those formerly considered to be British subjects with a free right of entry into the United Kingdom, explained that the advantage of the legislation was that on the surface it did not seem discriminatory, but that 'its restrictive effect is intended to, and would in fact, operate on coloured people almost exclusively'.[104] Ten years later, Butler justified the imposition of controls on the basis of the need to restrict numbers in order to ensure integration.[105] This reasoning had by then become a commonplace, whichever government was in power. In the late 1960s, faced with the expulsion of Asians from former British colonies in Africa, the Labour Party, opposed to immigration control in 1962, looked for ways to restrict entry to Britain for these British passport holders. The Labour home secretary, James Callaghan, recognised the obligations Britain had to the Kenyan Asians but warned that

> So large an influx was more than we could absorb, especially since Asian immigrants tended to concentrate in particular localities in this country; and, unless the influx could be greatly reduced, there was a very real risk that our efforts to create a multi-racial society in this country would fail.[106]

Here the tension was stated explicitly. Britishness was available to finite numbers, and was threatened in addition by the ethnicity of the migrants themselves. It was possible to create a multi-racial Britishness, but black and Asian people were viewed as a problem within this project. There is a debate about the extent to which the state was responding to or creating public opinion in these matters,[107] but whichever is the case, most British people, whether white or black, came to accept the belief that immigration control was necessary, implying that national identity is finite. In addition, immigration legislation was framed with the intention of excluding as many black and Asian immigrants as possible. In the 1971 Immigration Act, the Conservative government of Ted Heath developed features of the 1968 Act to create a clear distinction between 'patrial' and 'non-patrial' status.[108] Only those with patrial status, that is a connection to the United Kingdom by birth, descent or settlement, would be allowed to enter.[109] This Act ended primary black and Asian migration to the UK. Subsequently, only the dependants of those migrants already resident in the UK were to be allowed entry. The Act built upon the assumption of the 1948 Royal Commission on Population, that migrants had to be able to assimilate with an existing version of Britishness, rather than to be allowed to adapt Britishness in new directions.

The British Nationality Act of 1981, even in its very name, established clearly these assumptions. The Act recognised a variety of British 'citizenships' but ensured that most overseas British citizens had no right to enter the United Kingdom. In addition, the Act swept away the right of those born in Britain to acquire British nationality automatically.[110]

Such legislation retains an implicit racialism, but generally the trend has been to move away from emphasis on 'race' towards a focus on cultural difference and incompatibility.[111] Within this view, Britishness has been seen as a particular kind of behaviour to which most black and Asian people were seen as incapable of conformity. Historians such as Alison Light and Raphael Samuel have argued that Englishness-Britishness was domesticated between the wars, as national identity turned towards a more feminised and home-centred form of imperialism.[112] The experience of the 'home front' in the Second World War further emphasised the link between the home and the nation, and the British came increasingly to portray their heroism as private, ordinary and home-loving. Hence, Chris Waters has argued, a new 'national fiction' emerged in the 1930s and 1940s, associating a cohesive national community with the home.[113] It was this national fiction that many Britons used against post-war immigrants from the Empire/Commonwealth.

Of course, such use of concepts of respectability associated with home and neighbourhood had been employed against previous groups of immigrants. The Irish were seen as especially incapable of respectable home life, preferring instead drunkenness and criminality.[114] Jewish migrants, too, were seen as displacing respectable British working-class families, through non-observance of the British Sunday and the conduct of anti-social businesses. In 1903, the Royal Commission on Alien Immigration heard evidence from a member of the British Brothers' League, who, in league with Major Evans-Gordon, an anti-alien Conservative MP and member of the Commission, described the process of destruction of native communities:

> 9680. Have you suffered in your business? [asked Evans-Gordon] – Very much indeed.

> 9681. How? – In these last two years alone . . . I can give the names and addresses of over 200 residents in the Borough of Stepney who have been driven out of this parish by the alien immigration.

> 9686. The 200 customers that you speak of, have they in all cases been displaced by foreigners? – In all cases they have been displaced. The system by which they are driven off is much the same system as I am suffering from now. Next door to me there has come a pickled herring yard . . . I have never tasted one, but the odour from them is something dreadful . . . all day on Sunday these pickled herring barrels are being thrown in and out of the shed. I want to live, as I consider myself a decent working man, and I want to live in a respectable neighbourhood. I always thought Exmouth Street was a respectable street, but they are turning the street into one of the worst streets I know of in the neighbourhood.[115]

By 1951, however, a Mass-Observation report revealed that attitudes towards Jews had substantially changed. Two hundred gentiles were asked what they thought were 'the best things about Jews'. That they were 'home-loving' emerged as the third most popular response, after 'look[ing] after each other' and being 'good at business'.[116] On the whole, while anti-Semitism remained widespread in British society, it was no longer based on a sense that Jews were incapable of conforming to British norms of behaviour in relation to the home.

The home had taken on greater meaning in representations of Britishness during the Second World War, which through aerial bombardment also contributed to the politicisation of the issue of house building. In 1945, 1950 and

1951, the Labour and Conservative parties contested each other's abilities to build houses in sufficient numbers to provide homes for the heroes and heroines of the war. By 1953, the Conservative government was able to achieve its promise to build 300,000 houses each year, yet there remained a significant housing shortage in some areas, which was exacerbated by the arrival of black and Asian people. In some of these areas, such as west London, this contributed to anti-black hostility and violence. As with the British Brothers' League in the early 1900s, the issue of housing provided racist organisations with culturally loaded ammunition against immigrants. The claim was made that the black and Asian immigrants could occupy houses but could not make homes. Leaflets were issued declaring 'House Britons, not Blacks', and graffiti was scrawled demanding 'KBW', meaning 'Keep Britain [sometimes Brixton] White.'[117] In 1964, Peter Griffiths successfully utilised the supposed contrast between blackness and neighbourhood, linking the defence of Britishness to his Conservatism. Such campaigns were often aimed at local authorities, which were accused of housing 'immigrants' before 'local' people. However, even greater emphasis was placed on the damage done to owner-occupied housing by the arrival of immigrants, and in turn to the neighbourhood and wider civic community. This was expressed clearly by 'Mrs X, an Englishwoman standing at a bus-stop', interviewed by Humphry and John:

> I have lived in Handsworth for fifty years. I was born here. I inherited my father's property. Handsworth is no longer a place to be proud of. This used to be one of the nicest areas of Birmingham. We have this lovely park there and I am afraid to go and sit in it. I used to spend many hours in the park but now with all these darkies running around you never know what they would do to you, do you . . . And there's all this talk about crime. I am afraid to walk the streets. I think it is terrible, and the police are not doing enough about it.[118]

Such concerns were shaped against the backdrop of social studies of the new immigrant communities, which in turn fed off the sense that national character could be studied scientifically.[119] In the mid-1950s a Sunday tabloid newspaper had commissioned a major study of the English people by Geoffrey Gorer, an anthropologist. Published in 1955, his report was entitled *Exploring English Character*. Based on 11,000 questionnaires, it suggested that the English had an essential shyness and desire for privacy.[120] In this way, Englishness-Britishness was constructed as a set of behavioural norms against which the lives of black and Asian immigrants could be measured. Sheila Patterson, examining Brixton, portrayed an idealised view of British working- and lower-middle-class life:

> [The] respectable residents expect a tolerable and at least superficial conformity to 'our ways', a conformity to certain standards of order, cleanliness, quietness, privacy, and propriety. Clean lace curtains are hung at clean windows, dustbins are kept tidy and out of sight . . . and house fronts

are kept neat. Houses do not give the impression of being packed to the brim with temporary and noisy strangers of both sexes . . . Except for the children, people . . . 'keep themselves to themselves' and life is lived quietly.[121]

By the end of the 1960s, such notions about English-British behaviour had become prevalent. It was to these themes that Powell turned in his prophecy of racial violence. Powell claimed to speak for the white working class whose behaviour (or culture) had been described, without overt racist intention, by Gorer, Patterson and others. Powell claimed that

A week or two ago I fell into conversation with a constituent, a middle-aged, quite ordinary working man employed in one of our nationalised industries. After a sentence or two about the weather, he suddenly said: 'If I had the money to go, I wouldn't stay in this country . . . I have three children, all of them been through grammar school and two of them married now, with family. I shan't be satisfied till I have seen them all settled overseas. In this country in 15 or 20 years' time the black man will have the whip hand over the white man.'[122]

Powell's constituent felt his masculinity to be threatened, but it was very much a domestic masculinity, located in the home and family.[123] He was ordinary and national, but no longer felt able to conduct successful family life because of immigrants. Powell's other example of a victim of government policy on immigration was even less able to defend herself. He quoted a letter from another constituent, with a narrative of neighbourhood and national decline:

Eight years ago in a respectable street in Wolverhampton a house was sold to a Negro. Now only one white (a woman old-age pensioner) lives there. She lost her husband and both sons in the war . . . [T]he immigrants moved in. With growing fear, she saw one house after another taken over. The quiet street became a place of noise and confusion . . . She is becoming afraid to go out. Windows are broken. She finds excreta pushed through her letter box. When she goes to the shops, she is followed by children, charming, wide-grinning picaninnies. They cannot speak English, but one word they know. 'Racialist,' they chant.[124]

In Powell's construction, immigrants are incapable of ordinary and decent family life. While the working-class man's chief concern was his children, the children of immigrants ran wild; they were not part of a family but were an element of an invasion. In the 1970s, the association of street crime and mugging further developed a contrast between uncontrolled young black people and law-abiding white people. In 1984 the black poet E. A. Markham drew out this contrast in the depiction of the 'potential mugger / on a quiet English street'.[125]

Across the twentieth century, therefore, many Britons have sought to maintain British national identity as closed and exclusive. Some of the themes employed, such as a sense of decency and respectability, have a long history. The emphases have been changed, particularly as war and affluence placed home life at the centre of a sense of national culture. Immigrants, and their descendants, were constructed as incapable of participating in this normative form of Britishness that is located in an idealised suburban and semi-detached Britain.[126]

## Black and Asian identities in the UK

Much of this chapter so far has focused upon the response of the 'host community' to immigration. Such an approach on its own implies that immigrants and their descendants passively face the discourses on national identity, accepting the judgements of the host community. This has been far from the case. Discussions of national identity in Britain have involved all groups of migrants. Each group has negotiated, contested and forced discussions about national identity, seeking to engage with the discourses that have taken place within a geographically bounded polity. The position of immigrants and their descendants has not been equal to some of the more dominant voices within such discourses, and immigrants have often been victims of the decisions of the powerful in relation to national identity. In 1926, William Joynson-Hicks offered choices to immigrants about their relationship to Britishness:

> If two brothers come to this country and one settles in a district where only aliens live, continues to speak his native language, marries a woman from his own country, sends his child to a school where only foreign children are taught, keeps his account in a foreign bank, employs only foreign labour, while the other brother marries an Englishwoman, sends his children to an English school, speaks English, employs British labour, keeps his account in a British bank, it is the second brother, not the first who will stand to obtain naturalization.[127]

Such an attitude could be contested, but that Joynson-Hicks was home secretary of a Conservative government with a secure parliamentary majority suggests that resisting such assimilationist demands and gaining citizenship was unlikely to be easy. Nonetheless, in an examination of Britishness since 1870, the identities adopted by immigrants and their descendants have especial significance, since national identities rest to a great extent upon the consent of individuals. The strength or weakness of Britishness can, therefore, be discerned from the identities of those people who had alternative identities of place available to them. Of course, this applies to local, regional and national identities within the UK, but there has been a long relationship of compatibility between those identities. The hostility faced by immigrants could act as a discouragement to take up British identities. This was certainly the case among some of the Irish migrants to Britain in the early twentieth century. Hence Bill Naughton, whose father migrated from Mayo to Bolton in 1914, remembered that 'At any time in school when we were gathered to sing "God Save the King", I would sing "God Save Ireland" to myself.'[128]

Other responses to Britishness have been more ambiguous. Certainly, the legacy of imperial education and socialisation had major repercussions on immigrants' senses of identity and the response to these by the 'host community'. For the latter, the Empire suggested superiority. A seventy-year-old railway worker explained the legacy of imperial education for many white Britons:

> We believed we were better than blacks and that is why we had the right to rule them. Then they arrived to work with us on the railways. They were good men, but you never could forget what you learnt all your life about them, that they could never be as good as white men. They came to live next to us. We were just expected to live with that. They [the government] never asked us how we felt. I am not saying we should not have let them in, no Ma'am. My grandchild is half Jamaican and he's family.[129]

Salman Rushdie has suggested that this belief in imperial superiority was transferred into a 'new empire within Britain', in which:

> Four hundred years of conquest and looting, four centuries of being told that you are superior to the Fuzzy-Wuzzies and the wogs, leave their stain. This stain has seeped into every part of the culture, the language and daily life.[130]

A survey in the 1960s suggested that two-thirds of white Britons considered the British superior to Africans and Asians. Less than a quarter considered Americans inferior, and just above one-third considered Europeans inferior.[131] There was a clear sense of British superiority, linked in many ways to imperialism. Dilip Hiro related how, 'With very few exceptions they [the white British] all shared a notion that the British . . . gave the natives railways, hospitals, schools and roads and what is more taught them how to administer their countries.'[132]

In another direction, the Empire resulted in a globalised sense of Britishness, if only by its impact on familial relationships. Humphry and John described the background of Hubert Thomas, who migrated to Manchester from Jamaica in 1953:

> His family snapshot album shows that his father could pass for a white man because *his* father was a Chinese from Hong Kong and his mother was half Welsh and half Negro. On Hubert's mother's side his grandfather was a Scotsman called Forester and his grandmother a Negro . . . With so much British blood in his veins, and with Jamaica a British Crown colony from 1666 until independence within the Commonwealth in 1962, he considered himself as near British as makes no difference.[133]

Walter Lothen, another migrant from Jamaica, recalled that 'When I came here I didn't have a status as a Jamaican. I was British and going to the mother country was like going from one parish to another. You had no conception of it being different.'[134] On the other hand, the adoption of the label 'British' could act as a rejection of imperialism. Bernie Grant, the black council leader and MP for Tottenham in the 1980s, declared himself British because 'it includes other oppressed peoples, like the Welsh or Scots. It would stick in my throat to call myself English.'[135] These identities make explicit the connection between Empire and national identity in post-imperial Britain. David Dabydeen has expressed that link flawlessly: 'You cannot be Guyanese without being British.' But as he continues, white Britons are equally imperial in background: 'And you cannot be British without being Guyanese or Caribbean.'[136] Yasmin Alibhai-Brown has made a similar assertion about the impact of Empire on all British identities. She has argued that 'There is no modern British identity without Indian food, black music, Salman Rushdie and Trevor Phillips.'[137]

These sorts of identity have rejected entirely the notion of a single national identity adopted by exclusivist Britons, like Tebbit. He has made clear that he does not think it is possible to hold allegiance to more than one nation.[138] Yet the British Empire was built on the very assumption that emigrants would build new nations in the four corners of the world and would adopt dual identities – as British and Australian, as British North Americans, and so on.[139] White Britons, for a time, had 'double consciousness', as Paul Gilroy has described multiple identities. 'Double consciousness', Gilroy argues, has also been at the centre of black identities in the 'black Atlantic', including Britain. Some black people have identified themselves as black, national and hemispheric.[140] Likewise Tariq Modood has noted how '"being British" and "being Pakistani" etc. do not strongly compete with each other'.[141] It is in this context, of the confident assertion of 'second-generation immigrants', that the self-identifying labels of 'British Muslim' and 'Black British' have emerged. Modood found that nearly two-thirds of visible ethnic groups in Britain agreed with the statement 'In many ways I think of myself as British.' African Asians agreed most, at 71 per cent, while, aside from the Chinese, Bangladeshis agreed least, at 60 per cent. Among the Chinese, nearly half considered themselves to be British.[142] Given that primary immigration was virtually stopped by the 1971 Act an increasing proportion of black and Asian people in Britain are British born. Two-thirds of those of Caribbean origin, one-third of those of Chinese origin and the majority of children born to every other visible ethnic group in the United Kingdom have been born here.[143] Given the constant questioning of the Britishness of immigrants and their descendants over the last 130 years it is unsurprising that there has often been an air of defensiveness about the adoption of British identities. Baron Baker explained the impact of racist violence on his identity in the 1950s: 'Before the [Notting Hill] riots I was British – I was born under the Union Jack. But the race riots made me realise who I am and what I am. They turned me into a staunch Jamaican.'[144] Such 'dissociative' strategies[145] – a response to the refusal of some white Britons to accept black people as British – has in turn led to greater accusations of disloyalty. In many ways, black Britons have been in a no win situation. Lal, a twenty-year-old South Asian living in Newcastle upon Tyne, expressed this to an interviewer in 1976:

> In England, when you live in England, no doubt all the time you're scared in case someone comes up to you and says, 'Who are you to say such?' If you say something about the country, you're always scared in case someone comes up to you and says, 'Who are you to say this – such and such a thing about this country? You don't belong here.'[146]

For those who migrated to the UK decades ago, and for 'second generation immigrants', 'the only home [they] know is Britain'.[147] Anant Ram, a Punjabi migrant to the West Midlands and founding member of the Indian Workers' Association, told an oral historian in response to his questions: 'What are your views of England and life over here? Would you regret dying here?':

> This is a country of good life and I am quite contented with my life. Our family is into the third generation, my grandchildren are now well settled here. I do not think I could have done any better. No, I think I would not regret dying here. Many of our Punjabi people now die here. It is the same for all of us. I am part of our community. This is our home now, isn't it?[148]

There is an element here of ambiguity. It is not entirely clear which community is meant – a Punjabi community or a British one – but in addition there is that slight defensiveness about England being 'our home'. Jenny, a fifteen-year-old black girl, commenting on her identity, elaborated on the ambiguities of identity for black people living in Britain:

> Well, I am British, I was born in London, but I am not the same as English people, it's like I'm a different kind of English – a different way. I mean we have different ways – a different culture. But I am still British.[149]

The difference in the 1990s and in the early years of the new century seems to be that being a 'different kind of British' has become increasingly appropriate and welcomed. In 1993, for example, an opinion poll suggested that three-quarters of white people (and 88 per cent of young people) would not mind if one of their close relatives married an Afro-Caribbean.[150] A survey conducted for the *Daily Express* newspaper in 1995 seemed to provide disturbing evidence. Two-thirds of white people said they were at least a little racist, and 26 per cent said they might vote for a party like Le Pen's French National Front. However, 63 per cent of respondents said that ethnic minorities made a healthy contribution to society.[151]

From the 1990s there was a new confidence from black and Asian people in asserting their claim to Britishness. In a survey in 1990, nearly 60 per cent of

Asian parents and 75 per cent of young Asians said that Britain was their 'home country'. Most immigrants continued to feel Indian or Pakistani but 43 per cent of young Asians described themselves as 'primarily British'.[152] There is certainly an element of change here. Amrit Wilson's important book of the late 1970s, *Finding a Voice: Asian Women in Britain*, hardly touched on issues of British national identity, and when it did it was to reject the adoption of Englishness-Britishness. One chapter concludes with Meena, a schoolgirl from Acton, declaring 'I never regard myself as English. I am Indian in every way.'[153] The crisis of Britishness invoked by devolution has, though, been accompanied by a demand for Britishness by black and Asian Britons. Stuart Hall has remarked that 'Fifteen years ago we didn't care, or at least I didn't care, whether there was any black in the Union Jack. Now not only do we care, we must.'[154] Modood has argued that Asian teenagers in Bradford, Brick Lane and Southall are asserting similar feelings: 'So far it is we who have had to make all the changes, now it is the turn of the British to accept our existence.'[155] It might be argued that young black and Asian Britons have shrugged off the burden of imperialism to become more positively assertive about their identities. In turn, academics and journalists such as Parekh, Modood, Yasmin Alibhai-Brown, and Mike and Trevor Philips have championed a civic, rather than ethnic, Britishness that recognises and includes diversity rather than seeking to subordinate difference.[156] Phillips has argued that black people living in Britain should be saying: 'We are black English people, this is the kind of English people we are; as such we are part of this state and this state should reform its identity to allow for that.'[157] Parekh, as chair of the Runnymede Trust's commission on the Future of Multi-Ethnic Britain, was accused of seeking to end Britishness because of its innate racial connotations (as he said, that did not mean 'racist'). Yet he clarified that he sought the 'decoupling [of] Britishness from whiteness, so that black and Asian people in Britain do not feel excluded'. This would enable black Britishness.[158] This confidence has provided the context of the Blair Labour government's desires to create a 'New Britain'. This has strengthened the reshaping of the nation to include black and Asian people more centrally within national identity. In April 2001, the foreign secretary, Robin Cook, made a speech that symbolised the spirit of these new times. In what widely became know as the 'Chicken Tikka Massala speech', he outlined an inclusive version of Britishness, incorporating a variety of pluralism. Devolution and European integration were accommodated, but the main thrust of his speech celebrated ethnic and cultural pluralism. 'This pluralism', he argued, 'is not a burden we must reluctantly accept. It is an immense asset that contributes to the cultural and economic vitality of the nation.'[159] He continued that 'Chicken Tikka Massala is now a true British national dish, not only because it is the most popular, but because it is a perfect illustration of the way Britain absorbs and adapts external influences. Chicken Tikka is an Indian dish. The Massala sauce was added to satisfy the desire of British people to have their meat served with gravy.'[160]

It is, of course, necessary to clarify the limits of this acceptance of pluralism.

From the right of the Conservative Party, a 'maverick' MP, John Townend declared at almost the same time:

> Our homogenous Anglo-Saxon society has been seriously undermined by the massive immigration – particularly Commonwealth immigration – that has taken place since the war. Illegal immigrants have got a new ploy. They call themselves asylum-seekers. In my view the only way to deal with them is to send them back quickly.[161]

Hence, an essentialised and racial view of Britishness continued to be represented in British politics. This is a complex quote. In the first part, Townend referred to New Commonwealth immigration, a legal and recognised movement of black and Asian people to Britain. In the second half, he referred to illegal and largely white migration of asylum seekers, many of whom were from eastern Europe. The New Labour government condemned the racism explicit in this statement, but stressed the strong stance it would take in dealing with asylum seekers. Acquiescence in one part of the sentiment, however, implied defensiveness about the other. This attack on pluralism was extended by David Blunkett as home secretary, who implied that ethnic tensions in Britain's northern cities were the fault of Asians who refused to integrate. He went so far as to suggest that Asians should speak English inside their homes.[162] A similar tone had been adopted over the Rushdie affair in 1989. Salman Rushdie's novel *Satanic Verses* deeply offended many Muslims, in Britain and around the world. One response to the public protests in which the book was symbolically burnt was to stress the Britishness of free speech and, by implication, the foreignness of Muslims in Britain.[163] In addition, much of the discussion of Britain's ethnic pluralism had been conducted in the wake of the murder of Stephen Lawrence, a young black south Londoner. The police subsequently mismanaged the murder investigation to the extent that nobody was convicted, and the government was forced to hold a public inquiry that went to the heart of institutional racism in Britain.[164] Such events make it necessary to bear in mind the potential for a disparity between formal citizenship (or Britishness) and the substantive everyday rights that might be expected by all Britons and those with permission to reside in the United Kingdom.[165]

Nonetheless, despite this disparity, most white Britons have, after half a century of black and Asian immigration and descendancy, begun to come to terms with the need to define a new way of being British, because black and Asian Britons have insisted that they do so. Many, probably most, British people, white and black, have seen the experience of immigration and ethnic diversity as a positive benefit to British culture and identity.

# 7 Outer Britain

The United Kingdom of Great Britain and Northern Ireland is not a name that has encouraged loyalty. Indeed it hardly even conjures up an image of a country to be loved, as 'England', 'Scotland', 'Wales' and 'Ulster' have done for many people. Yet this difficulty for Britishness can be seen as one of its strengths. The United Kingdom as a nation-state flourished between the early eighteenth and mid-twentieth centuries because it allowed a broad diversity of identities within itself. 'The incredible vagueness of being British', as Robin Cohen has called it,[1] was not part of a crisis of identity but was one of the ways in which the British have tackled the complexities of an integrated yet diverse multi-national polity, formed over centuries, yet only fleetingly 'complete' between 1801 and 1922. Acts of Union had been passed with Wales in 1536 and 1543, with Scotland in 1707, and with Ireland in 1800. In 1922 Ireland became the Irish Free State, and neutrality in the Second World War and its declaration of itself as a Republic in 1949 completed the separation. Yet while the impact of the struggle for Irish separation between the 1880s and 1920s caused much political conflict in Britain, its completion was greeted with relief and the United Kingdom was restructured to accommodate a Home Rule parliament in the new 'statelet' of Northern Ireland with remarkably little trauma until the late 1960s.[2]

This chapter examines the relationship of identities within 'outer Britain'. I take this term from Hugh Kearney, who uses it to refer to Scotland, Wales and Ireland as well as to the north and south-west of England, expressing a sense of a subordinate relationship to the centre of the United Kingdom in London and the south-east.[3] An alternative term might have been the 'Celtic fringe', including also the Isle of Man and Cornwall while excluding the non-Celtic regions, but still suggesting the difference between the 'periphery' and the 'core'.[4] Murray Pittock has argued that the term 'Celtic fringe' is useful because it conveys the 'otherness' of the Gaelic parts of the British Isles to Britishness dominated by Englishness.[5] He quotes Gwynfor Evans, of Plaid Cymru, who in 1981 articulated this sense of the external nature of Britishness to Welsh, Scottish and Irish identities:

> What is Britishness? The first thing to realize is that it is another word for Englishness; it is a political word which arose from the existence of the

British state and which extends Englishness over the lives of the Welsh, the Scots and the Irish. If one asks what the difference is between English culture and British culture one realises that there is no difference. They are the same. The British language is the English language. British education is English education. British television is English television. The British press is the English press. The British Crown is the English Crown, and the Queen of Britain is the Queen of England . . . Britishness is Englishness.[6]

Evans' analysis is problematic in that it overemphasises the commonality of the relationships of the Welsh, Scottish and Irish to Britishness. Scotland's experience of education, the press and the crown is substantially different from that of Wales, for example.

I have retained the phrase 'outer Britain' because it enables discussion of those people who did not feel other to Britishness despite their geographical distance from the core, but it does seem to convey a sense of rule from the centre. It also enables a discussion of differences as well as similarities between Wales, Scotland and Ireland. This chapter examines a series of factors affecting the ways in which the non-English nations related to the United Kingdom. Hence economics, the British Empire, politics, the monarchy, the experiences of war and the mechanisms of the media are discussed in order to weigh up the relative importance of such differences and similarities of identity to an overall British identity. The chapter recognises the problems, tensions and disparate identities and the rejection of Englishness-Britishness that have existed across the period since 1870, but also seeks to show that Britishness has been a simultaneous identity for many, indeed most, people in Wales and Scotland since 1870, even perhaps for most people in Ireland until the First World War. After 1922, a large minority in Northern Ireland rejected Britishness entirely, but the majority held a deepened sense of allegiance to their British identity. This chapter therefore seeks to address the central issues of this whole book – what Britishness is and the extent to which it has been part of the lived identities of the peoples of the United Kingdom in the last 130 years.

## Holding together or pulling apart?

The multi-national nature of the United Kingdom is seen as being at the heart of the break-up of Britain at the end of the twentieth century. It has become fashionable since the 1970s therefore to begin to look to the past to find signs of internal strain, as acts in the unravelling of the United Kingdom, with the implication that the process of collapse was the inevitable end product of the existence of a state containing many nations. The experiences of eastern Europe and especially the fragmentation of the Soviet Union and Yugoslavia have provided comparisons. So Tom Nairn has asked 'why has the old British state system lasted so long, in the face of such continuous decline and adversity?' Christopher Harvie confines 'the moment of British nationalism' only to the years 1939 to 1970.[7] In such views, all signs of national identity in Scotland and

Wales are seen as different only in quantity rather than quality from successful Irish separatist nationalism, and the question asked then becomes why Wales and Scotland 'failed' to produce Home Rule and nationalist movements comparable to those of Ireland. There is a tendency to presume that Scotland and Wales *should* have produced nationalist movements earlier than they did. Such approaches see all forms of the assertion of non-English national identity as an implication of nationalism, but find the seriousness of that nationalism wanting. This chapter argues that it was often compatible to assert Scottishness, Welshness and even Irishness, without being a nationalist with a separatist political programme.

## Wales

Wales has the longest history of integration into the British state, and for some this is seen as accounting for the relative contentment with the continuing merger. Wales was a small nation; its population in 1871 was 1.4 million compared to the 21 million of its English neighbour. Wales had no national institutions of its own; it was subordinated to England to the extent that an infamous nineteenth-century edition of the *Encyclopaedia Britannica* had no separate entry for Wales. Instead, it advised, 'For Wales, see England.'[8] Yet in the period from the late nineteenth to the mid-twentieth century, there were few demands for any form of autonomy of government in Wales, and fewer still for complete separation. Despite this, most Welsh people felt themselves to be culturally distinct from the English, but most felt themselves to be British at the same time.

The chief factor in explaining Wales' continued integration into Britain in the nineteenth century was that it shared in the experience of the industrial revolution. This is not to suggest an economic determinism here, but there was a relationship between economy and identity. Wales was integrated into the British and imperial economy in such a way that the Welsh benefited from being British. But industrialisation also divided Wales within itself between industrial and rural areas. By 1900, 80 per cent of the Welsh population lived in urban communities and it was the rural 20 per cent who were most likely to retain the most distinctive feature of Welshness, the Welsh language, which is discussed below. In the second half of the nineteenth century, South Wales was transformed, most obviously by coal mining. In 1854, 4.5 million tons had been extracted from the ground; by 1913, it was 56 million tons. On the eve of the First World War there were 210,000 miners employed in Wales out of a population of just over 2 million. Other important industries were copper, iron, tin-plate and later steel.[9] These were exactly those industries upon which British prosperity was based – the staple, export industries that made Britain the 'workshop of the world'. Wales was part of this: half of the coal mined in Wales was exported, and Cardiff was the largest coal exporting port in the world. With a population of 180,000 in 1911, it was second only to London in its proportion of foreign-born inhabitants, including an early black community in Tiger Bay.[10]

Industrial expansion enabled Wales to retain its own population in a way

that Ireland could not after the famine of the 1840s. The rural counties of mid-
and North Wales did see migration. In 1890, 100,000 Welsh people lived in the
USA, and 228,000 Welsh natives lived in England.[11] Often these migrants contributed directly to the formation of Welsh identity. E. Vincent Evans, for
example, was secretary of the Honourable Society of Cymmrodorion, formed in
1888, in London. Evans moved from his native Wales to London in 1872,
where he pursued a successful managerial career and was involved in many
Welsh cultural institutions, including the National Eisteddfod Society. Evans
saw his Welshness as lying fully within the boundaries of Britain and its Empire,
and especially its monarchy. He told one national eisteddfod that 'it affords me
more than ordinary pleasure to take the chair at the gathering of a people who
are justly proud of their nationality, and who have always been conspicuous by
their loyalty and attachment to the Crown'.[12]

Most Welsh migrants, however, remained within Wales. This allowed industrial South Wales (and even more so the industrialised part of North Wales) to
remain distinctively Welsh, despite the migration of many English to the new
employment opportunities. As Brockliss and Eastwood point out, 'the industrial
revolution helped to mix up the population of these islands more than had been
the case for many centuries'.[13]

In large part this Welshness was based on Nonconformity in both rural and
urban Wales. The established church was Anglican and the preserve of an
Anglicised aristocracy and gentry. In contrast Nonconformity could claim 80 per
cent of churchgoers in 1851 (though half the population did not attend at all).
While Nonconformity divided between four main denominations – in order of
size: Calvinist Methodists, Congregationalists, Baptists and Wesleyan Methodists
– it was united in a style of worship and in hostility to the Established church.[14]
Nonconformity also helped maintain the use of the Welsh language in chapel
services and associated activities. In 1901 50 per cent of the population could
speak Welsh, and while the proportion fell to 44 per cent in 1911, the absolute
number of Welsh speakers had risen from 930,000 to 977,000 as the population
rose.

Nonconformity was culturally important because it provided an associational
culture that extended beyond Sunday services, enabling the speaking of Welsh
to retain an importance even when English was making inroads. Sunday schools
for adults as well as children, weeknight meetings, literary societies and choral
singing produced a populist and popular culture.[15] The chapels were also
central to the eisteddfodau, local, regional and national competitive festivals of
literature and music that platformed a distinctive and unique Welsh culture and
contributed enormously to a sense of Welsh identity. But as with E. Vincent
Evans, much of this identity was located within the British context. Sir
J. Prichard Jones told the national eisteddfod at Colwyn Bay that

> For generations the Eisteddfod has been the pivot around which Welsh
> nationalism has catered to us who are of Wales . . . that Nationalism is a
> living thing, by it and for it we strive to attain higher things, not in a mean

provincial spirit, but in a spirit that teaches us to do the best we can, not only for Wales, not only for Britain but for that wider British community, all over the world of which we form a part.[16]

How then was this cultural nationalism related to political nationalism?[17] As would be expected, Nonconformity made Liberalism an obvious political choice and the dominant force in Wales. After the widening of the franchise in 1867 and 1884, Liberalism expanded enormously. In 1868 the Liberals won twenty-four of the thirty-three Welsh seats, in 1885 they won thirty of the thirty-four seats. In 1900, a bad year for Liberalism across Britain, Welsh Liberals won twenty-eight seats, and, in 1906, an especially good year for British Liberalism, they won thirty-three out of the thirty-four seats, with the remaining seat going to Keir Hardie, the Labour candidate in Merthyr Tydfil. Liberalism was in turn linked to what were seen as Welsh causes: disestablishment, land reform, Welsh control over education, temperance and the demand for the creation of national cultural institutions. Welsh Home Rule barely figured in this list. In the mid-1890s, Tom Ellis and David Lloyd George had led the Cymru Fydd movement which grew out of cultural nationalism to demand political autonomy. Cymru Fydd was based on the agricultural counties of mid- and North Wales and failed to convert the South Wales Liberal Federation, which was industrial, urban and more Anglicised, to its cause. This was to be the recurring problem for political nationalism based on the needs of rural, Welsh Wales. The vision of the Welsh people as *gwerin* or 'cultivated, educated . . . responsible, self-disciplined, respectable but on the whole genially poor' never overcame its association with rural Wales, however much it sought to incorporate the miners and other industrial workers.[18]

But of equal importance was that the British Liberal Party was able to gain power and deliver much of what Welsh Liberals wanted. The Welsh Sunday Closing Act of 1881 satisfied the temperance movement and provided Wales with its first piece of distinctively Welsh legislation since the Acts of Union. In 1907 a national library and museum were founded in Aberystwyth and Cardiff respectively. A federal, national University of Wales was created. Disestablishment was taken up by the Edwardian Liberal governments, and was achieved in 1920. Welsh Liberals were incorporated in British Liberal governments; most obviously Lloyd George was chancellor of the exchequer after 1908 and prime minister from 1916 to 1922. Kenneth Morgan has explained: 'Welsh radicals were essentially British Liberals rather than Celtic nationalists.'[19] This description contrasts Welshness and Britishness, yet as D. A. Hamer has argued Wales was an 'interest' *within* the Liberal Party.[20] Samuel T. Evans, briefly Liberal MP for a seat in mid-Glamorgan, showed the way in which he embedded his Welsh identity within Liberalism and the Union. In January 1910, his election address called for Free Trade as 'essential' to 'the maintenance of the prosperity of the United Kingdom', and for reform of the House of Lords to enable Welsh disestablishment to proceed. He backed this up with a view of Welsh history that spelt out his contentment with the Union:

> The nation, since the Union, has escaped those internecine quarrels and feuds which theretofore ravaged it, and at the present day it presents a vigour and an individuality in its national life which should enable it, with noble ideals and worthy efforts, to achieve a high destiny in the future history and civilisation of the world.[21]

The First World War confirmed Welsh loyalty to Britain; the proportions volunteering for the army in Wales were higher than in England and Scotland. The plight of Belgium and Serbia appealed to Wales as a small nation; as Lloyd George told a meeting of the London Welsh, it was a war for five-foot-five nations.[22] Lloyd George was also responsible for ensuring that a distinct Welsh division (the 38th) was created within the British army, and its 'national' status was confirmed in its nickname as 'Lloyd George's Welsh Army'.[23]

This national unity was, however, marked by a growing class-consciousness and division in Wales. The class harmonious consensus of Liberalism, which sought to incorporate mine owner and worker, was breaking up. Since 1898 there had been a series of bitter industrial disputes owing to low productivity in mining, characterised by rank and file militancy, with some Marxist and syndicalist influence. Most mine owners were Liberals, indeed some were Liberal MPs, and in 1908 the South Wales Miners' Federation affiliated to the Labour Party.[24] In the general election of 1918 Labour secured 31 per cent of the vote in Wales, compared with 22 per cent across the United Kingdom. Social divisions were therefore emerging in Wales which were potentially disruptive of national identity.

These were exacerbated in the interwar years because Wales' export-dominated economy was severely hit by the world depression. Unemployment averaged 20 per cent between 1925 and 1938, and hit 35 per cent in 1932 (with individual towns seeing three-quarters of the workforce unemployed). Around 430,000 people, mostly young and active, migrated from Wales to the Midlands, the south of England and especially London. The mines continued to see poor industrial relations, culminating in the 1926 general strike and miners' strike. Combined with this, Welsh culture seemed to be increasingly under threat. Howell and Baber cite the decline of Nonconformity, the economic dislocation of the 1920s and 1930s, the influence of Anglicised and American radio and cinema, tourism and contraception as causes.[25]

In these circumstances, it was little wonder that a Welsh nationalist party emerged. Plaid Genedlaethol Cymru was formed in 1925 at the national eisteddfod.[26] Saunders Lewis, its president from 1926 to 1939, dominated the party. His most daring act was setting fire to an RAF bombing school in the Lleyn peninsula, to mark the four-hundredth anniversary of the Act of Union.[27] With two others he was tried at the Old Bailey (a Welsh court, the attorney-general of the National government felt, would be biased) and refused to make a defence since the trial was conducted in English. The three defendants were jailed for nine months, but received much Welsh support because the bombing school caused such damage to local farming and because of a wider pacifism in the 1930s. But Plaid Cymru did not move out of the political margins. While it had 2,000 members in 1939, they were mostly from the Welsh intellectual elite and Plaid Cymru enjoyed no electoral success, fighting only the seat of Caernarfonshire in 1935, where it gained 7 per cent of the vote.

This weakness can be explained mainly by referring back to the divide between rural and urban Wales. Significant parts of Plaid Cymru believed the answer to Wales' economic and cultural problems was the deindustrialisation of Wales, which Lewis believed was necessary for 'the moral and physical welfare of its population'.[28] The party romanticised the Welsh rural past, and stressed the importance of the Welsh language when it seemed to many of the Welsh that English was the way to social advancement. This nostalgia for the past was combined with the Catholicism of many of Plaid Cymru's leader, including Lewis, an irony in Nonconformist Wales. Plaid Cymru was also accused of having Fascist sympathies, for some leading members admired the French Catholic right and during the Second World War refused the right of an English government to conscript Welsh men and women.

Plaid Cymru was also hostile to the labour movement, and by the 1920s it was to the Labour Party that most Welsh people looked. Labour remained an all-British party; throughout the 1930s and 1940s it looked to national planning for solutions to economic problems. The experience of the Second World War, which restored full employment to Wales under state direction, resulted in Labour securing 58.5 per cent of the Welsh vote (compared to 48 per cent nationally). Labour's manifesto in 1945 pledged some form of devolution for Scotland, but leading Welsh Labour figures such as Aneurin Bevan were opposed to similar moves for Wales. James Griffiths, minister of national insurance in Attlee's government, has explained that Bevan was 'impatient of nationalisms which divided peoples and enslaved nations within their narrow geographical and spiritual frontiers. He feared that devolution of authority would divorce Welsh political activity from the main stream of British politics.'[29] There were risks in such a strategy, with which the cabinet agreed.[30] The Council of Wales was established with Huw T. Edwards, a leading North Wales trade union leader, as its chairman, but its powers were limited, and were further restricted by the Conservative government in the 1950s. Both Labour and the Conservatives sorely tested Edwards' loyalties. He had been severely wounded in the First World War; he could be relied upon to offer advice on the award of (British) honours to Welsh people,[31] or suggestions as to the routes of royal visits to Wales.[32] Yet he felt that Wales was not getting its full due. In December 1946 he sent an open letter to Attlee urging some devolution of power, since 'my country is solidly behind the Labour Government and is entitled to expect [from] the Government of its choice a sympathetic recognition of her special problems'.[33] Edwards continued as chairman until 1958, when he resigned because of the Conservative government's disregard for the Council.[34] Edwards left the Labour Party in the same year, and joined Plaid Cymru, although he returned to Labour when the creation of the office of the Secretary of State for Wales by the Wilson government suggested a real commitment to Welsh issues (the post went to James Griffiths).

In the post-war period, Labour's welfare state and mixed economy contributed significantly to a sense of Britishness.[35] Bevan ensured that the hospitals would be nationalised and controlled by the National Health Service; the coal mines were brought under the National Coal Board. A parallel tendency emerged in which a Welsh-language-based infrastructure emerged, in part in response to the politicisation of the language issue in the 1960s.[36] The Welsh Language Society organised direct action to secure the legal recognition of Welsh, and in 1967 the Labour government passed the Welsh Language Act giving equal validity to English and Welsh in Wales. Welsh-language cultural organisations such BBC Teledu Cymru (1964), the Welsh Arts Council (1967), Bwrdd Ffilmiau Cymraeg (Welsh Film Board, 1972) and S4C (1982) signified Welsh difference from English-Britain, and encouraged the emergence of a Welsh-speaking middle class, but at the same time amplified the divide between English- and Welsh-speakers within Wales.[37] In such circumstances Plaid Cymru was able to grow, even if it remained separate from the language campaigns. In a by-election in July 1966 the first Welsh Nationalist MP was elected at Carmarthen. For the 1970 general election Plaid Cymru's manifesto pointed to some of the reasons for its growth. The economy in Wales was stagnating – unemployment in Wales stood at 4 per cent, while in England it was only 2 per cent – and yet the national theatre, opera house, national art gallery and national orchestra suggested a revitalisation of Welsh cultural identity.[38] Labour felt itself under threat, even if 'For Plaid Cymru, 1970 was a turning-point at which Welsh politics obstinately refused to turn.'[39] Plaid Cymru had secured 11.5 per cent of the vote but lost its seat and twenty-five deposits. From the mid-1960s to the present, Labour has sought to make concessions to Welsh national feeling based on different levels of sincerity. The March 1979 referendum on Labour's devolution act showed that the majority of the Welsh were not enthused by the prospect of separate political forms – the vote was 956,000 against to 243,000 for – even if the vote signified little or nothing about the national identities of the Welsh. In the subsequent general election in May, the Conservatives gained eleven seats, their highest number of seats in Wales since 1935.

The Conservatives, as their Welsh historian suggests, suffered in Wales because of their association with Englishness and English interests.[40] In addition, Liberals and Labour attacked them for being the party of the aristocracy and land. However, that did not prevent some British aristocrats from wishing to display their own Welshness. In 1893 a meeting at the Mansion House, London, resolved 'to form a committee for the purpose of promoting a National Presentation from the People of Wales and from Welshmen to HRH the Duke of York and Princess Mary on their approaching marriage'. While the Liberal Vincent Evans became secretary, subscriptions came from the Conservatives the Marquess of Bute, Lord Tredegar and Lord Penrhyn.[41] In 1909 such unionist aristocrats took their engagement with Welshness further than subscribing to a public collection. In that year the National Pageant of Wales was staged in Cardiff, with around 5,000 amateur performers taking part. The aristocracy took prominent positions, suggesting they sought national leadership. Lord Tredegar played Owen Glyndwr and the Marchioness of Bute, as Dame Wales, led 'a number of ladies of high social distinction' representing the counties of Wales.[42] The Bute family had played a major role in the reconstruction of Cardiff to a status fit to become a city, granted by the Conservative government of Arthur Balfour in 1903.[43]

A similar event combining civic and national ideals occurred fifty years later to celebrate Prince Charles becoming Prince of Wales. The Festival of Wales in 1958 saw 'an ingenious tableau, proudly marching men, bands playing joyous music and a giant Welsh dragon breathing smoke passed triumphantly through the sun-lit streets of Cardiff',[44] which had been granted capital city status in 1955.[45] In the same year the Empire and Commonwealth Games were hosted in Cardiff. Whereas in the Olympic games, Welsh (and Scottish) athletes were subsumed in a Great British team, in the Commonwealth Games they had separate national teams. Wales, therefore, was able to retain multiple identities into the second half of the twentieth century. Wales was Welsh, but it was also British. The majority of people in Wales remained comfortable with dual and simultaneous identities, and even the 1997 referendum saw only a wafer-thin majority of 50.3 per cent in a turnout of only 51 per cent for the creation of a Welsh assembly. As Arthur Aughey has remarked, '"Welsh" Wales backed devolution; "British" Wales opposed or equivocal. Apathy decided the issue.'[46]

## Scotland

This section relates a narrative for the failure of Scottish nationalism until the late twentieth century (which shares much in common with the factors behind Welsh integration), but it also focuses on the construction of Scottish identities, an invented Scottishness, that in many ways did not come into conflict with the acceptance of Scotland as North Britain (in the nineteenth century this was frequently shortened in postal addresses to N.B.). In Wales, Welsh national identity was seen as democratic and popular, while in Scotland the aristocracy not only embraced but dominated notions of Scottishness.

The Scottish-Marxist-nationalist commentator Tom Nairn argued in *The Break-up of Britain* that the success of the Scottish middle class and intelligentsia within the British state and economy prevented the emergence of political nationalism until comparatively late. Since Scotland retained some of its national institutions after the Union, the legal, religious and educational systems for example, Scotland lacked the grievances around which middle-class nationalists in Wales and Ireland mobilised. However Nairn, among others, seems to imply that it was only the Scottish working class who were innocent of the British connection, that somehow to be involved in profiting from the British Empire or capitalist economy precluded Scottishness. Instead, it is argued here that the Scottish middle class/intelligentsia formed a consciousness of Scottish nationality that was compatible with being British. Through mobilisation by the United Kingdom labour movement much of the Scottish working class also took a route of distinct Scottish identity *within* Britishness. This was not an even and enduring process. In the 1870s and 1880s there was land agitation in the Highlands and Islands to match that in Ireland. The crofters elected half a dozen MPs and secured specific legislation from Westminster to tackle their problems.[47] Between the wars a series of developments resulted in a crisis of identity in Scotland,[48] and at the end of the twentieth century large numbers of the Scottish people supported a major transformation of the relationship of Scotland to the United Kingdom.

By the late nineteenth century the Scottish and British economies were integrated, because like parts of Wales and Ulster, Scotland shared in the industrial revolution.[49] Strathclyde, Lothian, Fife and central Scotland became centres of coal mining, iron and steel, textiles, engineering and shipbuilding. In 1913 the Clyde launched one-fifth of the world's ship tonnage, and Scottish Gross National Product per capita stood at 95 per cent of the UK figure. W. D. Rubinstein has pointed out that six of the forty largest British fortunes between 1809 and 1914 were Scottish, Edinburgh was the third wealthiest town in Britain, and Glasgow was the fifth.[50] If Scotland was a colony of England, it was a rich colony in which the native elite was sharing the wealth of the metropolis.

Indeed the complicity of many of the Scottish in imperialism was utilised as a method of enhancing a distinctive Scottish identity, but at the same time Scottish men made the Empire truly British.[51] Scotland provided governors of colonies, such as Lord Dalhousie, governor-general of India in the 1840s and 1850s, and Lord Minto, governor-general of Canada and viceroy of India in the early twentieth century, as well as imperial heroes such as David Livingstone, whose remains were interred in Westminster Abbey. We could add to this list John Buchan, author of *The Thirty-Nine Steps*, member of Lord Milner's kindergarten reconstructing British rule in South Africa after the Boer War of 1899–1902 and governor-general of Canada in the late 1930s. In addition he was creator of the Scottish fictional character Richard Hannay, who saved the Empire again and again from its external and internal enemies, ensuring Scotland's contribution came before the attention of readers and filmgoers alike.[52] Finally we could add to this Glasgow's proud boast that it was 'the second city of the Empire' and its hosting of an imperial exhibition in 1938.[53]

In addition to the Scottish contribution to Empire, Keith Robbins has argued that British government can be described as Anglo-Scottish. Gladstone played up his Scottish connections, Lord Rosebery held his estates near Edinburgh, and Sir Henry Campbell-Bannerman was the first Scottish commoner to become prime minister of Britain. In the Conservative Party, A. J. Balfour was half Scottish and Andrew Bonar Law with his Ulster Scot background (combined with residence in Canada) signifies the Britannic nature of British politics. In the Labour Party, as well as pioneers such as J. Keir Hardie, can be found a Scottish prime minister, James Ramsay MacDonald.[54]

Politicians from right and left combined sub-national identities with their Britishness. The Unionists (Conservatives and Liberal Unionists) at the turn of the century believed that progress meant the absorption of small by larger nations, but the aggregation of states within the United Kingdom did not mean the amalgamation of identities to create a single British identity exclusive of all other identities of place. As Joseph Chamberlain explained, 'the separate nationalities of Welsh, Scots and English were now merely local divisions of the developing British/English imperial race', but those divisions were acceptable and beneficial nonetheless.[55] Unionism tolerated and celebrated different identities as long as they remained subsidiary to British national identity. This is apparent in Balfour's explanation of his identities and their relationships:

> If I consider the case I know best (namely my own), I find that within a general regard for mankind, which I hope is not absent nor weak, I am moved by a feeling, especially patriotic in its character for a group of nations who are the authors and guardians of western civilization, for the subgroup which speaks the English language, and whose laws and institutions are rooted in British history, for the communities which compose the British Empire, for the United Kingdom of which I am a citizen, and for Scotland, where I was born, where I live, and where my fathers lived before me. Where patriotisms such as these are not forced into conflict, they are not only consistent with each other, but they may mutually reinforce each other.[56]

Unionism resulted from the desire to hold the United Kingdom together, emerging in response to the apparent threat to the Union posed by Irish nationalists from the 1880s, and it was more a product of outer Britain than it was of England. Ulster was very close to Scotland, both geographically and culturally. The eighth Duke of Argyll told the House of Commons in 1893 that

> I have been spending the last few weeks in a part of Scotland whence we can look down on the fields of Antrim. We can see the colour of their fields and in the sunset we can see the glancing of the light upon the windows of their cabins. This is the country, I thought the other day, which the greatest English statesman [Gladstone] tells us must be governed as we govern the Antipodes. Was there ever such a folly?[57]

As with Wales, the interwar depression hit Scotland's export industries extremely hard. Unemployment in Scotland stood at higher than the national average in every year between 1927 and 1939, reaching 26.1 per cent in 1931, compared to the UK average of 21.3 per cent.[58] This led to a questioning of Scotland's continued ability to exist as an identifiable national identity. The economic situation stood at the heart of this anxiety, but was accompanied by concerns over health and housing, population decline and Irish immigration, and the drift of Empire.[59]

Again, as in Wales, the crisis saw the establishment of a nationalist party in 1934, when the National Party of Scotland and the Scottish Party merged.[60]

There had of course been an element of nationalism in politics prior to the 1930s, going back to the National Association for the Vindication of Scottish Rights formed in 1853, but as Smout has pointed out, it was concerned with the rectification of trivial abuses such as the flying of the wrong flag. Such symbolic politics found a further expression in the objections to the Prince of Wales calling himself Edward VII rather than Edward I, since Edward VI had ruled only England.[61]

British parties of the left were strong in Scottish politics, as they were in Wales, and it was through the Liberals and Labour that nationalist demands had been expressed. Taylor Innes in 1887 had thought it enough to declare that 'I am a Liberal because I am a Scotchman.'[62] When the Liberal Party was defeated in the 1900 general election, a new Liberal group was organised 'to stir interest in progressive politics'.[63] It was called the Young Scots Society, and while it campaigned against 'English' MPs taking Scottish seats and for Home Rule for Scotland (in 1914 a Scottish Home Rule Bill passed its second reading), its celebration of British Liberal heroes such as Gladstone and Cobden suggests the ways in which it was embedded into the politics of the Union.[64] The Liberal Party was, as Biagini has observed, a multi-national 'coalition' party. Its pluralist view of national identities within the Union enabled it to act as the true United Kingdom party to the Unionists' more narrowly English viewpoint.[65]

The early Labour Party inherited this pluralist vision of Britishness, and was committed to Home Rule for Scotland until the 1920s, when the advance of the party at an all-British level suggested that social, indeed socialist, transformation would be a British phenomenon.[66] Labour supplanted the Liberals as the dominant left-wing force in Scotland during and after the First World War as a series of industrial disputes hit industrial Scotland, creating the myth of 'Red Clydeside'.[67] This in turn led to strong Scottish Labour representation at Westminster, but this only increased the confidence in socialist advance. The apogee of Scottish Labour's power came with Churchill's appointment of Thomas Johnston as Secretary of State for Scotland in 1941.[68] Johnston rejected the form of nationalism 'which had lost itself in the Jacobite mists'. Instead, he said, 'Scotland's hope lay not in heraldic restoration but in social ownership of soil, industry, and finance, and there was one political route and one only to the social ownership: it was through the British Labour Party.'[69] In 1945 Labour's manifesto included a pledge for Scottish self-government, partly in response to the electoral success of the SNP in wartime, culminating in the victory of Dr Robert Macintyre in Motherwell in April 1945 (he lost the seat at the general election in July).[70] Even when that pledge was reneged upon, and 2 million people had added their names to the Scottish Covenant desiring self-government, though within the framework of 'loyalty to the Crown', Labour's support in Scotland improved rather than declined in 1950 and 1951.[71]

Despite Labour's strength, the impact of the First World War and the economic problems of the interwar years did not lead to the collapse of Unionism in Scotland. Indeed the Unionists enjoyed a remarkable strength in Scotland for the four decades after 1918. The First World War had vindicated the Conservatives' brand of belligerent patriotism, and the war had proved popular in Scotland. As has been remarked by Fuller, the 'nation' soldiers fought for was often localised.[72] Hence one soldier wrote to George Dott, who was later a Scottish nationalist:

> The description of your visit to Lauder was splendid. It brought the dear old sleepy place back to me as clear as could be. No one writes like you, old man. No one could express in such a realistic and amusing [style?] the life and nature of my country. I hope you don't come to France old man. I shall miss your letters of home so much.[73]

But the war did bring the constituent nations of the UK together. The same soldier wrote:

> So there they lie rows of them five miles up and down the line. Our dead, killed in September. Men of the Wilts, Kents, Suffolks, Gordons, English regiments mostly. The Scots dead lie out of sight two miles *behind* the German line. The ground taken by them was afterwards lost through a blundering staff . . . There will be more British dead.[74]

Here he was expressing a pride in Scottish achievement, but in a British context. Most Scots fought for the United Kingdom, because Scotland formed a part of it. The war brought to the surface the perceptions of the underlying characteristics that the British had constructed for themselves, because Germany was constructed as the opposite, as the other. The vocabulary of nation was confused in Britain, and often the reverse of Germanness was described as Englishness, yet the other British nations could subscribe to the virtues associated with being in the right against Germany. Wales had its democratic nature and Scotland had its sense of sturdy independence; both could contribute moral rectitude, manliness and martial values.[75] Hence the Scottish nationalist journal, *Thistle*, could declare in 1914:

> [W]e of Scotland, like our Irish brethren, freely admit and duly acknowledge that in this great crisis we must place our national wrongs to a great extent in the background, and allow our Scottish patriotism to be submerged, to a large extent at least, in that of the wider current of British patriotism.[76]

The Scottish did not want to merge their contribution entirely. As with the Empire they wished to record their own distinct national role. One way in which this could occur was through memorialising the dead.[77] Hence the Duke of Atholl, hearing of the plans for the establishment of a national war museum in London, 'expressed the emphatic opinion that Scotland ought to have its own National War Museum'.[78] The memorial, located in Edinburgh castle, was opened in 1927 and by 1931 £144,000 had been raised by public subscription.[79]

The war might have radicalised parts of the Scottish working class, but it encouraged the nationalisation of the Scottish middle class, who, faced with the fragmentation of Liberalism, turned increasingly to Unionism, which under prominent figures like Walter Elliot and John Buchan offered a moderate and Scottish Conservatism. Faced with a challenge from right-wing nationalism, particularly from Cathcart Unionists, the Conservative government in London responded by transferring Scottish administration to Edinburgh, opening St Andrew's House in 1939, and reminding the Scottish of the importance of imperialism with the Glasgow Empire Exhibition of 1938.[80] The Second World War repaired the Scottish economy, temporarily at least, and again allowed Scotland to play a distinct role, as Walter Elliot said in a radio broadcast to the Empire: 'The demand nowadays, above everything, is for ships . . . Scotland feels her chief craft honoured again, and rises to it.'[81] In the post-war period the Unionists continued to combine attachment to the United Kingdom with a sense of Scottish national identity, which could be utilised against the centralising force of Labour's socialism. Combined with the world economic boom of the 1950s, this approach succeeded. In the 1950s, the *lowest* share of the vote the Unionists received was 44.8 per cent, and in 1955 they won 50.1 per cent of the votes, and a majority of the seats.[82] British Unionism recognised the strength of the contribution of Scottish Unionism, using Lady Tweedsmuir, MP for Aberdeen, to make election broadcasts to the whole of the United Kingdom in 1951 and 1959, because she was Scottish and a woman.[83] In 1959 she stressed that 'The Prime Minister has also placed Scotland's affairs – wherever possible – in Scottish hands, for we do not want too much central control. Above all – we do not want nationalisation.'[84] The Unionists counterpoised their Scottish (unionist) nationalism against the socialist Britishness of Labour.

This strategy ultimately failed.[85] When the Unionist decline in Scotland began it was Labour rather than the nationalists who benefited. Labour's share of the vote, resting on the greater importance of the public sector and welfare state in Scotland, even among the middle class, never suffered the ignominies of Labour in England in the 1980s. The SNP did begin to emerge in the 1960s as a challenge to Labour, whose response seemed to have the air of panic about it. Having abandoned Home Rule in the 1940s, the Wilson government set up the Crowther (later Kilbrandon) committee on the British constitution.[86] The SNP benefited from the stagnation of the Scottish economy in the 1960s and particularly from the failure of Labour's all-British planning to secure a remedy, but while in October 1974 the SNP secured more than 30 per cent of the vote, buoyed up by the discovery of North Sea oil, they seemed to take votes from the Liberals rather than Labour.[87] Even the Conservatives in the 1970s seemed to be manoeuvring cynically to capture Scottish votes, having slipped to only 32 per cent in October 1974. It was, however, the uncompromising Unionism of Margaret Thatcher and John Major and their attacks on the welfare state, which had been a major contributor to a sense of Britishness in Scotland since the 1940s,[88] that took the Conservatives to the depths of humiliation. In 1955 they had won thirty-six seats, a majority. In 1997 they failed to win a single seat (a contemporary joke had it that at last the Conservatives truly were the party of 'one nation' – England), and regained only one in 2001, though nearly one in five of those who voted supported the Conservatives. Major's claims that Scotland would still play a world role within the United Kingdom, 'in helping to liberate Kuwait, to safeguard the Kurds, to promote the UN, to help build democracy in the old Soviet Union and to put Europe on the right path', suggested that he shared the view that the end of Empire was having a disruptive role within the Union.[89]

In the last part of this section, the discussion turns to the construction of Scottish identities. The dominant image of Scotland has been that of the Highlands. Before 1750 more than a third of the Scottish population lived north of the Highland line, but by 1939 only 6.5 per cent did so.[90] Already by 1901 half the population (of 4.5 million) lived in the Glasgow conurbation. In the eighteenth and nineteenth centuries some features of traditional Highland life were invented and most features were assigned to represent the whole of Scottishness, and were given official approval by the affection Queen Victoria displayed for such emblems of Scottishness. The effect of this, as Murray Pittock has pointed out, has been that images of a Celtic past were emptied of political content.[91]

Hugh Trevor-Roper, in a provocative essay, has made it known that an English Quaker industrialist invented the kilt in the mid-eighteenth century, and that the notion that different clans had distinct tartans can be ascribed to a combination of conmen and commercialism. The sense of timelessness of the kilt and tartan was reinforced by the Hollywood film *Braveheart* (1996), of which the film historian Jeffery Richards has noted, 'the Scots wear woad a thousand years too late and clan tartan five hundred years too early'.[92] The popularity of Highland fashions was spread by Highland Regiments which played a part in the Napoleonic Wars, by Sir Walter Scott's novels and by royal patronage. Representations of the Highlands became part of the Romantic movement of the nineteenth century, as the noble savage was elevated to stand for spirituality in the face of materialist industrialisation. Rural Scotland, like rural England, Wales and Ireland, became a place of the imagination for the pleasure of the leisured elite. Victoria's purchase of Balmoral in 1847 effectively incorporated this version of Scottishness into Britishness.[93] Because Scotland's elite did so well out of English-led industrialisation and imperialism they were happy to live within this paradigm. This was contested of course: by John Maclean, Marxist revolutionary who refused to subsume himself within the Communist Party of Great Britain, preferring to go it alone in Scotland, arguing that the clans were organised along primitive communist lines, and Hugh MacDiarmid, leading figure within the inter-war Scottish Renaissance in literature, who in 1945 could write an approving article entitled 'A Scottish Communist looks at Bonny Prince Charlie'.[94] But what seems to have happened is that symbols of the Highlands became bowdlerised but accepted as representative of Scottishness. As Smout argues, 'for most people, by the mid-twentieth century, being Scottish was mainly a matter of identifying with tartan and bagpipes . . . with the accordions of BBC Scotland's "Scottish country dance music," and with certain football teams'.[95] Richards has shown that cinematic representations of Scotland and Scottishness have rested on the three depictions of tartanry, kailyard and faery, in films such as *I Know Where I'm Going* (1945) and *Whisky Galore* (1949), and more recently *Local Hero* (1983) and *Braveheart* (1995). Richards calls the latter film 'a contrived one-dimensional and schematic distortion of the known facts of life of the thirteenth century Scots patriot William Wallace', yet notes its commercial success in Scotland (and elsewhere), attested to by the *MacBraveheart* website.[96]

The demands for some form of political autonomy in Wales and Scotland grew significantly in the 1980s, and with Labour's conversion from expediency to United Kingdom pluralism and its election in 1997, the renegotiation of the terms of the Union got underway. The meaning of devolution in the 1990s has been disputed. Richard Finlay, the foremost historian of Scottish nationalism, has written that 'although Scotland is still part of the United Kingdom, it is important to recognize that it is so under a *new* union'.[97] Others have been less nuanced. Andrew Marr has described 'the day Britain died', and Nairn now argues that we are in a period 'after Britain'.[98] The resurgence of political nationalism has been accompanied by a cultural renaissance in Scotland and Wales that has found its way into popular culture. The Manic Street Preachers, the Stereophonics and (the now defunct) Catatonia positively celebrated their Welshness, with Catatonia declaring in a song mostly in Welsh that, 'Everyday that I wake up I thank the lord I'm Welsh.'[99] This renaissance, however, has not always straightforwardly embraced a sense of national identity. In the film *Trainspotting*, the heroin addict Renton displayed his alienation from Englishness, but he did not adopt Scottishness as an antidote:

> Doesn't it make you proud to be Scottish? [Tommy asks, as he stands against a backdrop of mountains.]
>   It's shite being Scottish. We're the lowest of the low. The scum of the fucking earth. The most wretched, miserable, servile, pathetic trash ever shat on civilisation. Some people hate the English. I don't. They're just wankers. We on the other hand are colonised by wankers. Can't even find a decent culture to be colonised by. We're ruled by effete arseholes. It's a shite state of affairs to be in, Tommy, and all the fresh air in the world won't make any fucking difference.[100]

Renton's critique of English imperialism and its effect on the Scottish is that the end of English rule might lead to a restoration of pride in Scottishness, and the logic of the 'after Britain' view is that it has led to a strengthening of Welsh and Scottish identities, at the expense of Britishness. But not all Scots and Welsh people see devolution as signifying the end of Britain. Margo Macdonald, leading member of the Scottish National Party, argued in 1995 that:

> there's enough Britishness to keep the people who live in these islands together because I think Britishness should be a thing of the spirit . . . you

will only maintain it if you have the proper political expression and proper community expression for the different nations which exist inside the British Isles.[101]

Devolution might therefore be seen as enabling Britishness to survive, and this has clearly been the Labour government's intention. Devolution in this sense is a form of unionism.[102] But this should not necessarily be seen as an English imposition on the Scottish and Welsh. The Scottish chancellor of the exchequer Gordon Brown has been deeply involved in the formulation of a 'New Britain' and 'New Britishness', declaring himself 'Scottish and British' and seeking reform of the state to accommodate the 'old' nationalities of Scottishness, Welshness and Englishness as well as the 'new nationalities, that is people who have come to this country'.[103] Wendy Alexander, Labour Member of the Scottish Parliament, has expressed the belief that there is a continuing place for Britishness post-devolution alongside a reinvigorated Scottishness because it is 'better placed to cultivate modern diverse citizenship'.[104] It has been suggested that Scottishness will accommodate itself as a political or civic identity alongside an emerging ethnic Britishness.[105] Certainly in 1997, while nearly a quarter of respondents to opinion polling were declaring themselves as 'Scottish not British', just over a quarter identified themselves as 'equally Scottish and British'. When those people who replied that they were 'more British than Scottish' (4 per cent) and 'British not Scottish' (4 per cent) are included, it suggests that more than one in three of the population of Scotland consider their Britishness as at least as important as their Scottishness.[106]

## Ireland and Northern Ireland

The vast majority of the Welsh and Scottish saw themselves as British for most of the twentieth century. In 1986, an opinion poll in Scotland suggested that while 39 per cent saw themselves as Scottish and not British, 53 per cent continued to see themselves as British as well as Scottish (and an additional 6 per cent saw themselves as British not Scottish).[107] In 1999 a similar poll suggested that the numbers rejecting Britishness had fallen to 27 per cent, though those considering themselves more Scottish than British had risen from 30 to 38 per cent.[108] In Northern Ireland, however, only 10 per cent of Catholics declared themselves British in the 1990s.[109] If many Scottish and Welsh people have felt comfortable about multiple identities which included Britishness, then in Ireland the relationship has been more complex and problematic.

The concern of this section is with southern Ireland only until 1922 when the Irish Free State was established. After that date the Irish were no longer British, whether the definition applied is legal or cultural.[110] Therefore this section examines the period from the 1880s to 1920s, because that period saw the creation of a new nation that outgrew the connection with the United Kingdom. But of equal importance is a discussion of the six counties of north-east Ireland that in 1921 became Northern Ireland. The entire population of

the six counties remained legally British. The majority, mainly Protestant, identified themselves as such, but a substantial minority, largely Catholic, refused to
do so. Northern Ireland therefore provides an acute example to discuss in terms
of consent and conflict over nationhood.

Ireland was formally joined to the United Kingdom under the Act of Union
that came into force in 1801. It was expected that Ireland would become an
integrated region of Britain in the way that Wales and Scotland were thought to
have done so. But Ireland faced the problem that the majority of its population
was Catholic. Religion has had a tremendous impact on national identities
within the United Kingdom, and what needs to be taken into account is, as
Linda Colley has argued, that Protestantism was a key component in the creation of a sense of Britishness in the eighteenth century (and before).[111] A long
series of wars had been fought against the Catholic nations of Europe, and
Ireland had been annexed to Britain as an act of national security. The Catholicism of the majority of the Irish population was seen as potentially subversive of
the integrity of Britain. While a number of Protestants played a part in Irish
nationalism, the Catholic Church played a more prominent role. Even the
Catholic Marxist revolutionary James Connolly never renounced his religion
and in the end subordinated his socialism to his Irish nationalism in the Easter
Rising of 1916.[112] Perhaps the major problem for the Catholic Irish was the
realisation that they would form a permanent minority within the frequently
hostile United Kingdom.

The obverse side of this was that the Protestant Irish, in both southern and
north-eastern Ireland, realised that in an independent Ireland they would form
a permanent minority.[113] Whereas in four counties in the historic province of
Ulster, Protestants formed a majority, elsewhere they were spread 'in a thin,
uneven film'.[114] For most Irish Protestants the connection with the United
Kingdom remained of paramount importance as the source of their identity.
Irish Protestants saw themselves as British, not least because of their role in the
formative experiences in the creation of Britishness, most obvious being their
role in the Glorious Revolution of 1688–90. In 1689 Londonderry had been
besieged for 105 days by the Catholic James II; in 1690 James II was defeated
at the Battle of the Boyne, establishing William III's control over Ireland.
Protestant identity was, therefore, tied in with the constitutional development of
Britain, including the Act of Union that appeared to guarantee protection from
renewed Catholic persecution. Unionists felt that their ancestors had played a
major role in the creation of Britain. Hence the *Belfast Newsletter* argued in 1892
(when the prospect of Home Rule had reappeared) that 'If there had been no
Londonderry and no Enniskillen and no Newtownbutler two hundred years ago
. . . there would be no United Kingdom today.'[115] Unionists further tied themselves into a wider British identity by utilising events out of Scottish history. In
1912, faced with the introduction of the third Home Rule Bill, a quarter of a
million Ulstermen signed the Solemn League and Covenant which echoed the
seventeenth-century Scottish Covenants.[116] Protestantism, politics and British
national identity therefore merged. In the north-eastern counties, the image of

Protestantism was bolstered by the economic success of the Union. Ulster exported flax, linen and ships through the trade routes of the British Empire, and this economic growth was linked in Unionist vocabulary with 'progress'. The Belfast Chamber of Commerce told Gladstone in 1893:

> All our progress has been made under the union. We were a small, insignificant town at the end of the last century, deeply disaffected and hostile to the British empire. Since the union and under equal laws, we have been wedded to the empire and made a progress second to none . . . Why should we be driven by force to abandon the conditions which have led to that success?[117]

While later Ulster loyalist identity has been seen as anachronistic and atavistic, much of its coherence and strength lay in its realistic assessment of the economic conditions of the United Kingdom in contrast to those of rural Ireland. Ulster loyalism has in addition been overwhelmingly an urban identity, associated in particular with Belfast, whose civic pride was well represented in the building of City Hall in 1905 at a cost of £360,000.[118] Augustine Birrell, the pro-Home Rule Chief Secretary for Ireland in the Liberal government that finally passed Home Rule, remarked of his tour of Ulster in late 1913 that the civic culture of Belfast drew it apart from Ireland and towards Britain:

> [I]f you wind up, as we did, in Belfast, which is really a great Protestant effort, with a Town Hall as fine as Glasgow or Manchester and shrewd level-headed business men managing its affairs, you realise what a thing it is you are asking these conceited unimaginative, Protestant citizens to do, when you expect them to throw in their lot with such a place as Dublin, with its fatuous and scandalous Corporation and senseless disputes about the Irish language![119]

Furthermore, the 'Ulster' character was constructed as 'dour but hospitable, shrewd, self-reliant, steadfast and industrious, blunt of speech, and gifted with the capacity to govern less fortunate peoples'.[120] In the nineteenth century, all of these fitted happily in with the dominant Liberal version of British national identity, adaptable to the local circumstances of the constituent parts of the United Kingdom and ready to embrace the advantages of industrialisation and urbanisation. With Gladstone's conversion to Home Rule in the 1880s, however, Ulster loyalist identity began its divorce from the forces of 'progress' and its exclusion from the English rural idyll, especially since its industrial decline led to increasing urban decay and violence.

A Protestant sense of Britishness was heightened by the feeling of insecurity caused by the ascendancy of political nationalism in southern Ireland in the nineteenth century. In 1801 the Catholic Irish had expected the removal of legal restrictions that prevented them from office holding. It took a concerted and threatening campaign led by Daniel O'Connell to secure Catholic emancipation in 1829. This seemed to set the seal on how Irish politics would operate in the nineteenth century. Britain would deny the Irish full citizenship resulting in Catholic and nationalist agitation, which would in turn convince some nationalists that only full independence could achieve Irish liberty, while Irish Protestants would believe that concessions made to Catholics threatened their own position.

Nationalism in Ireland took two main forms: constitutional or parliamentary nationalism and physical force or republican nationalism. The boundaries between these were often blurred: by the violent nature of the land wars of the 1870s and 1880s, by the need for parliamentary leaders to pay lip service to the heroes of physical force nationalism, and by the role of militants in the constitutional movement. Both forms of nationalism in Ireland, though, were Catholic and political. From the 1870s nationalism's destiny and development were tied in with the fortunes of the Home Rule party founded in the 1870s but given dynamism by Charles Stewart Parnell's leadership in the 1880s.[121] The success of the Irish Parliamentary Party, as it was also known, brought into the open the conflict over Britishness. In the late nineteenth century there were three main strands of thought on national identity. First, there was the Gladstonian or Liberal view of Britishness. When Gladstone converted his party to Home Rule in the 1880s it was not because he wished to see the destruction of the Union, but because he believed a measure of autonomy in domestic affairs would strengthen an Irish sense of Britishness. The Liberals accepted the multi-national nature of the United Kingdom and hoped that Irish Home Rule would allow the Irish to follow Scotland and Wales in embracing their own particular patriotism with a wider British patriotism. Second, there was the conception that acceptance of Britishness would mean the extinction of the Irish nation through the complete Anglicisation of Ireland. The exact balance within Irish nationalism varied here, for while Parnell was prepared to cooperate with Gladstone he feared the success of the Liberal version of British national identity within Ireland.[122] In 1890 Parnell was involved in the O'Shea divorce case and was driven from the leadership of nationalism by a combination of British Liberal Nonconformist and Irish Catholic morality. This led to a division within constitutional nationalism, allowing the emergence of a cultural nationalism in Ireland, for example in the Gaelic Athletic Association and the Gaelic League (which sought to defend the declining Irish language).[123] Such nationalism suggested a 'racial' difference between the Irish and the English, reinforcing the more militant brands of nationalism that urged complete separation from Britain.[124]

Irish nationalism, like state-sponsored forms of nationalism, was concerned with the invention of tradition in this period. The centenary of the 1798 rebellion marked one such occasion, when nationalist Ireland commemorated the physical force 'tradition'. This was an exercise in nation-building, and the organising committee made clear that Ireland's capital lay in neither London nor Belfast, but Dublin:

As the National Capital will be the scene of this historic demonstration of a Nation's affection for, and gratitude to, those peerless sons of her pride who strove to place on her brow the sovereign crown of Nationhood . . . it is fitting that every effort should be made to bedeck the metropolis in its brightest array on this occasion.[125]

The Irish *Independent*, too, noted the significance of the commemoration when it remarked that 'Monday, August 15th, will be a good day for Ireland. Maybe not for the British Ireland within our Ireland, but it will be a gladsome day for National Ireland.'[126] Such commemoration of Ireland's separate history and the opposition to the Boer War and royal visits to Dublin in the early years of the new century gave a tremendous boost to radical nationalism.[127] The cultural nationalism of the Gaelic League, Gaelic Athletic Association and Sinn Féin rejected the Liberal pluralist version of Britishness in favour of a Gaelicised (and mainly Catholic) Irishness.[128]

Ireland was not totally isolated from wider European cultural currents in this period, and cultural nationalism absorbed a glorification of war associated with Social Darwinism. Hence Patrick Pearse, a devout Catholic and teacher at an Irish bilingual school, declared in 1913: 'We may make mistakes in the beginning and shoot the wrong people; but bloodshed is a cleansing and satisfying thing, and the nation which regards it as the final horror has lost its manhood. There are many things more horrible than bloodshed; and slavery is one of them.'[129] Such declarations were given added importance because of the militarisation of Irish politics after 1910.[130] After the general elections of that year the reunited Irish parliamentary party held the balance of power in the Commons, and in 1912 the third Home Rule Bill was introduced. Whereas those of 1886 and 1893 had failed, this bill was assured success by the removal of the absolute veto of the House of Lords under the Parliament Act of 1911.

This brought the third conception of Britishness to the fore. English, Irish and Ulster Unionists believed that there was but a single British identity with regional rather than national diversity. Hence no concession of political autonomy would be made to Ireland, as it was not made to Yorkshire or the south-west of England.[131] The Irish were 'West Britons' as the Scots were 'North Britons'.[132] The parliamentary alliance of 1910 seemed to them to be a corrupt and treacherous bargain to subvert the constitution. In Ulster, the threat of Home Rule had forged a cross-class Unionist coalition, as aristocrats and industrialists saw their future as dependent on the connection with the British and imperial economy, and the Protestant working class faced competition for employment from Catholics. They all saw themselves as British, and saw the Union as essential to being British. The Unionist song, 'For Union and King', declared that 'Freedom's eyes are dim with anguish,/ But her voice sings loud and clear,/ And she calls her children round her,/ British kinsmen, do you hear?/ Yes, we hear; the cry goes upward/ And we rally to that cry.'[133] In order to defend the Union they were prepared to go against parliament, by force of arms if necessary. In 1912 the Ulster Volunteer Force was established and began

to arm itself. How did Unionists square this with being British, with the attachment to constitutional forms explicit within so much Britishness?

They did so by giving allegiance to the crown rather than to parliament,
which was capable of falling into the hands of the Liberal–Labour–Irish
alliance. Loyalty to the crown was the mark of loyalty to Britain and was contrasted with the disloyalty of nationalism, which they branded as republican.[134]
The Unionist MP Hugh Minford declared in the 1940s: 'There are only two
classes in Northern Ireland, the loyal and the disloyal. The loyal people are the
Orangemen, the disloyal people are the Socialists, Communists and Roman
Catholics.'[135] The loyalty of Unionists to the crown was therefore doubly
important because of the existence of a disloyal minority.

With nationalists responding to the arming of Ulster Unionism by establishing
the Irish Volunteers, and the British Conservative Party apparently supporting
the right of Ulster to resist parliament's will by force, the situation in Ireland in
1914 was extremely tense.[136] In August 1914 general European war broke out.
Naturally, Unionists immediately declared their loyalty. But so too did John
Redmond for the Irish Parliamentary Party, still the dominant force within
nationalism. While in part both sides were positioning themselves for resumption
of the Irish conflict after what they expected to be a short war, it was also the
case that most Irish accepted the Liberal version of Britishness, particularly in the
circumstances that Britain seemed to be fighting for the rights of small nations to
independence. The passing of the Home Rule Act in September 1914 enabled
Redmond to express the loyalty to which he and other moderate nationalists had
aspired.[137] He told an Irish audience in Manchester that

> Ireland has been admitted by the democracy of England upon equal terms
> to her proper place in the Empire, which she had as much to do in the
> building of as England or Scotland (loud applause); and already as a result
> she has taken her proper place with perfect and absolute good faith and
> loyalty.[138]

Redmond's support for the British war effort led to a division in the nationalist
movement, but of 180,000 Volunteers only 10,000 broke with the Irish Parliamentary Party. Redmond was certainly not alone in his desire to gain the
benefits of association with Britain within the Empire. George Berkeley, a Volunteer organiser in Belfast, described the Home Rule Act as 'restor[ing] a
Parliament to our country after so many generations of toil, the Act which
would enable Ireland to take her place willingly, and therefore without loss of
honour, in the circle of self-governing states which form the British Empire'.[139]

The war continued the confirmation of Protestant Ulster's sense of Britishness. The Ulster Volunteer Force was allowed to form a separate Ulster Division
(whereas recruits from Catholic Ireland were spread across the army).[140] Many
Ulster Protestants perceived a religious nature to the war; the first day of the
battle of the Somme fell on the anniversary of the Battle of the Boyne.[141] The
16th (Ulster) Division suffered 5,500 casualties. The report in the *Northern Whig*

symbolised the grief *and* patriotism that characterised loyal Ulster's response to this tragedy:

> There are aching hearts among those who still wait in mingled hope and dread for news, and over the whole body of the people there is a feeling of sad expectancy. Yet through it all there runs a thrill, we will not say of pride. Rather it is of exaltation, at the thought that the Ulster Loyalist stock has now added to its long record of soldier service to King and country such a glorious fighting episode.[142]

The war also confirmed loyal Ulster's view that Catholics were disloyal, because of the Easter Rising of 1916. On Easter Monday 1916, led by the Irish Republican Brotherhood, around 2,000 of those Volunteers who had split from the Redmondites rose against British rule and proclaimed an Irish republic. After a week the rising was defeated, and the execution of sixteen of the leaders roused immense sympathy in nationalist Ireland. The blood sacrifice ideal of Pearse had been proved; 'from the graves of patriot men and women spring living nations', he had said in 1915.[143] The failure of the government to grant Home Rule in the aftermath of the rising spelled the demise of the Irish Parliamentary Party and the attempt, in 1918, to impose conscription on Ireland destroyed the last vestiges of Britishness in nationalist Ireland. To loyal Ulster, the nationalist opposition to conscription, in Ireland but also in the white dominions once more confirmed Catholic disloyalty. In the 1918 general election, Sinn Féin won seventy-three of the hundred Irish seats and refused to go to Westminster, setting up the Dáil Éireann in Dublin instead. Alongside the cultural rejection of Britishness, Sinn Féin was attempting to assert Ireland's legal rejection through the establishment of an alternative sovereign institution. The war of independence developed gradually and the use of the Black and Tans, an auxiliary police force of ex-soldiers brutalised by the experience of war on the Western Front, further suggested to the Irish that the government never quite considered them to be full British citizens.

In 1921 a compromise was reached that ended the Anglo-Irish war: Ireland was partitioned, with twenty-six counties being granted dominion status on the condition that allegiance was sworn to the British crown. The establishment of the Irish Free State took the majority of Irish people out of the United Kingdom, and therefore out of the realm of the discussion of this chapter. Even so, there continued to be vestigial Britishness in southern Ireland. Around 200,000 Irish had served in the British Army in the First World War and 27,000 had been killed. While the memorialisation of the war dead was controversial in Ireland, high poppy sales, a network of branches of the British Legion and large Armistice Parades in the 1930s and again between 1945 and 1970, suggest the continuing desire of some to remember Ireland's 'British' past. During the Second World War around 50,000 Irish men and women were recruited from Eire into the British armed forces, and while many motives underlay these individual decisions some at least represented a residual 'loyalism'.[144]

Northern Ireland also received a separate parliament, and while it had never wanted it, seeing partition as a method of preventing Home Rule for all Ireland, it came to welcome this parliament as a way of ensuring the continuation of Britishness within its own part of Ireland.[145] Captain Charles Craig (brother of Sir James Craig), explained the position to the House of Commons:

> We would much prefer to remain part and parcel of the United Kingdom. We have prospered, we have made our province prosperous under the union, and under the laws passed by this House . . . We do not in any way desire to recede from a position which has been in every way satisfactory to us, but we have many enemies in this country, and we feel that an Ulster without a parliament of its own would not be in nearly as strong a position as one in which a parliament had been set up . . . We profoundly distrust the labour party and we profoundly distrust the right hon. gentleman the Member for Paisley (Mr Asquith). We believe that if either of those parties, or the two in combination, were once more in power our chances of remaining a part of the United Kingdom would be very small indeed.[146]

Loyalty to Stormont (the parliament house built in the 1930s) replaced the already much weakened loyalty to Westminster. Loyalty to the crown remained, especially as George V opened the Northern Ireland parliament in June 1921, providing an alternative focus for Britishness, but Ulster had excluded itself from the mainstream Whig interpretation of the Westminster parliament as central to Britishness. It was instead a body viewed with increasing suspicion.

The Ulster Unionist governments that ruled for the following fifty years rejected the Britishness of the Catholic minority, and openly discriminated on the basis that Catholics offered no loyalty either to the crown or to Britain.[147] The neutrality of Eire (as the Free State became in 1937) during the Second World War allowed Protestant Ulster once more to confirm its Britishness. Ulster's industrial identity aided its integration into the British war effort, as did its experience of bombing.[148] Harry Midgley, of the Northern Ireland Labour Party, explained the themes of unity and shared experience in wartime:

> Here in Northern Ireland [he wrote] we regard ourselves as being in the front line of defence and attack with Great Britain . . . To-day all industry and commerce in this area is increasingly being harnessed to the national cause and successful prosecution of the war . . . We are determined that these great industries . . . shall once again play an important part in smashing tyranny and liberating the peoples of the earth.[149]

Midgley went on, in 1943, to become the first non-Unionist member of the Stormont government, campaigning in the 1945 general election on the basis of a programme of social reform and 'the maintenance of Ulster's position as an integral part of the United Kingdom'.[150]

The Second World War also presented problems. It distanced Ulster from mainland versions of Britishness. In a war about social unity, democracy and tolerance, Ulster Protestant narrowness, sectarianism and zeal did not sit happily with the 'people's war' version of patriotism.[151] Therefore, despite declarations of support for the Union from both Conservative and Labour governments after 1922, Ulster's British Protestant population could never quite lose its anxiety over its constitutional status because its Britishness was in some measure different from the Britishness of mainland Britons. In many ways, Protestant Ulster's links had been with Scotland rather than with England, and its Britishness had been formulated in this light.[152] In 1949 Ireland left the Commonwealth, and to reassure the loyalist population the Labour government of Clement Attlee passed the Ireland Act (1949), 'which affirmed the province's territorial integrity within the United Kingdom'.[153] In addition the Stormont parliament was given a veto over ejection from the UK, a case of devolution being used to hold Britain together.

It also enabled the Westminster parliament to ignore discrimination against the Catholic part of the population as internal matters were ruled the responsibility of Stormont. In the 1960s, inspired by civil rights campaigns in the United States, Catholics and socialists mounted marches and demonstrations seeking to gain full and equal citizenship (even though that did not entail the demand for Britishness). Many Protestants saw these marches as simply another sign of Catholic disloyalty and the auxiliary police force, the B Specials, and others used mounting violence against the civil rights movement. In August 1969, the Wilson government at Westminster sent in the army to restore order on the streets of Belfast. It was widely perceived at the time that the army's role was to protect Catholics, and this led many Unionists to feel that the Westminster governments had lessened their commitment to the maintenance of the Britishness of Ulster. The actions of both Labour and Conservative governments seemed to Unionists to be heading towards compromise with the Republic of Ireland in the south and republicans in the north. While the army became regularly engaged in policing the Catholic population, culminating in internment in 1971 and Bloody Sunday in January 1972, when paratroops killed thirteen people on a routine civil rights demonstration, loyalists perceived a threat to their legal Britishness, especially when the Stormont parliament was abolished and Direct Rule was imposed. This led to a revival of loyalist hostility to the British parliament and a reassertion of loyalty to the British crown. George Graham, a Democratic Unionist Party assemblyman, explained his allegiance in 1976:

My loyalty is to the British Throne being Protestant. I have no loyalty to any Westminster government. I have no loyalty to a government which prorogued a democratically elected government [Stormont], destroyed our security forces and left us prey to the IRA. Nor have I loyalty to a British government going over the heads of our people, conniving and double-dealing behind our backs with a foreign government.[154]

But between 1969 and 1977 there were no royal visits to Northern Ireland, which was seen as a further lessening of Westminster governments' commitment to the Britishness of the province. In 1977, to mark the silver jubilee, the Queen did visit the province. While the intention was to confirm the integration of Northern Ireland into the nation through royal celebration, the need for special security measures against the Irish Republican Army pointed to division rather than union.[155] The crown at least continued to reward Ulster loyalism, with twenty-one further visits between 1977 and 1985, and after the Anglo-Irish Agreement alienated Unionists further, there were sixty-one visits between 1985 and 1993.[156]

Loyalism and Unionism have not been monolithic identities. While the Unionist establishment remained firmly in control from the 1920s to the 1960s, then the divisions were often between those seeking to assert sectional interests within unionism, such as the demands of labour and trade unionism. From the late 1960s, though, there have been sections of Unionism which have sought a more determined defence of Protestant and unionist identity, often associating any concession to the Republic of Ireland or nationalism within Northern Ireland with catastrophe. The symbolism of marches, so long of importance in northern identities, escalated in the 1990s, with that in Drumcree attracting annual attention each July. The march of the Orange Lodge down the Garvaghy Road became a crucial symbol for radical Protestants. As Ian Paisley explained in 1995, 'If we don't win this battle all is lost . . . It is a matter of Ulster or the Irish Republic, it is a matter of freedom or slavery.' James Loughlin uses this quote to exemplify the 'immobilism' and 'totalising' nature of such Unionist identities, of which Paisley has been leader since the late 1960s.[157]

The sense of siege from without and within has contributed to a search for a wide range of new identities. From the early 1970s some unionists have sought increasingly to stress their identity with Ulster. In part this was connected with the belief that England was letting them down, but in addition social developments on the mainland were not welcomed in the conservative north of Ireland. Two Londonderry Unionist groups declared, in a publication of 1973, that 'Great Britain has been sinking into a pagan cesspool of iniquity and to all appearances is now utterly devoid of honour and decency.'[158] The choice of words, so usually associated with Englishness-Britishness, showed that alienation from 'permissiveness' accompanied the hostility to the imposition of Direct Rule. 'Since Merrie England dearly wishes to "sell out" loyal Ulster', the pamphlet continued, 'all Protestants must prepare for the worst.' Protestants, it declared, 'are prepared to go it alone'.[159] Since the 1970s the use of the Northern Ireland flag has become prominent, further emphasising the desire to stress an Ulster identity. It has also resulted in the construction of myths about the events of 1912 to 1914 when Unionism defended the six counties against Home Rule.[160] This certainly has not meant alienation from Britishness however, but a delineation of Ulster Britishness. As John Hobson, Stormont MP, explained shortly before that parliament's prorogation: 'I have been British all my life and I wish to remain British. I consider myself to be Irish-British, just as there are

Scottish-British and Welsh-British, but I am first and foremost British, and British I want to remain.'[161] As Tom Hennessey points out though, a frequent trajectory among Protestants has been away from Irishness, as Catholics have increasingly asserted their own Irishness.[162]

The direct involvement of the Westminster governments in the affairs of the province for the first time since the 1920s had therefore further encouraged the politicisation of day-to-day national identities in Northern Ireland. Rule from Westminster was not accompanied by any serious or successful attempts by British mainland parties to engage in Northern Irish constituency politics, and hence the politicisation of identities in Ireland was more 'Irish' than 'British'. Across the decades from the formation of the statelet in 1921, Catholics had been suspected as disloyal and had often identified themselves as Irish rather than British. But by the 1960s there had been some sort of rapprochement with the state that had removed support from the IRA.[163] The behaviour of Protestant mobs in the late 1960s and the British army after 1969, however, brought about the 'progressive alienation of the Catholic working class from the British state'.[164] Fionnuala O Connor quotes a woman whose memories of living in Derry (the very names of the city – Derry to nationalists but Londonderry to loyalists – reflects the day-to-day conflict over identity) went back over seven decades:

> You didn't think about being Irish, you *were* Irish. It was only after the Troubles started you began to think about it. Before that, you were just Catholic, and you were in Northern Ireland, and you weren't part of it. So, yes, you were a nationalist too. Or republican. But you didn't stick the 'Northern' in first. Of course we were Northerners, and proud of it, proud of the North.[165]

This wonderfully explains the change in identity, from a latent Irishness, taken for granted until the late 1960s, transforming itself into an Irish nationalism of the north. But in addition it reveals the multi-layered identity entailed, since while it rejects the Northern Irish (Protestant) state it adopts an Irish northern regional identity. The frequent run-ins with the British state brought Irish identities to the forefront for a significant majority of the Catholic population, which was called and identified itself as the 'nationalist' community. Varying proportions of the 'nationalist' electorate gave their support to the moderate Social and Democratic Labour Party and the radical Sinn Féin, the latter associating itself with the physical force tradition that had gone so far in expelling the British from the twenty-six counties of the south. Sinn Féin has had varying electoral fortunes. In the 1982 Assembly, elections gave Sinn Féin over 10 per cent of the vote, in the wake of the hunger strikes of 1981, which saw ten republican prisoners die in pursuit of political status. In 1986, following the Anglo-Irish Agreement of the previous year, Sinn Féin secured only 6.6 per cent in by-elections brought about by the unionist resignation of seats. In recent years, since the Good Friday Agreement (1998), Sinn Féin has won as much as

17.6 per cent of votes cast in Assembly elections. On the other side, unionism has become increasingly fragmented between official and unofficial forms of loyalism. This clearly confirms the fluid nature of the impact of national identity on politics, even where allegiance has been seen as so firm and historically rooted.

## The end of Britain?

Since the 1870s, identities in Wales, Scotland, Ireland and Northern Ireland have not been fixed. Across that period, they have had a changing relationship with Britishness. That relationship has certainly not been externally imposed. Britishness, often in the guise of unionism, has been embraced by significant portions of the people of 'outer Britain'. Neither has the process been one of the inevitable unravelling of the United Kingdom or Britishness across the last 130 years. The economic prosperity of the late nineteenth and early twentieth centuries did provide a base upon which the national identity was politicised in Wales and Scotland as demands were made for cultural distinctiveness, but that was possible alongside a sense of integration, of Britishness. The view in Wales and Scotland, and among unionists in Ireland too, was the pluralistic view of national identities championed by Gladstone, the Liberals and the Labour Party. In the case of the Ulster Unionists, political change did not come into the equation of plural identities and hence they moved closer and closer to a view that lessened differences between Ulster and British identities. This was not only an economic relationship however, since the inter-war depression (and continuing decline of heavy industry after 1945) did not create significant support for the newly emerged Scottish and Welsh nationalist parties. Indeed, in some ways, decline tied the Welsh and Scottish left more firmly into the Britishness of the Labour Party, through the belief in planning and especially through the welfare state. The creation of a consciously 'national' and 'British' system of welfare and state responsibility gave a sense of 'community' to all areas of Britain. The impact of Thatcherism on the welfare state had repercussions in 'outer Britain'. Her monolithic unionism, a political rather than an economic force, created the conditions for the resurgence of Welsh and, even more so, Scottish distinctiveness. Through the 1990s, Labour returned to pluralism. In part, this was a question of expediency, but to deny the sincerity of the newly emerging Welshness and Scottishness of numerous party activists and MPs is untenable. The success of devolution in the 1990s, when it failed in the 1970s, is partly to be attributed to the more deeply held sense of Welsh and Scottish national identities of Labour. It is noteworthy that the pressure for devolution, therefore, came from a party that since its formation has seen itself as an all-British party, and it is that fact that should perhaps draw us short of suggesting that devolution is equivalent to the 'break-up of Britain'. The unravelling of Britain argument also runs into the sand in Northern Ireland. The process there has not been in the direction of 'progress', a contested concept, but meaning here the path towards devolution. Power was devolved to Northern Ireland in

1921. The existence of a separate parliament in the United Kingdom enhanced the Britishness of the majority unionist (often Protestant) population but alienated the minority nationalist (mostly Catholic) population. While the latter has more usually been associated with the idea that 'progress' comes from the political left, it has been Unionists who have associated themselves with the constitutional 'progress' of Whig history. The imposition of Direct Rule in 1972, therefore, alienated many loyalists from the British parliament, and confirmed that to be from Ulster implied a different kind of Britishness. Identities were confirmed as simultaneous, while allegiances were in many ways divorced. The 'peace process' in Northern Ireland has certainly not ended the deep sense of difference between loyalist and nationalist 'communities', who still imagine themselves to be dissimilar. Devolution in Northern Ireland though, this time around, is based more on recognition of diversity rather than on the simple imposition of Protestant rule.

There is a tendency in the discussions of 'the end of Britain' to consider that people as members of a variety of nations within the United Kingdom *ought* to be acting in particular ways, that they *should* be becoming more Welsh, Scottish and Irish. This tendency has marginalised those people (in the historiography of devolution), such as the unionists in Wales, Scotland and Ulster, who have 'resisted' such historical forces and suggested that their behaviour is in some way backward-looking. The tendency to presume identity as leading towards an exclusive sense of Welshness, Scottishness or Irishness also discounts the potential for multiple and simultaneous identities among those who would consider themselves to be, for example, Scottish and British at the same time, though in varying degrees in relation to the context in which the individual finds him or herself. Identities of place are adaptive feelings, and Britishness, while certainly not as paramount in identities as it was, say, during the First and Second World Wars, still retains a powerful hold alongside other identities of place within the United Kingdom.

# Conclusion

If the nineteenth century can be characterised as the age of nationalism, then the late twentieth century may be said to have experienced a crisis of the national identities that emerged out of that period of nation-building. On almost every continent, the meaning of belonging to particular nations has been contested. Some of the conflicts have become open war, as in the Palestine–Israel conflict, the war in the former Yugoslavia, in various parts of the former Soviet Union, in the Indian sub-continent and in Africa. Other conflicts have centred on 'History Wars'.[1] In France, the battle of words has been over collaboration and resistance under the Vichy regime in the Second World War (as well as the impact of the end of Empire).[2] In Germany, the site of encounter has been the place of Nazism and the Holocaust in German history and identity.[3] In Spain, there has been the need for a 'delicate balance' between the regional-national demands for autonomy and the desire for centralism and unity of the Spanish nation.[4] Even apparently stable countries have seen remarkably bitter controversies. Australian national identity has been torn by disputes over the influence of Britishness, Aboriginal rights, proximity to Asia and Asian immigration.[5] Territorial politics have become more and more complex, with few nations being so ethnically homogenous as to face no demands for devolution of powers. Regionalism and sub-nationalisms within existing nation-states have combined with the politics of immigration to mean that few (western) nations can take themselves for granted in the twenty-first century. At the same time, economic globalisation and supra-national political integration have added to the sense of crisis. This certainly points to Robert Colls' argument, referred to at the beginning of this book, that all national identities are unstable.[6] But it is too easy to throw the baby out with the bath water. There are tensions in all multiple identities, but that does not make multiple identities fundamentally incompatible. The primacy of particular identities may change, so that someone living in Germany might feel 'German' at times, but Bavarian or Prussian at others, or feel attached to localities through the numerous festivals held in each city, town and village. At other times, larger identities of place might be adhered to, such as being European. Sometimes, frequently, most often, it is possible and often necessary to feel many identities simultaneously. Examples could be multiplied endlessly, for each nation. It is in this international context of uncertainty that the current 'crisis of Britishness' needs to be viewed. This is not to add to a complacent British myth of moderation and common sense. The war in Northern Ireland has claimed 3,000 lives since the late 1960s and violent racism is a feature of many multi-ethnic areas of British cities. In almost every area discussed in this book it is possible to find signs that the collective national identity of the British people is weakening fast. The monarchy is less secure now as a core feature of Britishness than at any time since the 1870s. The geographical reality of the British Empire, which certainly provided common purpose to many of the English, Scots and Welsh and some of the Irish, has come to an end. Surveys reveal ignorance about Empire that shocks traditionalists.[7] In terms of culture, A. H. Halsey in his social trends survey of 2000 declared British society 'hopelessly Americanised'.[8] On the other hand, football hooliganism is frequently associated with Englishness. Devolution of power to Scotland and Wales has emerged from the electoral growth of nationalist parties. English nationalism and regionalism have emerged, weakly, on to the political agenda. The 'peace process' in Northern Ireland has not brought Catholics and Protestants, nationalists and unionists together, though it has brought a military truce. Clearly, Britishness has faced a range of serious challenges in the last three decades.

Many historians have concluded that Britishness cannot and will not see off these challenges. Norman Davies argues that, by the late 1990s, 'the prospect for "Britishness" was bleak indeed'.[9] Weight argues that Scottishness, Welshness and Englishness are becoming increasingly important, at the expense of Britishness.[10] Robert Colls focuses on the 'problem' of Englishness in the break-up of Britain.[11] However, most people living in the United Kingdom of Great Britain and Northern Ireland still consider themselves to be British, alongside other identities. Political scientists use the Moreno question to analyse national identities in the multi-national United Kingdom. The question asks whether respondents consider themselves to be (a) Scottish/Welsh/English, not British, (b) more Scottish/Welsh/English than British, (c) equally Scottish/Welsh/English and British, (d) more British than Scottish/Welsh/English, or (e) British, not Scottish/Welsh/English. As part of the 1997 British Election Study, for example, the question was asked of 3,600 people.[12] Of the 2,383 people asked in England 74 per cent considered themselves to be at least equally British and English. If the figures accurately reflected the feelings of the 50 million people living in England, then 37.5 million of the 60 million living in the United Kingdom would still retain Britishness as an important part of their identity. But we can go further than that. In Wales, 56 per cent considered themselves at least equally British with their Welshness. Even in Scotland, the crucial nation in the break-up of Britain argument, 35 per cent identified themselves as at least equally British and Scottish. But can we go still further for Scotland. An additional 33 per cent answered that they were 'more Scottish than British'. Since they were given the option to declare themselves 'not British', as 33 per cent did, this means that two-thirds of those living in Scotland in 1997 still considered themselves in some ways British, even if it was not their primary identity. There are, of course, many problems with such polls, but they are frequently used to establish that Britishness is in terminal decline. They can be used instead to consider the readjustment of Britishness to a changed situation.

Britishness is certainly going through a period of instability. It is worth reiterating that Britishness has never been a solid and uncontested concept. Between the 1870s and the 1920s it was fundamentally challenged by the struggle for Irish Home Rule and independence,[13] but Britishness was also strengthened by the experience of the First and Second World Wars. Across the period, different classes, genders, ethnic groups and political parties contested ownership of the concept of Britishness. Certainly, the persistence and depth of these contests has been greater in the last three decades, but nonetheless Britishness has been a highly adaptive identity in the past. It has never been static and fixed, but has fluctuated in meaning as different Britons have made claims upon it.

There are some who cling to the notion of an unchanging Britishness, forged long in the past. Some of these dispute the attempts of 'new' Britons to shape a national identity that sits comfortably with other identities, of place or memory (even myth) of place, of ethnicity, and so on. In no way should the persistent racism of some British people be underestimated, and a narrative of a progressive acceptance of immigrants and their descendants as Britons would be untenable. In the wake of the terrorist attacks on the United States on 11 September 2001 Muslims in Britain and elsewhere were demonised, with inevitable consequences.[14] However, at the end of the twentieth century, one poll at least suggested that a large majority believed that Englishness, so frequently seen as an ethnic rather than a civic identity, was available to immigrant and non-white people. While 29 per cent considered it 'mattered a great deal to being English' to be born in England, only 12 per cent considered that being white was important.[15] Most black, Asian and white people in Britain would share the view of a Bradford resident faced with a National Front march in the mid-1970s:

> It was we immigrants who brought Bradford back to life. We worked in the foundries, textiles, the health and transport services. We put the economy back on its feet. Now they don't want us. They can threaten us, but we are here to stay.[16]

The most frequent 'write-in' on the question about ethnicity in the 2001 census was 'black British'.[17] To see such contests as part of the inevitable decline of Britishness as the United Kingdom unravelled is to impose a grand narrative of the inevitable triumph of the nation-state that is more suited to the nineteenth century than the twenty-first. On the other hand, to expect Britishness to remain fixed and pure would be to deny the constructed and reconstructed nature of national identities. This is indeed the way in which many on the right have approached the issue. Britishness is no longer the unquestioned primary identity of the majority of the British people, as it probably was between the late nineteenth century and the 1970s, but it remains an important part of the population of the United Kingdom's identities of place at the beginning of the twenty-first century. If the question is asked, 'when was Britain?' then the answer must be that it still is.[18]

# Notes

## Introduction

1 The literature on nationalism, nation formation and national identities is huge, but see, for example, G. Balakrishnan (ed.), *Mapping the Nation*, London, Verso, 1996; S. Ben-Ami, Y. Peled and A. Spektorowski (eds), *Ethnic Challenges to the Modern Nation State*, Basingstoke, Macmillan, 2000; R. Brubaker, *Nationalism Reframed: Nationhood and the National Question in the New Europe*, Cambridge, Cambridge University Press, 1996; E. Hobsbawm, *Nations and Nationalism since 1780: Programme, Myth, Reality*, Cambridge, Cambridge University Press, 1990; B. Jenkins and S. Sofos (eds), *Nation and Identity in Contemporary Europe*, London, Routledge, 1996; T. Oommen (ed.), *Citizenship and National Identity: From Colonialism to Globalism*, New Delhi, Sage, 1997; M. Teich and R. Porter (eds), *The National Question in Europe in Historical Context*, Cambridge, Cambridge University Press, 1993.
2 C. Harvie, 'The moment of British nationalism, 1939–1970', *Political Quarterly*, 71, 2000, pp. 328–40.
3 T. Nairn, *The Break-Up of Britain: Crisis and Neo-Nationalism*, London, New Left Books, 1977, revised edition, London, Verso, 1981; T. Nairn, *After Britain: New Labour and the Return of Scotland*, London, Granta, 1999. For a discussion of the answers to the question 'When was Britain?' see A. Aughey, *Nationalism, Devolution and the Challenge to the United Kingdom State*, London, Pluto, 2001.
4 J. Redwood, *The Death of Britain?*, Basingstoke, Macmillan, 1999; A. Marr, *The Day Britain Died*, London, Profile, 2000; P. Hitchens, *The Abolition of Britain: The British Cultural Revolution from Lady Chatterley to Tony Blair*, London, Quartet, 1999; R. Scruton, *England: An Elegy*, London, Chatto and Windus, 2000. See also A. Marr, *The Day Britain Died*, London, Profile, 2000; J. Redwood, *The Death of Britain?*, Basingstoke, Macmillan, 1999; K. Sutherland, (ed.), *The Rape of the Constitution?*, Thorverton, Imprint Academic, 2000.
5 S. Heffer, *Nor Shall My Sword: The Reinvention of England*, London, Weidenfeld and Nicholson, 1999.
6 Redwood, *Death of Britain?*
7 *White Tribe*, Channel 4, 1999.
8 Redwood, *Death of Britain?*, p. 191.
9 Y. Alibhai-Brown, *Who Do We Think We Are? Imagining the New Britain*, London, Penguin, 2001.
10 S. Haseler, *The English Tribe: Identity, Nation and Europe*, Basingstoke, Macmillan, 1996, p. viii. See also A. Brown, D. McCrone and L. Paterson, *Politics and Society in Scotland*, Basingstoke, Macmillan, 1996, pp. 39–40.
11 Haseler, *English Tribe*, p. 109. The classic statement of this position is M. Hechter, *Internal Colonialism: The Celtic Fringe in British National Development*, New Brunswick, NJ, Transaction, 1999.

12  L. Colley, *Britons: Forging the Nation 1707–1837*, London, Pimlico, 1994, p. 6.

13  K. Robbins, *Nineteenth-Century Britain: England, Scotland, and Wales – The Making of a Nation*, Oxford, Oxford University Press, 1989, ch. 1.

14  See N. Davies, *The Isles: A History*, Basingstoke, Papermac, 2000, pp. xxiii–xli, for a discussion of the confusion over the nomenclature of the UK nation. Legally, strictly speaking, Northern Irish people are not 'British', but are subjects of the United Kingdom of Great Britain and Northern Ireland. The (bare) majority, however, adopt Britishness as a major part of their identity. The British world also extended into the Empire, with millions claiming Britishness long after migrating from Britain or being born overseas, see for example, C. Bridge and K. Fedorowich (eds), *The British World: Diaspora, Culture and Identity*, London, Frank Cass, 2003.

15  H. Bhabha, *Nation and Narration*, 1990, p. 3, quoted in J. Vernon, 'Englishness: the narration of nation', *Journal of British Studies*, 36, 1997, pp. 245–6.

16  It is invidious but necessary to give an example: J. Foster, *Class Struggle and the Industrial Revolution*, London, Weidenfeld and Nicolson, 1974, starts from the assumption that the proletariat *should* have been revolutionary but was not, and seeks, with rigorous historical method, to explain why that was so.

17  Haseler, *English Tribe*, p. 49.

18  L. Brockliss and D. Eastwood, 'Introduction: a union of multiple identities', in their *A Union of Multiple Identities: The British Isles, c.1750–c.1850*, Manchester, Manchester University Press, 1997, p. 2.

19  Aughey, *Nationalism*, p. 56.

20  J. Curtice, 'Is Scotland a nation and Wales not?', in B. Taylor and K. Thomson (eds), *Scotland and Wales: Nations Again?* Cardiff, University of Wales Press, 1999, p. 122.

21  Sinn Féin were unopposed in twenty-three of the hundred Irish seats, suggesting that their vote would have exceeded 50 per cent of the electorate.

22  Quoted in T. Wilson (ed.), *The Political Diaries of C. P. Scott, 1911–1928*, London, Collins, 1970, p. 217, diary entry 6–8 June 1916. John Redmond was leader of the devolutionist Home Rule party.

23  D. McCrone, 'Who do we think we are? Identity politics in modern Scotland', http://www.britcoun.de/e/education/studies/scot2994.htm#scot, 9 September 2002.

24  Davies, *The Isles*, pp. 857–61.

25  H. Kearney, *The British Isles: A History of Four Nations*, Cambridge, Cambridge University Press, 1995; K. Robbins, *Great Britain: Identities, Institutions and the Idea of Britishness*, London, Longman, 1998; J. Black, *A History of the British Isles*, Basingstoke, Macmillan, 1996; Davies, *The Isles*; J. Pocock, 'British history: a plea for a new subject', *New Zealand Journal of History*, 8, 1974, pp. 3–21.

26  See for example R. Finlay, 'Review article: New Britain, new Scotland, new history? The impact of devolution on the development of Scottish historiography', *Journal of Contemporary History*, 36, 2001, pp. 383–93.

27  Most recently in Robbins, *Great Britain*.

28  See for example, G. Newman, *The Rise of English Nationalism: A Cultural History, 1740–1830*, London, Weidenfeld and Nicolson, 1987; R. Colls and P. Dodd (eds), *Englishness: Politics and Culture 1880–1920*, London, Croom Helm, 1986 (which is actually wider in attention than its title suggests); J. Giles and T. Middleton (eds), *Writing Englishness 1900–1950: An Introductory Sourcebook on National Identity*, London, Routledge, 1995; R. Colls, *Identity of England*, Oxford, Oxford University Press, 2002; K. Kumar, *The Making of English National Identity*, Cambridge, Cambridge University Press, 2003.

29  For example, M. Pittock, *Celtic Identity and the British Image*, Manchester, Manchester University Press, 1999.

30  See Hobsbawm, *Nations and Nationalism since 1780: Programme, Myth, Reality*, second edition, 1992, ch. 1, 'The nation as novelty'. For the alternative view see, for

example, A. Hastings, *The Construction of Nationhood: Ethnicity, Religion and Nationalism*, Cambridge, Cambridge University Press, 1997, especially pp. 35–65; A. Grant and K. Stringer (eds), *Uniting the Kingdom: The Making of British History*, London, Routledge, 1995; A. Murdoch, *British History 1660–1832*, Basingstoke, Macmillan, 1998.

31  R. Samuel (ed.), *Patriotism: The Making and Unmaking of British National Identity*, 3 volumes, London, Routledge, 1989.

32  R. Weight, *Patriots: National Identity in Britain 1940–2000*, Basingstoke, Macmillan, 2002; Colls, *Identity of England*. The phrase 'Englishness-Britishness' is used here to describe the elision of English and British national identities in some discussions.

33  Weight, *Patriots*, p. 1.

34  Weight, *Patriots*, p. 11.

35  Weight, *Patriots*, p. 733.

36  Robbins, *Nineteenth-Century Britain*; Colley, *Britons?*

37  Colls, *Identity of England*, p. 377

38  Colls, *Identity of England*, p. 283.

39  Colls, *Identity of England*, p. 379.

40  Colls, *Identity of England*, p. 196.

41  Colls, *Identity of England*, pp. 185–6.

42  R. Rose, *National Pride: Cross National Surveys*, Glasgow, Centre for the Study of Social Policy, University of Strathclyde, 1984, pp. 3, 4, 5.

43  E. Renan, 'What is a nation?' (1882) in H. Bhabha (ed.), *Nation and Narration*, London, Routledge, 1990, pp. 20, 19.

## 1  Monarchy and Empire

1  Quoted in J. Golby and A. Purdue, *The Monarchy and the British People 1760 to the Present*, London, Batsford, 1988, p. 94. For Empire Day, see J. Mangan, '"The grit of our forefathers": invented traditions, propaganda and imperialism', in John M. MacKenzie (ed.), *Imperialism and Popular Culture*, Manchester, Manchester University Press, 1986, pp. 113–39, and D. Hume, 'Empire Day in Ireland 1896–1962', in K. Jeffery (ed.), *'An Irish Empire'? Aspects of Ireland and the British Empire*, Manchester, Manchester University Press, 1996.

2  D. Cannadine, 'The context, performance and meaning of ritual: the British monarchy and the "invention of tradition", c.1820–1977', in E. Hobsbawm and T. Ranger (eds), *The Invention of Tradition*, Cambridge, Cambridge University Press, 1983, p. 153.

3  Quoted in J. Cannon and R. Griffiths, *The Oxford Illustrated History of the British Monarchy*, Oxford, Oxford University Press, 1988, p. 577.

4  J. MacKenzie, *Propaganda and Empire: The Manipulation of British Public Opinion 1880–1960*, Manchester, Manchester University Press, 1984, pp. 174–5.

5  D. Cannadine, *Ornamentalism: How the British Saw Their Empire*, London, Allen Lane, 2001, p. 105

6  Sir John Stokes, 'Keep the Queen', in A. Barnett (ed.), *Power and the Throne: The Monarchy Debate*, London, Vintage, 1984, p. 81.

7  MacKenzie, *Imperialism and Popular Culture*, introduction, p. 8.

8  J. Benson, *The Rise of Consumer Society in Britain 1880–1980*, Harlow, Longman, p. 159.

9  M. Billig, *Banal Nationalism*, London, Sage, 1995, p. 6.

10  R. Samuel, *Theatres of Memory Volume III Island Stories: Unravelling Britain*, London, Verso, 1998, pp. 74–97. For the impact of imperialism on urban Britain see F. Driver and D. Gilbert (eds), *Imperial Cities: Landscape, Display and Identity*, Manchester, Manchester University Press, 1999, and J. Schneer, *London 1900: The Imperial Metropolis*, New Haven, CT, Yale University Press, 1999.

11  Cannadine, *Ornamentalism*, p. 103.

12 Manchester University Press publishes a series of books called 'Studies in Imperialism' that cover the domestic aspects of imperialism. The series is edited by MacKenzie.

13 For post-war imperial films see MacKenzie, *Propaganda and Empire*, p. 90, and J. Richards, 'Imperial heroes for a post-imperial age: films and the end of Empire', in S. Ward (ed.), *British Culture and the End of Empire*, Manchester, Manchester University Press, 2001, pp. 128–44. Richards sees *Zulu* as a rejection of some of the values of imperialism, pp. 138–9. See E. Said, *Culture and Imperialism*, London, Chatto and Windus, 1993, for a global examination of the relationships between the two.

14 R. Price, *An Imperial War and the British Working-Class: Working-Class Attitudes and Reactions to the Boer War 1899–1902*, London, Routledge and Kegan Paul, 1972, p. 237. See also Henry Pelling, 'British Labour and British imperialism', in his *Popular Politics and Society in Late Victorian Britain*, London, Macmillan, 1968.

15 B. Porter, *The Lion's Share: A Short History of British Imperialism 1850–1995*, third edition, London, Longman, 1996, pp. 138, 290.

16 R. Price, 'Society, status and jingoism', in G. Crossick (ed.), *The Lower Middle Class in Britain*, London, Croom Helm, 1977.

17 P. Marshall, 'Imperial Britain', in P. Marshall (ed.), *The Cambridge Illustrated History of the British Empire*, Cambridge, Cambridge University Press, 1996.

18 MacKenzie, *Propaganda and Empire*, p. 2.

19 King George's Jubilee Trust circular to local authorities, 1936. The circular, in the archives of the London County Council, accompanied a dummy copy of the programme, which was in fact never produced because of Edward VIII's abdication. London Metropolitan Archives LCC/CL/GP/1/88.

20 H. Nicolson's *King George the Fifth: His Life and Reign*, London, Constable, 1952, is official. For an example of the scholarly see B. Pimlott, *The Queen A Biography of Elizabeth II*, London, HarperCollins, 1997.

21 T. Nairn, *The Enchanted Glass: Britain and Its Monarchy*, London, Hutchinson Radius, 1988; S. Haseler, *The End of the House of Windsor*, London, I. B. Tauris, 1993. E. Wilson, *The Myth of the British Monarchy*, London, Journeyman/Republic, 1989, says on p. 1. that 'The main purpose of this book is to show that there is no good reason why the British monarchy should be as popular as, apparently, it is.'

22 H. Jennings and C. Madge (eds), *May the Twelfth: Mass-Observation-Day Surveys 1937*, London, Faber and Faber, 1987 [1937].

23 Cannadine, 'The context, performance and meaning of ritual', pp. 134–7.

24 W. Kuhn, *Democratic Royalism: The Transformation of the British Monarch, 1861–1914*, Basingstoke, Macmillan, 1996, p. 10. For the Liberal purpose behind the investiture of the Prince of Wales in 1911 see J. Ellis, 'Reconciling the Celt: British national identity, empire, and the 1911 Investiture of the Prince of Wales', *Journal of British Studies*, 37, 1998, pp. 391–418.

25 F. Prochaska, *Royal Bounty: The Making of a Welfare Monarchy*, New Haven, CT, Yale University Press, 1995, pp. 75, 133, 266, 262–4, 187.

26 E. Shils and M. Young, 'The meaning of the Coronation', *Sociological Review*, 1, 1953, pp. 63–81.

27 Cannadine, 'The context, performance and meaning of ritual', p. 120.

28 Cannadine, 'The context, performance and meaning of ritual', pp. 142, 159. Examinations of new media and monarchy and imperialism can be found in MacKenzie, *Propaganda and Empire*, ch. 3; J. Richards, 'Boy's own empire: feature films and imperialism in the 1930s', and J. MacKenzie, '"In touch with the infinity": the BBC and the Empire 1923–1953', in MacKenzie, *Imperialism and Popular Culture*; J. Bourke, *Working-Class Cultures in Britain 1890–1960: Gender, Class and Ethnicity*, London, Routledge, 1994, pp. 188–9.

29 Jennings and Madge, *May the Twelfth*, pp. 267–9.

30 A. Aldgate and J. Richards, *Best of British: Cinema and Society from 1930 to the Present*, London, I. B. Tauris, 1999, p. 51.

31 Jennings and Madge, *May the Twelfth*, p. 120.

32 For a report on the event see London County Council minutes, 11–12 July 1911 and Deborah S. Ryan, 'Staging the imperial city: the Pageant of 1911', in Driver and Gilbert, *Imperial Cities*, pp. 117–35.

33 London Metropolitan Archives, LCC/EO/GEN/1/163, H. J. Newton to R. Blair, 7 June 1911; LCC/GL/GP/1/89, letter, 10 February 1953.

34 Imperial War Museum Department of Documents, 90/10/1, Mrs E. M. Bilbrough, unpublished war diary, 4 November 1917.

35 Imperial War Museum Department of Documents, 86/20/1, handwritten memoir, 1943, Mrs H. Lightfoot.

36 Nicolson, *King George the Fifth*, p. 252. For a hierarchy of forms of contact with royalty see P. Ward, '"Women of Britain say go": women's patriotism in the First World War', *Twentieth Century British History*, 12, 2001, pp. 37–9.

37 W. Bagehot, *The English Constitution*, 1867, quoted in Golby and Purdue, *The Monarchy and the British People*, p. 13.

38 D. Thompson, 'Queen Victoria, the monarchy and gender', in her *Outsiders: Class, Gender and Nation*, London, Verso, 1993, p. 175.

39 Thompson, 'Queen Victoria, the monarchy and gender', p. 182.

40 Golby and Purdue, *The Monarchy and the British People*, p. 13.

41 Prochaska, *Royal Bounty*, p. 92.

42 Cannon and Griffiths, *History of the British Monarchy*, p. 582.

43 See Cannon and Griffiths, *History of the British Monarchy*, pp. 600–9; Golby and Purdue, *The Monarchy and the British People*, pp. 107–12.

44 R. Brunt, 'The family firm restored: newsreel coverage of the British monarchy 1936–45', in C. Gledhill and G. Swanson (eds), *Nationalising Femininity: Culture, Sexuality and British Cinema in the Second World War*, Manchester, Manchester University Press, 1996, p. 141.

45 Golby and Purdue, *The Monarchy and the British People*, p. 114.

46 J. Richards, *The Age of the Dream Palace: Cinema and Society 1930–1939*, London, Routledge and Kegan Paul, 1984, pp. 264–6.

47 See Brunt, 'The family firm restored', for the centrality of Queen Elizabeth's role in wartime.

48 Brunt, 'The family firm restored', discusses Woolf's description.

49 J. Davies, 'Victoria and Victorian Wales', in G. Jenkins and J. Beverley Smith (eds), *Politics and Society in Wales, 1840–1922*, Cardiff, University of Wales Press, 1988, pp. 7–28.

50 *Manchester Daily Despatch*, 24 January 1953, 30 January 1953; *Evening Standard*, 29 January 1953; *Newcastle Journal*, 24 January 1953; *Eastbourne Gazette*, 28 January 1953; London Metropolitan Archives, LCC/EO/GEN/1/224 Assembly of Children Press Cuttings file.

51 Cannon and Griffiths, *History of the British Monarchy*, pp. 560, 639.

52 Ellis, 'Reconciling the Celt', pp. 395, 393.

53 Ellis, 'Reconciling the Celt', p. 404.

54 Pimlott, *The Queen*, pp. 18–20, 71–3.

55 R. Finlay, 'The rise and fall of popular imperialism in Scotland, 1850–1950', *Scottish Geographical Magazine*, 113, 1997, pp. 13–21. See also J. MacKenzie, 'Empire and national identities: the case of Scotland', *Transactions of the Royal Historical Society*, 6th series, 8, 1993, pp. 215–31.

56 See D. Hempton, *Religion and Culture in Britain and Ireland from the Glorious Revolution to the Decline of Empire*, Cambridge, Cambridge University Press, 1996, pp. 160–1.

57 Quoted in S. Paseta, 'Nationalist responses to two royal visits to Ireland, 1900 and 1903', *Irish Historical Studies*, 124, 1999, p. 491.

58 Quoted in Jeffery, *An Irish Empire*, Introduction, p. 2.
59 K. Robbins, *Great Britain: Identities, Institutions and the Idea of Britishness*, Harlow, Longman, 1998, pp. 213–14.
60 E. Buettner, 'Haggis in the Raj: private and public celebrations of Scottishness in late imperial India', *Scottish Historical Review*, 81, 2002, pp. 212–39.
61 J. MacKenzie, '"The Second City of the Empire": Glasgow – imperial municipality', in Driver and Gilbert, *Imperial Cities*, pp. 215–37.
62 J. Loughlin, *Ulster Unionism and British National Identity since 1885*, London, Pinter, 1995, p. 43. For opposition to the visit see Paseta, 'Nationalist responses to two royal visits'.
63 Alick Crawford to Major Crawford, Crawford papers, D/1700/5/17/1/41A, Public Record Office of Northern Ireland. See also *Irish Times*, 15 July 1897: 'Ireland cannot be said to have been lavishly treated to the sunshine of the Sovereign's presence since the Act of Union', in 'Walsh Royal Visits Press Cuttings', MS 11672, National Library of Ireland.
64 Nicolson, *King George the Fifth*, pp. 348–52.
65 Pimlott, *The Queen*, pp. 73–4.
66 'Charles to revive Scots loyalty', *The Times*, 20 May 2000.
67 'Scottish Politics', http://www.alba.org.uk/polls/opinionpollnopper.html, 17 January 2003.
68 Quoted in C. Powell, *Juan Carlos of Spain: Self-Made Monarch*, Basingstoke, Macmillan, 1996, pp. 95–6. See also pp. 185–91.
69 Schneer, *London 1900*, pp. 240–8.
70 D. Thompson, 'Mourning for a better monarchy', in M. Merck (ed.), *After Diana: Irreverent Elegies*, London, Verso, 1998, p. 34.
71 See D. Lomax, 'Diana Al-Fayed: ethnic marketing and the end(s) of racism', in J. Richards, S. Wilson and L. Woodhead (eds), *Diana: The Making of a Media Saint*, London, I. B. Tauris, 1999, pp. 74–97, and R. McKibbin, 'Mass observation in The Mall', in Merck, *After Diana*, p. 17. Lomax points out that in part the image of Diana as 'England's rose' was constructed from a racism towards the Al-Fayeds.
72 J. Taylor, *Diana, Self-Interest and British National Identity*, Westport, CT, Praeger, 2000.
73 *Daily Mirror*, 4 September 1997, quoted in J. Davies, *Diana Cultural History: Gender, Race, Nation and the People's Princess*, Basingstoke, Palgrave, 2001, p. 181.
74 Marshall, 'Imperial Britain', pp. 331–3.
75 MacKenzie, *Propaganda and Empire*, pp. 104, 109–11.
76 Quoted in Bourke, *Working-Class Cultures*, pp. 175–6.
77 See W. Reader, *At Duty's Call: A Study in Obsolete Patriotism*, Manchester, Manchester University Press, 1988.
78 T. Richards, 'The image of Victoria in the year of jubilee', *Victorian Studies*, 31, 1987, p. 10.
79 Prochaska, *Royal Bounty*, p. 75.
80 George V to Miss G. Storey, 14 March 1919, 86/36/1, Imperial War Museum Department of Documents.
81 Prochaska, *Royal Bounty*, p. 174.
82 Golby and Purdue, *The Monarchy and the British People*, p. 111; Prochaska, *Royal Bounty*, p. 191.
83 *News Chronicle*, 6 April 1937, in Jennings and Madge, *May the Twelfth*, p. 6.
84 Prochaska, *Royal Bounty*, p. 185; Fire Brigade Committee, Silver Jubilee 1935, LCC/FB/GEN/1/63, London Metropolitan Archives.
85 Nicolson, *King George the Fifth*, p. 526.
86 See Brunt, 'The family firm restored'.
87 A. Calder, *The Myth of the Blitz*, London, Pimlico, 1992, p. 250.
88 See Cannadine, *Ornamentalism*.

89  I. Hayden, *Symbol and Privilege: The Ritual Context of British Royalty*, Tucson, University of Arizona Press, 1987.

90  Pimlott, *The Queen*, pp. 274–83, discusses the contents of Altrincham's article and the reaction it provoked; on pp. 285–6 he discusses Muggeridge.

91  Cannadine, 'The British monarchy and the invention of tradition', pp. 118–19.

92  Golby and Purdue, *The Monarchy and the British People*, p. 66.

93  F. Prochaska, 'George V and republicanism, 1917–1919', *Twentieth Century British History*, 10, 1999, pp. 27–51.

94  A. Taylor, *'Down with the Crown': British Anti-monarchism and Debates about Royalty since 1790*, London, Reaktion, 1999, p. 99.

95  Nicolson, *King George the Fifth*, pp. 307, 309.

96  F. Harcourt, 'Gladstone, monarchism and the "new" imperialism, 1868–74', *Journal of Imperial and Commonwealth History*, 14, 1985, pp. 20–51.

97  Ellis, 'Reconciling the Celt'.

98  See P. Ward, *Red Flag and Union Jack: Englishness, Patriotism and the British Left, 1881–1924*, Woodbridge, Royal Historical Society/Boydell, 1998, pp. 182–4.

99  M. Pugh, 'The rise of Labour and the political culture of Conservatism, 1890–1945', *History*, 87, 2002, pp. 514–37, esp. pp. 525–6.

100  *Daily Herald*, 13 May 1937.

101  Quoted in Taylor, *Down with the Crown*, p. 216.

102  P. Richards, *Long to Reign Over Us?*, London, Fabian Society, 1996, p. 4.

103  Richards, *Long to Reign Over Us?* pp. 20–1.

104  Keith Laybourn kindly provided these figures.

105  Schneer, *London 1900*, ch. 10, discusses the election in London; these quotes are taken from p. 230. Also see Price, *An Imperial War and the British Working Class*, for a scepticism that the Conservative landslide was based on imperial feeling.

106  For the opposition to the war, see Stephen Koss (ed.), *The Pro-Boers: The Anatomy of an Anti-War Movement*, Chicago, University of Chicago Press, 1973.

107  C. Midgley, 'Female emancipation in an imperial frame: English women and the campaign against sati (widow burning) in India, 1813–30', *Women's History Review*, 9, 2000, pp. 95–121.

108  S. Howe, *Anti-colonialism in British Politics: The Left and the End of the Empire, 1918–1964*, Oxford, Oxford University Press, 1993.

109  MacKenzie, *Propaganda and Empire*, p. 63; D. Feldman, 'Nationality and ethnicity', in P. Johnson (ed.), *Twentieth-Century Britain: Economic, Social and Cultural Change*, London, Longman, 1994, pp. 137–8.

110  G. Stewart, 'Tenzing's two wrist-watches: the conquest of Everest and late imperial culture in Britain 1921–1953', *Past and Present*, 149, 1995, pp. 170–97. In response, Peter H. Hansen argues that the imperial master-narrative was always questioned, contested and opposed, see 'Debate', *Past and Present*, 157, 1997, pp. 159–77. Surely, the significance is that the Empire in 1953 was so fragile that any questioning was more likely to bring down the imperial cultural edifice.

111  L. Harris, *Long to Reign Over Us?* 1966, p. 137, quoted in Cannadine, 'The British monarchy and the invention of tradition', p. 156.

112  MacKenzie, 'In touch with the infinity', p. 184.

113  M. Leonard, *Britain: Renewing Our Identity*, London, Demos, 1997, p. 12.

114  See the collection of essays in Ward, *British Culture and the End of Empire*.

115  For France, see for example R. Gildea, *France since 1945*, Oxford, Oxford University Press, 1996, pp. 16–29.

116  See K. Morgan, *Labour in Power, 1945–1951*, Oxford, Oxford University Press, 1985, ch. 5 and R. Hyam, 'Africa and the Labour Government, 1945–1951', *Journal of Imperial and Commonwealth History*, 16, 1988, pp. 148–72.

117  J. Darwin, 'The fear of falling: British politics and imperial decline since 1900', *Transactions of the Royal Historical Society*, 5th series, 36, 1986, p. 39.

118 K. Robbins, *History, Religion and Identity in Modern Britain*, London, Hambledon, 1993, p. 292, and *Great Britain*, pp. 299–307.

119 R. Weight, *Patriots: National Identity in Britain 1940–2000*, London, Macmillan, 2002, p. 357.

120 Quoted in Davies, *The Isles*, p. 763.

121 Darwin, 'The fear of falling', p. 42.

122 Quoted in P. Hennessy and Z. Masani, *Out of the Midday Sun? Britain and the Great Power Impulse*, Glasgow, University of Strathclyde, 1992.

123 Quoted in Ward, *British Culture and the End of Empire*, Introduction, p. 9.

124 T. Nairn, *The Break-Up of Britain*, revised edition, London, New Left Books, 1981.

125 Robbins, *History, Religion and Identity*, pp. 283, 290.

126 J. Torrence, *Scotland's Dilemma: Province or Nation?*, Edinburgh, Belhaven, 1937, p. 5. See R. Finlay, '"For or against?" Scottish Nationalists and the British Empire, 1919–39', *Scottish Historical Review*, 71, 1992, pp. 184–206.

127 H. Edwards, *What Is Welsh Nationalism?*, second edition, Cardiff, Plaid Cymru, 1954.

128 F. Ridley in P. Berresford Ellis (ed.), *The Creed of Celtic Revolution*, London, Medusa, 1969.

129 Quoted in A. Aughey, *Nationalism, Devolution and the Challenge to the United Kingdom*, London, Pluto, 2001, p. 44. Norman Davies shares a similar view, *The Isles*, p. 882.

130 R. Scruton, *England: An Elegy*, London, Chatto and Windus, 2000.

131 C. Patten, 'Who do they think we are? Being British', British Council Annual Lecture, 28 June 2001, p. 1.

132 Cannadine, *Ornamentalism*, p. 176.

133 S. Rushdie, *Imaginary Homelands*, London, Granta, 1991, p. 131. Richards, 'Imperial heroes for a post-imperial age', argues that anti-imperialism was a dominant motif in many 1980s films such as *Happy Valley* (1985) and *White Mischief* (1986). See also J. McBratney, 'The Raj is all the rage: Paul Scott's *The Raj Quartet* and colonial nostalgia', *North Dakota Quarterly*, 55, 1987, pp. 204–9.

134 N. Femenia, *National Identity in Times of Crisis: The Scripts of the Falklands-Malvinas War*, New York, Nova Science, 1996, p. 121.

135 Leader, *The Guardian*, 5 June 2002.

136 Leader, *The Guardian*, 5 June 2002.

137 Quoted in *The Times*, 6 June 2002.

138 P. Kelso, *The Guardian*, 5 June 2002.

## 2 Gender and national identity

1 See, for example, B. Harrison, *Separate Spheres: The Opposition to Women's Suffrage in Britain*, London, Croom Helm, 1978, ch. 4, for one political deployment of this term.

2 R. Shoemaker and M. Vincent (eds), *Gender and History in Western Europe*, London, Arnold, 1998, gathers together some of the most important essays.

3 See M. Dresser, 'Britannia', in R. Samuel (ed.), *Patriotism: The Making and Unmaking of British National Identity, III: National Fictions*, London, Routledge, 1989, pp. 26–49. For a masculine representation of national symbolism, see M. Taylor, 'John Bull and the iconography of public opinion in England, c.1712–1929', *Past and Present*, 134, 1994, pp. 93–128.

4 J. Springhall, 'Building character in the British boy: the attempt to extend Christian manliness to working class adolescents, 1880–1914', in J. Mangan and J. Walvin (eds), *Manliness and Morality: Middle-Class Masculinity in Britain and America 1800–1940*, Manchester, Manchester University Press, 1987, p. 61.

5 J. Mangan (ed.), *'Benefits Bestowed'? Education and British Imperialism*, Manchester, Manchester University Press, 1988.

6 J. MacKenzie, *Propaganda and Empire: The Manipulation of British Public Opinion 1880–1960*, Manchester, Manchester University Press, 1984, pp. 180–1.

7 Quoted in J. MacKenzie, 'The imperial pioneer and hunter and the masculine stereotype in late Victorian and Edwardian times', in Mangan and Walvin, *Manliness and Morality*, p. 176.

8 J. Bourke, *Working-Class Cultures in Britain 1890–1960: Gender, Class and Ethnicity*, London, Routledge, 1994, p. 182.

9 Quoted in J. Mackay and P. Thane, 'The Englishwoman', in R. Colls and P. Dodd (eds), *Englishness, Politics and Culture 1880–1920*, London, Croom Helm, 1986, p. 196.

10 Springhall, 'Building character in the British boy', argues that this national manliness did not percolate down to the working-class male as was intended by its creators.

11 Quoted in J. Giles and T. Middleton (eds), *Writing Englishness 1900–1950: An Introductory Sourcebook on National Identity*, London, Routledge, 1995, p. 117.

12 Examples of such an approach include A. Wiltsher, *Most Dangerous Women: Feminist Peace Campaigners of the Great War*, London, Pandora, 1985, and J. Liddington, *The Long Road to Greenham: Feminism and Anti-militarism in Britain since 1820*, London, Virago, 1989.

13 Bourke, *Working-Class Cultures*, p. 198; Mackay and Thane, 'The Englishwoman', pp. 191–2n.

14 See, for example, A. Burton, 'The feminist quest for identity: British imperial suffragism and "global sisterhood", 1900–1915', *Journal of Women's History*, 3, 1991, pp. 46–81; A. Summers, *Angels and Citizens: British Women as Military Nurses 1854–1914*, London, Routledge and Kegan Paul, 1988; P. Ward, 'Women of Britain say go: Women's patriotism in the First World War', *Twentieth Century British History*, 12, 2001, pp. 23–45.

15 Burton, 'The feminist quest for identity', pp. 46, 66.

16 Summers, *Angels and Citizens*, p. 8.

17 J. Bush, *Edwardian Ladies and Imperial Power*, Leicester, Leicester University Press, 2000, provides a detailed examination of women's involvement in imperial propaganda.

18 See the papers of the British Women's Patriotic League, BO 5/3, Imperial War Museum, Women's Work Collection.

19 Quoted in Bush, *Edwardian Ladies*, p. 50.

20 J. Winter, 'British national identity and the First World War', in S. Green and R. Whiting (eds), *The Boundaries of the State in Modern Britain*, Cambridge, Cambridge University Press, 1996, p. 266.

21 The anti-war left joined in the condemnation of Germany's aggression as 'Prussianism', see for example P. Ward, *Red Flag and Union Jack: Englishness, Patriotism and the British Left 1881–1924*, Woodbridge, Royal Historical Society/Boydell, 1998, pp. 121–2.

22 Quoted in Ward, 'Women of Britain say go'. Many of the themes discussed in this section are expanded in this article.

23 Viola Bawtree, 'Episodes of the Great War 1916 from the Diaries of Viola Bawtree', unpublished diary, 23 Feb. 1916, Imperial War Museum Department of Documents, 91/5/1.

24 See the papers of Miss A. and Miss R. McGuire, letter, 9 May 1915, Imperial War Museum Department of Documents, 96/31/1.

25 K. Robert, 'Gender, class, and patriotism: women's paramilitary units in First World War Britain', *International History Review*, 19, 1997, pp. 52–65.

26 For women workers see G. Braybon, *Women Workers in the First World War: The British Experience*, London, Croom Helm, 1981, which downplays working women's patriotism, and A. Woollacott, *On Her Their Lives Depend: Munition Workers and the Great War*, Berkeley, University of California Press, 1994, esp. pp. 192–7.

27 Liddington, *The Long Road to Greenham*, p. 117.

28  Mrs E. M. Bilbrough, unpublished First World War diary, 11 Nov. 1918, Imperial War Museum Department of Documents, 90/10/1.

29  Quoted in Ward, 'Women of Britain say go', p. 27.

30  M. Ward, *Unmanageable Revolutionaries: Women and Irish Nationalism*, London, Pluto, 1983, p. 88; Kent, *Gender and Power*, pp. 263–6.

31  K. Tynan, 'A trumpet call to Irish women', in W. Fitzgerald (ed.), *The Voice of Ireland: A Survey of the Race and Nation from All Angles*, Dublin, Virtue, n.d., p. 174.

32  A. John, '"Run like blazes": the suffragettes and Welshness', *Llafur*, 6, 1994, pp. 29–43.

33  John, 'Run like blazes', p. 38.

34  Quoted in K. Cook and N. Evans, '"The petty antics of the bell-ringing boisterous band"? The women's suffrage movement in Wales, 1890–1918', in A. John (ed.), *Our Mothers' Land: Chapters in Welsh History, 1830–1939*, Cardiff, University of Wales Press, 1991, p. 165.

35  E. King, 'The Scottish women's suffrage movement', in E. Breitenbach and E. Gordon, *Out of Bounds: Women in Scottish Society 1800–1945*, Edinburgh, Edinburgh University Press, 1992, p. 140.

36  BO2/52/16, Imperial War Museum Department of Printed Books.

37  The exclusion from electoral registers of women under thirty, the group most likely to have played an active part in the war effort, should be sufficient to make such an argument untenable. See M. Pugh, *Women and the Women's Movement in Britain 1914–1959*, Basingstoke, Macmillan, 1992, pp. 34–42.

38  A. Light, *Forever England: Femininity, Literature and Conservatism between the Wars*, London, Routledge, 1991, p. 8. See also R. Samuel, 'Introduction: exciting to be English', in Raphael Samuel (ed.), *Patriotism: The Making and Unmaking of British National Identity Volume 1 History and Politics*, London, Routledge, 1989, pp. xx–lxvii.

39  Light, *Forever England*, p. 11.

40  Bourke, *Working-Class Cultures*, pp. 188, 186.

41  See S. Constantine, '"Bringing the Empire Alive": the Empire Marketing Board and imperial propaganda 1926–33', in J. MacKenzie (ed.), *Imperialism and Popular Culture*, Manchester, Manchester University Press, 1986, pp. 192–231.

42  J. MacKenzie, '"In touch with the infinity": The BBC and the Empire 1923–1953', in MacKenzie, *Imperialism and Popular Culture*, pp. 181–2.

43  Quoted in A. Gregory, *The Silence of Memory: Armistice Day 1919–1946*, Oxford, Berg, 1994, p. 33.

44  Winter, 'British national identity and the First World War', pp. 270–5.

45  See N. Gullace, 'White feathers and wounded men: female patriotism and the Great War', *Journal of British Studies*, 36, 1997, pp. 178–206; S. Kent, *Making Peace: The Reconstruction of Gender in Interwar Britain*, Princeton, Princeton University Press, 1994.

46  G. Dawson, 'The blond bedouin: Lawrence of Arabia, imperial adventure and the imagining of English-British identity', in M. Roper and J. Tosh (eds), *Manful Assertions: Masculinities since 1800*, London, Routledge, 1991, pp. 113–44; J. Rutherford, *Forever England: Reflections on Race, Masculinity and Empire*, London, Lawrence and Wishart, 1997, ch. 4.

47  See J. Bourke, *Dismembering the Male: Men's Bodies, Britain, and the Great War*, London, Reaktion, 1996.

48  Quoted in Dawson, 'The blond bedouin', p. 123.

49  See J. Bourke, *An Intimate History of Killing: Face-to-Face Killing in the Twentieth Century*, London, Granta, 1999, pp. 306–7.

50  Miss H. M. Harpin, Letters, 3 May 1918, Imperial War Museum, Department of Documents, CON SHELF.

51  C. Playne, *Society at War 1914–1916*, 1931, p. 143, quoted in Bourke, *Intimate History of Killing*, p. 312.

52 See M. Andrews, '"For home and country": feminism and Englishness in the Women's Institute movement, 1930–60', in R. Weight and A. Beach (eds), *The Right to Belong: Citizenship and National Identity in Britain, 1930–1960*, London, I. B. Tauris, 1998, pp. 116–35.

53 S. Kent, *Gender and Power in Britain, 1640–1990*, London, Routledge, 1999, p. 313.

54 See for example G. Braybon and P. Summerfield, *Out of the Cage: Women's Experiences in Two World Wars*, London, Pandora, 1987.

55 L. Noakes, *War and the British: Gender, Memory and National Identity*, London, I. B. Tauris, 1998, is an exception. For representations of women see C. Gledhill and G. Swanson (eds), *Nationalising Femininity: Culture, Sexuality and British Cinema in the Second World War*, Manchester, Manchester University Press, 1996; A. Lant, *Blackout: Reinventing Women for Wartime British Cinema*, Princeton, NJ, Princeton University Press, 1991.

56 Noakes, *War and the British*, p. 64.

57 Gledhill and Swanson, *Nationalising Femininity*, p. 20.

58 S. Rose, 'Sex, citizenship, and the nation in World War II Britain', *American Historical Review*, 103, 1998, p. 1164.

59 S. Rose, *Which People's War? National Identity and Citizenship in Wartime Britain 1939–1945*, Oxford, Oxford University Press, 2003, pp. 73–92 examines representations of 'good-time girls' as a threat to Britishness.

60 Mass-Observation Report no. 520, 'Women and morale', December 1940, in D. Sheridan (ed.), *Wartime Women: An Anthology of Women's Wartime Writing for Mass-Observation 1937–45*, London, Mandarin, 1991, p. 117.

61 Gledhill and Swanson, *Nationalising Femininity*, p. 9.

62 P. Summerfield, *Reconstructing Women's Wartime Lives*, Manchester, Manchester University Press, 1998, pp. 54–5.

63 R. McKibbin, *Class and Cultures: England 1918–1951*, Oxford, Oxford University Press, 2000, p. 434.

64 Richards, *Films and British National Identity: From Dickens to Dad's Army*, Manchester, Manchester University Press, pp. 123–5, and Lant, *Blackout*. McKibbin notes that the popularity of the film lay in the suburbs. This was a middle-class film. *Class and Cultures*, p. 433.

65 Rose, *Which People's War?*, ch. 5.

66 Braybon and Summerfield, *Out of the Cage*, p. 162.

67 Noakes, *War and the British*, p. 98.

68 Quoted in Braybon and Summerfield, *Out of the Cage*, p. 188.

69 See H. Smith, 'The effect of the war on the status of women', in H. Smith (ed.), *War and Social Change*, Manchester, Manchester University Press, 1986.

70 Quoted in Sheridan, *Wartime Women*, p. 36.

71 Quoted in Braybon and Summerfield, *Out of the Cage*, p. 201.

72 S. Brooke, 'Gender and working class identity in Britain during the 1950s', *Journal of Social History*, 34, 2001, pp. 773–95.

73 P. Thane, 'Women since 1945', in P. Johnson (ed.), *Twentieth-Century Britain: Economic, Social and Cultural Change*, London, Longman, 1994, p. 395.

74 Thane, 'Women since 1945', p. 398.

75 See Summerfield, *Reconstructing Women's Wartime Lives*, pp. 119–21.

76 J. Ramsden, 'Refocusing "the people's war": British war films of the 1950s', *Journal of Contemporary History*, 33, 1998, pp. 35–63.

77 Noakes, *War and the British*, p. 103.

78 Sir Ernest Barker, *The Character of England*, 1947, quoted in Giles and Middleton, *Writing Englishness*, p. 59.

79 M. Francis, 'The Labour Party: modernisation and the politics of restraint', in B. Conekin, F. Mort and C. Waters (eds), *Moments of Modernity: Reconstructing Britain 1945–1964*, London, River Orams Press, 1999, pp. 153–4.

80  G. Gorer, *Exploring English Character*, London, Cresset, 1955, p. 293.
81  M. Collins, 'The fall of the English gentleman: the national character in decline, c.1918–1970', *Historical Research*, 75, 2002, p. 101.
82  The themes raised here are explored further in chapter 6.
83  W. Webster, *Imagining Home: Gender, 'Race' and National Identity 1945–64*, London, UCL Press, 1998, p. xii.
84  E. Huxley, *Back Street New Worlds: A Look at Immigrants in Britain*, 1964, quoted in Webster, *Imagining Home*, p. 65. See C. Waters, '"Dark strangers" in our midst: discourses of race and nation in Britain, 1947–1963', *Journal of British Studies*, 36, 1997, 36, pp. 207–38.
85  For a discussion of the limits of permissiveness see T. Newburn, *Permission and Regulation: Law and Morals in Post-war Britain*, London, Routledge, 1992.
86  J. Weeks, *Sex, Politics and Society: The Regulation of Sexuality since 1800*, second edition, London, Longman, 1989, pp. 240–1.
87  Quoted in Kent, *Gender and Power*, p. 280.
88  Collins, 'The fall of the English gentleman', pp. 102–3.
89  R. Scruton. *England: An Elegy*, London, Chatto and Windus, 2000, p. 245.
90  S. Ward, 'Introduction', in S. Ward (ed.), *British Culture and the End of Empire*, Manchester, Manchester University Press, 2001, p. 12
91  Kent, *Gender and Power*, pp. 346–53.
92  R. Colls, *Identity of England*, Oxford, Oxford University Press, 2002, p. 185.

## 3  Rural, urban and regional Britishness

1  S. Baldwin, *On England*, 1926, quoted in J. Giles and T. Middleton (eds), *Writing Englishness 1900–1950: An Introductory Sourcebook on National Identity*, London, Routledge, 1995, p. 101.
2  G. Orwell, 'The lion and the unicorn: socialism and the English genius', 1941, in *Collected Essays, Journalism and Letters, II: My Country Right or Left 1940–1943*, London, Penguin, 1970, pp. 75–6.
3  C. Masterman (ed.), *The Heart of the Empire*, 1901, quoted in S. Meacham, *Regaining Paradise: Englishness and the Early Garden City Movement*, New Haven, CT, Yale University Press, 1999, p. 2.
4  P. Dunleavy, *The Politics of Mass Housing in Britain, 1945–1975*, Oxford, Clarendon, 1981, p. 2.
5  P. Abercrombie, *The Preservation of Rural England*, 1926, quoted in P. Lowe, 'The rural idyll defended: from preservation to conservation', in G. Mingay (ed.), *The Rural Idyll*, London, Routledge, 1989.
6  J. Darracott (ed.), *The First World War in Posters*, New York, Dover, 1974, pp. 55, xxii.
7  See for example 'The discovery of rural England', in Colls and Dodd, *Englishness*. A. Potts, '"Constable country" between the wars', in R. Samuel (ed.), *Patriotism: The Making and Unmaking of British National Identity, III: National Fictions*, London, Routledge, 1989, pp. 160–86; A. Calder, *The Myth of the Blitz*, London, Pimlico, 1992, ch. 9, 'Deep England'. The range of primary source materials for celebrations of rural Englishness is enormous. A selection can be found in Giles and Middleton, *Writing Englishness*, ch. 2 'Versions of rural England'.
8  M. Wiener, *English Culture and the Decline of the Industrial Spirit, 1850–1980*, Cambridge, Cambridge University Press, 1981. Quotes from p. 6.
9  P. Mandler, 'Against "Englishness": English culture and the limits to rural nostalgia, 1850–1940', *Transactions of the Royal Historical Society*, 6th series, 7, 1997, pp. 155–76.
10  D. Lowenthal, 'Heritage and the English landscape', *History Today*, 41, 1991, p. 8.
11  Lord Elton, *The Life of James Ramsay MacDonald (1866–1919)*, London, Collins, 1939, pp. 126–7.

12  J. Ramsay MacDonald, *Wanderings and Excursions*, London, Cape, 1929, p. 43.

13  *Listening to Britain: A Jennings Trilogy*, London, Imperial War Museum/Central Office of Information, 1991.

14  Mass-Observation File Report 878, 'What does Britain mean to you[?]', August 1941.

15  Quoted in P. Mandler, *The Fall and Rise of the Stately Home*, New Haven, CT, Yale University Press, 1997, p. 335.

16  J. Marsh, *Back to the Land: The Pastoral Impulse in England from 1880 to 1914*, London, Quartet, 1982, p. 6.

17  J. Lowerson, 'Battles for the countryside', in F. Gloversmith (ed.), *Class, Culture and Social Change: A New View of the 1930s*, Sussex, Harvester, 1980, pp. 268, 273–4.

18  D. Matless, *Landscape and Englishness*, London, Reaktion, 1998, pp. 16, 62–3.

19  H. Morton, *In Search of England*, London, Methuen, 1984, p. 1.

20  Morton, *In Search of England*, pp. 1–2.

21  Morton, *In Search of England*, p. 2.

22  M. Bartholomew, 'Englishness: the case of H. V. Morton (1892–1979)', in K. Dockray and K. Laybourn (eds), *The Representation and Reality of War: The British Experience*, Stroud, Sutton, 1999, p. 205.

23  There is a picture in H. Dalton, *The Fateful Years*, London, Muller, 1957, opp. p. 144.

24  *Improved Means of Locomotion as a First Step towards the Cure of the Housing Difficulties of London*, London, Macmillan, 1901.

25  For Webb, see for example, A. Briggs, *Victorian Cities*, Harmondsworth, Penguin, 1971, ch. 8, 'London: the World City'; for Morrison see B. Donoughue and G. Jones, *Herbert Morrison: Portrait of a Politician*, London, Phoenix, 2001.

26  See for example L. Gomme, *The Making of London*, Oxford, Clarendon, 1912, and H. Sherlock, *Cities Are Good for Us*, London, Paladin/Transport 2000, 1991, which praise London from very different standpoints.

27  See D. McNeill, 'Livingstone's London: Left politics and the world city', *Regional Studies*, 36, 2002, pp. 75–91; C. Nuttall, 'Livingstone's London', *Architecture*, 90, no. 9, 2001, pp. 49–52, 149. Livingstone's inauguration speech can be read at http://www.london.gov.uk/approot/mayor/speeches/2000/m_speech.jsp, 23 February 2002.

28  See Calder, *Myth of the Blitz*; M. Smith, *Britain and 1940: History, Myth and Popular Memory*, London, Routledge, 2000, ch. 5; and S. Rose, *Which People's War? National Identity and Citizenship in Wartime Britain 1939–1945*, Oxford, Oxford University Press, 2003, ch. 2.

29  H. Midgely, 'Northern Ireland reactions to the first year of war', draft of radio broadcast, Harry Midgley Papers, D/4089/3/1/1, Public Record Office of Northern Ireland. See also W. Elliot, broadcast, 'Calling Australia and New Zealand', 9 July 1942, Walter Elliot papers, Acc. 6721/1/3, National Library of Scotland.

30  S. Bader, *Visionaries and Planners: The Garden City Movement and the Modern Community*, New York, Oxford University Press, 1990, p. 36.

31  R. Barry Parker and R. Unwin, *The Art of Building a Home*, 1901, quoted in S. Meacham, 'Raymond Unwin (1863–1940): designing for democracy in Edwardian England', in S. Pedersen and P. Mandler (eds), *After the Victorians: Private Conscience and Public Duty*, London, Routledge, 1994, p. 89.

32  Rev. Canon Barnett, *The Ideal City*, Bristol, Arrowsmith, n.d., pp. 5, 6, 21.

33  R. Bremner, *The Housing Problem in Glasgow*, Glasgow, Scottish Centre for Women's Trades, n.d.

34  M. Girouard, *The English Town*, New Haven, CT, Yale University Press, 1990, ch. 11.

35  Borough of Chelmsford, *Coronation of King George V and Queen Mary, June 22nd 1911 Order of Procession and Service. Programme of Festivities*, Chelmsford, 1911.

36  London County Council (subsequently LCC) Minutes of Proceedings, January–June 1910, p. 1,112, London Metropolitan Archives.

37  Quoted in Howkins, 'The discovery of rural England', p. 66.

38  M. Freeman, 'The provincial survey in Edwardian Britain', *Historical Research*, 75, 2002, p. 75.

39  G. Searle, *The Quest for National Efficiency: A Study in British Politics and Political Thought, 1899–1914*, London, Ashfield, 1990.

40  Chesterfield Fabian Society, *Town Planning for Chesterfield*, Chesterfield, Fabian Society, 1910, p. 3.

41  E. Howard, *Garden Cities of Tomorrow*, 1902, in Giles and Middleton, *Writing English-ness*, pp. 199–202.

42  South Wales Garden Cities and Town Planning Association, Minute Book, Edgar Chappell papers, A5/1, National Library of Wales. See also M. Swenarton, *Homes Fit for Heroes: The Politics and Architecture of Early State Housing in Britain*, London, Heinemann, 1981.

43  Earl Compton, 'The homes of the people', *New Review*, June 1889, p. 47.

44  J. Burnett, *The Social History of Housing 1815–1985*, second edition, London, Rout-ledge, 1986, p. 225.

45  See A. Light, *Forever England: Femininity, Literature and Conservatism*, London, Rout-ledge, 1991, for lived conservatism and conservative modernity emerging from the use of domestic appliances.

46  M. Swenarton, *Artisans and Architects: The Ruskinian Tradition in Architectural Thought*, Basingstoke, Macmillan, 1989, ch. 6.

47  K. Adam, 'The government of London 1889–1939', *Fortnightly Review*, March 1939, in K. Young and P. Garside, *Metropolitan London: Politics and Urban Change 1837–1981*, London, Edward Arnold, 1982, p. 180.

48  Quoted in K. Laybourn, *Britain on the Breadline: A Social and Political History of Britain 1918–1939*, Stroud, Sutton, 1998, p. 83.

49  Mandler, 'Against "Englishness"', pp. 170–1; R. Porter, *London: A Social History*, London, Hamish Hamilton, 1994, p. 318.

50  *Metro-land*, BBC, 1973. For Betjeman's England see D. Brown, *John Betjeman*, Ply-mouth, Northcote House, 1999, ch. 3.

51  I owe this information to Margot Holt, one of my third-year students in 2002, who undertook a project on gardening in the Second World War.

52  A. Saint, 'The New Towns', in B. Ford (ed.), *The Cambridge Cultural History of Britain, IX: Modern Britain*, Cambridge, Cambridge University Press, 1992, p. 147.

53  Quoted in Matless, *Landscape and Englishness*, p. 200.

54  Quoted in Matless, *Landscape and Englishness*, p. 232.

55  The esteem with which the Soviet Union was held even in the early post-war period suggests that this was the work of conservatives. Saint, 'The New Towns', p. 152.

56  Mass-Observation Archive, File Reports Series, 2375. Stevenage, 17 April 1946 (microfilm).

57  Mass-Observation Archive, File Reports Series, 2375. Stevenage, 17 April 1946 (microfilm).

58  M. Glendinning and S. Muthesius, *Tower Block: Modern Public Housing in England, Scotland, Wales and Northern Ireland*, New Haven, CT, Yale University Press, 1994, p. 220.

59  T. Knight, *Let Our Cities Live*, 1960, in P. Mandler, 'New Towns for old: the fate of the town centre', in B. Conekin, F. Mort and C. Waters (eds), *Moments of Modernity: Reconstructing Britain 1945–1964*, London, River Orams, 1999, p. 221.

60  Mandler, 'New Towns for old', p. 227.

61  *Western Mail*, 21 August 1911.

62  See P. Gruffudd, 'Prospects of Wales: contested geographical imaginations', in

R. Fevre and A. Thompson (eds), *Nation, Identity and Social Theory: Perspectives from Wales*, Cardiff, University of Wales Press, 1999, pp. 149–67.

63  K. Morgan, *Rebirth of a Nation: A History of Modern Wales*, Oxford, Oxford University Press, 1981, pp. 335, 382.

64  'A Garden Capital for Wales', n.d. Edgar Chappell papers, A5/1, National Library of Wales.

65  For a critical account see H. Thomas, 'Spatial restructuring in the capital: struggles to shape Cardiff's built environment', in Fevre and Thompson, *Nation, Identity and Social Theory*, pp. 168–88.

66  K. Jones, *Catherine Cookson: The Biography*, London, Constable, 1999, pp. 5, 299, 315, 297. See also R. Williams, *The Country and the City*, London, Hogarth, 1993 [1973] for rural and urban literature.

67  J. Harris, *Private Lives, Public Spirit: Britain 1870–1914*, London, Penguin, 1994, pp. 18–19.

68  E. Royle, 'Introduction: regions and identities', in E. Royle (ed.), *Issues of Regional Identity*, Manchester, Manchester University Press, 1998, pp. 4, 10.

69  K. Wales, 'North and South: a linguistic divide?', Inaugural Lecture, 10 June 1999, http://www.leeds.ac.uk/reporter/439/kwales.htm, 12 March 2002.

70  J. B. Priestley, *English Journey*, London, William Heinemann, 1949 [1934], p. 154.

71  S. Rawnsley, 'Constructing "the north": space and sense of place', in N. Kirk (ed.), *Northern Identities: Historical Interpretations of 'The North' and 'Northernness'*, Aldershot, Ashgate, 2000.

72  Quoted in H. Kearney, *The British Isles: A History of Four Nations*, Cambridge, Cambridge University Press, 1995, p. 267.

73  Richards, *Films and British National Identity*, p. 255.

74  See file, 'Assembly of children: press cuttings', London County Council Papers, LCC/EO/GEN/1/124, London Metropolitan Archives.

75  *Halifax Courier*, 29 March 1965, quoted in J. Hargreaves, '"Long to reign over us"; changing attitudes towards the monarchy in Halifax from the golden jubilee of King George III in 1809 to the golden jubilee of Queen Elizabeth II in 2002', *Transactions of the Halifax Antiquarian Society*, 11, 2003, forthcoming.

76  C. Waters, 'J. B. Priestley (1894–1984): Englishness and the politics of nostalgia', in S. Pedersen and P. Mandler (eds), *After the Victorians: Private Conscience and Public Duty*, London, Routledge, 1994, pp. 208–26.

77  *We Speak for Ourselves*, 'Lancashire Folk', 27 October 1940, in D. Cardiff and P. Scannell, '"Good luck war workers!" Class, politics and entertainment in wartime broadcasting', in T. Bennett, C. Mercer and J. Woollacott (eds), *Popular Culture and Social Relations*, Milton Keynes, Open University Press, 1986, pp. 100–1.

78  See G. Stedman Jones, 'The "cockney" and the nation, 1780–1988', in D. Feldman and G. Stedman Jones (eds), *Metropolis London: Histories and Representations since 1800*, London, Routledge, 1989, pp. 272–324; D. Thoms, 'The Blitz, civilian morale and regionalism, 1940–1942', in P. Kirkham and D. Thoms (eds), *War Culture: Social Change and Changing Experience in World War Two Britain*, London, Lawrence and Wishart, 1995, pp. 3–12.

79  J. B. Priestley, *Let the People Sing*, London, Mandarin, 1996 [first published 1939].

80  W. Pickles, *Between You and Me*, London, Werner Laurie, 1949, p. 151.

81  A. Hughes and P. Trudgill, *English Accents and Dialects: An Introduction to Social and Regional Varieties of English in the British Isles*, London, Arnold, 1996, p. 8.

82  Jones, 'The "cockney" and the nation'.

83  See J. Richards, *Films and British National Identity: From Dickens to Dad's Army*, Manchester, Manchester University Press, 1997, ch. 9; J. Richards, *The Age of the Dream Palace: Cinema and Society in Britain 1930–1939*, London, Routledge and Kegan Paul, 1984, chs 10 and 11.

84 M. Luckett, 'Image and nation in 1990s British cinema', in R. Murphy (ed.), *British Cinema of the 1990s*, London, British Film Institute, 2000, pp. 88–99.

85 See P. Taylor, 'The meaning of the north: England's "foreign country" within?', *Political Geography*, 12, 1993, p. 145. I owe thanks to Katherine Lewis for drawing my attention to her partner Graeme's exclusive 'Geordieness'.

86 *Your Region, Your Choice: Revitalising the English Regions*, Cd 5511, 2002, preface.

87 J. Vernon, 'Border crossings: Cornwall and the English (imagi)nation', in G. Cubitt (ed.), *Imagining Nations*, Manchester, Manchester University Press, 1998, p. 154.

88 See also Gruffudd, 'Prospects of Wales', pp. 150–6.

89 The Hovis advertisement was filmed on Gold Hill, Shaftsbury, Dorset, associated with the Wessex region fictionalised by Thomas Hardy.

90 R. Lumley, *The Museum Time Machine*, London, Routledge, 1988, p. 64. I owe this reference to Ellen Cass.

91 D. Frost, 'West Africans, black Scousers and the colour problem in inter-war Liverpool', *North West Labour History*, 20, 1995/96, p. 56.

92 Quoted in S. Fielding, *Class and Ethnicity: Irish Catholics in England, 1880–1939*, Buckingham, Open University Press, 1993, p. 15.

## 4 Spare time

1 See for example, J. Richards, *Imperialism and Music: Britain 1876–1953*, Manchester, Manchester University Press, 2002. R. Weight, *Patriots: National Identity in Britain 1940–2000*, London, Macmillan, 2002, pp. 396–7, discusses popular music in the post-war period, seeing it as a focus for a post-imperial Britishness in the 1960s, through the Beatles for example. For fashion see C. Breward, B. Conekin and C. Cox (eds), *The Englishness of English Dress*, Oxford, Berg, 2002.

2 This chapter concentrates on football, rugby and cricket, as well as some Gaelic sports. For other sports see J. Lowerson, 'Golf and the making of myths', in G. Jarvie and G. Walker (eds), *Scottish Sport in the Making of the Nation: Ninety Minute Patriots?*, Leicester, Leicester University Press, 1994, pp. 75–90.

3 A. Williams, *Life in a Railway Factory*, 1915, quoted in H. Moorhouse, 'One state, several countries: soccer and nationality in a "United" Kingdom', in J. Mangan (ed.), *Tribal Identities: Nationalism, Europe, Sport*, London, Frank Cass, 1996, p. 56.

4 For a discussion of identities of place in relation to football see J. Bale, 'Playing at home: British football and a sense of place', in J. Williams and S. Wagg (eds), *British Football and Social Change: Getting into Europe*, Leicester, Leicester University Press, 1991.

5 D. Russell, 'Associating with football: social identity in England 1863–1998', in G. Armstrong and R. Giulianotti (eds), *Football Cultures and Identities*, Basingstoke, Macmillan, 1999, pp. 17–19.

6 See J. Hargreaves, *Sport, Power and Culture: A Social and Historical Analysis of Sports in Britain*, Cambridge, Polity Press, 1986, pp. 154–5, and G. Whannel, *Fields in Vision: Television Sport and Cultural Transformation*, London, Routledge, 1992, pp. 13–20.

7 J. Hill and F. Varrasi, 'Creating Wembley: the construction of a national monument', http://www2.umist.ac.uk/sport/3_art3.htm (27 June 2003). See *Metro-land*, BBC, 1973, for newsreel footage of the opening of the exhibition.

8 Quoted in R. Holt, *Sport and the British: A Modern History*, Oxford, Clarendon, 1992, p. 206. This is the standard work on sport and nation in the British Isles.

9 Quoted in M. Rosenthal, *The Character Factory: Baden-Powell and the Origins of the Boy Scout Movement*, London, Collins, 1986, p. 97. For the links between sport and imperialism, see especially J. A. Mangan, *Athleticism in the Victorian and Edwardian Public School*, third edition, London, Frank Cass, 2000, and R. MacDonald, *The Language of Empire: Myths and Metaphors of Popular Imperialism, 1880–1918*, Manchester, Manchester University Press, 1994, pp. 20–1.

10  Holt, *Sport and the British*, p. 208.
11  Holt, *Sport and the British*, pp. 222, 233–4; H. Perkin, 'Teaching the nations how to play: sport and society in the British Empire and Commonwealth', *International Journal of the History of Sport*, 6, 1989, pp. 145–53.
12  M. Polley, *Moving the Goalposts: A History of Sport and Society since 1945*, London, Routledge, 1998, p. 44. For the causes of decline in England's sporting performance see R. McKibbin, *Class and Cultures: England 1918–1951*, Oxford, Oxford University Press, 2000, pp. 377–83.
13  G. Orwell, 'The sporting spirit', *Tribune*, 14 December 1945, in S. Orwell and I. Angus (eds), *The Collected Essays, Journalism and Letters of George Orwell, II:* Harmondsworth, Penguin, 1970, p. 62.
14  Weight, *Patriots*, pp. 457–9.
15  For a discussion of the significance of this act for Englishness see L. Back, T. Crabbe and J. Solomos, '"Lions and black skins": race, nation and local patriotism in football', in B. Carrington and I. MacDonald (eds), *'Race', Sport and British Society*, London, Routledge, 2001, pp. 94–5.
16  Hargreaves, *Sport, Power and Culture*, p. 191. Wilson, it is said, carried a photograph of the 1922 team that won the FA Cup.
17  Hill and Varrasi, 'Creating Wembley', p. 6.
18  Holt, *Sport and the British*, p. 137.
19  B. Roberts, 'Welsh identity in a former mining valley: social image and imagined communities', in R. Fevre and A. Thompson (eds), *Nation, Identity and Social Theory: Perspectives from Wales*, Cardiff, University of Wales Press, 1999, p. 118.
20  See G. Williams, 'From popular culture to public cliché: image and identity in Wales, 1890–1914', in J. Mangan (ed.), *Pleasure, Profit, Proselytism: British Culture and Sport at Home and Abroad 1700–1914*, London, Frank Cass, 1988, pp. 128–43.
21  Holt, *Sport and the British*, p. 249.
22  *South Wales Daily News*, 18 December 1905, quoted in D. Andrews and J. Howell, 'Transforming into a tradition: rugby and the making of imperial Wales, 1890–1914', in A. Ingham and J. Loy (eds), *Sport in Social Development: Traditions, Transitions, and Transformations*, Champaign, Ill., Human Kinetics, 1993, p. 83.
23  K. Morgan, *Rebirth of a Nation: A History of Modern Wales*, Oxford, Oxford University Press, 1982, p. 134.
24  Andrews and Howell, 'Transforming into a tradition', p. 79.
25  Williams, 'From popular culture to public cliché', p. 138.
26  Quoted in Polley, *Moving the Goalposts*, p. 60.
27  Morgan, *Rebirth of a Nation*, pp. 348, 405.
28  Holt, *Sport and the British*, pp. 253–4. G. Jarvie, 'Royal games, sport and the politics of the environment', in Jarvie and Walker, *Scottish Sport in the Making of the Nation*, pp. 154–72; J. Buchan, *John MacNab*, London, Hodder and Stoughton, 1967 [1925].
29  C. Harvie, *Scotland and Nationalism: Scottish Society and Politics 1707–1994*, second edition, London, Routledge, 1994, p. 19.
30  Holt, *Sport and the British*, pp. 257–9. See also A. Bairner, 'Football and the idea of Scotland', in Jarvie and Walker, *Scottish Sport in the Making of the Nation*, p. 12.
31  Quoted in Jarvie and Walker, *Scottish Sport in the Making of the Nation*, p. 1.
32  C. Harvie, 'Sport and the Scottish state', in Jarvie and Walker, *Scottish Sport in the Making of the Nation*, p. 47.
33  Holt, *Sport and the British*, p. 240. See also M. Cronin, *Sport and Nationalism in Ireland: Gaelic Games, Soccer and Irish Identity since 1884*, Dublin, Four Courts, 1999.
34  A. Jackson, *Ireland 1798–1998*, Oxford, Blackwell, 1999, p. 183.
35  http://www.gaa.ie/ (14 February 2002).
36  Cronin, *Sport and Nationalism in Ireland*, p. 143.
37  Quoted in J. Williams, '"One could literally have walked on the heads of the

people congregated there." Sport, the town and identity', in K. Laybourn (ed.), *Social Conditions, Status and Community 1860–c.1920*, Stroud, Sutton, 1997, p. 133.

38 Quoted in T. Mason, 'Football, sport of the North?', in J. Hill and J. Williams (eds), *Sport and Identity in the North of England*, Keele, Keele University Press, 1996, p. 47.

39 This passage on Rugby League is based on T. Mason (ed.), *Sport in Britain*, Cambridge, Cambridge University Press, 1989, pp. 7–9.

40 This section relies heavily on D. Russell, 'Sport and identity: the case of Yorkshire County Cricket Club, 1890–1939', *Twentieth Century British History*, 7, 1996, pp. 206–30.

41 Russell, 'Sport and identity', p. 214.

42 Williams, 'Sport, the town and identity', p. 125.

43 Quoted in Polley, *Moving the Goalposts*, p. 56. See also H. F. Moorhouse, 'On the periphery: Scotland, Scottish football and the new Europe', in J. Williams and S. Wagg (eds), *British Football and Social Change: Getting into Europe*, Leicester, Leicester University Press, 1991, pp. 204–5.

44 P. Dimeo and G. Finn, 'Racism, national identity and Scottish football', in Carrington and MacDonald, *'Race', Sport and British Society*, pp. 29–47.

45 Jarvie and Walker, *Scottish Sport in the Making of the Nation*, p. 5.

46 Other Scottish cities also had separate Protestant and Catholic teams, such as Hearts and Hibernian in Edinburgh and Dundee and Dundee United.

47 J. Bradley, 'Sport and the contestation of cultural and ethnic identities in Scottish society', in M. Cronin and D. Mayall (eds), *Sporting Nationalisms: Identity, Ethnicity, Immigration and Assimilation*, London, Frank Cass, 1998, pp. 127–50, provides a good discussion of Celtic's place in Scottish society.

48 Quoted in Dimeo and Finn, 'Racism, national identity and Scottish football', p. 37.

49 F. Madox Ford, *The Spirit of the People: An Analysis of the English Mind*, 1907, in I. Baucom, *Out of Place: Englishness, Empire and the Locations of Identity*, Princeton, NJ, Princeton University Press, 1999, pp. 16–17.

50 Polley, *Moving the Goalposts*, p. 135.

51 Dimeo and Finn, 'Racism, national identity and Scottish football', pp. 38–43.

52 Quoted in Polley, *Moving the Goalposts*, p. 143.

53 Back, Crabbe and Solomos, 'Lions and black skins', p. 98.

54 Polley, *Moving the Goalposts*, p. 153; T. Mason, *Sport in Britain*, London, Faber and Faber, 1988, pp. 15–17.

55 Polley, *Moving the Goalposts*, p. 136.

56 Quoted in Back, Crabbe and Solomos, 'Lions and black skins', p. 83.

57 *The Works of Rudyard Kipling*, Ware, Wordsworth, 1994, p. 302.

58 *Guardian*, 10 November 2000. See also J. Williams, 'Having an away day: English football spectators and the hooligan debate', in Williams and Wagg, *British Football and Social Change*, pp. 160–1.

59 J. Hill, 'Rite of spring: Cup Finals and community in the north of England', in Hill and Williams, *Sport and Identity in the North*, p. 87.

60 J. Paxman, *The English*, London, Penguin, 1999, pp. 245–8.

61 C. Dickens, *Barnaby Rudge: A Tale of the Riots of 'Eighty*, London, Oxford University Press, 1954 [1841]; S. Connor, 'Space, place and the body of riot in *Barnaby Rudge*', in S. Connor (ed.), *Charles Dickens*, London, Longman, 1996, p. 227.

62 Mason, *Sport in Britain*, pp. 22–35; J. Williams, 'Having an away day', pp. 164–5.

63 R. Giulianotti, 'Hooligans and carnival fans: Scottish football supporter cultures', in Armstrong and Giulianotti, *Football Cultures*, pp. 29–40.

64 Mason, *Sport in Britain*, p. 29.

65 Quoted in J. de Groot, '"What should they know of England who only England know?" Kipling on the boundaries of gender, art and empire', in G. Cubitt (ed.), *Imagining Nations*, Manchester, Manchester University Press, 1998, p. 184.

66  G. Rose, *Feminism and Geography*, Cambridge, Polity Press, 1993, p. 116, quoted in A. Pritchard, 'Ways of seeing "them" and "us": tourism representation, race and identity', in M. Robinson *et al.*, *Expressions of Culture, Identity and Meaning in Tourism*, Sunderland, Centre for Travel and Tourism, 2000, p. 246. See also L. Colley, 'Britishness and otherness and national identity: an argument', *Journal of British Studies*, 31, 1992, pp. 309–29.

67  J. Urry, *The Tourist Gaze: Leisure and Travel in Contemporary Societies*, London, Sage, 1990, p. 6.

68  R. Shields, *Places on the Margin: Alternative Geographies of Modernity*, London, Routledge, 1991, especially pp. 73, 83.

69  J. Walton, *Blackpool*, Edinburgh, Edinburgh University Press/Carnegie, 1998, p. 69. The release from restraint was also a theme in Mass-Observation's social survey of Blackpool, see G. Cross (ed.), *Worktowners at Blackpool: Mass-Observation and Popular Leisure in the 1930s*, London, Routledge, 1990 and P. Gurney, '"Intersex" and "dirty girls": Mass-Observation and working-class sexuality in England in the 1930s', *Journal of the History of Sexuality*, 8, 1997, pp. 256–90.

70  R. Beck, 'Review of Marjorie Morgan, *National Identities and Travel in Victorian Britain*, H-Albion, H-Net Reviews, October 2002. URL http://www.h-net.msu.edu/reviews/showrev.egi? path-233971037026788, 12 November 2002.

71  Cross, *Worktowners*, p. 19.

72  J. Drower, *Good Clean Fun: The Story of Britain's First Holiday Camp*, London, Arcadia, 1982.

73  Cross, *Worktowners*, p. 137.

74  See J. Richards, *The Age of the Dream Palace: Cinema and Society in Britain 1930–1939*, London, Routledge, 1984, pp. 19–22.

75  See K. Lindley, *Seaside Architecture*, London, Hugh Evelyn, 1973, and L. F. Pearson, *The People's Palaces: The Story of the Seaside Pleasure Buildings of 1870–1914*, Buckingham, Barracuda, 1991.

76  Walton, *Blackpool*, p. 108.

77  J. Walvin, *Beside the Seaside: A Social History of the Popular Seaside Holiday*, London, Allen Lane, 1978, p. 101.

78  For example, G. Orwell, 'The lion and the unicorn: Socialism and the English genius', in S. Orwell and I. Angus (eds), *The Collected Essays, Journalism and Letters of George Orwell, II*, Harmondsworth, Penguin, 1970, p. 78.

79  Shields, *Places on the Margin*, p. 93.

80  Walvin, *Beside the Seaside*, p. 11; Pearson, *The People's Palaces*, p. 11.

81  Quoted in Richards, *Age of the Dream Palace*, pp. 247–8.

82  *Time and Tide*, 7 September 1940 in *Collected Essays, II*, p. 191n.

83  Quoted in Urry, *The Tourist Gaze*, p. 29.

84  J. Culler, 'Semiotics of tourism', *American Journal of Semiotics*, 1, 1981, quoted in Urry, *The Tourist Gaze*, p. 3.

85  Pritchard, 'Ways of seeing "them" and "us"'.

86  Quoted in J. Presley, '"Frizzling in the sun": Robert Graves and the development of mass tourism in the Balearic Islands', in Robinson, *Expressions of Culture*, p. 231.

87  M. Palin, *Around the World in 80 Days*, London, BBC, 1989.

88  H.-M. Teo, 'Wandering in the wake of empire: British travel and tourism in the post-imperial world', in S. Ward (ed.), *British Culture and the End of Empire*, Manchester, Manchester University Press, 2001, p. 167.

89  D. Reynolds, *Britannia Overruled: British Policy and World Power in the Twentieth Century*, London, Longman, 1991, p. 21.

90  See, for example, L. Trotsky, 'Anglo-American rivalry and the growth of militarism', 1924, in R. Chappell and A. Clinton (eds), *Leon Trotsky: Collected Writings and Speeches on Britain, I*, London, New Park, 1974, pp. 145–52.

91  R. Seitz, *Over Here*, London, Weidenfeld and Nicolson, 1998, p. 347.

92 Quoted in A. Davies, 'Cinema and broadcasting', in P. Johnson (ed.), *Twentieth-Century Britain: Economic, Social and Cultural Change*, London, Longman, 1994, p. 271.

93 See J. Richards, 'The British Board of Film Censors and content control in the 1930s: images of Britain', *Historical Journal of Film, Radio and Television*, 1, 1981, pp. 95–116.

94 Quoted in J. Springhall, *Youth, Popular Culture and Moral Panics: Penny Gaffs to Gangsta-Rap, 1830–1996*, Basingstoke, Macmillan, 1998, p. 114.

95 R. Hoare, *This Our Country*, 1935, quoted in Richards, *Age of the Dream Palace*, p. 57.

96 J. B. Priestley, *English Journey*, London, Heinemann, 1949, p. 401.

97 Quoted in S. Fielding, '"But westward, look, the land is bright": Labour's Revisionists and the imagining of America, *c.*1945–1964', in J. Hollowell (ed.), *Twentieth-Century Anglo-American Relations*, Basingstoke, Palgrave, 2001, p. 88.

98 D. Reynolds, *Rich Relations: The American Occupation of Britain 1942–1945*, London, Phoenix, 2000, p. 432.

99 Mass-Observation, 'Anti-Americanism', 1947.

100 Quoted in Reynolds, *Rich Relations*, p. 457.

101 Importing Hollywood films meant the export of sterling. The government sought to impose a 75 per cent duty to offset the deficit. Hence their motives were both economically and culturally nationalist. See McKibbin, *Classes and Cultures*, pp. 429–30.

102 Quoted in Weight, *Patriots*, p. 179.

103 Much of this section relies on Springhall, *Youth, Popular Culture and Moral Panics*, pp. 141–5.

104 Quoted in Springhall, *Youth, Popular Culture and Moral Panics*, p. 142.

105 Facsimile in P. Kitchen (ed.), *For Home and Country: War, Peace and Rural Life as seen through the Pages of the* W.I. Magazine *1919–1959*, London, Ebury, 1990, pp. 126–7.

## 5 Politicians, parties and national identity

1 See B. Brivati, 'The end of decline: the Blair-Brown governments and contemporary British history', unpublished inaugural lecture, Kingston University, 2003.

2 For Labour's challenge see M. Pugh, 'The rise of Labour and the political culture of Conservatism, 1890–1945', *History*, 87, 2002, pp. 514–37, and P. Ward, *Red Flag and Union Jack: Englishness, Patriotism and the British Left, 1881–1924*, Woodbridge, Boydell, 1998.

3 For these processes see L. Colley, *Britons: Forging the Nation 1707–1837*, New Haven, CT, Yale University Press, 1992, and G. Newman, *The Rise of English Nationalism: A Cultural History 1740–1830*, London, Weidenfeld and Nicolson, 1987.

4 P. Mandler, *The Fall and Rise of the Stately Home*, New Haven, CT, Yale University Press, 1997.

5 E. P. Thompson, *The Making of the English Working Class*, Harmondsworth, Penguin, 1980, remains the classic account of radicalism during the industrial revolution. For the positive connotations of Anglo-Saxonism see C. Hill, 'The Norman yoke', in his *Puritanism and Revolution*, Harmondsworth, Penguin, 1986, pp. 58–125.

6 Ward, *Red Flag and Union Jack*, p. 15

7 *Northern Star*, 29 September 1839, in F. Mather (ed.), *Chartism and Society: An Anthology of Documents*, London, Bell and Hyman, 1980, pp. 57–62. For the role of the Irish in Chartism, see D. Thompson, *Outsiders: Class, Gender and Nation*, London, Verso, 1993.

8 R. McWilliam, *Popular Politics in Nineteenth Century England*, London, Routledge, 1998, pp. 85–6, and M. Finn, *After Chartism: Class and Nation in English Radical Politics 1848–1874*, Cambridge, Cambridge University Press, 1993.

9 H. Cunningham, 'The language of patriotism', in R. Samuel (ed.), *Patriotism: The Making and Unmaking of British National Identity Volume 1: History and Politics*, London, Routledge, 1989, pp. 57–89.

10 R. McWilliam, 'Radicalism and popular culture: the Tichborne case and the politics of "Fair Play", 1867–1886', in E. Biagini and A. Reid (eds), *Currents of Radicalism*, Cambridge, Cambridge University Press, 1991, pp. 44–64.

11 F. Harcourt, 'Gladstone, monarchism and the "new" imperialism, 1868–74', *Journal of Imperial and Commonwealth History*, 14, 1985, pp. 20–51.

12 P. Joyce, *Work, Society and Politics: The Culture of the Factory in Later Victorian England*, Brighton, Harvester, 1980.

13 Cunningham, 'Language of patriotism', pp. 74–5. See also J. Parry, 'Disraeli and England', *Historical Journal*, 43, 2000, pp. 699–728.

14 Cunningham, 'Language of patriotism', p. 76.

15 McWilliam, *Popular Politics*, p. 96.

16 M. Pugh, *The Tories and the People 1880–1935*, Oxford, Blackwell, 1985.

17 McWilliam, *Popular Politics*, p. 94.

18 H. Cunningham, 'The Conservative Party and patriotism', in R. Colls and P. Dodd (eds), *Englishness: Politics and Culture 1880–1920*, London, Croom Helm, 1986, p. 284.

19 K. Morgan, *Rebirth of a Nation: A History of Modern Wales*, Oxford, Oxford University Press, 1981, p. 30.

20 D. Feldman, 'Nationality and ethnicity', in P. Johnson (ed.), *Twentieth-Century Britain: Economic, Social and Cultural Change*, London, Longman, 1994, p. 137.

21 See illustration for Gladstone's golden wedding album in W. Crane, *An Artist's Reminiscences*, London, Methuen, 1907, p. 195.

22 D. G. Boyce, 'The marginal Britons: the Irish', in Colls and Dodd, *Englishness*, p. 236.

23 5 August 1910, quoted in E. John, *National Self Government: How Wales Stands to Gain by It*, 1910.

24 See E. F. Biagini, *Gladstone*, Basingstoke, Macmillan, 2000, and chapter 7 below.

25 D. Lloyd George, *Patriotism and Free Trade*, 1904, in Feldman, 'Nationality and ethnicity', pp. 137–8.

26 R. Price, *An Imperial War and the Working Class*, has argued that the result was not the outcome of a successful Unionist appeal to patriotism, but for a corrective to this view see P. Readman, 'The Conservative Party, patriotism and British politics: the case of the general election of 1900', *Journal of British Studies*, 40, 2001, pp. 107–45.

27 C. H. Norman, *Nationality and Patriotism*, Manchester, National Labour Press, 1915, p. 6.

28 Ward, *Red Flag and Union Jack*, ch. 2.

29 C. Benn, *Keir Hardie*, London, Hutchinson, 1992, p. 257.

30 K. Robbins, *Great Britain: Identities, Institutions and the Idea of Britishness*, London, Longman, 1998, p. 270.

31 See for example J. Masterman, *The House of Commons: Its Place in National History*, London, John Murray, 1908. R. Miliband, *Parliamentary Socialism: A Study in the Politics of Labour*, second edition, London, Merlin, 1972, remains the classic polemical account of the effect of this celebration of parliament on the Labour Party.

32 R. Quinault, 'Westminster and the Victorian constitution', *Transactions of the Royal Historical Society*, 6th series, 2, 1992, pp. 79–104.

33 *The Queen's Speech, on the Opening of the Neath Parliament*, Neath, 1883.

34 R. McKibbin, *The Ideologies of Class*, Oxford, Oxford University Press, 1991, p. 22.

35 Of course in Britain it was the role of the monarch to call on a minister to form a government. For Germany, see V. Berghahn, *Germany and the Approach of War in 1914*, Basingstoke, Macmillan, 1973, pp. 5–25, and H.-U. Wehler, *The German Empire 1871–1918*, Leamington Spa, Berg, 1985, pp. 52–70.

36 J. Ramsden, *An Appetite for Power: A History of the Conservative Party since 1830*, London, HarperCollins, 1998, pp. 222–9.

37 Ward, *Red Flag and Union Jack*, pp. 169–70.

38 *Daily Herald*, 3 August 1914.

39  Quoted in P. Snowden, *An Autobiography, I: 1864–1919*, London, Ivor Nicholson and Watson, 1934, p. 364.

40  M. Hilson, 'Women voters and the rhetoric of patriotism in the British general election of 1918', *Women's History Review*, 10, 2001, pp. 325–47.

41  R. Blake, *The Conservative Party from Peel to Thatcher*, London, Fontana, 1985, p. 216.

42  For this argument, see J. Ramsden, *The Age of Balfour and Baldwin 1902–1940: A History of the Conservative Party*, London, Longman, 1978, pp. 207–15.

43  McKibbin, *Ideologies of Class*, pp. 259–93.

44  S. Nicholas, 'The construction of a national identity: Stanley Baldwin, "Englishness" and the mass media in inter-war Britain', in M. Francis and I. Zweiniger-Bargielowska (eds), *The Conservatives and British Society, 1880–1990*, Cardiff, University of Wales Press, 1996, p. 131.

45  G. Ward-Smith, 'Baldwin and Scotland: more than Englishness', *Contemporary British History*, 15, 2001, pp. 61–82.

46  R. McKibbin, *The Evolution of the Labour Party 1910–1924*, Oxford, Clarendon, 1974, pp. 167–70.

47  *New Leader*, 29 December 1922.

48  J. Ramsay MacDonald, *Labour's Policy versus Protection: The Real Issues of the General Election*, London, Labour Party, n.d. [1923], p. 9. Original emphasis.

49  Recent books on British Communism and Fascism include K. Laybourn and D. Murphy, *Under the Red Flag: A History of Communism in Britain, c.1849–1991*, Stroud, Sutton, 1999, and R. Thurlow, *Fascism in Modern Britain*, Stroud, Sutton, 2000.

50  A. Thorpe (ed.), *The Failure of Political Extremism in Inter-War Britain*, Exeter, Exeter University Press, 1989, p. 10.

51  K. Laybourn, *Britain on the Breadline: A Social and Political History of Britain 1918–1939*, Stroud, Sutton, 1991, supports the traditional view, while C. Cook and J. Stevenson, *Britain in the Depression: Society and Politics, 1929–1939*, London, Longman, 1994, see the 1930s in the revisionist light. M. Smith, *Democracy in a Depression: Britain in the 1920s and 1930s*, Cardiff, University of Wales Press, 1998, discusses the politics of the historiography of the 1930s.

52  R. McKibbin, 'Class and conventional wisdom: the Conservative Party and the "public" in inter-war Britain', in his *Ideologies of Class*.

53  Labour Party, *Annual Conference Report*, 1924, pp. 187–8.

54  Quoted in R. Skidelsky, *Oswald Mosley*, London, Macmillan, 1975, p. 370.

55  O. Mosley, *My Life*, London, Nelson, 1970, p. 319.

56  Skidelsky, *Mosley*, p. 386.

57  Quoted in N. Fielding, *The National Front*, London, Routledge and Kegan Paul, 1981, p. 21.

58  K. Morgan, *Against Fascism and War: Ruptures and Continuities in British Communist Politics 1935–41*, Manchester, Manchester University Press, 1989, pp. 41–2.

59  This section relies on J. Baxendale, '"You and I – All of us ordinary people": renegotiating "Britishness" in wartime', in N. Hayes and J. Hill (eds), *Millions Like Us? British Culture in the Second World War*, Liverpool, Liverpool University Press, 1999, and M. Smith, *Britain and 1940: History, Myth and Popular Memory*, London, Routledge, 2000.

60  Quoted in Baxendale, 'You and I', p. 309.

61  J. Ramsden, *Man of the Century: Winston Churchill and His Legend since 1945*, London, HarperCollins, 2002. Foot is quoted on p. 60n.

62  'Cato', *Guilty Men*, London, Victor Gollancz, 1940, p. 19.

63  See P. Ward, 'Preparing for the people's war: the left and patriotism in the 1930s', *Labour History Review*, 67, 2002, pp. 171–86.

64  G. Field, 'Social patriotism and the British working class: appearance and disappearance of a tradition', *International Labour and Working-Class History*, 42, 1992, pp. 20–39.

65 E. Bevin, *The Job to Be Done*, 1940, quoted in Smith, *Britain and 1940*, p. 56.

66 G. Orwell, 'The lion and the unicorn: socialism and the English genius', 1941, in *Collected Essays, Journalism and Letters, II: My Country Right or Left 1940–1943*, London, Penguin, 1970.

67 Quoted in Baxendale, 'You and I', p. 316.

68 Churchill speech to House of Commons, 13 May 1940, 'Modern History Sourcebook', http://www.fordham.edu/halsall/mod/churchill-blood.html (17 January 2001).

69 S. Fielding, P. Thompson and N. Tiratsoo, *England Arise! The Labour Party and Popular Politics in 1940s Britain*, Manchester, Manchester University Press, 1995.

70 J. Ramsden (ed.), *The Oxford Companion to Twentieth-Century British Politics*, Oxford, Oxford University Press, 2002, p. 598.

71 M. Taylor, 'Labour and the constitution', in D. Tanner, P. Thane and N. Tiratsoo (eds), *Labour's First Century*, Cambridge, Cambridge University Press, 2000, pp. 151–80 argues that Labour has had a long-term commitment to constitutional reform.

72 Quoted in K. Morgan, *The People's Peace: British History 1945–1990*, Oxford, Oxford University Press, 1992, p. 108.

73 Pugh, 'The rise of Labour', p. 524.

74 R. Hewison, *Culture and Consensus: England, Art and Politics since 1940*, London, Methuen, 1995, pp. 60–1.

75 See D. Reynolds, *Britannia Overruled: British Policy and World Power in the 20th Century*, Harlow, Longman, 1991, and P. Kennedy, *The Realities behind Diplomacy: Background Influences on British External Policy 1865-1980*, London, Fontana, 1981.

76 J. Monnet, *Memoirs*, London, Collins, 1978, p. 362.

77 Quoted in Morgan, *The People's Peace*, p. 134.

78 See J. Darwin, *Britain and Decolonisation: The Retreat from Empire in the Post-war World*, Basingstoke, Macmillan, 1978, pp. 329–35.

79 Quoted in P. Hennessy, *Never Again: Britain 1945-1951*, London, Vintage, 1993, p. 268.

80 Quoted in Morgan, *The People's Peace*, p. 127.

81 See S. Greenwood, *Britain and European Integration since the Second World War*, Manchester, Manchester University Press, 1996, and S. George, *Britain and European Integration since 1945*, Oxford, Blackwell, 1991.

82 Labour Party Conference, 5 October 1960, p. 201.

83 Quoted in Morgan, *People's Peace*, pp. 338-9.

84 D. Powell, *Nationhood and Identity: The British State since 1800*, London, I. B. Tauris, 2002, p. 237.

85 Quoted in Hewison, *Culture and Consensus*, p. 9.

86 S. Haseler, *The English Tribe: Identity, Nation and Europe*, London, Macmillan, 1996, p. 144.

87 Quoted in A. Seldon, *Major: A Political Life*, London, Weidenfeld and Nicolson, 1997, p. 370.

88 Hewison, *Culture and Consensus*, p. 194.

89 See Philip Lynch, *The Politics of Nationhood: Sovereignty, Britishness and Conservative Politics*, Basingstoke, Macmillan, 1999.

90 Samuel, 'Exciting to be English', in Samuel, *Patriotism, I*, p. xxxiv.

91 'Christianity and wealth', speech to the Church of Scotland General Assembly, 21 May 1988, http://www.fordham.edu/halsalVmod/1988thatcher.html (5 July 2002).

92 K. Robbins, *Present and Past: British Images of Germany in the First Half of the Twentieth Century and Their Historical Legacy*, Göttingen, Wallstein Verlag, 1999, pp. 13–14.

93 J. Kürnig, 'The mass media in the age of globalisation: implications for Anglo-German relations', unpublished Reuters lecture, University of Kent, 1999. I owe this reference to John Ramsden.

94  C. Collette, *The International Faith: Labour's Attitudes to European Socialism 1918-39*, Aldershot, Ashgate, 1998, and Ward, *Red Flag and Union Jack*.

95  T. Blair, 'My vision for Britain', in G. Radice (ed.), *What Needs to Change: New Visions for Britain*, London, HarperCollins, 1996, p. 8.

96  A. Giddens, *The Third Way: The Renewal of Social Democracy*, Cambridge, Polity Press, 1998, p. 130.

97  *Guardian*, 12 November 1998, quoted in Y. Alibhai-Brown, 'Muddled leaders and the future of the British national identity', *Political Quarterly*, 71, 2000, p. 29. See also S. Richards, 'The NS interview: Gordon Brown', *New Statesman*, 19 April 1999, pp. 18–19.

98  For a contemporary critique from the left see Tristam Hunt, *New Statesman*, 27 August 2001. On the right, William Hague, briefly Conservative leader, argued that Labour's policies ran 'counter to the essential character of the British people. They are the third way not the British way': BBC News Online, 19 January 1999, http://news.bbc.co.uk/low/English/uk_politics/~ewsid-257000/257646.stm (4 July 2000).

99  P. Griffith and M. Leonard (eds), *Reclaiming Britishness*, London, Foreign Policy Centre, 2002.

100  *Guardian*, 28 March 2000.

101  Quoted in S. Breese, 'In search of Englishness: in search of votes', in J. Arnold, K. Davies and S. Ditchfield (eds), *History and Heritage: Consuming the Past in Contemporary Culture*, Shaftsbury, Donhead, 1998, p. 155.

## 6  A new way of being British: ethnicity and Britishness

1  Powell is often seen as honourable for 'daring' to speak out. In fact, he hid behind the racism of others, always quoting 'constituents' rather than declaring his own racism.

2  This quote is from Powell's 'rivers of blood' speech in Birmingham in April 1968. The full text is in *New Statesman*, 17 April 1998, pp. 14–19.

3  The politics of the use of terminology such as 'immigrants' has been much discussed. See B. Parekh, 'The report on the future of multi-ethnic Britain', which outlines with exactitude the use of language. See also Y. Alibhai-Brown, *Who Do We Think We Are? Imagining the New Britain*, London, Penguin, 2001, pp. vii–xi.

4  P. Fryer, *Staying Power: The History of Black People in Britain*, London, Pluto, 1984, p. 395.

5  P. Panayi, *Racial Violence in Britain in the Nineteenth and Twentieth Centuries*, London, Leicester University Press, 1996, pp. 17–18.

6  G. John and D. Humphry, *Because They're Black*, Harmondsworth, Penguin, 1972, p. 55.

7  Quoted in J. Zubrzycki, *Polish Immigrants in Britain: A Study of Adjustment*, The Hague, Martinus Nijhoff, 1956, p. 207.

8  Quoted in Zubrzycki, *Polish Immigrants*, p. 209.

9  Zubrzycki, *Polish Immigrants*, pp. 210–13.

10  Quoted in T. Sewell, *Keep on Moving: The Windrush Legacy: The Black Experience in Britain from 1948*, London, Voice Enterprises, 1998, p. 57.

11  E. Rose and N. Deakin, *Colour and Citizenship: A Report in British Race Relations*, London, Oxford University Press, 1969, pp. 552–3.

12  A. Travis, 'Blunkett in race row over culture tests', 10 December 2001, http://www.guardian.co.uk/uk_news/story/0,3604,616214,00.html (17 January 2003). See also D. Blunkett, 'Integration with diversity: globalisation and the renewal of democracy and civil society', in P. Griffith and M. Leonard (eds), *Reclaiming Britishness*, London, Foreign Policy Centre, 2002, pp. 65–77. For the Crick proposals see *Guardian*, 4 September 2003. For Tebbit and cricket see M. Marqusee, *Anyone but England: Cricket, Race and Class*, London, Two Heads, 1998.

13  H. Kureishi, 'London and Karachi', in R. Samuel (ed.), *Patriotism: The Making and Unmaking of British National Identity, II: Minorities and Outsiders*, London, Routledge, 1989, p. 286.

14  T. Modood, 'Culture and identity', in T. Modood and R. Berthoud (eds), *Ethnic Minorities in Britain: Diversity and Disadvantage*, London, Policy Studies Institute, 1997, p. 290.

15  D. Mason, *Race and Ethnicity in Modern Britain*, second edition, Oxford, Oxford University Press, 2000, p. 12; S. Fielding, *Class and Ethnicity: Irish Catholics in England, 1880–1939*, Buckingham, Open University Press, 1993, p. xii.

16  Quoted in D. Beriss, Review of G. Baumann, *Contesting Culture: Discourses of Identity in Multi-Ethnic London*, Cambridge, Cambridge University Press, 1996, H-ALBION @H-NET.MSU.EDU (18 December 1999). For hybridity see P. Werbner and T. Modood (eds), *Debating Cultural Hybridity*, London, Zed, 1997.

17  R. Cohen, *Frontiers of Identity: The British and the Others*, London, Longman, 1994, p. 1. My emphasis.

18  Z. Layton-Henry, *The Politics of Immigration*, Oxford, Blackwell, 1992, p. 3.

19  Fryer, *Staying Power*, p. 1.

20  R. Visram, *Asians in Britain: 400 Years of History*, London, Pluto, 2002.

21  T. Kushner. 'Heritage and ethnicity: an introduction', in *The Jewish Heritage in British History: Englishness and Jewishness*, London, Frank Cass, 1992, p. 11.

22  P. Panayi, *Immigration, Ethnicity and Racism in Britain 1815–1945*, Manchester, Manchester University Press, 1994, pp. 24, 51–2.

23  The Irish, like the migrants from the former Empire and Commonwealth after 1948, were legally subjects of the monarch and were therefore 'British'.

24  Fielding, *Class and Ethnicity*, p. 21.

25  J. Bourke, *Working-Class Cultures in Britain 1890–1960: Gender, Class and Ethnicity*, London, Routledge, 1994, p. 193.

26  Fielding, *Class and Ethnicity*, p. 15.

27  D. Fitzpatrick, 'A curious middle place: the Irish in Britain, 1871–1921', in S. Gilley and R. Swift (eds), *The Irish in Britain, 1815–1939*, London, Pinter, 1989, pp. 10–59.

28  Fitzpatrick, 'A curious middle place', p. 14.

29  Quoted in Fitzpatrick, 'A curious middle place', p. 29.

30  Fitzpatrick, 'A curious middle place', p. 35.

31  Quoted in M. Lennon, M. MacAdam and J. O'Brien, *Across the Water: Irish Women's Lives in Britain*, London, Virago, 1998, pp. 146–55.

32  Gilley and Swift, *The Irish in Britain*, p. 3.

33  J. Walvin, *Passage to Britain*, Harmondsworth, Penguin, 1984, p. 59.

34  Fielding, *Class and Ethnicity*, pp. 40, 62.

35  Bourke, *Working-Class Cultures*, p. 192.

36  See for example, D. Feldman, *Englishmen and Jews: Social Relations and Political Culture 1840–1914*, New Haven, CT, Yale University Press, 1994.

37  L. Grade, *Still Dancing*, 1987, pp. 18–20, in D. Englander (ed.), *A Documentary History of Jewish Immigrants in Britain, 1840–1920*, Leicester, Leicester University Press, 1994, pp. 23–4.

38  R. Voeltz, '"A good Jew and a good Englishman": the Jewish Lads' Brigade 1894–1922', *Journal of Contemporary History*, 23, 1988, pp. 119–27.

39  *Jewish World*, 28 January 1910, in Voeltz, 'A good Jew and a good Englishman', p. 120.

40  Quoted in Englander, *Documentary History of Jewish Immigrants*, pp. 341–2.

41  Voeltz, 'A good Jew and a good Englishman', p. 124.

42  See D. Cohen, 'Who was who? Race and Jews in turn-of-the-century Britain', *Journal of British Studies*, 41, 2002, pp. 460–83.

43  Mass-Observation File Report 788, 'Tiger Bay', July 1941. These figures are only

of those registered for employment at Bute Docks employment exchange. See Fryer, *Staying Power*, p. 295 and Walvin, *Passage to Britain*, pp. 72–3.

44  J. Richards, *The Age of the Dream Palace: Cinema and Society in Britain 1930–1939*, London, Routledge, 1984, p. 112.

45  L. Tabili, *'We Ask for British Justice': Workers and Racial Difference in Late Imperial Britain*, Ithaca, NY, Cornell University Press, 1994, p. 6.

46  D. Feldman, 'There was an Englishman, an Irishman and a Jew . . . : immigrants and minorities in Britain', *Historical Journal*, 26, 1983, p. 186.

47  Bourke, *Working-Class Cultures*, pp. 203–11.

48  Quoted in Panayi, *Immigration, Ethnicity and Racism*, p. 152.

49  Quoted in Tabili, *We Ask for British Justice* p. 81.

50  Quoted in J. Clegg, *Fu Manchu and the 'Yellow Peril': The Making of a Racist Myth*, Stoke-on-Trent, Trentham, 1994, p. 10.

51  Richards, *Age of the Dream Palace*, p. 138.

52  Mass-Observation File Report 2411, 'Anti-Semitism and free speech', 25 July 1946.

53  Panayi, *Racial Violence in Britain*, p. 3.

54  Panayi, *Racial Violence in Britain*, p. 11.

55  Bourke, *Working-Class Cultures*, p. 210.

56  Mass-Observation File Report 79, 'Public feeling about aliens', 25 April 1940.

57  Mass-Observation File Report 184, 'Anti-Italian riots in Soho', 11 June 1940.

58  Mass-Observation File Report 1669Q, 'Attitudes to foreigners', April 1943.

59  Mass-Observation File Report 2248, 'German atrocities', May 1945. 'German atrocities' had been the phrase used to describe German actions against civilians in Belgium and France during the First World War. As between the war many of these stories had been disproved, the phrase had gone out of use and the British propaganda machine was more reluctant in the Second World War to utilise such material, which was readily available from those who had witnessed the concentration and extermination camps. The use of the phrase 'atrocities' by Mass-Observation seems to serve the purpose of stressing continuities of German behaviour.

60  M. Smith, *Britain and 1940: History, Myth and Popular Memory*, London, Routledge, 2000.

61  S. Rose, *Which People's War? National Identity and Citizenship in Wartime Britain 1939–1945*, Oxford, Oxford University Press, 2003, interrogates wartime unity.

62  C. Waters, '"Dark strangers" in our midst: discourses of race and nation in Britain, 1947–1963', *Journal of British Studies*, 36, 1997, p. 212.

63  A. Bonnett, *White Identities: Historical and International Perspectives*, Harlow, Prentice Hall, 2000, ch. 2.

64  Quoted in Bonnett, *White Identities*, p. 28.

65  P. Ward, *Red Flag and Union Jack: Englishness, Patriotism and the British Left, 1881–1924*, Woodbridge, Boydell, 1998.

66  Bonnett, *White Identities*, p. 40.

67  See for example, Rose and Deakin, *Colour and Citizenship*, p. 571.

68  Quoted in Mason, *Race and Ethnicity*, p. 133.

69  See W. Webster, 'The Empire answers: imperial identity on radio and film, 1939–45', unpublished paper, 'The British World 2 conference', University of Calgary, July 2003.

70  I am grateful to John Ramsden for this information.

71  These details are from Walvin, *Passage to Britain*, pp. 96–7, and I. Spencer, 'World War Two and the making of multiracial Britain', in P. Kirkham and D. Thoms (eds), *War Culture: Social Change and Changing Experience in World War Two Britain*, London, Lawrence and Wishart, 1995, pp. 209–18.

72  Quoted in John and Humphry, *Because They're Black*, p. 29.

73  C. Holmes, 'Immigration', in T. Gourvish and A. O'Day (eds), *Britain since 1945*, Basingstoke, Macmillan, 1991, p. 211.

74  *New Statesman*, 17 April 1998, pp. 14–15.

75  Quoted in Fryer, *Staying Power*, p. 38.

76  B. Parekh, 'Defining British national identity', *Political Quarterly*, 71, 2000, p. 5. See, for contrast, L. Colley, 'Britishness and otherness: an argument', *Journal of British Studies*, 31, 1992, pp. 309–29. Parekh does not, however, argue that his identity has an essential and timeless core; the constitution of his identity is formulated and not given.

77  S. Patterson, *Dark Strangers: A Study of West Indians*, Harmondsworth, Penguin, 1965, p. 17.

78  Patterson, *Dark Strangers*, p. 209.

79  Report of the Royal Commission on Population, Cd 7695, London, HMSO, 1949, paragraphs 329–30, quoted in K. Paul, 'From subjects to immigrants: black Britons and national identity, 1948–62', in R. Weight and A. Beach (eds), *The Right to Belong: Citizenship and National Identity in Britain, 1930–1960*, London, I. B. Tauris, 1998, p. 236.

80  See P. Gilroy, *'There Ain't No Black in the Union Jack': The Cultural Politics of Race and Nation*, London, Routledge, 1987.

81  See the documents in P. Panayi (ed.), *The Impact of Immigration: A Documentary History of the Effects and Experiences of Immigrants in Britain since 1945*, Manchester, Manchester University Press, 1999, pp. 129–30, 146–51.

82  See R. Thurlow, *Fascism in Britain: From Oswald Mosley's Blackshirts to the National Front*, second edition, London, I. B. Tauris, 1998.

83  Quoted in John and Humphry, *Because They're Black*, p. 163.

84  Layton-Henry, *Politics of Immigration*, pp. 32, 34, 72–4.

85  Holmes, 'Immigration', p. 219.

86  Speech in Eastbourne, *The Times*, 18 November 1968, quoted in T. Kushner and K. Lunn, 'Introduction', in T. Kushner and K. Lunn (eds), *Traditions of Intolerance: Historical Perspectives on Fascism and Race Discourse in Britain*, Manchester, Manchester University Press, 1989, p. 6.

87  Quoted in Holmes, 'Immigration', p. 225.

88  Kushner and Lunn, 'Introduction', p. 7.

89  *World in Action*, 30 January 1978, quoted in Layton-Henry, *Politics of Immigration*, p. 94.

90  See M. Thatcher, *The Path to Power*, 1995, quoted in Panayi, *The Impact of Immigration*, p. 153.

91  Kushner and Lunn, 'Introduction', p. 4. See also Thurlow, *Fascism in Britain*, pp. 255–6.

92  Layton-Henry provides an analysis of Thatcher's 'racecraft' in *Politics and Immigration*, ch. 8.

93  *The Sun*, 22 December 1989, quoted in Clegg, *Fu Manchu and the 'Yellow Peril'*, p. 48.

94  Fielding, *Class and Ethnicity*, p. 80.

95  J. Wolffe, '"And there's another country . . . " Religion, the state and British identities', in G. Parsons (ed.), *The Growth of Religious Diversity: Britain from 1945*, London, Routledge/Open University, 1994, p. 95.

96  G. Searle, *Corruption in British Politics 1895–1930*, Oxford, Clarendon, 1987, pp. 119–20, 172–200, 210–11.

97  Quoted in Wolffe, 'And there's another country', p. 96.

98  Tabili, *We Ask for British Justice*, p. 12.

99  Quoted in Tabili, *We Ask for British Justice*, p. 15.

100  Quoted in Walvin, *Passage to Britain*, p. 125.

101  Parekh, 'Defining British national identity', p. 10.

102  The poster is in T. Sewell, *Keep on Moving*, p. 99.

103  Paul, 'From subjects to immigrants', p. 228.

104 CAB 129/107 C(61) 153, 6 October 1961, Commonwealth Migrants: Memorandum by the Secretary of State for the Home Department', quoted in Paul, 'From subjects to immigrants', p. 236.

105 R. Butler, *The Art of the Possible*, Harmondsworth, Penguin, 1973, pp. 207–8.

106 CAB 128/43, 15 February 1968, http://www.pro.gov.uk/docimages/CAB/128_43_13a.gif, 18 January 1999.

107 See for example, Y. Alibhai-Brown, *True Colours: Public Attitudes to Multiculturalism and the Role of Government*, London, Institute for Public Policy Research, 1999.

108 See Layton-Henry, *Politics of Immigration*, p. 79.

109 Holmes, 'Immigration', p. 219.

110 Cohen, *Frontiers of Identity*, p. 19. See also I. Baucom, *Out of Place: Englishness, Empire, and the Locations of Identity*, Princeton, NJ, Princeton University Press, 1999, p. 13.

111 For the 'new racism' see Gilroy, *Ain't No Black in the Union Jack*.

112 A. Light, *Forever England: Femininity, Literature and Conservatism between the Wars*, London, Routledge, 1991; R. Samuel, 'Introduction: exciting to be English', in Raphael Samuel (ed.), *Patriotism: The Making and Unmaking of British National Identity, I: History and Politics*, London, Routledge, 1989, pp. xx–lxvii.

113 Waters, 'Dark strangers', pp. 210–13.

114 See Bourke, *Working-Class Cultures*, p. 204.

115 Quoted in Englander, *Documentary History of Jewish Immigrants*, p. 92.

116 Mass-Observation Anti-Semitism Survey, April 1951. Only 2 per cent responded that Jews were the 'same as other people', compared to 19 per cent of Jewish respondents.

117 Bourke, *Working-Class Cultures*, p. 207.

118 Quoted in Humphry and John, *Because They're Black*, pp. 23–4. This ought to be contrasted with 'Mr Jones, a white man in a Handsworth pub': 'I have lived here twenty-three years. It's changed a lot you know. Of course I saw lots of white people move out . . . I don't mind black people. I know a few of them where I work and some round where I live. I have never felt I wanted to move out', p. 24.

119 This section relies heavily on Waters, 'Dark strangers', pp. 223–4.

120 G. Gorer, *Exploring English Character*, London, Cressett, 1955.

121 Patterson, *Dark Strangers*, pp. 178–9, quoted in Waters, 'Dark strangers', p. 224.

122 *New Statesman*, 17 April 1998, p. 14.

123 See W. Webster, '"There'll always be an England": representations of colonial wars and immigration, 1948–1968', *Journal of British Studies*, 40, 2001, pp. 557–84, for the linked and gendered nature of the discourses on the loss of colonies and black immigration.

124 *New Statesman*, 17 April 1998, p. 16. Stuart Hall picks apart Powell's speech in the same issue of *New Statesman*.

125 E. Markham, 'A mugger's game', 1984, in J. Proctor (ed.), *Writing Black Britain 1948–1998: An Interdisciplinary Anthology*, Manchester, Manchester University Press, 2000, p. 83. See also S. Hall, C. Critcher, T. Jefferson, J. Clarke and B. Roberts, 'Policing the crisis', 1978, p. 171, in the same volume.

126 W. Webster, *Imagining Home: Gender, 'Race' and National Identity 1945–64*, London, UCL Press, 1998. See chapter 2 above.

127 *Jewish Chronicle*, 2 April 1926, quoted in Bourke, *Working-Class Cultures*, p. 195

128 Quoted in Fielding, *Class and Ethnicity*, p. 101.

129 Quoted in Alibhai-Brown, *True Colours*, p. 52.

130 S. Rushdie, *Imaginary Homelands: Essays and Criticism 1981–1991*, London, Penguin/Granta, 1991, p. 130.

131 Rose and Deakin, *Colour and Citizenship*, p. 567.

132 Quoted in S. Lahiri, 'South Asians in post-imperial Britain: decolonisation and imperial legacy', in S. Ward (ed.), *British Culture and the End of Empire*, Manchester, Manchester University Press, 2001, p. 205.

133  Humphry and John, *Because They're Black*, pp. 32–3.
134  Quoted in Sewell, *Keep on Moving*, p. 31.
135  Quoted in J. Paxman, *The English*, London, Penguin, 1999, p. 74.
136  Quoted in K. Davey, *English Imaginaries*, London, Lawrence and Wishart, 1999, p. 143
137  Y. Alibhai-Brown, 'Muddled leaders and the future of British national identity', *Political Quarterly*, 71, 2000, p. 29.
138  See Davey, *English Imaginaries*, p. 14.
139  See for example, S. Ward, *Australia and the British Embrace*, Carlton South, Melbourne University Press, 2001.
140  P. Gilroy, *The Black Atlantic: Modernity and Double Consciousness*, London, Verso, 1993, pp. 1, 126–7.
141  Modood, 'Culture and identity', p. 329.
142  Modood, 'Culture and identity', p. 329.
143  Alibhai-Brown, *True Colours*, p. 16.
144  Quoted in Sewell, *Keep on Moving*, p. 52.
145  See Modood, 'Culture and identity', p. 330.
146  Quoted in J. Taylor, *The Half-Way Generation: A Study of Asian Youths in Newcastle upon Tyne*, Windsor, NFER, 1976, p. 204.
147  Sewell, *Keep on Moving*, p. 72. See also K. Gardner and A. Shukur, '"I'm Bengali, I'm Asian, and I'm living here." The changing identity of British Bengalis', in R. Ballard (ed.), *Desh Pardesh: The South Asian Presence in Britain*, London, Hurst, 1994, pp. 142–64.
148  D. Singh Tatla, 'This is our home now: reminiscences of a Punjabi migrant in Coventry', *Oral History*, 21, 1993, p. 73.
149  Quoted in Sewell, *Keep on Moving*, p. 109.
150  Institute of Public Policy Research/NOP survey, October–November 1996, in Alibhai-Brown, *True Colours*, p. 33.
151  Alibhai-Brown, *True Colours*, p. 26.
152  M. Stopes-Roe and R. Cochrane, *Citizens of the Country: The Asian British*, Clevedon, Philadelphia, Multilingual Matters, 1990, pp. 169–72.
153  A. Wilson, *Finding a Voice: Asian Women in Britain*, London, Virago, 1984, p. 102.
154  S. Hall, 'New ethnicities', in J. Donald and A. Rattansi (eds), *'Race', Culture and Difference*, London, Sage/Open University, 1992, p. 259.
155  T. Modood, 'British Asian Muslims and the Rushdie affair', in Donald and Rattansi, *'Race', Culture and Difference*, p. 264.
156  The best known of the more sustained arguments is Alibhai-Brown, *Who Do We Think We Are?*
157  Quoted in Panayi, *The Impact of Immigration*, p. 161.
158  B. Parekh, 'Changing what it means to be British', *Daily Telegraph*, 18 October 2000. Only a couple of pages of the report itself dealt with Britishness. Most of the report made recommendations about reducing racism.
159  R. Cook, 'Extracts from a speech by the foreign secretary, to the Centre for the Open Society, Social Market Foundation, London', 19 April 2001, http://www.fco.gov.uk/news/speechtext.asp?49 (30 April 2002).
160  Cook, 'Extracts from a speech', p. 3. Panayi argues that the impact of immigration on the blandness of English food has been hugely beneficial, *The Impact of Immigration*, pp. 165–73.
161  Quoted in 'Chicken tikka timebomb', *Observer*, 22 April 2001, *Guardian Unlimited*, 20 August 2001, http://www.guardian.co.uk/Archive/Article/0,4273,4173765,00.html.
162  See A. Singh, 'Speak to us, Mr Blunkett', 22 September 2002, http://www.observer.co.uk/race/story/0,11255,796912,00.html (17 January 2003).
163  See Modood, 'British Asian Muslims and the Rushdie affair'; Layton-Henry, *Politics of Immigration*, pp. 171–4.

164  *The Stephen Lawrence Inquiry: Report of an Inquiry by Sir William Macpherson of Cluny*, London, HMSO, 1999.

165  Mason, *Race and Ethnicity*, p. 121. See also L. Burroughs, '"Dirty Babylon": reflections on the experience of racism and some lessons from social work', in A. Marlow and B. Loveday (eds), *After Macpherson: Policing after the Stephen Lawrence Inquiry*, Lyme Regis, Russell House, 2000, pp. 53–9, for a personal account of racism in daily life in north London from the 1960s onwards.

## 7  Outer Britain

1  R. Cohen, 'Review article: the incredible vagueness of being British/English', *International Affairs*, 76, 2000, pp. 575–82.

2  In Northern Ireland, of course, the Catholic population suffered institutionalised discrimination, but this rarely concerned the rest of Britain.

3  H. Kearney, *The British Isles: A History of Four Nations*, Cambridge, Cambridge University Press, 1995, pp. 269–70.

4  See M. Hechter, *Internal Colonialism: The Celtic Fringe in British National Development*, New Brunswick, NJ, Transaction, 1999.

5  M. Pittock, *Celtic Identity and the British Image*, Manchester, Manchester University Press, 1999, pp. 10–12.

6  Pittock, *Celtic Identity*, p. 104. Pittock also quotes the graffito from Northern Ireland in the 1970s 'KAI' or 'Kill All Irish', and remarks that 'one cannot make the Gaelic Celt more "other" than that', p. 12.

7  T. Nairn, *The Break-Up of Britain: Crisis and Neo-Nationalism*, second edition, London, Verso, 1981, p. 14; C. Harvie, 'The moment of British nationalism 1939–1970', *Political Quarterly*, 71, 2000, pp. 328–40.

8  K. Morgan, *Rebirth of a Nation: A History of Modern Wales*, Oxford, Oxford University Press, 1981, p. 4.

9  D. Howell and C. Baber, 'Wales', in F. M. L. Thompson (ed.), *The Cambridge Social History of Britain 1750–1950, I: Regions and Communities*, Cambridge, Cambridge University Press, 1990, pp. 300–6; Morgan, *Rebirth*, pp. 59–71.

10  P. Fryer, *Staying Power: The History of Black People in Britain*, London, Pluto, 1984, pp. 303–4.

11  Morgan, *Rebirth*, p. 6. For Welsh migrants in England see M. Jones, 'Long-distance migrants and cultural identity: the example of a Welsh colony in South Yorkshire', *Local Historian*, 26, 1996, pp. 223–36.

12  Sir E. Vincent Evans papers, Talks and Lectures c.1890–1930, N1, National Library of Wales.

13  L. Brockliss and D. Eastwood (eds), *A Union of Multiple Identities: The British Isles, c.1750–c.1850*, Manchester, Manchester University Press, 1997, p. 4.

14  Morgan, *Rebirth*, pp. 14–18, 134–7.

15  Howell and Baber, 'Wales', p. 330.

16  Sir E. Vincent Evans papers, Talks and Lectures c.1890–1930, N12, National Library of Wales.

17  This section relies heavily on K. O. Morgan, *Wales in British Politics 1868–1922*, Cardiff, University of Wales Press, 1991.

18  The definition comes from G. Williams, *When Was Wales?* London, Black Raven Press, 1985, p. 237. See also D. Adamson, 'The intellectual and the national movement in Wales', in R. Fevre and A. Thompson (eds), *Nation, Identity and Social Theory: Perspectives from Wales*, Cardiff, University of Wales Press, 1999, pp. 58–60, 63–4.

19  Morgan, *Rebirth*, p. 113.

20  D. Hamer, *Liberal Politics in the Age of Gladstone and Rosebery*, Oxford, Clarendon, 1972, p. 2.

21 Samuel T. Evans papers, 'Wales in Tudor Times', ts, n.d. [1908–9], National Library of Wales.

22 G. Phillips, 'Dai Bach Y Soldiwr: Welsh soldiers in the British Army 1914–1918', *Llafur*, 6, 1993, pp. 94–105. See also K. Morgan, 'England, Britain and the audit of war', *Transactions of the Royal Historical Society*, 6th series, 7, 1997, pp. 141–2, which argues that the impact of war on Wales impacted negatively upon its integration into Britain.

23 J. Davies, *A History of Wales*, London, Penguin, 1990, pp. 512–13.

24 See C. Williams, *Capitalism, Community and Conflict: The South Wales Coalfield 1898–1947*, Cardiff, University of Wales Press, 1998.

25 Howell and Baber, 'Wales', pp. 307–9, 327, 335.

26 D. Hywell Davies, *The Welsh Nationalist Party 1925–1945: A Call to Nationhood*, Cardiff, University of Wales Press, 1983, provides a detailed account of the party's early years. The party is referred to here as Plaid Cymru, which it became in 1945.

27 Saunders Lewis, 'The case for Welsh nationalism', *The Listener*, 13 May 1936, pp. 915–16.

28 Saunders Lewis, *The Ten Points of Policy*, 1934, in Davies, *The Welsh Nationalist Party*, p. 101.

29 J. Griffiths, *Pages from Memory*, London, Dent, 1969, p. 162.

30 See Morgan, *Rebirth*, pp. 377–8.

31 See for example, Huw T. Edwards papers, letters to William Whitely MP, 20 February 1947, 11 November 1947, A2/10, A2/14, National Library of Wales.

32 See for example, Huw T. Edwards papers, letters to H. A. Strutt, 8 September 1952, 24 October 1952, A2/69, A2/71, National Library of Wales.

33 Huw T. Edwards papers, 'An open letter to the Prime Minister and the Cabinet', 16 December 1946, A4/3, National Library of Wales.

34 See Huw T. Edwards papers, 'Personal Statement', 24 October 1958, E10, National Library of Wales.

35 R. Finlay, *A Partnership for Good? Scottish Politics and the Union since 1880*, Edinburgh, John Donald, 1997, p. 136.

36 C. Aull Davies, *Welsh Nationalism in the Twentieth Century: The Ethnic Option and the Modern State*, New York, Praeger, 1989.

37 Davies, *Welsh Nationalism*; Morgan, *Rebirth*, p. 360. See also 'The Welshness of Wales', *The Listener*, 6 February 1964, pp. 228–9.

38 *Action for Wales*, Bangor, Plaid Cymru, n.d. [1970].

39 Morgan, *Rebirth*, p. 393.

40 F. Aubel, 'The Conservatives in Wales, 1880–1935', in M. Francis and I. Zweiniger-Bargielowska (eds), *The Conservatives and British Society 1890–1980*, Cardiff, University of Wales Press, 1996, pp. 105–6.

41 Sir E. Vincent Evans papers, 'The Royal Wedding: Welsh National Presentation', AC1, National Library of Wales.

42 E. A. Murphy, *Official Souvenir of the National Pageant of Wales, Cardiff, 26th July to 7th August 1909*, Cardiff, 1909, National Library of Wales ex. 1469.

43 See N. Evans, 'The Welsh Victorian city: the middle class and civic and national consciousness in Cardiff, 1850–1914', *Welsh History Review*, 12, 1984–5, pp. 350–87.

44 *Western Mail*, 5 May 1958. See 'Festival of Wales 1958' folder, ex. 1047, National Library of Wales.

45 H. Thomas, 'Spatial restructuring in the capital: struggles to shape Cardiff's built environment', in Fevre and Thompson, *Nation, Identity and Social Theory*, pp. 168–88.

46 A. Aughey, *Nationalism, Devolution and the Challenge to the United Kingdom State*, London, Pluto, 2001, p. 149.

47 T. Devine, *The Scottish Nation 1700–2000*, London, Allen Lane, 1999, ch. 18, discusses Highland and crofting societies from the 1840s to the 1940s.

48 R. Finlay, 'National identity in crisis: politicians, intellectuals and the "End of Scotland", 1920–1939', *History*, 79, 1994, pp. 242–59.

49 This section relies heavily on T. Smout, 'Scotland 1850–1950', in Thompson, *Cambridge Social History of Britain 1750–1950*, I, pp. 212–21.

50 Cited in Smout, 'Scotland', p. 217.

51 There is now a wealth of material on Scotland's contribution to the British Empire: see for example J. M. MacKenzie, 'Empire and national identities: the case of Scotland', *Transactions of the Royal Historical Society*, 6th series, 8, 1998, pp. 215–31; R. Finlay, 'The rise and fall of popular imperialism in Scotland 1850–1950', *Scottish Geographical Magazine*, 113, 1997, pp. 13–21; C. Harvie, *Scotland and Nationalism: Scottish Society and Politics, 1707–1994*, second edition, London, Routledge, 1994, pp. 56–72.

52 See the correspondence between Alexander Korda and John Buchan in 1938–9 about imperial films, Acc. 11628/283, National Library of Scotland.

53 J. MacKenzie, '"The Second City of the Empire": Glasgow – imperial municipality', in F. Driver and D. Gilbert (eds), *Imperial Cities: Landscape, Display and Identity*, Manchester, Manchester University Press, 1999, pp. 215–37.

54 K. Robbins, *Great Britain: Identities, Institutions and the Idea of Britishness*, Harlow, Longman, 1998, p. 370.

55 Quoted in J. Loughlin, *Ulster Unionism and British National Identity since 1885*, London, Pinter, 1995, p. 30.

56 A. Balfour, *Nationality and Home Rule*, London, Longmans, Green and Co., 1913, pp. 10–11.

57 Kearney, *The British Isles*, p. 256. See also J. McCaffrey, 'The origins of Liberal Unionism in the West of Scotland', *Scottish Historical Review*, 50, 1971, pp. 47–71.

58 Smout, 'Scotland', pp. 221–7.

59 Finlay, 'National identity in crisis', pp. 242–59.

60 For the fortunes of nationalism in the 1920s and 1930s see R. Finlay, 'Pressure group or political party? The nationalist impact on Scottish politics, 1928–1945', *Twentieth-Century British History*, 3, 1992, pp. 274–97.

61 Smout, 'Scotland', p. 268. Concerns were raised in Scotland over the naming of Queen Elizabeth II since Elizabeth I had not ruled Scotland: see Walter Elliot papers, Box 6 F6 'Letters on the Queen's Title 1953', National Library of Scotland.

62 Smout, 'Scotland', p. 230.

63 Quoted in K. Webb, *The Growth of Nationalism in Scotland*, Harmondsworth, Penguin, 1978, p. 64.

64 See the Young Scots postcard in John W. Gulland papers, Acc. 6868, National Library of Scotland.

65 E. Biagini (ed.), *Citizenship and Community: Liberals, Radicals and Collective Identities in the British Isles, 1865–1931*, Cambridge, Cambridge University Press, 1996, introduction; E. Biagini, *Gladstone*, Basingstoke, Macmillan, 2000, p. 97.

66 M. Keating and D. Bleiman, *Labour and Scottish Nationalism*, Basingstoke, Macmillan, 1979, pp. 52, 59.

67 See, for example, I. McLean, *The Legend of Red Clyde*, Edinburgh, John Donald, 1983.

68 See C. Harvie, 'Labour in Scotland during the Second World War', *Historical Journal*, 26, 1983, pp. 921–44.

69 Undated speech, Thomas Johnston papers, Acc. 5862/8, National Library of Scotland.

70 I. Hutchison, *Scottish Politics in the Twentieth Century*, Basingstoke, Palgrave, 2001, p. 85. See also A. Calder, *The Myth of the Blitz*, London, Pimlico, 1992, pp. 72–5, for the SNP in wartime.

71 See A. Marr, *The Battle for Scotland*, London, Penguin, 1992, pp. 96–7; Richard Weight, *Patriots: National Identity in Britain 1940–2000*, London, Macmillan, 2002, p. 129.

72　J. Fuller, *Troop Morale and Popular Culture in the British and Dominion Armies, 1914–1918*, Oxford, Clarendon, 1991.

73　Claude Henry to George Dott, 27 March 1916, George Dott papers, Acc. 8371/4, National Library of Scotland.

74　Henry to Dott, 3 February 1916, George Dott papers, Acc. 8371/4, National Library of Scotland.

75　See J. Winter, 'British national identity and the First World War', in S. J. D. Green and R. C. Whiting (eds), *The Boundaries of the State in Modern Britain*, Cambridge, Cambridge University Press, 1996, pp. 261–77.

76　Quoted in J. Hunter, 'The Gaelic connection: the Highlands, Ireland and nationalism 1873–1922', *Scottish Historical Review*, 54, 1975, p. 196.

77　Honouring the living could also provide opportunities for marking the Scottish involvement. Captain Walter Elliot for example was presented with 'a miniature reproduction of the statue of the Scots Grey in Princes Street, Edinburgh' by his brother officers: *Scots Pictorial*, 17 August 1918.

78　Duke of Atholl, *Narrative of the Scottish National War Memorial Scheme*, Edinburgh, privately published, 1923, p. 3. The London war museum became the Imperial War Museum, marking the imperial rather than English contribution to the war.

79　*Report of the Committee on the Utilisation of Edinburgh Castle for the Purpose of a Scottish National War Memorial*, Cd 279, London, HMSO, 1919; Scottish National War Memorial folder, Acc. 4714, National Library of Scotland.

80　Hutchison, *Scottish Politics in the Twentieth Century*, pp. 41–3, 48; Finlay, 'National identity in crisis', pp. 258–9.

81　'Calling Australia and New Zealand', typescript of radio broadcast, 9 July 1942, Acc. 6721/1/3, National Library of Scotland.

82　C. Harvie, 'Scottish politics', in A. Dickson and J. Treble (eds), *People and Society in Scotland, III, 1914–1990*, Edinburgh, John Donald, 1992, pp. 244, 248; Hutchison, *Scottish Politics in the Twentieth Century*, pp. 70–1.

83　Oliver Poole to Lady Priscilla Tweedsmuir, 7 August 1959, Tweedsmuir papers, Dep. 337, National Library of Scotland.

84　Transcript of General Election Broadcast, 28 September 1959, Tweedsmuir papers, Dep. 337, National Library of Scotland.

85　See for example D. Seawright and J. Curtice, 'The decline of the Scottish Conservative and Unionist Party 1950–92: religion, ideology or economics?' *Contemporary Record*, 9, 1995, pp. 319–42.

86　Harvie, *Scotland and Nationalism*, pp. 187–8; Bleiman and Keating, *Labour and Scottish Nationalism*, ch. 5.

87　Hutchison, *Scottish Politics in the Twentieth Century*, pp. 119–25.

88　Finlay, *Partnership for Good*, p. 1.

89　J. Major, *Scotland in the United Kingdom*, London, Conservative Political Centre, 1992, p. 5.

90　Kearney, *The British Isles*, p. 222.

91　M. Pittock, *The Invention of Scotland: The Stuart Myth and the Scottish Identity, 1638 to the Present*, London, Routledge, 1991.

92　J. Richards, *Films and British National Identity from Dickens to Dad's Army*, Manchester, Manchester University Press, 1997, p. 185.

93　H. Trevor Roper, 'The invention of tradition: the Highland tradition of Scotland', in E. Hobsbawm and T. Ranger (eds), *The Invention of Tradition*, Cambridge, Cambridge University Press, 1984, pp. 15–41; C. Withers, 'The historical creation of the Scottish Highlands', in I. Donnachie and C. Whatley (eds), *The Manufacture of Scottish History*, Edinburgh, Polygon, 1992, pp. 143–56.

94　Pittock, *Invention of Scotland*. For Maclean see D. Howell, *A Lost Left: Three Studies in Socialism and Nationalism*, Manchester, Manchester University Press, 1986.

95　Smout, 'Scotland', p. 278.

96  Richards, *Films and British National Identity*, p. 185; http://www.macbraveheart.co.uk/index.htm (19 July 2001).

97  R. Finlay, 'Review article: new Britain, new Scotland, new history? The impact of devolution on the development of Scottish historiography', *Journal of Contemporary History*, 36, 2001, p. 385.

98  A. Marr, *The Day Britain Died*, London, Profile, 2000; T. Nairn, *After Britain: New Labour and the Return of Scotland*, London, Granta, 2001.

99  Catatonia, International Velvet (compact disc), Warner Brothers UK, 1998.

100  *Trainspotting* (dir. D. Boyle, 1995).

101  BBC TV, *The Big Picture: Is Britain Breaking Up?* 1995.

102  For a critique of this unionism, see Nairn, *After Britain*.

103  S. Richards, 'The NS interview: Gordon Brown', *New Statesman*, 19 April 1999, pp. 18–19.

104  W. Alexander, 'See Scotland, sea change? Our identity, our governance and our future', RSA lecture, August 2000.

105  A. Ichijo, 'Civic or ethnic? The evolution of Britishness and Scottishness', unpublished paper, British Island Stories conference, University of York, April 2002.

106  D. McCrone, 'Who do we think we are? Identity politics in modern Scotland', http://www.britcoun.de/e/education/studies/scot2994.htm#scot (9 September 2002).

107  J. Kellas, *The Politics of Nationalism and Ethnicity*, Basingstoke, Macmillan, 1991, p. 17.

108  A. Harrington, 'Survey confirms no Scots identity crisis', http://www.theherald.co.uk/news/archive/8-3-1990-0-26-18.html (19 July 2001).

109  T. Hennessey, *A History of Northern Ireland 1920–1996*, Basingstoke, Macmillan, 1997, pp. 24–49.

110  Of course, the Irish had only ever been subjects of the British crown, since while Ireland is geographically located within the British Isles it never constituted part of Great Britain, but rather was an addition to the United Kingdom of Great Britain and Ireland.

111  L. Colley, *Britons: Forging the Nation 1707–1837*, London, Pimlico, 1994.

112  Howell, *A Lost Left*. For the wider subordination of labour to nationalist politics in Ireland see C. Fitzpatrick, 'Nationalising the ideal: Labour and Nationalism in Ireland, 1909–1923', in Biagini, *Citizenship and Community*, pp. 276–304.

113  D. Boyce, '"The Marginal Britons": the Irish', in R. Colls and P. Dodd (eds), *Englishness: Politics and Culture 1880–1920*, London, Croom Helm, 1986, p. 233. The following section on the 'loyal' community in Ireland is based on A. Jackson, 'Unionist myths 1912–1985', *Past and Present*, 136, 1992, pp. 164–85; Loughlin, *Ulster Unionism and British National Identity*; P. Buckland, *Irish Unionism 2: Ulster Unionism and the Origins of Northern Ireland 1886–1922*, Dublin, Gill and Macmillan, 1973.

114  I. D'Alton, 'Southern Irish Unionism: a study of Cork unionists, 1884–1914', *Transactions of the Royal Historical Society*, 5th series, 23, 1973, p. 77.

115  Loughlin, *Ulster Unionism and British National Identity*, p. 39.

116  Jackson, 'Unionist myths', p. 171. A further 234,046 signed the women's covenant, which did not commit women to such active resistance, but pledged them to 'stand by their menfolk in [their] determination' (*Covenant against Home Rule*, London, National Unionist Association of Conservative and Liberal Unionist Organisations, n.d. D 1238/212 PRONI). The image of Unionism remains remarkably masculine.

117  Quoted in Buckland, *Irish Unionism 2*, p. xxx. For a further references to the idea of 'progress', see Irish Unionist Alliance, *Ireland and the Union: A Short Sketch of the Political History of Ireland*, Dublin, Irish Unionist Alliance, 1914, ch. 2, 'The Union judged by results'. For a brief account of the interwar depression and the Northern Ireland economy see Kearney, *The British Isles*, p. 271.

118  Buckland, *Irish Unionism 2*, p. xxiv.

119  Quoted in L. Ó Broin, *The Chief Secretary: Augustine Birrell in Ireland*, London, Chatto and Windus, 1969, p. 83.

120  I. MacBride, 'Ulster and the British problem', in R. English and G. Walker (eds), *Unionism in Modern Ireland: New Perspectives on Politics and Culture*, Basingstoke, Macmillan, 1996, p. 7.

121  See for example F. Lyons, *Charles Stewart Parnell*, London, Fontana, 1978.

122  Boyce, 'Marginal Britons', pp. 236–7.

123  W. Mandle, *The Gaelic Athletic Association and Irish Nationalist Politics 1884–1924*, London, Croom Helm, 1987; J. Hutchinson, *The Dynamics of Cultural Nationalism: The Gaelic Revival and the Creation of the Irish Nation State*, London, Allen and Unwin, 1987.

124  Boyce, 'Marginal Britons', p. 239.

125  '98 Centenary Committee, 'Circular', 1 July 1898, J. P. Dunne papers, MS 1581, National Library of Ireland.

126  Undated press cutting in J. P. Dunne papers, MS 1581, National Library of Ireland.

127  See for example S. Paseta, 'Nationalist responses to two royal visits to Ireland, 1900 and 1903', *Irish Historical Studies*, 124, 1999, pp. 488–504. The impact of royal visits on maintaining Unionism should not be discounted either.

128  See T. Hennessey, *Dividing Ireland: World War I and Partition*, London, Routledge, 1998, pp. 29–35.

129  Quoted in F. Lyons, *Culture and Anarchy in Ireland 1890–1939*, Oxford, Oxford University Press, 1982, p. 90.

130  G. Ó Tuathaigh, 'Nationalist Ireland, 1912–1922: aspects of continuity and change', in P. Collins (ed.), *Nationalism and Unionism: Conflict in Ireland, 1885–1921*, Belfast, Institute of Irish Studies, 1996, pp. 47–73.

131  These are the two regions often referred to by both nationalists and unionists in the dispute over region versus nation. Hence in 1918 William Redmond remarked that 'Ireland is not like Yorkshire or Somerset. Ireland is a distinctive country' (Hennessey, *Dividing Ireland*, p. 223), and in 1975 the Ulster Workers' Council declared that 'as British Irish, and like other areas of the UK such as the West Country or Yorkshire, we do have a unique regional identity of our own' (Hennessey, *History of Northern Ireland*, p. 247).

132  'West Briton' was more frequently a term of abuse aimed at the Anglo-Irish rather than an accepted identification. See B. Inglis, *The Story of Ireland*, London, Faber and Faber, 1960, p. 20, and B. Inglis, *West Briton*, London, Faber and Faber, 1962.

133  The full song is in P. Buckland, *Irish Unionism 1885–1923: A Documentary History*, Belfast, HMSO, 1973, p. 167.

134  T. Hennessey, 'Ulster Unionism and loyalty to the Crown of the United Kingdom, 1912–74', in English and Walker, *Unionism in Modern Ireland*, pp. 115–29.

135  Quoted in Anti-Partition League, *The Six Counties: A Record 1921–1947*, undated pamphlet D1862/D/2 PRONI.

136  A good introduction to the events of 1910 to 1914 is provided by the essays in Collins *Nationalism and Unionism*.

137  The useful phrase 'aspirational loyalty' comes from Hennessey, *Dividing Ireland*, p. 22.

138  Volume of newspaper cuttings, 14 March 1915, MS 7450 National Library of Ireland.

139  Unpublished memoir [1917], Berkeley papers, MS 7880, National Library of Ireland.

140  For Redmond's efforts to provide a distinctive Irish element within the British Army see for example Redmond to General Sclater, 8 July 1915, John Redmond papers, MS 15225, National Library of Ireland.

141  According to the Julian calendar.

142 Quoted in Hennessey, *Dividing Ireland*, p. 198. See also Loughlin, *Ulster Unionism and British National Identity*, pp. 82–4.

143 Lyons, *Culture and Anarchy*, p. 92.

144 For veterans and the war dead, see J. Leonard, 'The twinge of memory: Armistice Day and Remembrance Sunday', in English and Walker, *Unionism in Modern Ireland*, pp. 99–114; J. Leonard, 'Facing "the finger of scorn": veterans' memories of Ireland after the Great War', in M. Evans and K. Lunn (eds), *War and Memory in the Twentieth Century*, Oxford, Berg, 1997, pp. 59–72; A. Jackson, *Ireland 1798–1998: Politics and War*, Oxford, Blackwell, 1999, p. 303.

145 Loughlin, *Ulster Unionism and British National Identity*, pp. 88–9.

146 House of Commons Debates, series 5, vol. cxxvii, 29 March 1920, columns 989–90 in Buckland, Irish Unionism 2, pp. 116–17.

147 A. Stewart, *The Narrow Ground: The Roots of Conflict in Ulster*, revised edition, London, Faber and Faber, 1989, p. 160.

148 For the impact of the Second World War on Northern Ireland see Loughlin, *Ulster Unionism and British National Identity*, pp. 121–5.

149 H. Midgley, 'Northern Ireland Reactions to the First Year of War', D/4089/3/1/1, Public Record Office of Northern Ireland. It is likely that this was a draft of Midgley's broadcast on the BBC Home Service, 27 September 1940.

150 H. Midgley, *Election Communication*, Belfast, William Stain, 1945, D/4089/4/1/25, Public Record Office of Northern Ireland.

151 Loughlin, *Ulster Unionism and British National Identity*, pp. 134–5.

152 MacBride, 'Ulster and the British problem', pp. 8–9.

153 S. Wichert, *Northern Ireland since 1945*, second edition, London, Longman, 1999, p. 44.

154 Quoted in S. Bruce, *God Save Ulster! The Religion and Politics of Paisleyism*, Oxford, Oxford University Press, 1986, p. 251.

155 Loughlin, *Ulster Unionism and British National Identity*, pp. 205–6.

156 Loughlin, *Ulster Unionism and British National Identity*, p. 222.

157 J. Loughlin, *The Ulster Question since 1945*, Basingstoke, Macmillan, 1998, p. 135.

158 Londonderry Command, U[lster] D[efence] A[ssociation] and Londonderry Branch Loyalist Association of Workers, *Through Seas of Blood*, Londonderry [1973], p. 3.

159 Londonderry UDA and LAW, *Through Seas of Blood*, pp. 24, 7.

160 Jackson, 'Unionist myths'.

161 Quoted in Hennessey, *History of Northern Ireland*, p. 247.

162 Hennessey, *History of Northern Ireland*, p. 246.

163 Wichert, *Northern Ireland*, p. 132.

164 Loughlin, *Ulster Question since 1945*, p. 54.

165 F. O Connor, *In Search of a State: Catholics in Northern Ireland*, Belfast, Blackstaff, 1993, p. 339.

## Conclusion

1 S. Macintyre, 'History wars and the imperial legacy', unpublished paper, British World 2 conference, University of Calgary, July 2003.

2 See P. Davies, *France and the Second World War*, London, Routledge, 2001, ch. 5; H. Rousso, *The Vichy Syndrome: History and Memory in France since 1944*, Cambridge, MA, Harvard University Press, 1991; R. Gildea, *France since 1945*, Oxford, Oxford University Press, 1996.

3 See M. Fulbrook, *German National Identity after the Holocaust*, Cambridge, Polity Press, 1999, and G. Knischewski and U. Spittler, 'Memories of the Second World War and national identity in Germany', in M. Evans and K. Lunn (eds), *War and Memory in the Twentieth Century*, Oxford, Berg, 1997, pp. 239–54.

4  C. Ross, *Contemporary Spain: A Handbook*, London, Arnold, 1997, ch. 3. See also B. Jenkins and S. Sofos (eds), *Nation and Identity in Contemporary Europe*, London, Routledge, 1996, for the varieties of conflict over national identity in Europe.

5  Macintyre, 'History wars'.

6  R. Colls, *Identity of England*, Oxford, Oxford University Press, 2002, p. 379.

7  J. Richards, 'Imperial heroes for a post-imperial age: films and the end of Empire', in S. Ward (ed.), *British Culture and the End of Empire*, Manchester, Manchester University Press, 2001, discusses a Gallup poll from 1997; see also 'Britannia's glory is fading from our memory', *The Daily Telegraph*, 25 August 2003.

8  *Guardian*, 27 January 2000.

9  N. Davies, *The Isles: A History*, London, Papermac, 2000, p. 867.

10  R. Weight, *Patriots: National Identity in Britain 1940–2000*, Basingstoke, Macmillan, 2002.

11  Colls, *Identity of England*.

12  J. Curtice, 'Is Scotland a nation and Wales not?' in B. Taylor and K. Thomson (eds), *Scotland and Wales: Nations Again?* Cardiff, University of Wales Press, 1999, p. 125.

13  K. Robbins, 'Devolution in Britain: will the United Kingdom survive?' *European Studies*, 16, 2001, pp. 53–65, considers the similarities and differences between the turns of the twentieth and twenty-first centuries.

14  See Z. Sardar, 'The excluded minority: British Muslim identity after 11 September', in P. Griffith and M. Leonard (eds), *Reclaiming Britishness*, London, Foreign Policy Centre, 2002, pp. 51–5.

15  J. Curtice and A. Heath, 'Is the English lion about to roar? National identity after devolution', in R. Jowell, J. Curtice, A. Park and others (eds), *British Social Attitudes: Focusing on Diversity. The 17th Report*, London, Sage, 2000, p. 169.

16  Quoted in A. Wilson, 'It's not like Asian ladies to answer back', 1976, in J. Proctor (ed.), *Writing Black Britain 1948–1998: An Interdisciplinary Anthology*, Manchester, Manchester University Press, 2000, p. 186.

17  C. Bryant, 'Speaking for England, claiming Scotland: alternative constructions of nation', unpublished paper, Understanding Britain Postgraduate Conference, University of Salford, September 2003.

18  G. Williams, *When was Wales?* London, Black Raven Press, 1985.

# Bibliography

**PRIMARY SOURCES**

For newspaper, TV, film and music sources see the notes to each chapter.

**Unpublished sources**

*Imperial War Museum Department of Documents*

Imperial War Museum, Women's Work Collection:
Viola Bawtree, 'Episodes of the Great War 1916 from the Diaries of Viola Bawtree', unpublished diary.
Mrs E. M. Bilbrough, unpublished First World War diary, 90/10/1.
Miss H. M. Harpin, Letters.
Mrs H. Lightfoot, handwritten memoir, 1943, 86/20/1.
Miss A. and Miss R. McGuire Papers.
Miss G. Storey, 86/36/1.

*Imperial War Museum Women's Work Collection, Department of Printed Books:*

British Women's Patriotic League, BO 5/3.
Flag Days, BO 2/52

*London Metropolitan Archives*

London County Council Papers.

*National Library of Ireland*

J. P. Dunne papers, MS 1581.
Berkeley papers, MS 7880.
John Redmond papers, MS 15225.
Volume of newspaper cuttings, MS 7450.
Walsh Royal Visit Press Cuttings, MS 11672.

*National Library of Scotland*

George Dott papers, Acc. 8371.
John Buchan Papers, Acc. 11628.
John W. Gulland papers, Acc. 6868.
Scottish National War Memorial folder, Acc. 4714.
Thomas Johnston papers, Acc. 5862.
Tweedsmuir papers, Dep. 337.
Walter Elliot papers, Acc 6721.

*National Library of Wales*

Edgar Chappell papers.
Huw T. Edwards papers.
Samuel T. Evans papers.
Sir E. Vincent Evans papers.

*Public Record Office of Northern Ireland*

Harry Midgley papers, D/4089.
Crawford papers, D/1700.

Mass-Observation Archive, File Reports Series (microfiche).


**Published sources**

*Official and institutional records and reports*

Labour Party, *Annual Conference Reports*.
*London County Council, Minutes of Proceedings*, London Metropolitan Archives.
*Report of the Committee on the Utilisation of Edinburgh Castle for the Purpose of a Scottish National War Memorial*, Cd 279, London, HMSO, 1919.
*The Stephen Lawrence Inquiry: Report of an Inquiry by Sir William Macpherson of Cluny*, London, HMSO, 1999.

*Memoirs, autobiographies, published diaries*

Butler, R., *The Art of the Possible*, Harmondsworth, Penguin, 1973.
Crane, W., *An Artist's Reminiscences*, London, Methuen, 1907.
Griffiths, J., *Pages from Memory*, London, Dent, 1969.
Monnet, J., *Memoirs*, London, Collins, 1978.
Pickles, W., *Between You and Me*, London, Werner Laurie, 1949.
Snowden, P., *An Autobiography, I: 1864–1919*, London, Ivor Nicholson and Watson, 1934.
Wilson, T. (ed.), *The Political Diaries of C. P. Scott, 1911–1928*, London, Collins, 1970.

*Books and articles*

Alexander, W., 'See Scotland, sea change? Our identity, our governance and our future', RSA lecture, August 2000.
Anon., *The Queen's Speech, on the Opening of the Neath Parliament*, Neath, 1883.
Anon., *Improved Means of Locomotion as a First Step Towards the Cure of the Housing Difficulties of London*, London, Macmillan, 1901.
Anon., 'The Welshness of Wales', *The Listener*, 6 Feb. 1964, pp. 228–9.
Anti-Partition League, *The Six Counties: A Record 1921–1947*, undated pamphlet D1862/D/2 PRONI.
Atholl, Duke of, *Narrative of the Scottish National War Memorial Scheme*, Edinburgh, 1923
Balfour, A., *Nationality and Home Rule*, London, Longmans, Green and Co., 1913.
Barnett, Rev. Canon, *The Ideal City*, Bristol, Arrowsmith, n.d.
Berresford Ellis, P. (ed.), *The Creed of Celtic Revolution*, London, Medusa, 1969.
Blair, T., 'My vision for Britain', in G. Radice (ed.), *What Needs to Change: New Visions of Britain*, London, HarperCollins, 1996, pp. 3–17.
Borough of Chelmsford, *Coronation of King George V and Queen Mary, June 22nd 1911 Order of Procession and Service. Programme of Festivities*, Chelmsford, 1911.
Bremner, R., *The Housing Problem in Glasgow*, Glasgow, Scottish Centre for Women's Trades, n.d.

'Cato', *Guilty Men*, London, Victor Gollancz, 1940.

Chesterfield Fabian Society, *Town Planning for Chesterfield*, Chesterfield, Fabian Society, 1910.

Compton, Earl, 'The homes of the people', *New Review*, June 1889, pp. 47–61.

Cross, G. (ed.), *Worktowners at Blackpool: Mass-Observation and Popular Leisure in the 1930s*, London, Routledge, 1990.

Edwards, H., *What is Welsh Nationalism?* Second edition, Cardiff, Plaid Cymru, 1954.

Elton, Lord, *The Life of James Ramsay MacDonald*, London, Collins, 1939.

Giddens, A., *The Third Way: The Renewal of Social Democracy*, Cambridge, Polity Press, 1998.

Gomme, L., *The Making of London*, Oxford, Clarendon, 1912

Gorer, G., *Exploring English Character*, London, Cresset, 1955.

Griffith, P. and M. Leonard (eds), *Reclaiming Britishness*, London, Foreign Policy Centre, 2002, pp. 65–77.

Heffer, S., *Nor Shall My Sword: The Reinvention of England*, London, Weidenfeld and Nicholson, 1999.

Hitchens, P., *The Abolition of Britain: The British Cultural Revolution from Lady Chatterley to Tony Blair*, London, Quartet, 1999.

Irish Unionist Alliance, *Ireland and the Union: A Short Sketch of the Political History of Ireland*, Dublin, Irish Unionist Alliance, 1914.

Jennings, H. and C. Madge (eds), *May the Twelfth: Mass-Observation-Day Surveys 1937*, London, Faber and Faber, 1987 [1937].

John, E., *National Self Government: How Wales Stands to Gain By It*, 1910.

John, G. and D. Humphry, *Because They're Black*, Harmondsworth, Penguin, 1972.

Kipling, R., *The Works of Rudyard Kipling*, Ware, Wordsworth, 1994.

Leonard, M., *Britain: Renewing Our Identity*, London, Demos, 1997.

Lewis, Saunders, 'The case for Welsh nationalism', *The Listener*, 13 May 1936, pp. 915–16.

Londonderry Command, U[lster] D[efence] A[ssociation] and Londonderry Branch Loyalist Association of Workers, *Through Seas of Blood*, Londonderry [1973].

MacDonald, J. Ramsay, *Labour's Policy versus Protection: The Real Issues of the General Election*, London, Labour Party, n.d. [1923].

MacDonald, J. Ramsay, *Wanderings and Excursions*, London, Jonathan Cape, 1929.

Major, J., *Scotland in the United Kingdom*, London, Conservative Political Centre, 1992.

Masterman, J., *The House of Commons: Its Place in National History*, London, John Murray, 1908.

Morton, H., *In Search of England*, London, Methuen, 1984.

Mosley, O., *My Life*, London, Nelson, 1970.

Murphy, E., *Official Souvenir of the National Pageant of Wales, Cardiff, 26th July to 7th August 1909*, Cardiff, 1909, National Library of Wales ex.1469.

National Unionist Association of Conservative and Liberal Unionist Organisations, *Covenant against Home Rule*, London, n.d. D 1238/212 PRONI.

Norman, C., *Nationality and Patriotism*, Manchester, National Labour Press, 1915.

Orwell, G., 'The lion and the unicorn: socialism and the English genius' (1941) in *Collected Essays, Journalism and Letters: Volume 2 My Country Right or Left 1940–1943*, London, Penguin, 1970, pp. 74–134.

Orwell, G., 'The sporting spirit', *Tribune*, 14 December 1945, in S. Orwell and I. Angus (eds), *The Collected Essays, Journalism and Letters of George Orwell Volume 4 In Front of Your Nose*, Harmondsworth, Penguin, 1970, pp. 61–4.

Palin, M., *Around the World in 80 Days*, London, BBC, 1989.

Patten, C., 'Who do they think we are? Being British', British Council Annual Lecture, 28 June 2001.

Patterson, S., *Dark Strangers: A Study of West Indians*, Harmondsworth, Penguin 1963.

Paxman, J., *The English*, London, Penguin, 1999.

Plaid Cymru, *Action for Wales*, Bangor, Plaid Cymru, n.d. [1970].

Priestley, J. B., *English Journey*, London, William Heinemann, 1949 [first published 1934].

Priestley, J. B., *Let the People Sing*, London, Mandarin, 1996 [first published 1939].

Redwood, J., *The Death of Britain?* Basingstoke, Macmillan, 1999.

Renan, E., 'What is a nation?' (1882), in H. Bhabha (ed.), *Nation and Narration*, London, Routledge, 1990, pp. 8–22.

Richards, P., *Long to Reign Over Us?* London, Fabian Society, 1996.

Richards, S., 'The NS interview: Gordon Brown', *New Statesman*, 19 April 1999, pp. 18–19.

Rose, E. and N. Deakin, *Colour and Citizenship: A Report in British Race Relations*, London, Oxford University Press, 1969.

Rushdie, S., *Imaginary Homelands: Essays and Criticism 1981–1991*, London, Penguin/Granta, 1991.

Scruton, R., *England: An Elegy*, London, Chatto and Windus, 2000.

Sherlock, H., *Cities Are Good for Us*, London, Paladin/Transport 2000, 1991.

Shils, E. and M. Young, 'The meaning of the Coronation', *Sociological Review*, 1, 1953, pp. 63–81.

Stokes, Sir J., 'Keep the Queen', in A. Barnett (ed.), *Power and the Throne: The Monarchy Debate*, London, Vintage, 1984, pp. 80–3.

Sutherland, K. (ed.), *The Rape of the Constitution?*, Thorverton, Imprint Academic, 2000.

Torrence, J., *Scotland's Dilemma: Province or Nation?*, Edinburgh, Belhaven, 1937.

Trotsky, L., 'Anglo-American rivalry and the growth of militarism' (1924), in R. Chappell and A. Clinton (eds), *Leon Trotsky: Collected Writings and Speeches on Britain Volume One*, London, New Park, 1974, pp. 145–52.

*Useful edited collections of primary sources*

Buckland, P., *Irish Unionism 1885–1923: A Documentary History*, Belfast, HMSO, 1973.

Englander, D. (ed.), *A Documentary History of Jewish Immigrants in Britain, 1840–1920*, Leicester, Leicester University Press, 1994.

Giles, J. and T. Middleton (eds), *Writing Englishness 1900–1950: An Introductory Sourcebook on National Identity*, London, Routledge, 1995.

Koss, S. (ed.), *The Pro-Boers: The Anatomy of an Anti-War Movement*, Chicago, University of Chicago Press, 1973.

Panayi, P. (ed.), *The Impact of Immigration: A Documentary History of the Effects and Experiences of Immigrants in Britain since 1945*, Manchester, Manchester University Press, 1999.

Sheridan, D. (ed.), *Wartime Women: An Anthology of Women's Wartime Writing for Mass-Observation 1937–45*, London, Mandarin, 1991.

*Internet sources*

Cabinet minutes, CAB 128/43, 15 February 1968, http://www.pro.gov.uk/docimages/CAB/128_43_13a.gif (18 January 1999).

'Chicken tikka timebomb', *The Observer*, 22 April 2001, http://www.guardian.co.uk/Archive/Article/0,4273,4173765,00.html (20 August 2001).

Churchill speech to House of Commons, 13 May 1940, 'Modern History Sourcebook', http://www.fordham.edu/halsall/mod/churchill-blood.html (17 January 2001).

Cook, R., 'Extracts from a speech by the foreign secretary, to the Centre for the Open Society, Social Market Foundation, London', 19 April 2001, http://www.fco.gov.uk/news/speechtext.asp?49 (30 April 2002).

Harrington, A., 'Survey confirms no Scots identity crisis', http://www.theherald.co.uk/news/archive/8-3-1990-0-26-18.html (19 July 2001).

http://www.macbraveheart.co.uk/index.htm (19 July 2001).

Singh, A., 'Speak to us, Mr Blunkett', *Guardian Unlimited*, 22 September 2002, http://www.observer.co.uk/race/story/0,11255,796912,00.html (17 January 2003).

Thatcher, M., 'Christianity and wealth', speech to the Church of Scotland General Assembly, 21 May 1988, http://www.fordham.edu/halsalVmod/1988thatcher.html (5 July 2002).

Travis, A., 'Blunkett in race row over culture tests', 10 December 2001, http://www.guardian.co.uk/uk_news/story/0,3604,616214,00.html (17 January 2003).


## SECONDARY SOURCES

Only those books, articles and essays that have proved particularly useful or important are listed here. For full details of secondary sources consulted see the notes to each chapter.


### General

Books and articles in this section were useful for more than one chapter. They are not repeated in the subject bibliographies.

Billig, M., *Banal Nationalism*, London, Sage, 1995.

Black, J., *A History of the British Isles*, Basingstoke, Macmillan, 1996.

Bourke, J., *Working-Class Cultures in Britain 1890–1960: Gender, Class and Ethnicity*, London, Routledge, 1994.

Brockliss, L. and D. Eastwood (eds), *A Union of Multiple Identities: The British Isles, c.1750–c.1850*, Manchester, Manchester University Press, 1997.

Colley, L., *Britons: Forging the Nation 1707–1837*, London, Pimlico, 1994.

Colls, R., *Identity of England*, Oxford, Oxford University Press, 2002.

Colls, R. and P. Dodd (eds), *Englishness: Politics and Culture 1880–1920*, London, Croom Helm, 1986.

Davies, N., *The Isles: A History*, Basingstoke, Papermac, 2000.

Feldman, D., 'Nationality and ethnicity', in P. Johnson (ed.), *Twentieth-Century Britain: Economic, Social and Cultural Change*, London, Longman, 1994, pp. 127–48.

Grant, A. and K. Stringer (eds), *Uniting the Kingdom: The Making of British History*, London, Routledge, 1995.

Harvie, C., 'The moment of British nationalism, 1939–1970', *Political Quarterly*, 71, 2000, pp. 328–40.

Haseler, S., *The English Tribe: Identity, Nation and Europe*, Basingstoke, Macmillan, 1996.

Hastings, A., *The Construction of Nationhood: Ethnicity, Religion and Nationalism*, Cambridge, Cambridge University Press, 1997.

Hobsbawm, E., *Nations and Nationalism since 1780: Programme, Myth, Reality*, second edition, Cambridge, Cambridge University Press, 1992.

Kearney, H., *The British Isles: A History of Four Nations*, Cambridge, Cambridge University Press, 1992.

Kumar, K., *The Making of English National Identity*, Cambridge, Cambridge University Press, 2003.

Nairn, T., *The Break-Up of Britain: Crisis and Neo-Nationalism*, London, New Left Books, 1977, second edition, London, Verso, 1981.

Nairn, T., *After Britain*, London, Granta, 1999.

Pocock, J., 'British history: a plea for a new subject', *New Zealand Journal of History*, 8, 1974, pp. 3–21.

Robbins, K., *Nineteenth-Century Britain: England, Scotland, and Wales – The Making of a Nation*, Oxford, Oxford University Press, 1989.

Robbins, K., *History, Religion and Identity in Modern Britain*, London, Hambledon, 1993.

Robbins, K., *Great Britain: Identities, Institutions and the Idea of Britishness*, Harlow, Longman, 1998.

Rose, S., *Which People's War? National Identity and Citizenship in Wartime Britain 1939–1945*, Oxford, Oxford University Press, 2003.

Said, E., *Culture and Imperialism*, London, Chatto and Windus, 1993.

Samuel, R. (ed.), *Patriotism: The Making and Unmaking of British National Identity*, 3 volumes, London, Routledge, 1989.

Samuel, R., *Theatres of Memory. Volume III: Island Stories: Unravelling Britain*, London, Verso, 1998.

Vernon, J., 'Englishness: the narration of nation', *Journal of British Studies*, 36, 1997, pp. 243–9.

Weight, R., *Patriots: National Identity in Britain 1940–2000*, London, Macmillan, 2002.


## Monarchy and empire

Cannadine, D., 'The context, performance and meaning of ritual: the British monarchy and the "invention of tradition", c.1820–1977', in E. Hobsbawm and T. Ranger (eds), *The Invention of Tradition*, Cambridge, Cambridge University Press, 1983, pp. 101–64.

Cannadine, D., *Ornamentalism: How the British Saw Their Empire*, London, Allen Lane, 2001.

Cannon, J. and R. Griffiths, *The Oxford Illustrated History of the British Monarchy*, Oxford, Oxford University Press, 1988.

Constantine, S., '"Bringing the Empire alive": the Empire Marketing Board and imperial propaganda 1926–33', in J. MacKenzie (ed.), *Imperialism and Popular Culture*, Manchester, Manchester University Press, 1986, pp.192–231.

Darwin, J., 'The fear of falling: British politics and imperial decline since 1900', *Transactions of the Royal Historical Society*, 5th series, 36, 1986, pp. 27–43.

Davies, J., 'Victoria and Victorian Wales', in G. Jenkins and J. Smith (eds), *Politics and Society in Wales, 1840–1922*, Cardiff, University of Wales Press, 1988, pp. 7–28.

Davies, J., *Diana Cultural History: Gender, Race, Nation and the People's Princess*, Basingstoke, Palgrave, 2001.

Driver, F. and D. Gilbert (eds), *Imperial Cities: Landscape, Display and Identity*, Manchester, Manchester University Press, 1999.

Ellis, J., 'Reconciling the Celt: British national identity, empire, and the 1911 Investiture of the Prince of Wales', *Journal of British Studies*, 37, 1998, pp. 391–418.

Finlay, R., '"For or against?" Scottish Nationalists and the British Empire, 1919–39', *Scottish Historical Review*, 71, 1992, pp. 184–206.

Finlay, R., 'The rise and fall of popular imperialism in Scotland, 1850–1950', *Scottish Geographical Magazine*, 113, 1997, pp. 13–21.

Golby, J. and A. Purdue, *The Monarchy and the British People: 1760 to the Present*, London, Batsford, 1988.

Hargreaves, J., '"Long to reign over us": changing attitudes towards the monarchy in Halifax from the golden jubilee of King George III in 1809 to the golden jubilee of Queen Elizabeth II in 2002', *Transactions of the Halifax Antiquarian Society*, forthcoming 11, 2003.

Howe, S., *Anti-colonialism in British Politics: The Left and the End of the Empire, 1918–1964*, Oxford, Oxford University Press, 1993.

Jeffery, K. (ed.), *'An Irish Empire'? Aspects of Ireland and the British Empire*, Manchester, Manchester University Press, 1996.

MacKenzie, J., *Propaganda and Empire: The Manipulation of British Public Opinion 1880–1960*, Manchester, Manchester University Press, 1984.

MacKenzie, J., '"In touch with the infinity": the BBC and the Empire 1923–1953', in J. MacKenzie (ed.), *Imperialism and Popular Culture*, Manchester, Manchester University Press, 1986, pp. 165–91.

MacKenzie, J., 'Empire and national identities: the case of Scotland', *Transactions of the Royal Historical Society*, 6th series, 8, 1993, pp. 215–31.

MacKenzie, J., '"The Second City of the Empire": Glasgow – imperial municipality', in F. Driver and D. Gilbert (eds), *Imperial Cities: Landscape, Display and Identity*, Manchester, Manchester University Press, 1999, pp. 215–37.

Marshall, P., 'Imperial Britain', in P. Marshall (ed.), *The Cambridge Illustrated History of the British Empire*, Cambridge, Cambridge University Press, 1996, pp. 318–37.

Nairn, T., *The Enchanted Glass: Britain and Its Monarchy*, London, Hutchison Radius, 1988.

Paseta, S., 'Nationalist responses to two royal visits to Ireland, 1900 and 1903', *Irish Historical Studies*, 124, 1999, pp. 488–504.

Pimlott, B., *The Queen: A Biography of Elizabeth II*, London, HarperCollins, 1997.

Price, R., *An Imperial War and the British Working Class: Working-Class Attitudes and Reactions to the Boer War 1899–1902*, London, Routledge and Kegan Paul, 1972.

Price, R., 'Society, status and jingoism', in G. Crossick (ed.), *The Lower Middle Class in Britain*, London, Croom Helm, 1977, pp. 89–112.

Prochaska, F., *Royal Bounty: The Making of a Welfare Monarchy*, New Haven, CT, Yale University Press, 1995.

Prochaska, F., 'George V and republicanism, 1917–1919', *Twentieth Century British History*, 1999, 10, pp. 27–51.

Schneer, J., *London 1900: The Imperial Metropolis*, New Haven, CT, Yale University Press, 1999.

Stewart, G., 'Tenzing's Two Wrist-Watches: the conquest of Everest and late imperial culture in Britain 1921–1953', *Past and Present*, 149, 1995, pp. 170–97.

Taylor, A., *'Down with the Crown': British Anti-monarchism and Debates about Royalty since 1790*, London, Reaktion, 1999.

Taylor, J., *Diana, Self-Interest and British National Identity*, Westport, CT., Praeger, 2000.

Thompson, D., 'Queen Victoria, the monarchy and gender', in her *Outsiders: Class, Gender and Nation*, London, Verso, 1993, pp. 164–86.

## Gender

Andrews, M., '"For Home and Country": feminism and Englishness in the Women's Institute movement, 1930–60', in R. Weight and A. Beach (eds), *The Right to Belong: Citizenship and National Identity in Britain, 1930–1960*, London, I. B. Tauris, 1998, pp. 116–35.

Bourke, J., *Dismembering the Male: Men's Bodies, Britain, and the Great War*, London, Reaktion, 1996.

Bourke, J., *An Intimate History of Killing: Face-to-Face Killing in the Twentieth Century*, London, Granta, 1999.

Brooke, S., 'Gender and working class identity in Britain during the 1950s', *Journal of Social History*, 34, 2001, pp. 773–95.

Brunt, R., 'The family firm restored: newsreel coverage of the British monarchy 1936–45', in Christine Gledhill and Gillian Swanson (eds), *Nationalising Femininity: Culture, Sexuality, and British Cinema in the Second World War*, Manchester, Manchester University Press, 1996.

Burton, A., 'The feminist quest for identity: British imperial suffragism and "global sisterhood", 1900–1915', *Journal of Women's History*, 3, 1991, pp. 46–81.

Bush, J., *Edwardian Ladies and Imperial Power*, Leicester, Leicester University Press, 2000.

Collins, M., 'The fall of the English gentleman: the national character in decline, c.1918–1970', *Historical Research*, 75, 2002, pp. 90–111.

Dawson, G., 'The blond bedouin: Lawrence of Arabia, imperial adventure and the imagining of English-British identity', in M. Roper and J. Tosh (eds), *Manful Assertions: Masculinities since 1800*, London, Routledge, 1991, pp. 113–44.

Francis, M., 'The Labour Party: modernisation and the politics of restraint', in B. Conekin, F. Mort and C. Waters (eds), *Moments of Modernity: Reconstructing Britain 1945–1964*, London, River Oram Press, 1999, pp. 153–70.

Gledhill, C. and G. Swanson (eds), *Nationalising Femininity: Culture, Sexuality and British Cinema in the Second World War*, Manchester, Manchester University Press, 1996.

Gullace, N., 'White feathers and wounded men: female patriotism and the Great War', *Journal of British Studies*, 36, 1997, pp. 178–206.

John, A., '"Run like blazes": the suffragettes and Welshness', *Llafur*, 6, 1994, pp. 29–43.

Kent, S., *Making Peace: The Reconstruction of Gender in Interwar Britain*, Princeton, NJ, Princeton University Press, 1994.

Kent, S., *Gender and Power in Britain, 1640–1990*, London, Routledge, 1999.

Lant, A., *Blackout: Reinventing Women for Wartime British Cinema*, Princeton, NJ, Princeton University Press, 1991.

Light, A., *Forever England: Femininity, Literature and Conservatism between the Wars*, London, Routledge, 1991.

Mackay, J. and P. Thane, 'The Englishwoman', in Robert Colls and Philip Dodd (eds), *Englishness, Politics and Culture 1880–1920*, London, Croom Helm, 1986, pp. 191–229.

Noakes, L., *War and the British: Gender, Memory and National Identity*, London, I. B. Tauris, 1998.

Ramsden, J., 'Refocusing "the people's war": British war films of the 1950s', *Journal of Contemporary History*, 33, 1998, pp. 35–63.

Robert, K., 'Gender, class, and patriotism: women's paramilitary units in First World War Britain', *International History Review* (Canada), 19, 1997, pp. 52–65.

Rose, S., 'Sex, citizenship, and the nation in World War II Britain', *American Historical Review*, 103, 1998, pp. 1147–76.

Summers, A., *Angels and Citizens: British Women as Military Nurses 1854–1914*, London, Routledge and Kegan Paul, 1988.

Ward, M., *Unmanageable Revolutionaries: Women and Irish Nationalism*, London, Pluto, 1983.

Ward, P., '"Women of Britain say go": women's patriotism in the First World War', *Twentieth Century British History*, 12, 2001, pp. 23–45.

Webster, W., *Imagining Home: Gender, 'Race' and National Identity 1945–64*, London, UCL Press, 1998.

### Rural, urban and regional Britishness

Bader, S., *Visionaries and Planners: The Garden City Movement and the Modern Community*, New York, Oxford University Press, 1990.

Bartholomew, M., 'Englishness: the case of H. V. Morton (1892–1979)', in K. Dockray and K. Laybourn (eds), *The Representation and Reality of War: The British Experience*, Stroud, Sutton, 1999, pp. 203–17.

Burnett, J., *The Social History of Housing 1815–1985*, second edition, London, Routledge, 1986.

Calder, A., *The Myth of the Blitz*, London, Pimlico, 1992.

Dunleavy, P., *The Politics of Mass Housing in Britain, 1945–1975*, Oxford, Clarendon, 1981.

Frost, D., 'West Africans, black Scousers and the colour problem in inter-war Liverpool', *North West Labour History*, 20, 1995/96, pp. 50–7.

Girouard, M., *The English Town*, New Haven, CT, Yale University Press, 1990.

Glendinning, M. and S. Muthesius, *Tower Block: Modern Public Housing in England, Scotland, Wales and Northern Ireland*, New Haven, CT, Yale University Press, 1994.

Gruffudd, P., 'Prospects of Wales: contested geographical imaginations', in R. Fevre and A. Thompson (eds), *Nation, Identity and Social Theory: Perspectives from Wales*, Cardiff, University of Wales Press, 1999, pp. 149–67.

Harris, J., *Private Lives, Public Spirit: Britain 1870–1914*, London, Penguin, 1994.

Howkins, A., 'The discovery of rural England', in R. Colls and P. Dodd (eds), *Englishness, Politics and Culture 1880–1920*, London, Croom Helm, 1986, pp. 62–88.

Jones, K., *Catherine Cookson: The Biography*, London, Constable, 1999.

Lowe, P., 'The rural idyll defended: from preservation to conservation', in G. Mingay (ed.), *The Rural Idyll*, London, Routledge, 1989, pp. 213–31.

Lowerson, J., 'Battles for the countryside', in F. Gloversmith (ed.), *Class, Culture and Social Change: A New View of the 1930s*, Sussex, Harvester, 1980, pp. 258–80.

Luckett, M., 'Image and nation in 1990s British cinema', in R. Murphy (ed.), *British Cinema of the 1990s*, London, British Film Institute, 2000, pp. 88–99.

Mandler, P., 'Against "Englishness": English culture and the limits to rural nostalgia, 1850–1940', *Transactions of the Royal Historical Society*, 6th series, 7, 1997, pp. 155–76.

Mandler, P., 'New Towns for old: the fate of the town centre', in B. Conekin, F. Mort and C. Waters (eds), *Moments of Modernity: Reconstructing Britain 1945–1964*, London, River Orams, 1999, pp. 208–27.

Matless, D., *Landscape and Englishness*, London, Reaktion, 1998.

Meacham, S., 'Raymond Unwin (1863–1940): designing for democracy in Edwardian England', in S. Pedersen and P. Mandler (eds), *After the Victorians: Private Conscience and Public Duty*, London, Routledge, 1994.

Meacham, S., *Regaining Paradise: Englishness and the Early Garden City Movement*, New Haven, CT, Yale University Press, 1999.

Porter, R., *London: A Social History*, London, Hamish Hamilton, 1994.

Potts, A., '"Constable country" between the wars', in R. Samuel (ed.), *Patriotism: The Making and Unmaking of British National Identity. Volume 3: National Fictions*, London, Routledge, 1989, pp. 160–86.

Rawnsley, S., 'Constructing "The North": space and sense of place', in N. Kirk (ed.), *Northern Identities: Historical Interpretations of 'The North' and 'Northernness'*, Aldershot, Ashgate, 2000.

Richards, J., *The Age of the Dream Palace: Cinema and Society in Britain 1930–1939*, London, Routledge and Kegan Paul, 1984.

Richards, J., *Films and British National Identity from Dickens to Dad's Army*, Manchester, Manchester University Press, 1997.

Royle, E. (ed.), *Issues of Regional Identity*, Manchester, Manchester University Press, 1998.

Saint, A., 'The New Towns', in B. Ford (ed.), *The Cambridge Cultural History of Britain Volume 9 Modern Britain*, Cambridge, Cambridge University Press, 1992, pp. 147–59.

Smith, M., *Britain and 1940: History, Myth and Popular Memory*, London, Routledge, 2000.

Stedman Jones, G., 'The "cockney" and the nation, 1780–1988', in D. Feldman and G. Stedman Jones (eds), *Metropolis London: Histories and Representations since 1800*, London, Routledge, 1989, pp. 272–324.

Swenarton, M., *Homes Fit for Heroes: The Politics and Architecture of Early State Housing in Britain*, London, Heinemann, 1981.

Swenarton, M., *Artisans and Architects: The Ruskinian Tradition in Architectural Thought*, Basingstoke, Macmillan, 1989.

Thomas, H., 'Spatial restructuring in the capital: struggles to shape Cardiff's built environment', in R. Fevre and A. Thompson (eds), *Nation, Identity and Social Theory: Perspectives from Wales*, Cardiff, University of Wales Press, 1999, pp. 168–88.

Vernon, J., 'Border crossings: Cornwall and the English (imagi)nation', in G. Cubitt (ed.), *Imagining Nations*, Manchester, Manchester University Press, 1998, pp. 153–72.

Wales, K., 'North and south: a linguistic divide?', Inaugural Lecture, 10 June 1999, http://www.leeds.ac.uk/reporter/439/kwales.htm (12 March 2002).

Waters, C., 'J. B. Priestley (1894–1984): Englishness and the politics of nostalgia', in S. Pedersen and P. Mandler (eds), *After the Victorians: Private Conscience and Public Duty*, London, Routledge, 1994, pp. 208–26.

Wiener, M., *English Culture and the Decline of the Industrial Spirit, 1850–1980*, Cambridge, Cambridge University Press, 1981.

Williams, R., *The Country and the City*, London, Hogarth Press, 1993 [1973].

**Spare time**

*Sport*

Andrews, D. and J. Howell, 'Transforming into a tradition: rugby and the making of imperial Wales, 1890–1914', in A. Ingham and J. Loy (eds), *Sport in Social Development: Traditions, Transitions, and Transformations*, Champaign, Ill., Human Kinetics, 1993, pp. 77–96.

Back, L., T. Crabbe and J. Solomos, '"Lions and black skins": race, nation and local patriotism in football', in B. Carrington and I. MacDonald (eds), *'Race', Sport and British Society*, London, Routledge, 2001, pp. 83–102.

Bairner, A., 'Football and the idea of Scotland', in G. Jarvie and G. Walker (eds), *Scottish Sport in the Making of the Nation: Ninety Minute Patriots?*, Leicester, Leicester University Press, 1994, pp. 9–26.

Bale, J., 'Playing at home: British football and a sense of place', in J. Williams and S. Wagg (eds), *British Football and Social Change: Getting into Europe*, Leicester, Leicester University Press, 1991, pp. 131–56.

Bradley, J., 'Sport and the contestation of cultural and ethnic identities in Scottish society', in M. Cronin and D. Mayall (eds), *Sporting Nationalisms: Identity, Ethnicity, Immigration and Assimilation*, London, Frank Cass, 1998, pp. 127–50.

Cronin, M., *Sport and Nationalism in Ireland: Gaelic Games, Soccer and Irish Identity since 1884*, Dublin, Four Courts, 1999.

Dimeo, P. and G. Finn, 'Racism, national identity and Scottish football', in B. Carrington and I. MacDonald (eds), *'Race', Sport and British Society*, London, Routledge, 2001, pp. 29–47.

Giulianotti, R., 'Hooligans and carnival fans: Scottish football supporter cultures', in G. Armstrong and R. Giulianotti (eds), *Football Cultures and Identities*, Basingstoke, Macmillan, 1999, pp. 29–40.

Hargreaves, J., *Sport, Power and Culture: A Social and Historical Analysis of Sports in Britain*, Cambridge, Polity Press, 1986.

Harvie, C., 'Sport and the Scottish state', in G. Jarvie and G. Walker (eds), *Scottish Sport in the Making of the Nation: Ninety Minute Patriots?*, Leicester, Leicester University Press, 1994, pp. 43–57.

Hill, J., 'Rite of spring: Cup Finals and community in the north of England', in J. Hill and J. Williams (eds), *Sport and Identity in the North of England*, Keele, Keele University Press, 1996, pp. 85–111.

Hill, J. and F. Varrasi, 'Creating Wembley: the construction of a national monument', http://mulder.umist.ac.uk/umist_sport/3_art3.htm (27 June 2003).

Holt, R., *Sport and the British: A Modern History*, Oxford, Clarendon, 1992.

Jarvie, G., 'Royal games, sport and the politics of the environment', in G. Jarvie and G. Walker (eds), *Scottish Sport in the Making of the Nation: Ninety Minute Patriots?*, Leicester, Leicester University Press, 1994, pp. 154–72.

Lowerson, J., 'Golf and the making of myths', in G. Jarvie and G. Walker (eds), *Scottish Sport in the Making of the Nation: Ninety Minute Patriots?*, Leicester, Leicester University Press, 1994, pp. 75–90.

Mangan, J., *Athleticism in the Victorian and Edwardian Public School*, third edition, London, Frank Cass, 2000.

Mason, T., *Sport in Britain*, London, Faber and Faber, 1988.

Mason, T. (ed.), *Sport in Britain*, Cambridge, Cambridge University Press, 1989.

Mason, T., 'Football, sport of the North?', in J. Hill and J. Williams (eds), *Sport and Identity in the North of England*, Keele, Keele University Press, 1996, pp. 41–52.

Moorhouse, H., 'On the periphery: Scotland, Scottish football and the new Europe', in J. Williams and S. Wagg (eds), *British Football and Social Change: Getting into Europe*, Leicester, Leicester University Press, 1991, pp. 201–19.

Moorhouse, H., 'One state, several countries: soccer and nationality in a "United"

Kingdom', in J. Mangan (ed.), *Tribal Identities: Nationalism, Europe, Sport*, London, Frank Cass, 1996, pp. 55–74.

Perkin, H., 'Teaching the nations how to play: sport and society in the British Empire and Commonwealth', *International Journal of the History of Sport*, 6, 1989, pp. 145–53.

Polley, M., *Moving the Goalposts: A History of Sport and Society since 1945*, London, Routledge, 1998

Russell, D., 'Sport and identity: the case of Yorkshire County Cricket Club, 1890–1939', *Twentieth Century British History*, 7, 1996, pp. 206–30.

Russell, D., 'Associating with football: social identity in England 1863–1998', in G. Armstrong and R. Giulianotti (eds), *Football Cultures and Identities*, Basingstoke, Macmillan, 1999, pp. 15–28.

Whannel, G., *Fields in Vision: Television Sport and Cultural Transformation*, London, Routledge, 1992.

Williams, G., 'From popular culture to public cliché: image and identity in Wales, 1890–1914', in J. Mangan (ed.), *Pleasure, Profit, Proselytism: British Culture and Sport at Home and Abroad 1700–1914*, London, Frank Cass, 1988, pp. 128–43.

Williams, J., 'Having an away day: English football spectators and the hooligan debate', in J. Williams and S. Wagg (eds), *British Football and Social Change: Getting into Europe*, Leicester, Leicester University Press, 1991, pp. 160–84.

Williams, J., '"One could literally have walked on the heads of the people congregated there." Sport, the town and identity', in K. Laybourn (ed.), *Social Conditions, Status and Community 1860–c.1920*, Stroud, Sutton, 1997, pp. 123–38.

*Holidays*

Beck, R., 'Review of Marjorie Morgan', *National Identities and Travel in Victorian Britain*, H-Albion, H-Net Reviews, October 2002. URL http://www.h-net.msu.edu/reviews/showrev.egi? path-233971037026788 (28 February 2003).

Drower, J., *Good Clean Fun: The Story of Britain's First Holiday Camp*, London, Arcadia, 1982.

Gurney, P., '"Intersex" and "dirty girls": Mass-Observation and working-class sexuality in England in the 1930s', *Journal of the History of Sexuality*, 8, 1997, pp. 256–90.

Lindley, K., *Seaside Architecture*, London, Hugh Evelyn, 1973.

Pearson, L., *The People's Palaces: The Story of the Seaside Pleasure Buildings of 1870–1914*, Buckingham, Barracuda, 1991.

Presley, J., '"Frizzling in the sun": Robert Graves and the development of mass tourism in the Balearic Islands', in M. Robinson, P. Long, N. Evans, R. Sharpley and J. Swarbrooke (eds), *Expressions of Culture, Identity and Meaning in Tourism*, Sunderland, Centre for Travel and Tourism, 2000, pp. 231–44.

Pritchard, A., 'Ways of seeing "them" and "us": tourism representation, race and identity', in M. Robinson *et al.*, *Expressions of Culture, Identity and Meaning in Tourism*, Sunderland, Centre for Travel and Tourism, 2000, pp. 245–62.

Shields, R., *Places on the Margin: Alternative Geographies of Modernity*, London, Routledge, 1991.

Teo, H.-M., 'Wandering in the wake of empire: British travel and tourism in the post-imperial world', in S. Ward (ed.), *British Culture and the End of Empire*, Manchester, Manchester University Press, 2001, pp. 163–79.

Urry, J., *The Tourist Gaze: Leisure and Travel in Contemporary Societies*, London, Sage, 1990.

Walton, J., *Blackpool*, Edinburgh, Edinburgh University Press/Carnegie, 1998.

Walvin, J., *Beside the Seaside: A Social History of the Popular Seaside Holiday*, London, Allen Lane, 1978.

*Americanisation*

Davies, A., 'Cinema and broadcasting', in P. Johnson (ed.), *Twentieth-Century Britain: Economic, Social and Cultural Change*, London, Longman, 1994, pp. 263–80.

Fielding, S., '"But westward, look, the land is bright": Labour's revisionists and the imagining of America, c.1945–1964', in J. Hollowell (ed.), *Twentieth-Century Anglo-American Relations*, Basingstoke, Palgrave, 2001.

Kitchen, P. (ed.), *For Home and Country: War, Peace and Rural Life as Seen through the Pages of the W.I. Magazine 1919–1959*, London, Ebury, 1990.

Reynolds, D., *Britannia Overruled: British Policy and World Power in the Twentieth Century*, London, Longman, 1991.

Reynolds, D., *Rich Relations: The American Occupation of Britain 1942–1945*, London, Phoenix, 2000.

Richards, J., 'The British Board of Film Censors and content control in the 1930s: images of Britain', *Historical Journal of Film, Radio and Television*, 1, 1981, pp. 95–116.

Richards, J., *The Age of the Dream Palace: Cinema and Society 1930–1939*, London, Routledge and Kegan Paul, 1984.

Springhall, J., *Youth, Popular Culture and Moral Panics: Penny Gaffs to Gangsta-Rap, 1830–1996*, Basingstoke, Macmillan, 1998.

## Politics

Baxendale, J., '"You and I – all of us ordinary people": renegotiating "Britishness" in wartime', in N. Hayes and J. Hill (eds), *Millions Like Us? British Culture in the Second World War*, Liverpool, Liverpool University Press, 1999, pp. 295–322.

Blake, R., *The Conservative Party from Peel to Thatcher*, London, Fontana, 1985.

Boyce, D., 'The "marginal Britons": the Irish', in R. Colls and P. Dodd (eds), *Englishness: Politics and Culture 188–1920*, London, Croom Helm, 1986, pp. 230–53.

Breese, S., 'In search of Englishness: in search of votes', in J. Arnold, K. Davies and S. Ditchfield (eds), *History and Heritage: Consuming the Past in Contemporary Culture*, Shaftsbury, Donhead, 1998, pp. 155–67.

Cook, C. and J. Stevenson, *Britain in the Depression: Society and Politics, 1929–1939*, London, Longman, 1994.

Cunningham, H., 'The Conservative Party and patriotism', in R. Colls and P. Dodd (eds), *Englishness: Politics and Culture 188–1920*, London, Croom Helm, 1986, pp. 283–307.

Cunningham, H., 'The language of patriotism', in R. Samuel (ed.), *Patriotism: The Making and Unmaking of British National Identity Volume 1: History and Politics*, London, Routledge, 1989, pp. 57–89.

Feldman, D., 'Nationality and ethnicity', in P. Johnson (ed.), *Twentieth-Century Britain*, London, Longman, 1994, pp. 127–48.

Field, G., 'Social patriotism and the British working class: appearance and disappearance of a tradition', *International Labour and Working-Class History*, 42, 1992, pp. 20–39.

Fielding, S., P. Thompson and N. Tiratsoo, *England Arise! The Labour Party and Popular Politics in 1940s Britain*, Manchester, Manchester University Press, 1995.

Finn, M., *After Chartism: Class and Nation in English Radical Politics 1848–1874*, Cambridge, Cambridge University Press, 1993.

George, S., *Britain and European Integration since 1945*, Oxford, Blackwell, 1991.

Greenwood, S., *Britain and European Integration since the Second World War*, Manchester, Manchester University Press, 1996.

Haseler, S., *The English Tribe: Identity, Nation and Europe*, London, Macmillan, 1996.

Hewison, R., *Culture and Consensus: England, Art and Politics since 1940*, London, Methuen, 1995.

Hill, C., 'The Norman yoke', in his *Puritanism and Revolution*, Harmondsworth, Penguin, 1986, pp. 58–125.

Hilson, M., 'Women voters and the rhetoric of patriotism in the British general election of 1918', *Women's History Review*, 10, 2001, pp. 325–47.

Laybourn, K., *Britain on the Breadline: A Social and Political History of Britain 1918–1939*, Stroud, Sutton, 1991.

McKibbin, R., *The Ideologies of Class*, Oxford, Oxford University Press, 1991.

McWilliam, R., 'Radicalism and popular culture: the Tichborne case and the politics of "fair play", 1867–1886', in E. Biagini and A. Reid (eds), *Currents of Radicalism*, Cambridge, Cambridge University Press, 1991, pp. 44–64.

McWilliam, R., *Popular Politics in Nineteenth Century England*, London, Routledge, 1998.

Miliband, R., *Parliamentary Socialism: A Study in the Politics of Labour*, second edition, London, Merlin, 1972.

Morgan, K., *Rebirth of a Nation: A History of Modern Wales*, Oxford, Oxford University Press, 1981.

Morgan, K., *The People's Peace: British History 1945–1990*, Oxford, Oxford University Press, 1992.

Newman, G., *The Rise of English Nationalism: A Cultural History 1740–1830*, New York, Weidenfeld and Nicolson, 1987.

Nicholas, S., 'The construction of a national identity: Stanley Baldwin, "Englishness" and the mass media in inter-war Britain', in M. Francis and I. Zweiniger-Bargielowska (eds), *The Conservatives and British Society, 1880–1990*, Cardiff, University of Wales Press, 1996, pp. 127–46.

Powell, D., *Nationhood and Identity: The British State since 1800*, London, I. B. Tauris, 2002.

Ramsden, J., *The Age of Balfour and Baldwin 1902–1940: A History of the Conservative Party*, London, Longman, 1978.

Ramsden, J., *An Appetite for Power: A History of the Conservative Party since 1830*, London, HarperCollins, 1998.

Ramsden, J., *Man of the Century: Winston Churchill and His Legend since 1945*, London, HarperCollins, 2002.

Readman, P., 'The Conservative Party, patriotism and British politics: the case of the general election of 1900', *Journal of British Studies*, 40, 2001, pp. 107–45.

Robbins, K., *Present and Past: British Images of Germany in the First Half of the Twentieth Century and Their Historical Legacy*, Göttingen, Wallstein Verlag, 1999.

Skidelsky, R., *Oswald Mosley*, London, Macmillan, 1975.

Smith, M., *Britain and 1940: History, Myth and Popular Memory*, London, Routledge, 2000.

Thompson, D., *Outsiders: Class, Gender and Nation*, London, Verso, 1993.

Thorpe, A. (ed.), *The Failure of Political Extremism in Inter-War Britain*, Exeter, Exeter University Press, 1989.

Ward, P., *Red Flag and Union Jack: Englishness, Patriotism and the British Left, 1881–1924*, Woodbridge, Boydell, 1998.

Ward, P., 'Preparing for the people's war: the left and patriotism in the 1930s', *Labour History Review*, 67, 2002, pp. 171–86.

Ward-Smith, G., 'Baldwin and Scotland: more than Englishness', *Contemporary British History*, 15, 2001, pp. 61–82.

## Ethnicity

Alibhai-Brown, Y., *True Colours: Public Attitudes to Multiculturalism and the Role of Government*, London, Institute for Public Policy Research, 1999.

Alibhai-Brown, Y., 'Muddled leaders and the future of British national identity', *Political Quarterly*, 71, 2000, pp. 26–30.

Alibhai-Brown, Y., *Who Do We Think We Are? Imagining the New Britain*, London, Penguin, 2001.

Bonnett, A., *White Identities: Historical and International Perspectives*, Harlow, Prentice Hall, 2000.

Clegg, J., *Fu Manchu and the 'Yellow Peril': The Making of a Racist Myth*, Stoke-on-Trent, Trentham, 1994.

Cohen, R., *Frontiers of Identity: The British and the Others*, London, Longman, 1994.

Colley, L., 'Britishness and otherness: an argument', *Journal of British Studies*, 31, 1992, pp. 309–29.

Davey, K., *English Imaginaries*, London, Lawrence and Wishart, 1999.

Feldman, D., 'There was an Englishman, an Irishman and a Jew . . . immigrants and minorities in Britain', *Historical Journal*, 26, 1983, pp. 185–99.

Feldman, D., *Englishmen and Jews: Social Relations and Political Culture 1840–1914*, New Haven, CT, Yale University Press, 1994.

Fielding, S., *Class and Ethnicity: Irish Catholics in England, 1880–1939*, Buckingham, Open University Press, 1993.

Fitzpatrick, D., 'A curious middle place: the Irish in Britain, 1871–1921', in S. Gilley and R. Swift (eds), *The Irish in Britain, 1815–1939*, London, Pinter, 1989, pp. 10–59.

Fryer, P., *Staying Power: The History of Black People in Britain*, London, Pluto, 1984.

Gardner, K. and A. Shukur, '"I'm Bengali, I'm Asian, and I'm living here": The changing identity of British Bengalis', in R. Ballard (ed.), *Desh Pardesh: The South Asian Presence in Britain*, London, Hurst, 1994, pp. 142–64.

Gilroy, P., *'There Ain't No Black in the Union Jack': The Cultural Politics of Race and Nation*, London, Routledge, 1987.

Gilroy, P., *The Black Atlantic: Modernity and Double Consciousness*, London, Verso, 1993.

Hall, S., 'New ethnicities', in J. Donald and A. Rattansi (eds), *'Race', Culture and Difference*, London, Sage/Open University, 1992, pp. 252–9.

Holmes, C., 'Immigration', in T. Gourvish and A. O'Day (eds), *Britain since 1945*, Basingstoke, Macmillan, 1991.

Kureishi, H., 'London and Karachi', in R. Samuel (ed.), *Patriotism: The Making and Unmaking of British National Identity Volume 2 Minorities and Outsiders*, London, Routledge, 1989, pp. 270–87.

Kushner, T. (ed.), *The Jewish Heritage in British History: Englishness and Jewishness*, London, Frank Cass, 1992.

Kushner, T. and K. Lunn (eds), *Traditions of Intolerance: Historical Perspectives on Fascism and Race Discourse in Britain*, Manchester, Manchester University Press, 1989.

Lahiri, S., 'South Asians in post-imperial Britain: decolonisation and imperial legacy', in S. Ward (ed.), *British Culture and the End of Empire*, Manchester, Manchester University Press, 2001, pp. 200–16.

Layton-Henry, Z., *The Politics of Immigration*, Oxford, Blackwell, 1992.

Lennon, M., M. MacAdam and J. O'Brien, *Across the Water: Irish Women's Lives in Britain*, London, Virago, 1998.

Marqusee, M., *Anyone but England: Cricket, Race and Class*, London, Two Heads, 1998.

Mason, D., *Race and Ethnicity in Modern Britain*, second edition, Oxford, Oxford University Press, 2000.

Modood, T., 'British Asian Muslims and the Rushdie affair', in J. Donald and A. Rattansi (eds), *'Race', Culture and Difference*, London, Sage/Open University, 1992, pp. 260–77.

Modood, T., 'Culture and identity', in T. Modood and R. Berthoud (eds), *Ethnic Minorities in Britain: Diversity and Disadvantage*, London, Policy Studies Institute, 1997, pp. 290–338.

Panayi, P., *Immigration, Ethnicity and Racism in Britain 1815–1945*, Manchester, Manchester University Press, 1994.

Panayi, P., *Racial Violence in Britain in the Nineteenth and Twentieth Centuries*, London, Leicester University Press, 1996.

Parekh, B., 'Defining British national identity', *Political Quarterly*, 71, 2000, pp. 4–14.

Paul, K., 'From subjects to immigrants: black Britons and national identity, 1948–62', in R. Weight and A. Beach (eds), *The Right to Belong: Citizenship and National Identity in Britain, 1930–1960*, London, I. B. Tauris, 1998, pp. 223–48.

Sewell, T., *Keep on Moving: The* Windrush *Legacy: The Black Experience in Britain from 1948*, London, Voice Enterprises, 1998.

Singh Tatla, D., 'This is our home now: reminiscences of a Punjabi migrant in Coventry', *Oral History*, 21, 1993, pp. 68–74.

Spencer, I., 'World War Two and the making of multiracial Britain', in P. Kirkham and

D. Thoms (eds), *War Culture: Social Change and Changing Experience in World War Two Britain*, London, Lawrence and Wishart, 1995, pp. 209–18.

Tabili, L., *'We Ask for British Justice': Workers and Racial Difference in Late Imperial Britain*, Ithaca, NY, Cornell University Press, 1994.

Taylor, J., *The Half-Way Generation: A Study of Asian Youths in Newcastle upon Tyne*, Windsor, NFER Publishing Co., 1976.

Thurlow, R., *Fascism in Britain: From Oswald Mosley's Blackshirts to the National Front*, second edition, London, I. B. Tauris, 1998.

Visram, R., *Asians in Britain: 400 Years of History*, London, Pluto, 2002.

Voeltz, R., '"A good Jew and a good Englishman": the Jewish Lads' Brigade 1894–1922', *Journal of Contemporary History*, 23, 1988, pp. 119–27.

Walvin, J., *Passage to Britain*, Harmondsworth, Penguin, 1984.

Waters, C., '"Dark strangers" in our midst: discourses of race and nation in Britain, 1947–1963', *Journal of British Studies*, 36, 1997, pp. 207–38.

Webster, W., *Imagining Home: Gender, 'Race' and National Identity 1945–64*, London, UCL Press, 1998.

Webster, W., 'The Empire answers: imperial identity on radio and film, 1939–45', unpublished paper, 'The British World 2 conference', University of Calgary, July 2003.

Wilson, A., *Finding a Voice: Asian Women in Britain*, London, Virago, 1984.

Wolffe, J., '"And there's another country . . . "': Religion, the state and British identities', in G. Parsons (ed.), *The Growth of Religious Diversity: Britain from 1945*, London, Routledge/Open University, 1994, pp. 84–121.

Zubrzycki, J., *Polish Immigrants in Britain: A Study of Adjustment*, The Hague, Martinus Nijhoff, 1956.

**Outer Britain**

*General*

Aughey, A., *Nationalism, Devolution and the Challenge to the United Kingdom State*, London, Pluto, 2001.

Biagini, E. (ed.), *Citizenship and Community: Liberals, Radicals and Collective Identities in the British Isles, 1865–1931*, Cambridge, Cambridge University Press, 1996.

Cohen, R., 'Review article: the incredible vagueness of being British/English', *International Affairs*, 76, 2000, pp. 575–82.

Harvie, C., 'The moment of British nationalism 1939–1970', *Political Quarterly*, 71, 2000, pp. 328–40.

Hechter, M., *Internal Colonialism: The Celtic Fringe in British National Development*, New Brunswick, NJ, Transaction, 1999.

Hunter, J., 'The Gaelic connection: the Highlands, Ireland and nationalism 1873–1922', *Scottish Historical Review*, 54, 1975, pp. 178–204.

Kellas, J., *The Politics of Nationalism and Ethnicity*, Basingstoke, Macmillan, 1991.

Morgan, K., 'England, Britain and the audit of war', *Transactions of the Royal Historical Society*, 6th series, 7, 1997, pp. 131–53.

Pittock, M., *Celtic Identity and the British Image*, Manchester, Manchester University Press, 1999.

Richards, J., *Films and British National Identity: From Dickens to Dad's Army*, Manchester, Manchester University Press, 1997.

Winter, J. M., 'British national identity and the First World War', in S. J. D. Green and R. C. Whiting (eds), *The Boundaries of the State in Modern Britain*, Cambridge, Cambridge University Press, pp. 261–77.

*Wales*

Adamson, D., 'The intellectual and the national movement in Wales', in R. Fevre and

A. Thompson (eds), *Nation, Identity and Social Theory: Perspectives from Wales*, Cardiff, University of Wales Press, 1999, pp. 48–68.

Aubel, F., 'The Conservatives in Wales, 1880–1935', in M. Francis and I. Zweiniger-Bargielowska (eds), *The Conservatives and British Society 1890–1980*, Cardiff, University of Wales Press, 1996, pp. 96–110.

Aull Davies, C., *Welsh Nationalism in the Twentieth Century: The Ethnic Option and the Modern State*, New York, Praeger, 1989.

Davies, J., *A History of Wales*, London, Penguin, 1990.

Evans, N., 'The Welsh Victorian city: the middle class and civic and national consciousness in Cardiff, 1850–1914', *Welsh History Review*, 12, 1984–85, pp. 350–87.

Howell, D. W. and C. Baber, 'Wales', in F. M. L. Thompson (ed.), *The Cambridge Social History of Britain 1750–1950. Volume I Regions and Communities*, Cambridge, Cambridge University Press, 1990, pp. 281–354.

Hywell Davis, D., *The Welsh Nationalist Party 1925–1945: A Call to Nationhood*, Cardiff, University of Wales Press, 1983.

Morgan, K., *Rebirth of a Nation: A History of Modern Wales*, Oxford, Oxford University Press, 1981.

Morgan, K., *Wales in British Politics 1868–1922*, Cardiff, University of Wales Press, 1991.

Phillips, G., 'Dai Bach Y Soldiwr: Welsh soldiers in the British Army 1914–1918', *Llafur*, 6, 1993, pp. 94–105.

Thomas, H., 'Spatial restructuring in the capital: struggles to shape Cardiff's built environment', in R. Fevre and A. Thompson (eds), *Nation, Identity and Social Theory: Perspectives from Wales*, Cardiff, University of Wales Press, 1999, pp. 168–88.

Williams, C., *Capitalism, Community and Conflict: The South Wales Coalfield 1898–1947*, Cardiff, University of Wales Press, 1998.

Williams, G., *When Was Wales?*, London, Black Raven Press, 1985.

*Scotland*

Finlay, R., 'Pressure group or political party? The nationalist impact on Scottish politics, 1928–1945', *Twentieth-Century British History*, 3, 1992, pp. 274–97.

Finlay, R., 'National identity in crisis: politicians, intellectuals and the "End of Scotland", 1920–1939', *History*, 79, 1994, pp. 242–59.

Finlay, R., *A Partnership for Good? Scottish Politics and the Union since 1880*, Edinburgh, John Donald, 1997.

Finlay, R., 'The rise and fall of popular imperialism in Scotland 1850–1950', *Scottish Geographical Magazine*, 113, 1997, pp. 13–21.

Finlay, R., 'Review article: New Britain, new Scotland, new history? The impact of devolution on the development of Scottish historiography', *Journal of Contemporary History*, 36, 2001, pp. 383–93.

Harvie, C., 'Labour in Scotland during the Second World War', *Historical Journal*, 26, 1983, pp. 921–44.

Harvie, C., 'Scottish politics', in A. Dickson and J. H. Treble (eds), *People and Society in Scotland, Volume III, 1914–1990*, Edinburgh, John Donald, 1992, pp. 241–60.

Harvie, C., *Scotland and Nationalism: Scottish Society and Politics, 1707–1994*, second edition, London, Routledge, 1994.

Howell, D., *A Lost Left: Three Studies in Socialism and Nationalism*, Manchester, Manchester University Press, 1986.

Hutchison, I., *Scottish Politics in the Twentieth Century*, Basingstoke, Palgrave, 2001.

Ichijo, A., 'Civic or ethnic? The evolution of Britishness and Scottishness', unpublished paper, British Island Stories conference, University of York, April 2002.

Keating, M. and D. Bleiman, *Labour and Scottish Nationalism*, Basingstoke, Macmillan, 1979.

McCrone, D., 'Who do we think we are? Identity politics in modern Scotland', http://www.britcoun.de/e/education/studies/scot2994.htm#scot (9 September 2002).

MacKenzie, J., 'Empire and national identities: the case of Scotland', *Transactions of the Royal Historical Society*, 6th series, 8, 1998, pp. 215–31.

MacKenzie, J., '"The second city of the empire": Glasgow – imperial municipality', in F. Driver and D. Gilbert (eds), *Imperial Cities: Landscape, Display and Identity*, Manchester, Manchester University Press, 1999, pp. 215–37.

McLean, I., *The Legend of Red Clyde*, Edinburgh, John Donald, 1983.

Marr, A., *The Battle for Scotland*, London, Penguin, 1992.

Marr, A., *The Day Britain Died*, London, Profile, 2000.

Nairn, T., *After Britain: New Labour and the Return of Scotland* , London, Granta, 2001.

Pittock, M., *The Invention of Scotland: The Stuart Myth and the Scottish Identity, 1638 to the Present*, London, Routledge, 1991.

Seawright, D. and J. Curtice, 'The decline of the Scottish Conservative and Unionist Party 1950–92: religion, ideology or economics?', *Contemporary Record*, 9, 1995, pp. 319–42.

Smout, T., 'Scotland 1850–1950', in F. M. L. Thompson (ed.), *The Cambridge Social History of Britain 1750–1950 Volume I Regions and Communities*, Cambridge, Cambridge University Press, 1990, pp. 209–80.

Trevor Roper, H., 'The invention of tradition: the Highland tradition of Scotland', in E. Hobsbawm and T. Ranger (eds), *The Invention of Tradition*, Cambridge, Cambridge University Press, 1984.

Webb, K., *The Growth of Nationalism in Scotland*, Harmondsworth, Penguin, 1978.

Withers, C., 'The historical creation of the Scottish Highlands', in I. Donnachie and C. Whatley (eds), *The Manufacture of Scottish History*, Edinburgh, Polygon, 1992, pp. 143–56.

*Ireland and Northern Ireland*

Boyce, D., '"The marginal Britons": the Irish', in R. Colls and P. Dodd (eds), *Englishness: Politics and Culture 1880–1920*, London, Croom Helm, 1986, pp. 230–53.

Bruce, S., *God Save Ulster! The Religion and Politics of Paisleyism*, Oxford, Oxford University Press, 1986.

Buckland, P., *Irish Unionism 2: Ulster Unionism and the Origins of Northern Ireland 1886–1922*, Dublin, Gill and Macmillan, 1973.

D'Alton, I., 'Southern Irish Unionism: a study of Cork Unionists, 1884–1914', *Transactions of the Royal Historical Society*, 5th series, 23, 1973, pp. 71–88.

Hennessey, T., 'Ulster Unionism and loyalty to the Crown of the United Kingdom, 1912–74', in R. English and G. Walker (eds), *Unionism in Modern Ireland: New Perspectives on Politics and Culture*, 1996, pp. 115–29.

Hennessey, T., *A History of Northern Ireland 1920–1996*, Basingstoke, Macmillan, 1997.

Hennessey, T., *Dividing Ireland: World War I and Partition*, London, Routledge, 1998.

Hutchinson, J., *The Dynamics of Cultural Nationalism: The Gaelic Revival and the Creation of the Irish Nation State*, London, Allen and Unwin, 1987.

Jackson, A., 'Unionist myths 1912–1985', *Past and Present*, 136, 1992, pp. 164–85.

Loughlin, J., *Ulster Unionism and British National Identity since 1885*, London, Pinter, 1995.

Loughlin, J., *The Ulster Question since 1945*, Basingstoke, Macmillan, 1998.

Lyons, F., *Culture and Anarchy in Ireland 1890–1939*, Oxford, Oxford University Press, 1982.

MacBride, I., 'Ulster and the British problem', in R. English and G. Walker (eds), *Unionism in Modern Ireland: New Perspectives on Politics and Culture*, Basingstoke, Macmillan, 1996, pp.1–17.

Mandle, W., *The Gaelic Athletic Association and Irish Nationalist Politics 1884–1924*, London, Croom Helm, 1987.

O Connor, F., *In Search of a State: Catholics in Northern Ireland*, Belfast, Blackstaff, 1993.

Ó Tuathaigh, G., 'Nationalist Ireland, 1912–1922: aspects of continuity and change', in

P. Collins (ed.), *Nationalism and Unionism: Conflict in Ireland, 1885–1921*, Belfast, Institute of Irish Studies, 1996, pp. 47–73.

Paseta, S., 'Nationalist responses to two royal visits to Ireland, 1900 and 1903', *Irish Historical Studies*, 124, 1999, pp. 488–504.

Stewart, A., *The Narrow Ground: The Roots of Conflict in Ulster*, revised edition, London, Faber and Faber, 1989.

Wichert, S., *Northern Ireland since 1945*, second edition, London, Longman, 1999.

# Index

abdication 21
Abercrombie, Patrick 55
accents 70, 89–90
Acts of Unions: with Ireland 2, 141, 158;
    with Scotland 2, 141; with Wales 141,
    146
Aden 32
advertising 15
Africa and Africans 26, 30, 31, 32, 34, 83,
    113, 116–7, 120, 123, 131, 170
air raids 42, 58–9
Albert, Prince 20, 23, 27, 28
Alexander, Wendy 157
Alexandra, Queen 20
Al-Fayed, Dodi 26
Alibhai-Brown, Yasmin 2, 137, 139
aliens *see* immigration
Alsace-Lorraine 1
Altrincham, Lord 28
Americanisation 2, 11, 48–9, 89–92, 146,
    171
Anderson, Viv 83
Angel of the North 71
Anglo-Irish War 163
Angry Young Men 52, 91
Anti-Nazi League 9
anti-Semitism 104, 115, 121, 128
Antrim 151
architecture 15, 58, 60, 65, 86–7
Argyll, Duke of 151
aristocracy 16, 27, 36, 57, 78, 93–4, 109,
    148–9
Armistice Day 28, 45, 74, 163
Armstrong, Aileen 66
army 47, 124, 146, 165; pride in 23, 155
Arsenal FC 80
Arts and Crafts Movement 55
Asian Britons 5, 12, 26, 71, 82–3, 113–4,
    115, 116, 117, 126, 131, 132–4,
    135–40, 172

Asquith, H. H. 100, 164
asylum 118, 140
Atholl, Duke of 153
Attlee, Clement 99, 107, 147, 165
Australia 19, 24, 137, 170
Austro-Hungarian empire 1

Bagehot, Walter 20–1
Baker, Baron 137
Baldwin, Stanley 21, 54, 57, 100–4, 106
Balfour, Arthur 14, 149, 150, 151
Balmoral 23, 155
*Bank Holiday* 87
Bannister, Roger 51
Barker, Sir Ernest 51
Barnett, Canon 60
Barnsley 67, 80
Bawtree, Viola 41–2
BBC 19, 28, 32, 45, 74, 89, 106
Belfast 45, 159, 162
Belgium 1, 98, 146
Bennett, Phil 78
Benson, John 15
Berkeley, George 162
Berkshire 58
Bethnal Green 25
Betjeman, John 63
Bevan, Aneurin 147
Beveridge, William 40
Bevin, Ernest 106, 108
Bhabha, Homi 3
Bhownaggree, Sir Mancherjee Merwanjee
    25
Bilbrough, Mrs E. M. 20
Birmingham 11, 22, 27, 124, 133
Birrell, Augustine 159
black Britons 5, 12, 35, 53, 83, 113–14,
    115, 116, 122, 129–30, 132–4, 135–40,
    172
Blackburn 22, 80

blackness 51–2, 113–14, 126
Blackpool 86, 87
Blair, Tony 2, 30, 32, 71, 93, 110–11, 139
Blatchford, Robert 31, 70, 97
Blitz, the 58–9, 68–9
Bloody Sunday 165
Blunkett, David 115, 140
Boer War 16, 30, 40, 61, 95, 96, 99, 119, 150, 161
Bonar Law, Andrew 150
Booth, Charles 58, 61
Bovril 27
Boy Scouts 39, 118
boys 37, 39, 119–20
Boys' Brigade 119
*Boy's Own Paper* 39
Bradford 11, 139, 172
*Brassed Off* 71
*Braveheart* 155, 156
break-up of Britain 33
Bremner, Robert 60
Brick Lane 119, 139
*Brief Encounter* 48–9
Brighton 86
Bristol 60
Britannia 38, 95
British Board of Film Censors 90, 117, 120, 121
British Brothers' League 127, 132, 133
British Council 34, 84
British Empire and Commonwealth 7–8, 10, 14–36, 37, 39, 44, 55, 74; 95, 111, 121, 130, 131, 136, 137, 142, 150, 171; *see also* imperialism
British Legion 163
British Muslims 137, 140, 172
British national identity *see* Britishness
British National Party 12
Britishness: contested 5, 93, 101, 105–8, 109, 135–40; crisis of 7, 142–3, 171; decline 6, 8; definitions 2–3, 5, 6, 9–10, 141; and ethnicity 50–2, 83, 110–1, 119, 125, 131–4, 135–40; and gender 37, 39–40, 41; and imperialism 24, 26, 32, 36, 75, 151; instability of 3, 141, 172; and monarchy 18, 23, 26, 29, 35, 164; and the other 3, 88, 116, 124, 126, 141, 153; persistence of 5, 7, 9, 12–13, 110, 168–9, 171–3; and politics 98, 102–5, 147, 163; and sport 75–6, 78, 81, 85; and urban life 58–9
British Union of Fascists 101–4, 122, 127
British Women's Patriotic League 40–1
Brixton 126, 133–4

Brown, Gordon 110, 157
Brummies 11
Buchan, John 46, 150, 154
Buckingham Palace 20, 28, 35, 42
Buckinghamshire 56
Budd, Zola 83
*Bulldog Drummond* 46
Burns, Robert 98
Bute, Marquess and Marchioness of 148–9
Butler, R. A. 130–1

Caernarvon 23
Caine, Michael 16, 76
Calder, Angus 28
Callaghan, James 109, 131
Callander 56
Campbell-Bannerman, Sir Henry 150
Canada 1, 24, 33, 150
Cannadine, David 14, 15, 17–18, 34
capitalism 6, 7, 30, 71, 94, 149
Cardiff 66, 120, 122, 143, 148–9
Carpenter, Edward 97
Catatonia 156
Catholicism and Catholics 12, 24, 25, 43, 79–80, 81–2, 117–18, 129, 147, 158, 160, 161, 163, 165, 167
Celtic FC 82, 83
Celtic fringe 22, 141
Celticness 33, 43, 65, 71, 98, 100, 155
Chamberlain, Joseph 28, 151
Chamberlain, Neville 106
Chappell, Edgar 65–6
character, national 75, 84, 100, 133–4
characteristics, national 54; free speech 127–8; moderation 66, 102, 103–4, 171
charity 18, 20, 27
Charles, Prince 25, 35, 149
Chartism 94
Chelmsford 60–1
Chelsea FC 82
Chesterfield 27, 62
children 19, 22, 38, 39, 41, 68, 134
China and the Chinese 26, 34, 120, 121, 128–9, 137
Christie, Agatha 45
Christie, Lynford 83
Christmas 45
Church Lads' Brigade 39, 119
Church of England 29, 76
Church of Scotland 25
*Church Times* 90
churches 15, 58
Churchill, Winston 105–8, 124, 128, 152

cinema 15, 22, 45, 47, 50, 70–1, 73, 86, 89–91, 120, 121, 146, 148, 156
citizenship 20, 37, 40, 47, 53, 62, 115, 127, 131, 157, 160, 163
civic pride 59–61, 67, 159
civil rights 165
Clark, Alan 34
class 4, 16, 22, 40, 47, 57, 70, 71, 80–1, 82, 86, 94–5, 102–3, 132, 146; and monarchy 26–8, 36
Clyde, River 24, 150
Clynes, J. R. 72
cockneys 61, 64, 70, 88
*The Colditz Story* 50
Cold War 11, 52, 92
Colley, Linda 3, 5, 6, 7, 158
Collins, Marcus 52
Colls, Robert 6–7, 170, 171
Colwyn Bay 144
comics 91–2
Communist Party of Great Britain 12, 100, 101–4, 155
Compton-Burnett, Ivy 45
Connolly, James 158
conscription *see* military service
Conservative Party 2, 8, 11, 12, 15, 40, 65, 92, 100–1, 108, 127, 133, 147; associated with Englishness 96, 100, 103–4, 106, 148; and Britishness 128, 130, 135, 140; and Europe 108–111; and imperialism 25, 30, 44, 45; and monarchy 14, 18, 29; and patriotism 93, 95–6, 99–100, 105–6; in Scotland 152–3, 154–5
Constantine, Learie 124
Cook, Robin 139
Cookson, Catherine 66
core and periphery 6, 141–2
Cornwall 57, 71
coronations: 1911 19, 40; 1937 17, 19, 27; 1953 14, 18, 19–20, 22, 31, 68
Cotswolds 55, 56, 57
Council of Wales 147
countryside 54, 55–8, 146–7, 155
Covenant, Scottish 152
Craig, Charles 164
Craig, Sir James 164
Crane, Walter 96
Crawford, Alick 24–5
Crick, Bernard 115
cricket 11, 38, 74–8, 80–4, 115, 124
crime 55, 121, 134
Cronin, A. J. 66
*The Cruel Sea* 50

Cumberland 56
Cymru Fydd 145

Dabydeen, David 137
Dáil Éireann 5, 163
*Daily Express* 138
*Daily Herald* 30
*Daily Mirror* 26
Dalhousie, Lord 150
Dalton, Hugh 57, 58, 106
*The Dam Busters* 50
Dark, Sidney 90
Davies, Clement 108
Davies, David 62
Davies, Norman 5, 171
decolonisation *see* end of Empire
decorations *see* honours
Derbyshire 56
Derry/Londonderry 158, 166, 167; Derry City FC 79
devolution 2, 8, 12, 25, 30, 71, 139, 148, 156, 157, 165, 168, 171
Diana, Princess 18, 25–6, 35
Dickens, Charles 66, 84
Dilke, Sir Charles 28
disestablishment 145
Disraeli, Benjamin 14, 29, 30, 95–6
domesticity 39, 44–5, 50–1, 131–4
Dott, George 153
Dover 20
Downing Street 42
Driberg, Tom 125
drugs 8
Drumcree 166
Dublin 24, 79, 159, 160–1
Dunkirk 106, 107
Dunleavy, Patrick 55

Ealing Films 91
Eastbourne 23
Easter Rising 1916 5, 43, 79, 158, 163
economy 6, 7–8, 24, 34, 56, 78, 79, 102, 108, 127, 142, 143–4, 146, 147, 148, 150, 151, 154, 159, 168, 172
Eden, Anthony 89
Edinburgh 45, 150, 153, 154
education *see* schools and schooling
Edward VII 21, 152
Edward VIII 17, 21, 24
Edwards, H. W. J. 33, 89–90
Edwards, Huw T. 147
eisteddfodau 144–5
elections: general 1868 145; 1885 145; 1900 11, 30, 97, 145, 152; 1906 11–12,

97, 145; 1910 161; 1918 44, 99, 146,
163; 1922 99; 1931 12; 1935 12, 147;
1945 12, 63, 107, 124, 132–3, 147;
1950 132–3; 1951 108, 132–3; 1955
154; 1959 154; 1964 127; 1970 148;
1974 154; 1979 8, 33, 148; 1983 130;
1997 9, 110, 154–5, 156; 2001 155
Elgar, Sir Edward 17
Elizabeth II 14, 20, 22, 23, 25, 28, 31, 35,
36, 152n61
Elizabeth, the Queen Mother 20, 21–2,
27, 30, 35
Elliot, Walter 154
Ellis, Tom 145
emigration 24, 40–1, 117, 134, 144, 146
empire 4; *see also* British Empire and
Commonwealth
Empire Day 14–15, 16, 45, 118
Empire Marketing Board 45
*Empire Windrush* 117, 124
'end of Britain' 2, 109, 142–3, 168–9
end of Empire 1, 2, 31, 32, 52, 76, 108
endowment of motherhood 40
Engels, Friedrich 117
England 15, 138, 141
*English Journey* 68
English nationalism 2, 34, 76, 171
Englishness 6, 7, 10, 41, 45, 67, 68, 96,
100, 137, 139, 171, 172; elision with
Britishness 45, 54, 141–2, 153; and
monarchy 22, 25; rural 54, 56, 57; and
sport 79
*Escape to Victory* 76
Esher, Viscount 17
Ethiopia 34
ethnicity 8, 12, 27, 49, 50–2, 110,
113–40, 172; definition 115–16
eugenicism 40
European integration 2, 12, 108–11, 128,
139, 155
Evans Gordon, Major 132
Evans, E. Vincent 144, 148
Evans, Gwynfor 141–2
Evans, Samuel T. 145–6
*Exploring English Character* 51, 133

Fabian Colonial Research Bureau 31
Fabian Society 31, 62
fair play 41, 74, 77, 84, 129
Falklands War 6, 8, 34, 50–1, 128
*The Far Pavilions*, 34
fascism 47, 101–4, 128, 147
femininity 44, 46, 47, 51
feminism, feminists 7, 37, 39, 53

Fenians 117
Festival of Britain 108
Festival of Wales 149
Fields, Gracie 70
Finlay, Richard 156
First World War 8, 11, 16, 20, 21, 24, 29,
37, 41, 52, 84, 87; 89, 95, 100, 120,
122, 146, 172; and gender 40, 42, 44–6;
and Ireland 162–3; and politics 98–100,
152, 152–3; and rural idyll 55–6, 57–8,
62–3, 100; and Scotland 152–4
Fitter, Richard 64
food and drink 8, 16, 26, 27, 31, 41–2,
45, 71, 73, 86, 91, 95, 119, 132, 139
Foot, Michael 105, 106
football 38, 72, 73–85, 154–5
Ford, Ford Madox 82
foreign policy 32–3, 42, 106, 108–11
Formby, George 70
*The Four Feathers* 46
France and the French 1, 3, 32, 88, 93–4,
98, 109, 110, 120, 170
freeborn Englishman 94
*The Full Monty* 71

Gaelic Athletic Association 79, 160
Gaelic League 117–18, 160
Gaelic symbols 42–3
Gaitskell, Hugh 109
*Gandhi* 34
garden cities 54, 59–60, 62–3, 64, 66
gardens 62, 63
gender 11, 20, 28, 37–53, 123, 149, 154;
*see also* women
General Strike 84, 100
gentleness 51, 52, 102
*The Gentle Sex* 123
Geordie identity 71, 72
George III 94
George V 14, 19, 20, 21, 25, 27, 28, 40,
45, 60–1, 74, 164
George VI 14–15, 17, 19, 21, 27, 28, 148
German atrocities 41, 107, 123, 123 n. 59
Germany and Germans 1, 4, 11, 40, 41,
42, 46, 49, 76, 87, 88, 98, 99, 101, 104,
109, 110, 121, 123, 153, 170
Gibson, David 65
Giddens, Anthony 110
Gilroy, Paul 137
Girl Guides 118
Gladstone, W. E. 29, 78, 95–6, 150, 151,
152, 159–60, 168
Glasgow 24, 44, 60, 65, 80, 81–2, 88,
122, 150, 155, 159

globalisation 7, 8, 12, 66, 71, 170
Gonne, Maud 43
Gorer, Geoffrey 51, 133
Grade, Lou 119
Graham, George 165
Grant, Bernie 137
Graves, Robert 88
Great War *see* First World War
Greater Britain 38
Greece and Greeks 120
Greenham Common 7, 53
Griffiths, James 147
Griffiths, Peter 127, 128, 133
*Guardian* 35, 111
Gulf War 51, 155
Guy Fawkes Day 118

Hadrian's Wall 116–7
Hall, Stuart 139
Hannay, Richard 150
Hardie, Keir 27, 98, 145, 150
Hardy, Thomas 55, 66
Harvie, Christopher 2, 79, 142
Harwich 20
Haseler, Stephen 3, 4, 17
Hattersley, Roy 90
*Heart of Britain* 56, 59
Heath, Edward 89, 128, 131
Henderson, Arthur 100
Hennessy, Peter 32
heritage 56, 71
Higgins, Anne
Highlands 57, 78, 150, 155
Hillary, Edmund 31, 51
Hiro, Dilip 136
history, used to support national identity
    5, 33, 43, 94, 95, 104, 105, 109, 111,
    115, 151, 158, 160–1
History Workshop 6
Hoare, Rawdon Sir 90
Hobson, John 166
Hogarth 84
holidays 11, 85–9
Hollywood 48, 89–91
home 15, 26, 51, 55–6, 62, 63, 131–5
Home Rule 143; Irish 25, 43, 78, 96–7,
    129, 158–9, 160–3, 172; Northern Irish
    141, 164; Scottish 152, 154; Welsh 145
homosexuality 26, 52
Hong Kong 26, 34, 127, 128–9, 136
Honourable Society of Cymmrodorion
    144
honours 20, 21, 27, 147
housing 55, 59–60, 63, 132–3

Howard, Ebenezer 62
Howe, Darcus 2
Huddersfield 9, 11, 76, 80; Choral Society
    56
humour 69, 87–8
Huxley, Elspeth 51
Hyamson, Dyan 119
Hyndman, H. M. 97

*I Know Where I'm Going* 156
immigration 2, 4, 5, 8, 12, 71–2, 109,
    113–22, 157, 172; Acts 130–1; hostility
    to 95, 113, 114–5, 120–1, 122; and
    monarchy 25–6; and women 39, 50–2;
    *see also* racism
imperial exhibitions 26, 74, 150, 154
imperialism 1, 6; 14–36, 38, 74–5, 84,
    86–7, 150, 151, 155, 156; and gender
    40–1, 44, 45; nostalgia for 34, 36, 89;
    opposition to 31; and sport 75, 84
Ince, Paul 83
Independent Labour Party 97
India and Indians 14, 19, 21, 24, 29, 30,
    82, 86, 106, 120, 124, 139, 150, 170
Indian Workers' Association 138
industrial unrest 27, 34, 84, 100, 109
Innes, Taylor 152
*In Search of England* 57–8
internationalism 9, 39, 53, 94, 97–8, 110
Ireland 2, 3, 5, 6, 12, 57, 97, 141,
    157–68; and gender 42–3; immigrants
    in Britain 94, 95, 117–18, 122, 125,
    126–7, 129, 132, 135–6; and
    imperialism 24; and monarchy 22, 24,
    29, 36; and sport 76, 79–80; *see also*
    Northern Ireland
Ireland Act 1949 165
Irish nationalism 5, 8, 24, 36, 42–3, 79,
    117, 129, 142–3, 151, 159–63, 167
Irishness 23, 100, 117–18, 135–6, 141–2,
    160–1, 167, 168–9
IRA *see* Provisional IRA
Irish Volunteers 162
Islam 26, 113
Italy and Italians 33, 101, 104, 120, 121,
    122

Jamaica 114, 120, 136, 137
Jennings, Humphrey 56, 59
*The Jewel in the Crown* 34
Jews 49, 95, 111, 115, 117, 118–22, 134;
    and Jewishness 129; *see also* anti-
    Semitism
Jewish Lads' Brigade 119–20

jingoism 30, 95
Johnston, Sir Charles 32
Johnston, Thomas 152
Jones, Sir J. Prichard 144–5
*Journey's End* 46
Joynson-Hicks, William 135
Juan Carlos, King of Spain 25
jubilees: 1935 19; 1977 34, 109, 166;
    2002 35, 36
juvenile and children's literature 15, 55

Kandinsky, Wassily 4
Kennedy, John F. 92
Kenyan Asians 131
Kilbrandon committee 154
Kilmarnock 83
Kinder Scout 57
King, Tom 121
Kipling, Rudyard 84, 85
knitting 21, 41
Korda, Alexander 46
Kureishi, Hanif 115

Labour: and Britishness 103, 107–8, 115,
    168; and devolution 156, 157; and
    Europe 108–11; governments 2, 5, 57,
    71, 108, 133, 139–40; and immigration
    125–6, 128, 129, 131; and imperialism
    30–1, 32, 45; and monarchy 19, 21, 22,
    27, 29–30, 32; movement 9, 100–1,
    106, 149–50; party 8, 63, 64, 100; and
    patriotism 92, 96–8, 99, 106, 111–12,
    124; in Scotland 152, 154; in Wales
    146, 147–8
Lake District 57
Lal 138
Lancashire 59, 67, 68, 69, 71, 95, 136
'Land of Hope and Glory' 19, 36
Lansbury, George 29–30
Lawrence, Stephen 140
Lawrence, T. E. 46
League of Empire Loyalists 28, 127
Leeds 22, 63, 120, 122
Leith Athletic 83
Leonard, Mark 32, 111
*Let the People Sing* 69
Lewis, Saunders 146, 147
Liberal Party 9, 98–9, 111; and
    imperialism 30–1, 95, 96; and Ireland
    159, 160–2; and monarchy 18, 23, 29;
    and pluralism 97, 152, 160, 168; in
    Scotland 152; in Wales 145–6; *see also*
    Gladstone
Light, Alison 44–7, 131–2

Lightfoot, Mrs 20
Limehouse 120
Linfield FC 80, 82
*The Lion and the Unicorn* 107
Liverpool 11, 42, 49, 63, 71, 117, 121,
    122
Livingstone, David 150
Lloyd George, David 97, 99, 129, 145,
    146
local government 19–20, 60–1, 63, 65, 67,
    133
*Local Hero* 156
Logan, David 117
London 9, 19–20, 22, 25, 27, 28, 49–50,
    55–6, 58, 59, 60, 61, 64, 67, 68, 69, 70,
    80, 95, 105, 113, 114, 119, 127, 132,
    133, 138, 144; Greater London
    Council 128; London County Council
    19–20, 58, 61, 63
*London Can Take It* 59
Londonderry 158, 166, 167
Lothen, Walter 137
*Lusitania* 42

MacDiarmid, Hugh 155
MacDonald, J. Ramsay 56, 98, 99, 100,
    101, 106, 150
Macdonald, Margo 156–7
Macintyre, Robert 152
MacKenzie, John 15–16, 16–17, 45
Maclean, John 155
Macmillan, Harold 89, 108
Mafeking 16, 119
magazines 47, 50, 91–2
Magna Carta Association 95
Major, John 8, 109, 154–5
Majorca 88
Man, Isle of 86
Manchester 22, 67, 80, 81, 118, 119, 136,
    159
Mandler, Peter 56, 65, 94
Manic Street Preachers 156
Marconi scandal 129
Margaret, Princess 35
Markievicz, Constance 43
Marple, Miss 45
Marquand, David 33
Marr, Andrew 156
Martin, Kingsley 17
Mary, Princess 68
Mary, Queen 21, 27, 61, 148
masculinity 7, 11, 21, 36, 37, 38–9, 43,
    46–7, 49, 50, 51, 71, 74, 84, 109, 134,
    161

Mason, A. E. W. 46
Mass-Observation 17, 19, 48, 49, 56–7, 64–5, 86, 90, 120, 122, 123, 132
Masterman, C. F. G. 55
May Day 97–8
medieval 6, 51
*Merrie England* 97
Merthyr Tydfil 27, 98, 145
Metroland 63
middle class 4, 16, 27, 40, 44, 51, 57, 96, 103, 109, 148, 149, 153
Midgley, Harry 59, 164
military service 39, 40, 99, 146
*Millions Like Us* 123
Milner, Lord 99, 123–4
miners and mining 7, 69, 103, 143, 145, 146, 150
Minford, Hugh 162
Ministry of Information 46, 56, 59, 124
Minto, Lord 150
modernity and anti-modernity 57–8, 62–3, 65, 92
Modood, Tariq 137, 139
monarchy 7–8, 10–11, 14–36, 94, 104, 142, 148–9, 162, 164, 165–6, 171; *see also* under individual monarchs
Monty Python 52, 89
Morrison, Herbert 30, 58, 107–8
Morrison, Mrs Arthur 44
Morton, H. V. 57–8
Mosley, Oswald 102, 104, 127
Motherwell 152
Muggeridge, Malcolm 28
multiple identities 4, 9, 10, 97, 110–11, 119, 143–5, 149–51, 153, 157, 166–7, 168–9, 170–1
museums 71; National Museum of Wales 27, 66, 145
music 34, 56, 73, 76, 89, 154–5, 156

Nairn, Tom 2, 7, 9, 17, 33, 142, 149, 156
names 4, 9, 124
National Association for the Vindication of Scottish Rights 132
national efficiency 12, 61
National Front 127, 128, 172
National Health Service 148
National governments 21, 63, 70, 103, 106
national identities 1
nationalism *see* English, Irish, Scottish, Welsh nationalism
National Pageant of Wales 148–9

National Service League 40
Naughton, Bill 135–6
Navy League 40
National Library of Wales 66, 145
Neagle, Anna 22
*New Statesman* 17, 87
new towns 63–4
New Zealand 24, 31, 77
Newbolt, Henry 75
Newbould, Frank 56
Newcastle upon Tyne 9, 11, 71, 138
Nicolson, Harold 20, 28
*1984* 92
Noakes, Lucy 47, 49, 50–1
Norgay, Tenzing 31
Norman, C. H. 97
North Britons 149, 161
'the North' and northernness 22, 56, 67, 77
Northern Ireland 3, 8, 12, 25, 79–80, 142, 157–8, 163–8, 171; and Second World War 59, 164–5
north–south divide 22–3, 67, 80–1
North York Moors 11
Norwich, John Julius 15
nursing 40, 114

O'Connell, Daniel 159–60
O'Connor, T. P. 5, 117
Oldham 69
opinion polls 5, 8, 25, 110, 138, 157, 171, 172
Orwell, George 54–5, 76, 87, 88, 92, 107, 109
Osbourne, Cyril 127
the other and otherness 3, 28, 41, 47, 51–2, 73, 80, 85, 88, 115–16, 122–3, 125–6, 141, 153
Oxford 51, 74

pacifism 39, 42, 53, 146–7
Paisley, Ian 166
Pakistan and Pakistanis 82, 111, 137, 138–9
Palin, Michael 89
Parekh, Bikhu 126, 139
parliament and parliamentary nature of Britishness 30, 42, 98, 99, 100–1, 104, 105, 107–8, 158
Parnell. Charles Stewart 160
Partick Thistle 80
*A Passage to India,* 34
patriarchy 40, 48
patriotic leagues 40–1, 44, 99

patriotism 6, 24, 39, 48, 87, 119, 129–30, 153, 163; and monarchy 20, 26, 61; radical 93–5, 106–7; 'true' 97
Patten, Chris 34
Patterson, Sheila 126, 133–4
Peak District 57
Pearse, Patrick 161, 163
Penhryn, Lord 148
'People's War' *see* Second World War
permissiveness 51–3, 166
Philip, Prince 22, 35
Phillips, Mike 139
Phillips, Trevor 137, 139
Pickles, Wilfred 69–70
Plaid Cymru 65, 146–8
Playne, Caroline 41, 46
Plymouth 84
Pocock, J. G. A. 5
Poland and the Polish 1, 114, 121, 126
police 84, 87, 94, 124, 140
Poor Law 94
Porter, Bernard 16
Potter, Beatrix 55
Powell, Enoch 113, 125, 127, 128, 130, 134
Power, O'Connor 117
Priestley, J. B. 59, 66, 67, 68, 69, 90, 107, 117
Primrose League 29, 40, 44, 96, 97
Princes of Wales 23, 29, 43, 149
privacy 51
Prochaska, Frank 18, 20–1, 27
Profumo, John 52
propaganda 45, 46, 47–8, 107
Protestantism 3, 6, 7, 23, 56, 80, 81–2, 118, 144, 158, 165, 166
Provisional IRA 9, 165, 166, 167

Quinlan, Sir Michael 32–3

Race Relations Acts 130
racism 26, 82–3, 89, 115, 123, 126–8, 131–2, 140, 172
radio 15, 19, 45, 69, 154
Ram, Anant 138
Redmond, John 5 n. 22, 79, 162
Redwood, John 2
regional identities 11, 15, 49–50, 55, 66–72, 161, 167
regions 35, 54
Reith, Lord 19
religion 3, 9, 10, 23, 26, 35, 98, 110, 117–18, 129, 144, 158
Renan, Ernest 12–13

republicanism 9, 25, 28–30; Irish 23–4, 160, 162
*Reynolds's Newspaper* 29
Ridley, Nicholas 110
riots 109, 137
Robbins, Keith 3, 5, 6, 7, 32, 33, 150
Roberts, Robert 14
Rose, Richard 8
Rosebery, Lord 96, 150
Rosyth 20
Rowntree, Seebohm 61
royal family 10, 18, 20–2, 35
royalty *see* monarchy
rugby 11, 38, 77–8
Runnymede Trust 139
Rutherford, Andrew 46
Rushdie, Salman 34, 136, 137, 140
Russia and Russians 95, 118–19, 121, 122
Russian Revolution 29, 101, 103
Rwanda 1

St Andrew's Day 24
St George's cross 76
St George's Day 74, 109
St Patrick's Day 118
Salford 14
Salim, Abdul 83
Salisbury, Lord 95–5; 1950s 108
Sampson, Anthony 33
Samuel, Raphael 6, 15, 131
Sandes, Flora 46
Sarwar, Rashid 83
*Satanic Verses* 140
Scapa Flow 20
Scarborough 87
schools and schooling 14, 15, 19, 52, 75, 79, 136, 142, 145, 149
Scotland 3, 6, 12, 15, 49, 69, 97, 117, 141, 149–57, 165, 170–1; and Britishness 111, 151, 155, 156–7, 168–9; and imperialism 23, 24, 33, 155, 156; and monarchy 22, 25, 27; and sports 76–9, 82, 83, 85, 154–5
Scott, Walter 155
Scottish National Party 25, 79, 151–2
Scottish National War Memorial 153
Scottish nationalism 8, 33, 142–3, 149, 151–4, 156–7, 168
Scottishness 5, 7, 23, 44, 56, 82, 98, 100, 141–2, 149–50, 153, 154, 155–7, 168–9
scouse identity 11, 71
Scruton, Roger 34, 52
seaside resorts 85–8

Second World War 2, 8, 11, 16, 28, 37–8, 55–6, 58–9, 63, 68–9, 74, 89, 105–7, 114, 122, 131–2, 141, 147, 154, 163, 170, 172; and gender 44, 47–50, 90
Seitz, Raymond 89
separate spheres 37, 41
Serbia 146
Sex Pistols 34
sexuality 47, 52
Sherriff, R. C. 46
shopping 41, 45, 71, 76, 114
Shurmer, Percy 22
Sillars, Jim 79, 82
Simpson, Wallis 21
*Sing as We Go* 70
singing and songs 16, 19, 36, 69, 70, 76, 83, 87, 135–6
Sinn Féin 5, 98, 161, 163, 167–8
*Sixty Glorious Years* 22
Smethwick 127, 128
Snowden, Philip 100
Social and Democratic Labour Party 167
Social Darwinism 17, 26, 61, 74, 161
Social Democratic Federation 97
socialism 9, 97–8, 106, 107, 110
Socialist Workers' Party 9
soldiers 20, 27, 62, 123–4, 153
South Africa 1, 12, 34, 96, 150
south east, the 56
*South Riding* 19
Spain and Spanish identities 4, 25, 33, 89, 120, 170
sport 11, 38–9, 52, 73–85, 149, 154–5
Stable, Sir Wintringham 125
Stallone, Sylvester 76
state identities 3, 7
Stereophonics 156
stereotypes 120–1, 132–3
Stevenage 64–5
Stewart, Gordon T. 31
stiff upper lip 26, 49, 86, 89
stoicism 48–9, 52, 123
Stokes, Sir John 15
Stopes, Marie 40
Storey, Miss 17
Stormont 164, 165
strikes *see* industrial unrest
suburbs 15, 47, 51, 63
Suez crisis 31, 32, 65, 89

Tariff Reform 12, 31, 96, 97, 101
tartan 23, 78, 85, 155
Taylor, A. J. P. 5

Taylor, Antony 29
Tebbit, Norman 82, 83, 115, 128–9, 137
television 142, 148 *see also* BBC
Thatcher, Margaret 6, 8, 33, 34, 53, 89, 109–10, 128, 130, 154, 168
*The Times* 45
theatre 15
Thomas, Hubert 136
Thomas, Lowell 46
Thompson, Dorothy 20, 26
Tichborne affair 95
Tiger Bay 120, 143
tolerance 51, 84, 127–8
Torrence, John 33
town planning 55, 62–4; *see also* garden cities
Townsend, Peter 127
*Trainspotting* 156
Tredegar, Lord 148
Troops Out of Ireland campaign 9
Trotsky, Leon 89
Tudor Walters Report 62
Tweedsmuir, Lady 154
Tynan, Katherine 43
Tyneside 66, 122

Ulster 141, 150, 151, 158, 163–8; Solemn League and Covenant 43, 158
Ulster Volunteer Force 161–2
unemployment 23, 34, 70, 101, 102, 109, 123, 146, 148, 151
uniforms 39
Union Jack 14, 44, 60–1, 70, 76, 83, 87, 108, 124, 127, 137, 139
Union of Soviet Socialist Republics 1, 76, 103–4, 142, 170
Unionism 2, 7, 8, 12, 24–5, 80, 82, 93, 96, 109, 168–9; Irish and Northern Irish 158–9, 161–2, 163–8; Scottish 150–1, 154–5
United Kingdom 3 n. 14, 141, 151, 152, 158, 164
United States of America 1, 4, 11, 31, 89, 144, 172
University of Wales 145
Unwin, Raymond 60
urban Britain and Britishness 11, 54, 55, 58, 164

Vaughan, Gwyneth 43
Victoria League 40–1
*Victoria the Great* 22
Victoria, Queen 14, 18, 20, 22, 23, 24, 27, 28–9, 155

violence 12, 84–5, 159, 171; racial 113, 114, 121–2, 134, 140
'Vitai Lampada' 75
Voluntary Aid Detachments 40, 42

Wales 3, 12, 15, 57, 90, 96, 97, 120, 122, 136, 137, 141, 143–9, 151, 153, 170–1; and Britishness 78, 111, 168–9; and imperialism 23, 33, 77; and monarchy 22, 24, 27, 29, 147, 148–9, 161; and sport 76–8, 79
Walker, John 83
Walsingham, Lord 61
wars *see* Falklands War, First World War, Gulf War, Second World War
Warwickshire 57
Watford and Watford Gap 67
Webb, Sydney 58
Weight, Richard 6, 7, 32, 171
welfare state 8, 39, 107, 124, 127, 148, 154, 168
Wells, H. G. 29
Welsh language 43, 144, 146, 147, 148
Welsh nationalism 8, 33, 78, 142–3, 145, 168
Welshness 16, 23, 62, 65–6, 100, 113–14, 141–9, 168–9; and gender 43–4, 149; and sport 77–8
Wembley 77, 78–9, 83, 84
Wessex 55, 66
West Britons 161
West Bromwich Albion 83
West Indies and West Indians 113, 114, 120, 124
West Midlands 127, 128, 134, 138; *see also* Birmingham
Western Front 46, 163
*Whisky Galore* 91, 156
Whitechapel 28

whiteness 36, 48, 51–2, 89, 114, 123–4, 136, 137
Wiener, Martin J. 56, 59
Wigan 80
Wilcox, Herbert 22
Wilson, Amrit 139
Wilson, Edgar 17
Wilson, Harold 76, 109, 128, 147, 154, 165
*Wind in the Willows* 55
Winter, J. M. 41, 46
women 7, 11, 37, 38, 50, 59, 69, 123; and military organisations 42, 46, 49; and miscegenation 47–8, 121; and monarchy 18, 20–1, 22, 26, 36; and suffrage 40, 43–4
Women's Institute 47, 91–2.
Women's Land Army 20
Women's Peace Crusade 42
Woolf, Virginia 22, 39
Worcestershire 57
working class 4, 16, 40, 48, 51, 57, 84–5, 96, 102, 132, 149; 161; and monarchy 22, 27–8; and regional identities 55, 70; and Second World War 49, 106, 123–4
World Cup 76
Wright, Ian 83

Yeats, W. B. 24
York 61
Yorkshire 11, 19, 20, 56, 68, 70, 71, 81, 88, 161
Yorkshire Dales 11
Young Scots Society 152
youth 51–2, 89; movements 15, 118, 119–20
Yugoslavia 1, 142, 170

Zinoviev letter 103
*Zulu* 16

.